D1345605

The Unfinished History of the Iran–Iraq War

The Islamic Revolutionary Guards Corps (IRGC), founded after the Iranian Revolution in 1979, is one of the most powerful and prominent but least understood organizations in Iran. In this book, Annie Tracy Samuel presents an innovative and compelling history of this organization and, by using the Iran–Iraq War as a focal point, analyzes the links between war and revolution.

Tracy Samuel provides an internal view of the IRGC by examining how the Revolutionary Guards have recorded and assessed the history of the war in the massive volume of Persian language publications produced by the organization's top members and units. This not only enhances our comprehension of the IRGC's roles and power in contemporary Iran but also demonstrates how the history of the Iran–Iraq War has immense bearing on the Islamic Republic's present and future. In doing so, the book reveals how analyzing Iran's history provides the critical tools for understanding its actions today.

ANNIE TRACY SAMUEL is a scholar specializing in the modern history of Iran and the Middle East. She is Assistant Professor in the Department of History at the University of Tennessee at Chattanooga and previously served as a research fellow at the Harvard Kennedy School's Belfer Center for Science and International Affairs. Her publications include journal articles in *International Security* and *Diplomatic History*; her commentary on current events has been published in Lawfare, *The Hill*, CNN, and *The Atlantic*; and she has delivered talks at universities and conferences and briefed government agencies in the United States, Europe, and the Middle East.

The Unfinished History of the Iran–Iraq War

Faith, Firepower, and Iran's Revolutionary Guards

ANNIE TRACY SAMUEL
University of Tennessee at Chattanooga

CAMBRIDGE
UNIVERSITY PRESS

CAMBRIDGE
UNIVERSITY PRESS

University Printing House, Cambridge CB2 8BS, United Kingdom

One Liberty Plaza, 20th Floor, New York, NY 10006, USA

477 Williamstown Road, Port Melbourne, VIC 3207, Australia

314–321, 3rd Floor, Plot 3, Splendor Forum, Jasola District Centre, New Delhi – 110025, India

103 Penang Road, #05–06/07, Visioncrest Commercial, Singapore 238467

Cambridge University Press is part of the University of Cambridge.

It furthers the University's mission by disseminating knowledge in the pursuit of
education, learning, and research at the highest international levels of excellence.

www.cambridge.org
Information on this title: www.cambridge.org/9781108478427
DOI: 10.1017/9781108777674

© Annie Tracy Samuel 2022

This publication is in copyright. Subject to statutory exception
and to the provisions of relevant collective licensing agreements,
no reproduction of any part may take place without the written
permission of Cambridge University Press.

First published 2022

A catalogue record for this publication is available from the British Library.

Library of Congress Cataloging-in-Publication Data
Names: Tracy Samuel, Annie, author.
Title: The unfinished history of the Iran–Iraq War : faith, firepower, and Iran's Revolutionary Guards
/ Annie Tracy Samuel, University of Tennessee at Chattanooga.
Other titles: Faith, firepower, and Iran's Revolutionary Guards
Description: Cambridge, United Kingdom ; New York, NY : Cambridge University Press, 2020.
| Includes bibliographical references and index.
Identifiers: LCCN 2021002453 (print) | LCCN 2021002454 (ebook) | ISBN 9781108478427
(hardback) | ISBN 9781108745789 (paperback) | ISBN 9781108777674 (epub)
Subjects: LCSH: Iran–Iraq War, 1980–1988 | Sipāh-i Pāsdārān-i Inqilāb-i Islāmī (Iran)–History.
| Iran–History, Military. | Iran–Politics and government–1997–
Classification: LCC DS318.85.T733 2020 (print) | LCC DS318.85 (ebook) | DDC 955.05/424–dc23
LC record available at https://lccn.loc.gov/2021002453
LC ebook record available at https://lccn.loc.gov/2021002454

ISBN 978-1-108-47842-7 Hardback

Cambridge University Press has no responsibility for the persistence or accuracy
of URLs for external or third-party internet websites referred to in this publication
and does not guarantee that any content on such websites is, or will remain,
accurate or appropriate.

Contents

Map of Iran

Notes on Translation, Transliteration, and Citation

In the text, transliterations of Persian words follow a simplified and modified version of the systems adopted by the journals *Iranian Studies* and the *International Journal of Middle East Studies* that omits diacritic marks and, in most cases, the hamza and 'ayn. Persian personal and proper names have been spelled as they are most commonly rendered in English and, for personal names, according to the preference of the given individual if such a preference could be determined. "Formal" transliterations follow the *International Journal of Middle East Studies* system. While using that system has some drawbacks, especially in terms of its rendering of Persian vowels and pronunciations, it allows words and their spellings to be presented with a high degree of precision.

Citations for sources are presented in a manner that seeks to balance the desire to present the bibliographic information as completely as possible with the desire to prevent the footnotes from overwhelming the text.

All sources published by the IRGC, including those published by and on the website of the Holy Defense Research and Documentation Center, which is abbreviated HDRDC, and by Imam Hossein University are in Persian. Citations for all Persian sources include only English translations. Non-IRGC Persian sources are identified as being in Persian with "(Persian)" following the citation.

For the IRGC and other Persian sources especially, the number of bibliographic elements that would need to be included to make each citation complete and the irregularity of how these elements are presented in these particular publications make the potential for unwieldiness in the notes more likely. For example, some, but not all, of the publications list individual writers or authors. Some list authors as well as a variety of other contributors, including supervisors and editors, and the manner in which these contributors are listed has changed over time and varies by publication. Therefore, in order to consolidate and standardize the citations in the footnotes, I have included titles, publishers, and publication years but have not listed individual contributors.

Several of the IRGC sources have been published in multiple editions. If no edition is listed in the footnote, then the edition used is the first or only edition.

Citations for English sources appear in a shortened form in the footnotes.

Most URLs are included in the Bibliography rather than in the footnotes.

Citations generally follow *The Chicago Manual of Style*, 17th edition.

Additional bibliographic information can be found in the Bibliography included herein.

Throughout the manuscript I have replaced dates and years based on the Iranian calendar, which are used throughout Iran and in the IRGC sources, with those based on the Gregorian calendar. In most cases, the converted dates are as precise and accurate as possible. However, in cases when only the Iranian year is provided, as is the case for the publication dates of most monographs, the corresponding year cannot always be determined with certainty, given that each Iranian year begins in March of the Gregorian year and therefore corresponds to two different Gregorian years. In such cases, either both possible years are provided or only the year more likely to correspond to the Iranian year has been included.

The singular personal pronoun in Persian is gender-neutral, which I have tried to replicate by using "their" instead of "he," "she," or "he/she" whenever possible.

For additional images and other information, visit https://sites .google.com/view/unfinished-history.

List of Abbreviations and Key Terms

Abadan	City in southwestern Iran
Artesh	Iran's regular military
Arvand Rud (Shatt al-Arab)	River that runs along the Iran–Iraq border
Basij Force	Paramilitary, part of the IRGC
Basra	City in southern Iraq
Faw	City and peninsula in southern Iraq
HDRDC	Holy Defense Research and Documentation Center
Imam Hossein University	Affiliated with the IRGC
IRGC	Islamic Revolutionary Guards Corps (Sepah)
JCPOA	Joint Comprehensive Plan of Action
Khorramshahr	City in southwestern Iran
Khuzistan	Southwestern province of Iran
Kurdistan	Northwestern province of Iran
Majlis	Iran's parliament
Quds Force	Elite IRGC force
SCWS	Supreme Council for War Support
SDC	Supreme Defense Council
Shatt al-Arab (Arvand Rud)	River that runs along the Iran–Iraq border
Tehran	Capital of Iran
UNSC	United Nations Security Council
UNSCR	United Nations Security Council Resolution
WMD	Weapons of Mass Destruction

Names of Key Figures

Unless otherwise noted, positions refer to the Iranian government. The descriptions in this list are not meant to be comprehensive but to provide the reader with a way to keep track of the main individuals and their roles in this history. For additional information on key figures in postrevolutionary Iran, see Boroujerdi and Rahimkhani, *Postrevolutionary Iran* (Syracuse University Press, 2018).

Amir-Entezam, Abbas – Provisional Government deputy prime minister and spokesman

Ansari, Mehdi – IRGC war researcher

Ardestani, Hossein – IRGC war researcher, HDRDC director (–2017)

Bani-Sadr, Abolhassan – First president of the Islamic Republic (1980–81)

Bazargan, Mehdi – Provisional Government prime minister (1979)

Doroodian, Mohammad – Early member of the IRGC Political Bureau, IRGC war researcher

Hussein, Saddam – President of Iraq, leader of the Ba'th regime (1979–2003)

Jafari, Mohammad Ali – IRGC commander-in-chief (2007–19)

Khamenei, Ali – Ayatollah, president (1981–89), Supreme Leader (1989–)

Khomeini, Ruhollah – Ayatollah, Imam, Supreme Leader (1979–89)

Lahouti, Hassan – Khomeini's representative in the IRGC (1979)

Lotfallah-Zadegan, Alireza – IRGC war researcher

Mansouri, Javad – First IRGC commander

Mohammadzadeh, Ibrahim Haji – An IRGC founder, first head of the Political Bureau

Mottaki, Manouchehr – Foreign minister (2005–10)

Mousavi, Mir-Hossein – Prime minister (1981–89)

Naini, Ali-Mohammad – HDRDC director (2017–)

Nakhai, Hadi – Early member of the IRGC Political Bureau, IRGC war researcher

Namjoo, Mousa – Artesh ground forces colonel during the war (died 1981)

Naqdi, Mohammad Reza – Basij Force commander-in-chief (2009–16)

Pahlavi, Mohammad Reza – Shah (King) of Iran (1941–79)

Pérez de Cuéllar, Javier – UN Secretary-General (1982–91)

Rafiqdust, Mohsen – IRGC minister (1982–88)

Rafsanjani, Akbar Hashemi – Speaker of Majlis (1980–89), de facto commander-in-chief during the war

Rashid, Gholam-Ali (G. Rashid) – A top IRGC commander, involved in the war history project

Rashid, Mohsen (M. Rashid) – A founder of the IRGC Political Bureau, IRGC war researcher

Rezaee, Mohsen – IRGC commander-in-chief (1981–97), involved in the war history project

Rouhani, Hassan – President (2013–21)

Safavi, Yahya Rahim – Head of the IRGC operations unit during the war, IRGC commander-in-chief (1997–2007)

Salami, Hossein – IRGC commander-in-chief (2019–)

Shirazi, Ali Sayad – Commander of the Artesh ground forces during the war

Soleimani, Qasem – IRGC Quds Force commander-in-chief (1997–2020), assassinated by the United States in January 2020

Vahidi, Ahmad – IRGC Quds Force commander-in-chief (1990s), defense minister (2009–13)

Yazdi, Ebrahim – Provisional Government deputy prime minister

Zarif, Mohammad Javad – Foreign minister (2013–21)

Chronology

1979

January 16	Shah leaves Iran
February 1	Khomeini returns to Iran
February 11	Shah's military and government collapse, revolution succeeds
March 30–April 1	National referendum and establishment of the Islamic Republic
April 22	Khomeini issues decree establishing IRGC
April 25	Passage of statute establishing IRGC
May 6	Official announcement of statute establishing IRGC
November 4	US Embassy in Tehran occupied by Khomeini supporters
November 5	Prime Minister Bazargan and his cabinet resign
November	Khomeini calls for creation of Basij Force
December 2–3	New Iranian constitution approved in referendum

1980

January 25	Bani-Sadr elected president of the Islamic Republic
April 7	United States severs ties with Iran
May 28	Majlis of the Islamic Republic convenes for the first time
September 17	Saddam Hussein abrogates the 1975 Algiers Agreement
September 22	Iraqi forces invade Iran; Iran–Iraq War begins
September 28	UNSC adopts Resolution 479 calling for a ceasefire in the war
October 26	Iraq occupies Khorramshahr

1981

January	IRGC assumes control of Basij
June	Bani-Sadr impeached
September	Iran breaks the siege of Abadan
October 2	Khamenei elected president
November 29 – December 7	Operation *Tariq al-Quds* (Toward Jerusalem), Iran retakes the city of Bostan

1982

March 22	Operation *Fath-ul-Mubin* (Undeniable Victory), Iran retakes the cities of Shush, Dezful, and Ahvaz
May 24	Operation *Bayt al-Muqaddas* (Jerusalem, literally the Holy Temple), Iran retakes Khorramshahr
June – July	Iranian mission to help counter the Israeli invasion of Lebanon
July 12	UNSC adopts Resolution 514 calling for a ceasefire in the war
July 14	Iran launches Ramadan (*Ramazan*) operation into Iraq

1983–85

	Stalemate in the war
November 1984	Iraq and the United States renew diplomatic relations
Spring – Summer 1985	Iran's diplomatic opening

1986

February	Iran takes Faw
March	Iran announces beginning of the "decisive year"
November	Iran-Contra Affair (Irangate or McFarlane's Adventure) becomes public

1987

January 9– February 23	Karbala 5 Operation toward Basra

Spring   Shift in Iran's focus from the southern to the
                    northern front
May   United States agrees to escort Kuwaiti oil
                    tankers in the Persian Gulf
May 17   Iraqi aircraft fires on the *USS Stark*
July 20   UNSC adopts Resolution 598 calling for an end
                    to the war
July 24   *USS Bridgeton*, serving as an escort for a
                    Kuwaiti tanker, strikes a mine in the Persian
                    Gulf
September   United States sinks the *Iran-Ajr* supply ship
                    being used to lay mines
November   Supreme Council for War Support announces
                    readiness week to confront America's
                    aggression

1988
January   *Bayt al-Muqaddas* (Jerusalem) 2 Operation,
                    Iran's major operation on the
                    northwestern front
February–   Fifth and final War of the Cities
  April
March   Operation Dawn (*Valfajr*) 10, launched by
                    Sepah and Iraqi Kurdish forces in the area of
                    Halabja
March 16   Iraqi chemical attack on Halabja
April 17   Iranian forces expelled from Faw
July 3   *USS Vincennes* shoots down Iranian civilian
                    airplane, killing all 290 people on board
July 18   Iran agrees to UNSCR 598
July 21   Khomeini declares end of the war
August 20   Iran–Iraq War ends, UNSCR 598 comes
                    into force

Acknowledgments

I very much appreciate the team at Cambridge University Press – especially Maria Marsh, Atifa Jiwa, and Natasha Whelan – for making this publication possible, and the anonymous peer reviewers who provided valuable feedback on the manuscript.

I am grateful for the many people who supported me, my passion for history, and this project over many years. I would like to thank the institutions, teachers, professors, mentors, advisors, colleagues, friends, and family members who provided assistance and encouragement. And, most especially, I thank Michael.

Introduction

On his official website, Iran's Supreme Leader Ayatollah Ali Khamenei periodically posts his views on a range of subjects, often presented as answers to questions, and in December 2012 he released a series of responses to questions about Iran's relationship with the United States. While for many Americans US relations with Iran are defined by disputes over the Islamic Republic's nuclear program and the two countries' often conflicting strategic interests in the Middle East, those were not the subjects that the Supreme Leader focused on.

Instead, he concentrated on history.

In answer to a question asking for "instances of hostility of the American government against our nation," Khamenei listed events that most Americans would know nothing about, and that would seem to have occurred too long ago to matter: "aid to Saddam [Hussein] during the war with Iran" and "the shooting down of an Iranian passenger airplane" in 1988. After further explaining the relevant history of US involvement in the 1980–88 Iran–Iraq War, of which those two events were part, the Supreme Leader concluded with two questions of his own: "Has our nation forgotten these things? Can it forget [these things]?"[1]

The answer to both questions is "No," as Khamenei clearly implied.

When discussing the same subject of US–Iran relations on ABC's *This Week* in September 2013, Iran's foreign minister Mohammad Javad Zarif went with assertion instead of implication. "We have not forgotten the fact, that when Iraq used chemical weapons [against] Iran [during the Iran–Iraq War], not only [did] the United States [not] condemn it, it went out of its way to blame us for the use of chemical weapons," Zarif said in response to George Stephanopoulos's question

---

[1] "The Leader of the Revolution's Answers to Ten Questions About the Historical Struggle of the Iranian Nation with America," Khamenei.ir, December 6, 2012 (Persian).

about why Iran insisted on maintaining a uranium enrichment capability if it wasn't interested in weaponizing its nuclear program. In a partial explanation of why he was talking about a decades-old war when the subject was uranium, Zarif proclaimed, "we cannot start history at the time of our choosing. The background has to be addressed, the historical aspects have to be addressed. The historical sources of Iran's very serious and deep mistrust of the behavior of the United States needs to be addressed." The foreign minister then summed up his point before letting Stephanopoulos get on with the interview. "So, these are all facts of history which are very fresh in the minds of Iranians," he said. "We may be willing [to] forgive as [former South African] President [Nelson] Mandela said once, but we're not going to forget."[2]

While Zarif was explaining the importance of the Iran–Iraq War and its history to Stephanopoulos and his American audience in New York, back in Iran Masoud Jazayeri, a commander in the powerful military conglomerate known as the Islamic Revolutionary Guards Corps (IRGC or Revolutionary Guards), was bringing the same message to the Iranian people. He asserted, like Zarif, that any future ties between Iran and the United States required that Iranians' historic distrust of US behavior and intentions be addressed. And, like both Khamenei and Zarif, Jazayeri traced the source of that distrust to the Iran–Iraq War. The United States' support for Iraq in that conflict meant that it was "complicit in all of the devastation and crimes that occurred during that period," he stated. Accordingly, "before America considers its future relations with the Islamic Republic of Iran," Jazayeri warned, "it must clear the many debts it has to the Iranian nation."[3]

The ongoing significance of the Iran–Iraq War is likely one of very few issues on which Khamenei, Zarif, and Jazayeri – leaders with very different backgrounds, ideologies, and visions for Iran's future – can agree. Even more important, however, is the fact that while all three leaders are part of a regime that has struggled to maintain its legitimacy among a deeply divided population, in this case all were very likely

---

[2] *This Week*, ABC, September 29, 2013.
[3] "Commander Jazayeri: Those Who Put Confidence in America Are Not Familiar with America or [Its] Policy," *Fars News*, September 24, 2013 (Persian).

speaking for the majority of Iranians when they said in agreement that the Iran–Iraq War's impact on Iran is present and profound.[4]

But the problem is that they don't agree. They all recognize that the war's legacies loom large, but they don't all agree on what those legacies mean, on what they should mean. And given that they all appreciate the significance and power, both real and potential, of the Iran–Iraq War and its history, they all understand that the ability to control Iran's future belongs to those who control its recent past, to those who give content and meaning to the history of the Iran–Iraq War.

This book examines that particular front in the struggle for Iran's future. It analyzes the IRGC's history of the Iran–Iraq War and how the Revolutionary Guards have recorded, assessed, and assigned a particular set of meanings to the conflict. Its central questions include how and why the Guards have documented and composed the history of the Iran–Iraq War; how the Guards explain the course and outcome of the war, the relationship between the war and Iran's 1979 Islamic Revolution, and their own roles in prosecuting the conflict; and what the answers to those questions reveal about the IRGC, the Iran–Iraq War, and the Islamic Republic.

The analysis is based on the massive volume of Persian-language publications on the war produced by top members and units of the IRGC, primarily by the IRGC's Holy Defense Research and Documentation Center (formerly the Center for War Studies and Research). Those publications provide us with the rare opportunity to go inside the IRGC and to understand Iran's recent history as the Revolutionary Guards understand it themselves. What we find when we enter upends much of what we thought we knew about the IRGC and the Islamic Republic.

The first thing we discover is that both the experience of the Iran–Iraq War and the project of composing the historical narrative of the war are fundamental to the IRGC and accordingly to understanding

---

[4] On the war's legacies see Narges Bajoghli, *Iran Reframed* (Stanford University Press, 2019); Arta Khakpour, Mohammad Mehdi Khorrami, and Shouleh Vatanabadi, eds., *Moments of Silence* (New York University Press, 2016); Pedram Khosronejad, ed., *Unburied Memories* (Routledge, 2013); Lawrence Potter and Gary Sick, eds., *Iran, Iraq, and the Legacies of War* (Palgrave Macmillan, 2004); Farhang Rajaee, ed., *Iranian Perspectives on the Iran–Iraq War* (University of Florida Press, 1997).

the organization. Their significance stems from several factors, including the ways in which the war and the ongoing revolutionary process in Iran influenced one another; the war's role in legitimizing and institutionalizing the IRGC and the new Islamic Republic as a whole; the expansion and evolution of the IRGC through its participation in the war into the powerful organization it is today; and the fact that the Revolutionary Guards view history as a vital tool for shaping national identity and power.

Secondly, and more broadly, the IRGC's assessments of the Iran–Iraq War remind us that history must be both made and written. The content of the past is not fixed or singular; it is determined by those who give it meaning and permanence. Indeed, the interpretation and significance of the war's history as it has been written by the Revolutionary Guards challenge many of the prevailing scholarly and popular characterizations of the Islamic Republic, which are often based on Western sources and perspectives. In particular, the latter have given much weight to the rhetoric Iranian leaders used during (and since) the war and to the importance of faith and revolutionary fervor in understanding the Islamic Republic and its prosecution of the conflict. However, the history of the war authored by the Revolutionary Guards demonstrates that this is an essentialized understanding based on a literalized interpretation of the regime's rhetoric, and one that is not reflected in the IRGC sources or the Islamic Republic's actions. Those reveal in contrast that the war was a weighty and calamitous matter for Iran that the Revolutionary Guards and others struggled to prosecute and survive, and that to do so they relied on all the tools at their disposal, which included both faith – religious commitment, revolutionary ideology, and popular morale – and firepower – careful strategic planning, organized force and offensive power, and military professionalism.

In the process of developing those central arguments, this book also explores several overarching themes that reveal how the analysis of the IRGC's history of the Iran–Iraq War provides extensive new insight into the Islamic Republic's past and present. First, throughout their sources, the Revolutionary Guards examine the close and complex connections between the war and the Islamic Revolution and argue that neither can be understood without the other. In exploring the links between war and revolution, the book contributes to theoretical examinations of those subjects and adds new dimensions to existing interpretations of the Iranian Revolution.

Second, the IRGC's sources on the war offer an internal view of the organization's mission and development, something that has been sorely lacking from existing assessments. The book's analysis of that internal view enhances our comprehension of the IRGC's roles and power in contemporary Iran, a subject that concerns scholars and policymakers alike. Finally, both the IRGC's history of the war and the book's analysis thereof reveal the power and necessity of understanding the past. The IRGC sources demonstrate that the history of the Iran–Iraq War has immense bearing on the Islamic Republic's present and future and therefore that command of the former facilitates the control of the latter. The book makes a complementary argument by revealing how analyzing Iran's history provides the critical tools for understanding its actions today.

In essence, then, this book presents an interwoven analysis of three main subjects – first, the IRGC's roles in the Iran–Iraq War and that conflict as a whole; second, the IRGC's history of the Iran–Iraq War; and third, the significance of that project. This is not a study wholly or exclusively of the Iran–Iraq War, of the IRGC, or of the war's legacy in Iran. Rather, it is a study of the conjunction of those three, of the IRGC's roles in and history of the Iran–Iraq War, and of the sources that contain that particular story.

Revolution, War, and the IRGC

The Iranian Revolution

The Iranian Revolution of 1978–79 was a movement of several different groups that were united most strongly in their opposition to the regime of Mohammad Reza Shah Pahlavi, whose policies generated substantial resistance along a variety of lines. The shah's rule was characterized by a lack of freedom and was maintained with a system of violent repression. Many sectors of Iranian society experienced dislocation and economic hardship as a result of the shah's efforts to rapidly modernize the country. Immense wealth was amassed in the hands of a few, especially in the hands of the shah and his family, which created gaping socioeconomic disparities.

Much of Iranian society was alienated from the regime by the shah's program of Westernization and secularization, a fact that helps explain the revolution's Islamic orientation. Over the course of his reign, the shah worked to limit the power of the ulama (Islamic clergy) and to promote secularism over Islamic norms and customs. He also oversaw a substantial increase in Western and US influence in Iran and its policies. As a result, many Iranians came to feel ostracized from their own country and culture, which prompted them to associate Westernization with suffering and dictatorship, to seek solace and identity in familiar traditions, and to put their faith in the solutions being advanced by Muslim religious leaders.[5]

The most prominent Muslim religious leader and the one who offered an Islamic answer to the problem of the shah was Ayatollah (Imam) Ruhollah Khomeini. Although the shah had him exiled for that very reason in 1964, Khomeini continued to play an important role in the opposition in the following years. The shah had responded to the massive demonstrations that preceded Khomeini's exile with a mix of partial reforms and increased repression, which allowed the monarch to hang on to power for another fifteen years. But his continued despotism and failure to implement meaningful change, combined with economic difficulties, led to the outbreak of opposition again in 1977 and 1978, which he was not able to survive. After a surging wave of demonstrations against the monarchy in the second half of 1978, the regime crashed rapidly and dramatically in the first six weeks of 1979, with the shah's departure from Iran on January 16, Khomeini's return on February 1, and the collapse of the shah's military and government on February 11.

Postrevolutionary rule in Iran was initially carried out by two competing authorities. The first was the Provisional Government headed by Prime Minister Mehdi Bazargan, and the second was the Council of the Islamic Revolution headed (informally) by Khomeini. Both authorities ruled for most of 1979 while the new regime took shape. A national referendum on March 30–31 led to the establishment of the Islamic Republic on April 1. Immediately following the occupation of the US Embassy in Tehran by students supporting Khomeini on November 4, Prime Minister Bazargan and his cabinet resigned, marking the demise of the Provisional Government and Khomeini's increasing domination of the new regime. The Council of the Revolution took control of the state, joined at the end of January 1980 by the Islamic Republic's first

---

[5] Nikki R. Keddie, *Modern Iran* (Yale University Press, 2003); Jalal Al-i Ahmad, *Occidentosis*, trans. R. Campbell (Mizan Press, 1984).

president, Abolhassan Bani-Sadr, and was then replaced mid-year when the new Majlis (parliament) convened for the first time.

As has been the case in other postrevolutionary regimes, the Islamic Republic was quick to take aim at the structures and policies that had defined the *ancien régime*, often moving far in the other direction. Social life was Islamicized, especially through the Cultural Revolution, which in spring 1980 began to transform Iran's universities. Political life was also reconstructed. After an acrimonious drafting process, a new constitution was approved in a referendum in December 1979.[6]

According to the constitution, the Islamic Republic is based on the system of *vilayat-i faqih*, or guardianship of the jurist.[7] The highest governing authority is the guardian jurist (*vali-i faqih*), more commonly known as the Supreme Leader, a role occupied by Khomeini for the duration of the Iran–Iraq War. Executive power is exercised by the president, a position held by Bani-Sadr until his impeachment in June 1981 and then by Ali Khamenei, who became Supreme Leader following Khomeini's death in 1989.[8] During the war and before the constitutional revisions of 1989, the president shared executive power with the prime minister, Mir-Hossein Mousavi. Legislative authority resides in the popularly elected Majlis, which for most of the 1980s was under the chairmanship of Akbar Hashemi Rafsanjani.

In the eighteen-month period between the victory of the revolution in February 1979 and the outbreak of the Iran–Iraq War in September 1980, the establishment of the Islamic Republic was accompanied by extensive conflict both within and against the new regime. The union of diverse groups that had come together to oust the shah gradually dissipated. There was little consensus on the nature and policies of the postrevolutionary state or the scope of religious leadership. Though many of the Iranians who had participated in the revolution supported the creation of an Islamic Republic and the leadership of Khomeini, most did not support the sort of absolute power that he and his allies were increasingly yielding. As Khomeini proved unwilling to accommodate conceptions of the Islamic Republic that differed from his own,

---

[6] Website of the Iranian Majlis. The constitution and governmental structure were changed in 1989.

[7] The concept is based on Khomeini's theory of Islamic government.

[8] Mohammad-Ali Rajai served as president for less than a month between Bani-Sadr and Khamenei.

his ascendancy was achieved in part by political and violent suppression of the groups that challenged his rule.

The Iran–Iraq War

Though ultimately its causes were political and proximate, the Iran–Iraq War is part of a long history of conflict between the various rulers and peoples of those lands. Iraq's border with Iran represents the eastern limit of the Arab world where it meets the Persian population that forms Iran's largest ethnic group.[9] Though both Iran and Iraq are majority-Shi'i-Muslim countries, before 2003, Iraq was ruled by governments composed of Sunni Muslims, while Shi'i Muslims have governed Iran for hundreds of years.

Empires have also fought it out in the territories that comprise Iraq and Iran. Wars between the Babylonian and Achaemenid Empires in the sixth century BCE, between Roman forces and the Parthian and then Sasanian Empires across several centuries, between Arab-Muslim forces and the Sasanian Empire in the seventh century, and between the Ottoman and Safavid Empires in the sixteenth and seventeenth centuries have bestowed upon the modern rulers of Iraq and Iran a history rich with political and strategic rivalry.

The frequent warring produced an often-shifting and much-disputed border. The importance of historical claims to territory is compounded by the importance of the river that runs along or close to that boundary. Known as the Shatt al-Arab (in Arabic) or Arvand Rud (in Persian), the river provides access to the Persian Gulf, which is of strategic significance for both countries. But while Iran has a long coastline along the Gulf, the modern state of Iraq has a very limited shoreline (of about thirty-six miles). The river is the latter's best outlet to the Gulf, and as a result Iraq's leaders have consistently sought control of it.[10]

Disputes over the river formed one of the main sources of contention in the decades prior to the Iran–Iraq War. The governments also clashed over leadership of the region, with both seeking a dominant role in the Middle East and especially in the Persian Gulf. Iraq joined

---

[9] Persians make up about 61 percent of the Iranian population. *CIA World Factbook: Iran.*

[10] *CIA World Factbook: Iraq.*

other Arab countries in loudly condemning Iran's seizure of three Gulf islands in 1971. There were also efforts by each government to undermine the other by fomenting instability in the Kurdish community that spans the northern regions of the two countries.

But despite these conflicts, the decades preceding the outbreak of hostilities in 1980 were marked not by war but by limited cooperation, even in the presence of rivalry. It was the Iranian Revolution that precipitated open conflict, and it was the revolution's results and reverberations that formed the Iran–Iraq War's most significant catalysts. As outlined earlier, Iran's postrevolutionary government was based on the centrality of Islam in public life, and Ayatollah Khomeini vowed to fight for the freedom of the oppressed throughout the world. Iraqi president Saddam Hussein – who presided over the Sunni-dominated, secular Ba'th regime ruling a Shi'i majority – saw the policies of the new Islamic Republic as a threat to his power.[11]

At the same time, Iran appeared to be in a vulnerable position, as violent disputes over the nature of the new regime persisted into its second year. Saddam decided to take the opportunity to launch what he hoped would be a quick military operation to defeat the revolution and safeguard his rule and, while he was at it, to seize the oil-rich territory in southwestern Iran and assert his leadership of the Arab world. So, after a year of steadily worsening relations and several months of clashes along the countries' shared border, Iraqi forces invaded Iran and initiated an aerial assault on Iranian bases on September 22, 1980, marking the beginning of the Iran–Iraq War.

What Saddam intended to be a swift and easy strike to check the revolutionary state quickly transformed into a brutal and drawn-out conflict that in fact revitalized the flagging revolution. After an initial series of victories allowed Iraqi forces to advance into Iran through the beginning of 1981, and to capture the strategic city of Khorramshahr and lay siege to the city of Abadan along the way, Iranian forces halted the Iraqis' march and retook most of their territory over the course of the next year. Iran then pursued the retreating forces into Iraq in the

---

[11] In 1980 Shi'is composed about 60 percent (between 55 and 65 percent) of the Iraqi population. Hanna Batatu, *The Old Social Classes and the Revolutionary Movements of Iraq* (Princeton University Press, 1978), 13–50; Helen Chapin Metz, ed., *Iraq: A Country Study* (GPO for the Library of Congress, 1988), 87–93; Yitzhak Nakash, *The Shi'is of Iraq* (Princeton University Press, 1994), 13–47.

summer of 1982 but was unable to gain much ground. As the war stalled, it also broadened to entangle the rest of the Middle East and both superpowers, and it spread from the land to a tanker war in the Persian Gulf and several series of aerial attacks on civilian areas, known as the Wars of the Cities.

The war continued largely as a bloody stalemate until the summer of 1988. It ended on August 20, 1988, when the ceasefire terms of United Nations Security Council Resolution 598 (of July 20, 1987) came into force. The end of the war restored the status quo ante, with both regimes still in power and without territorial adjustments. Neither side emerged as the clear victor, but the war had a profound impact on both countries. The conflict was exceedingly heinous, even by the standards of modern warfare, with the belligerents resorting to the most inhumane practices: Both parties targeted civilians and mistreated prisoners of war; Iraq used chemical weapons on a massive scale; Iran sent child soldiers to the fronts and employed unprotected frontal infantry assaults, or human wave attacks.[12]

It is indeed difficult to overstate the significance of the Iran–Iraq War for Iranians and for the Islamic Republic. Ending less than four decades ago, the war has touched, and is still with, nearly every individual Iranian. Hundreds of thousands fought. Tens, maybe hundreds, of thousands died. Many thousands more were wounded and live everyday with the scars of war.[13] Those who were exposed to chemical weapons are still sick from their effects.

If you yourself didn't fight, then your father or cousin or neighbor did. If you don't remember the frontlines or the airstrikes and weren't alive to experience a society at war in real time, then you live now in a society where the legacies of war are impossible to escape. The massive murals that tower over cities across the country display the scenes and faces of the war reanimated in epic visual fashion. Quotes from the country's leaders emphasizing the importance of the Iran–Iraq War and connecting it to everything from uranium enrichment to relations with the West and economic development appear daily in the news.

[12] See Ige F. Dekker and Harry H. G. Post, eds., *The Gulf War of 1980–1988* (Martinus Nijhoff, 1992).
[13] Estimates of Iranian deaths in the war range from about 170,000 to 750,000. The Peace Research Institute Oslo, "Battle Deaths Dataset"; The Correlates of War, "Inter-State War Data."

And occasionally there are indications that the war might not actually be over, because if it was over, if it had really ended decades ago, then the casualty numbers wouldn't still be increasing as a result of a wrong step onto one of the landmines littered along the western border, and there wouldn't still be funerals for soldiers who died in combat but whose bodies ended up in enemy hands and are only now coming home. The epithets Iranians use to describe the war clearly reveal how they understand the conflict and the nature of its significance. For them, the conflict was an Imposed War (*Jang-i Tahmili*); it was an attack undertaken by powers that opposed Iran's revolution and that were determined to prevent the country from asserting its independence and voicing its Islamic message. The conflict, therefore, was also a Holy Defense (*Difa'-i Muqaddas*) (also translated as Sacred Defense), a campaign made necessary by the imposition of war and by the need to defend both the Iranian nation and its Islamic Revolution.

And yet, as time marches forward, the war inevitably recedes further and further into the past.[14] The soldiers who survived will not do so indefinitely. Those who lived through the war will pass on and will be replaced by a generation of Iranians with no memory of the conflict or the revolution that preceded it. For them, living in a society where the legacies of war are impossible to escape can be, and has already started to become, onerous and alienating. The struggle to keep the memory of the war alive and to shape its significance in the present and future is accordingly both ongoing and evolving. And so as the war becomes history, Iran's Revolutionary Guards have become historians, determined to preserve and defend what many of them fought for many years ago.

The IRGC

The IRGC is the military and political organization that is charged with guarding the Islamic Republic and the revolution that brought it to power. On April 22, 1979, about three weeks after the national

---

[14] On war, history, and collective memory, see Alon Confino, "Collective Memory and Cultural History," *The American Historical Review* 102.5 (1997); Eric Davis, "The Uses of Historical Memory," *Journal of Democracy* 16.3 (2005); Wulf Kansteiner, "Finding Meaning in Memory," *History and Theory* 41.2 (2002); Jay Winter and Emmanuel Sivan, eds., *War and Remembrance in the Twentieth Century* (Cambridge University Press, 1999).

referendum that established the new regime, Ayatollah Khomeini issued a decree directing the governing Revolutionary Council to establish the IRGC, effectively consolidating various revolutionary militias into a formal organization. In accordance with the decree, the Council ordered the IRGC to guard the revolution against internal and external threats and to propagate the ideology of the revolution.[15]

The IRGC was further institutionalized in the Constitution of the Islamic Republic, which defines the IRGC's role as "guarding the revolution and its achievements" and which gives it responsibility "not only for defending the borders, but also for the ideological mission of holy war in the way of God and fighting to expand the rule of God's law in the world" (Introduction, Principle 150). Principle 110 names the Supreme Leader as commander-in-chief of the armed forces and gives him the power to appoint and dismiss the head of the IRGC. It also states that the latter shall be a member of the Supreme Defense Council organized and overseen by the Supreme Leader, which was the primary center of policy- and strategy-making during the Iran–Iraq War.[16]

The IRGC was not set up to replace Iran's regular military (Artesh). Rather, it was to function as an additional, revolutionary armed force. In the wake of the revolution, Iran's new leaders debated what form the Islamic Republic's armed forces should take. The regular military had just served as the army of the deposed shah, and many revolutionary leaders did not trust its loyalty to the new regime. Indeed, in the first years after the revolution, significant opposition to the Islamic Republic came from the military. Purges and ideological training helped transform the imperial armed forces into the armed forces of the Islamic Republic, but they also weakened the military, leaving Iran practically defenseless, and did not guarantee loyalty. The IRGC was set up in response to those circumstances. It was designed to be a force whose allegiance to the Islamic Republic would be beyond doubt and one that could check the power of the regular military.[17]

[15] *Chronology of the Iran–Iraq War 1* (HDRDC, 1997), 783–874.

[16] Constitution, Majlis Website. The Supreme Defense Council was replaced by the Supreme National Security Council (SNSC) when the constitution was revised.

[17] On civil–military relations and political development in Iran and in theory, see Diane E. Davis and Anthony W. Pereira, eds., *Irregular Armed Forces and Their Role in Politics and State Formation* (Cambridge University Press, 2003); Nader Entessar, "The Military and Politics in the Islamic Republic of Iran," in *Post-Revolutionary Iran,* eds. Hooshang Amirahmadi and Manoucher Parvin (Westview Press, 1988); Samuel Huntington, *Soldier and the State* (Harvard

During the first year after the revolution, the IRGC was occupied with combating internal opposition to the new Islamic Republic. With the outbreak of the Iran–Iraq War in September 1980, however, the Guards turned their attention to combating the external threat to the regime. They played significant roles in prosecuting the conflict, and were profoundly transformed by their participation. During the course of the war, the IRGC grew dramatically in size and developed from a disorganized militia into a complex and powerful organization with specialized armed forces, the resources to produce weaponry, and an array of economic, religious, and educational enterprises. In January 1981, the IRGC assumed control over the Basij (Organization for the Mobilization of the Oppressed), a massive popular force created to help defend the country and the revolution, particularly after the rupturing of diplomatic relations between Iran and the United States as a result of the occupation of the US Embassy in Tehran.[18]

Today the IRGC consists of an array of military, political, economic, and cultural organizations and is one of the most powerful institutions in Iran. Its members and former members hold positions throughout the government. It has substantial influence over Iran's military doctrine and how the state defines its security and national interests. It has units stationed throughout the country and its own army, navy, and air force. The IRGC commands the Quds Force, an elite unit specializing in unconventional and asymmetric warfare and responsible for supporting Iran's proxies and allies in Iraq, Lebanon, Syria, and elsewhere. The IRGC operates its own intelligence branch, oversees several universities, and owns companies in many sectors of the economy. It controls Iran's strategic-missile force, dominates ballistic missile production, and plays a central role in the state's nuclear program.[19]

University Press, 1957); Morris Janowitz, *The Military in the Political Development of New Nations* (University of Chicago Press, 1964); Nikola Schahgaldian, *The Iranian Military Under the Islamic Republic* (RAND, 1987); Sepehr Zabih, *The Iranian Military in Revolution and War* (Routledge, 1988).

[18] See Saeid Golkar, *Captive Society* (Columbia University Press, 2015).

[19] The IRGC military consists of at least 125,000 active service members, which include approximately 100,000 in the army, 20,000 in the navy, 5,000 in the Quds Force, and a small air force. Iran's regular military has an army of 350,000, navy of 18,000, and air force of 30,000. The IRGC's total numbers increase substantially with the inclusion of the Basij, which may include up to one million members. Those numbers do not, however, account for any of the

Contributions to Scholarship

While the power and significance of the IRGC have grown, scholarship on the organization has not kept pace. The IRGC's history of the Iran–Iraq War has not been researched or written about by scholars. There have been no works that have examined, or that have set out to examine, the central questions regarding the construction and content of the IRGC's history that drive the present study. Neglect of the IRGC sources can be attributed to several factors. First, much of the existing literature on the Iran–Iraq War was published during or shortly after the conflict and before the vast majority of the IRGC sources became available. Second, the IRGC publications are not widely accessible, especially outside of Iran. There are hardly any traces of them in existing studies, so researchers have little reason to be aware that they exist. Their imperceptibility is compounded by the popular image of the IRGC as an ideological military unlikely to invest in historical scholarship. Finally, all of the IRGC sources are in Persian, which many people writing about Iran do not read.

English-language scholarship on the IRGC is scant. Most of the monographs are limited and of relatively low but varying academic caliber. They discuss the IRGC as an institution and its roles in Iran's domestic politics but include little analysis of the Guards' involvement in the Iran–Iraq War and none on their history of the conflict.

The two foundational works on the IRGC are Kenneth Katzman's *The Warriors of Islam* (Westview Press, 1993) and *The Rise of the Pasdaran*, a 2009 RAND study. The former analyzes the IRGC's institutional strength and the latter traces the Guards' ascendancy within Iran. Both provide much useful information on the IRGC but include very little on the Guards' perspectives or their experiences in the war.

Three additional studies on the IRGC – Emanuele Ottolenghi's *The Pasdaran* (Foundation for the Defense of Democracies, 2011), Ali Alfoneh's *Iran Unveiled* (American Enterprise Institute, 2013), and Steven O'Hern's *Iran's Revolutionary Guard* (Potomac, 2012) – are all the product of the recent uptick in interest in the IRGC generated by

IRGC's non-military institutions. "Chapter Seven: Middle East and North Africa," *The Military Balance* (International Institute for Strategic Studies, 2017). See also additional reports by the International Institute for Strategic Studies and those by Anthony Cordesman at the Center for Strategic and International Studies.

the group's growing power. Like the Katzman and RAND studies, those by Ottolenghi and Alfoneh include useful data on the IRGC, particularly on its organizational structure. Unlike the former studies, however, these three monographs are guided by the goal of encouraging policymakers in the United States to recognize and counter the threat they argue the IRGC presents.[20]

Finally, three academic monographs on the IRGC were published in 2016, a fact that attests to the growing recognition of the need for additional and more rigorous scholarship on the organization. The best of these is Afshon Ostovar's *Vanguard of the Imam* (Oxford University Press), which is the most comprehensive study of the IRGC to date. Although *Vanguard of the Imam* represents a significant contribution to the scholarship on the IRGC, it certainly does not close the sizeable gap in the literature. Though he does cite some IRGC sources, Ostovar does not use those that form the basis of the present study, and the perspective is overall not that of the Guards themselves.

The other two 2016 studies of the IRGC – Hesam Forozan's *The Military in Post-Revolutionary Iran* and Bayram Sinkaya's *Revolutionary Guards in Iranian Politics* (both Routledge) – overlap substantially with one another. Both examine the IRGC's roles in Iranian politics and the reasons for its growing power, but not the Guards' perspectives and publications. Both authors rely heavily on theoretical and comparative methodologies that lead them to essentially the same conclusion – that the IRGC's ascent is the result of the way the organization has interacted with its domestic political environment. Finally, there are several shorter studies on the IRGC, as well as books and articles on Iran's armed forces, many of which make significant contributions to our understanding of those subjects and which are included in the bibliography.

Studies on the Iran–Iraq War, which similarly fail to examine the Revolutionary Guards' history of the conflict, are also limited by a number of temporal, thematic, and methodological shortcomings.

---

[20] Ottolenghi argues that Western "policymakers must … develop coherent policies to curb [the IRGC's] influence … and aggressively isolate its leadership and its tentacle-like reach both inside the country and beyond Iran's borders" (p. 74). Alfoneh writes that his "book aims at correcting the U.S. decision makers' understanding of the nature of the regime in Tehran by discussing how the IRGC is transforming the Islamic Republic into a military dictatorship" (p. 2).

Most of these are general monographs or edited volumes written during or right after the war.[21] Though a declining number of studies on the conflict have been published over time, several have come out since the late 1990s, a few of which merit mention here.[22]

Iran, Iraq, and the Legacies of War (Palgrave Macmillan, 2004), edited by Lawrence Potter and Gary Sick, is one of the best volumes on the war published to date. Of particular value is Farideh Farhi's chapter on "The Antinomies of Iran's War Generation," which references the IRGC publications on the war. Farhi notably mentions the studies produced by the IRGC's Holy Defense Research and Documentation Center and stresses that they deserve the attention of historians.

The Iran–Iraq War: New International Perspectives (Routledge, 2013), edited by Nigel Ashton and Bryan Gibson, is one of the few volumes that aims to reassess the existing scholarship on the war. Although that is an important goal, the editors overlook many of the most significant shortcomings and source-related issues in their review of the literature. They do not note, for example, the need to integrate Persian-language sources, which the volume's contributors likewise fail to utilize. This shortcoming is particularly evident in Rob Johnson's chapter on Iran. Instead of offering a new perspective, Johnson rehashes many of the common mischaracterizations of Iran's prosecution of the war without referencing Persian-language sources and while exposing a sketchy understanding of Iranian history.

The final recent addition to the literature is Peirre Razoux's *The Iran–Iraq War* (translated by Nicholas Elliott, Belknap Press/Harvard University Press, 2015), which is the most comprehensive study of the war to date. Its enumeration of the war's military and political developments, cataloging of many relevant statistics, and use of previously untapped sources are especially valuable. Razoux is also one of the few authors who recognize that, contrary to the conventional wisdom, the Iran–Iraq War demonstrates that "the Iranian leadership is perfectly rational and pragmatic" (pp. 484–85). My research significantly

---

[21] These include Shahram Chubin and Charles Tripp, *Iran and Iraq at War* (I.B. Tauris, 1988); Dilip Hiro, *The Longest War* (Grafton, 1989); Anthony Cordesman, *The Lessons of Modern War, Vol. II: The Iran–Iraq War* (Westview Press, 1991).

[22] These include Jerome Donovan, *The Iran–Iraq War* (Routledge, 2011); Robert Johnson, *The Iran–Iraq War* (Palgrave Macmillan, 2011).

bolsters that contention. Yet, as was true of those discussed earlier, Razoux's study leaves a plethora of subjects and sources unexplored and contains several factual and analytical errors. Of particular note is the lack of analysis of the war's nonmilitary dimensions, the perspectives of the combatants, and the conflict's longer-term and social impacts. There is no new information on the IRGC and no use of Persian-language sources.

As a whole, the existing literature has presented and perpetuated a series of misconceptions about the IRGC and the Iran–Iraq War: The Revolutionary Guards should be understood first and foremost as the uncompromising vanguards of the Islamic Revolution; they consistently rejected military professionalism and rationality because they believed that revolutionary and Islamic fervor alone would win the war for Iran; and they viewed the war as a vehicle for demonstrating the legitimacy and dynamism of the revolution, a goal to which all others were sacrificed. This book's analysis repudiates all of those claims. It should accordingly alter and complicate existing conceptions of the IRGC and the Iran–Iraq War and the way we understand the Islamic Republic of Iran.

Faith and Firepower

The theme of "faith and firepower" that runs through the analysis demonstrates well the significance of the book's contributions. I have derived the concept of faith and firepower from a wartime declaration attributed to de facto supreme war commander Akbar Hashemi Rafsanjani that "the faith of the Islamic troops is stronger than the superior firepower of Iraq's troops."[23] In much of the scholarship, a strictly literal interpretation of that and similar statements has been used to define the way Iranian leaders viewed the war. Without reference to the IRGC sources, the literature contends that Islamic fervor dictated the way the Revolutionary Guards fought the war, that the Guards were incapable of viewing the conflict in military terms, and that they were concerned only with faith, not at all with firepower.

---

[23] "*I'tiqād-i sarbāzān-i Islām qavītar az qudrat-i ātish-i bartar-i sarbāzān-i 'Irāqī ast.*" Quoted in Sayyed-Hossein Yahyavi, "War of the Cities," *Negin Iran* 10.36 (HDRDC, 2011), 31.

My analysis of the IRGC and its history of the war challenges those claims by demonstrating that the Guards' understanding of the relationship between faith and firepower is unlike and much more sophisticated than what existing studies suggest. In contrast to what has been asserted, it certainly was not based on whatever "mood" the Guards happened to be in; it did value professional military lessons and was very much shaped by "practical considerations [and] constraints."[24] The Guards in fact assert that faith and firepower are complementary rather than contradictory and that both were important in fighting the war.

But this does not mean that the Guards disagree with Rafsanjani's declaration, at least not when we refrain from interpreting it literally by presuming to know what Iranian leaders "really believed" or from seeing it as a statement of absolute fact instead of what it was – a slogan and a battle cry, an attempt to convince Iranians to fight in a war in which they were very likely to die.[25] Stripping Rafsanjani's statement of its falsely applied literalism also allows us to use it more productively as a way to examine the relationship between faith and firepower as the Guards define it in their own sources and thereby to better understand the IRGC.

Notes on Methodology

Making use of and analyzing the Revolutionary Guards' sources on the Iran–Iraq War is the essence of this book. Those sources comprise and contain the Guards' history of the war. In working to understand that history, I have been guided by several considerations.

The first relates to the nature and composition of the IRGC. As will be discussed in Chapter 2, the Revolutionary Guards' history of the war is largely the product of one part of the IRGC (the Holy Defense Research and Documentation Center). However, throughout the analysis I have endeavored to understand the IRGC sources both as a whole and as a collection, to analyze and draw conclusions about the IRGC history in its entirety and to distinguish between its different elements. In the book I refer to "IRGC authors," "IRGC sources," and

---

[24] Shahram Chubin, "The Last Phase of the Iran–Iraq War," *Third World Quarterly* 11.2 (1989), 3–4.
[25] Ibid.

the "IRGC history," and so it is important to note that when I do so I am referring to the organizations and individuals who are responsible for that history. I am not arguing that they represent the positions of all of the IRGC's other members, and I am not attempting to make sweeping generalizations about the organization as a whole. The IRGC is not monolithic and does not speak with one voice, and therefore does not have a single historical narrative of the war that encompasses all its members. Still, those responsible for the IRGC publications do represent some of the most prominent and influential Revolutionary Guards and thus can rightly be said to be producing the IRGC's "official" history that reflects the views of the organization's leaders.

A second consideration relates to the content and contextualization of the Guards' history. As noted earlier, this is a study of several main subjects, only one of which is the Iran–Iraq War. Accordingly, not all of the war's events are examined comprehensively, as I have focused on those that are most prominent in the IRGC histories and that are therefore most central to the book's main themes. In my analysis I have sought to place the IRGC sources in their proper factual, historical, and analytical contexts. I have used a number of other sources, particularly press reports and secondary literature, to assess their accuracy and have noted the discrepancies I did discover. Overall, though, the IRGC histories conform to the historical record as it has been reported in those other sources and their characterizations of events are firmly grounded in facts and realities.

At the same time, the IRGC publications must be understood as reflecting the Guards' organizational and political motives. Though this may limit the sources' value for other studies, it does not diminish their value here. That is because my aim is to investigate precisely what those sources provide – the IRGC's representations of the war, whatever they may be – and to gain insight into how the Revolutionary Guards understand the war and their roles in it. Further, it is essential not to dismiss the IRGC publications simply because they, like all sources, reflect the views and goals of their authors. Thus far, doing so has produced an incomplete and overly simplistic picture of the Revolutionary Guards and their roles in the war. In contrast, the careful and critical analysis of the IRGC sources that I present here is a substantial addition to the history and historiography of modern Iran.

I have also sought to put the IRGC histories in a larger analytical context by making use of additional Iranian and non-Iranian primary and secondary sources. Still, my focus is on the Revolutionary Guards' history of the war as it is presented in their own publications. It is therefore important to acknowledge that this is a study of a particular set of the Iran–Iraq War's participants and historians, and it accordingly relies on the particular set of sources most pertinent to those subjects. Although a full contextualization or comparative analysis of some or all of the IRGC's representations of the war with other Iranian or non-Iranian sources would certainly be worthwhile, it is well beyond the scope of the present study. Indeed, the Iran–Iraq War, as the defining event in the Islamic Republic's history, has been the subject of a vast amount of analysis, reflection, and commemoration in Iran (and elsewhere). As the IRGC publications have not received any focused attention, they must first be uncovered and the narrative they contain reconstructed and analyzed before they can be more fully contextualized or subjected to comparative analysis. That is precisely what this book sets out to do.

Finally, it should be noted that the present study examines subjects that have been the focus of theoretical literature on topics including armed forces, revolution, war, security, and collective memory. When deciding how to engage that literature, I have been guided by the goal of shedding as much light as possible on the specific subjects under examination and of employing the explanatory strategies that are the most elucidating. What my examinations of both the IRGC and the theoretical literature have shown more than anything is that the IRGC does not fit neatly into existing conceptual categories.[26] For this

[26] For example, the IRGC is an "irregular" armed force in that it does "much more than make war" but, and to a large extent because of the Iran–Iraq War, is a "regular" armed force because it is part of the centralized state and is involved in "fighting external aggressors." Further, the IRGC is much more than an armed force – regular or irregular – so defining its relationship to the rest of Iran's governing apparatus must take into account its expansive nature. Anthony W. Pereira, "Conclusion: Armed Forces, Coercive Monopolies, and Changing Patterns of State Formation and Violence," 394 and Diane E. Davis, "Contemporary Challenges and Historical Reflections on the Study of Militaries, States, and Politics," 32, both in *Irregular Armed Forces and Their Role in Politics and State Formation*, eds. Diane E. Davis and Anthony W. Pereira (Cambridge University Press, 2003). Katzman argued that the IRGC "refutes" many of the "assertions" presented in the theoretical literature because it "is far too unusual in its ideological outlook, method of operations, role

reason, and because the overarching aim of this study is to examine the IRGC and its history on their own terms and as fully as possible, a more theoretical examination of those subjects shall await further analysis.

A Note on Terminology

The name of the organization under examination, as it is literally translated, is the Islamic Revolution Guards Corps or the Corps of Guards of the Islamic Revolution (*Sipah-i Pasdaran-i Inqilab-i Islami*). In this study, that organization is usually referred to as the "IRGC," a singular noun formed from the acronym of its name as most commonly translated into English, Islamic Revolutionary Guards Corps. In certain contexts, however, "IRGC" is replaced by the term "Sepah," the most common transliteration of *Sipah*, or Corps, which is how the organization is commonly referred to in Iran and in the IRGC sources. "Sepah" has been deemed more appropriate than "IRGC" when the organization is the subject of discussion or an actor in historical events, while IRGC is used to describe the organization today, the one responsible for writing rather than performing the history of the Iran–Iraq War. Thus, for example, I refer to the "IRGC sources" on the war but to the formation of the "Sepah." "Sepah" is also used when discussing the organization in conjunction with the Islamic Republic's regular military. The latter is referred to as the "Artesh," the most common transliteration of *Artish*, which is how the military is commonly referred to in Iran and in the IRGC sources. The members of the IRGC are referred to in the plural as the "Revolutionary Guards" (*Pasdaran-i Inqilabi*) or "Guards" (*Pasdaran*). However, all the terms outlined here (IRGC, Sepah, Revolutionary Guards, Guards) refer to the same organizational group.

Chapters and Themes

This book analyzes the construction and content of the IRGC's history of the Iran–Iraq War and explains the significance of that project for understanding both, as well as for understanding the Islamic Republic of Iran more broadly. It begins in Chapters 1 and 2 by introducing the

functions in Iranian society and politics, and developmental history to conform easily to traditional approaches of politico-military analysis." Katzman, *The Warriors of Islam*, 7–8, 1.

22

Introduction

book's main protagonists, the guards and historians. These chapters trace the development of the IRGC and of its efforts to document the Iran–Iraq War, including the people, units, activities, and publications that make up that project. In doing so, these chapters demonstrate that the development of the IRGC's documentation of the war mirrors the evolution of both the Iran–Iraq War and the IRGC as a whole, which highlights how the project emblematizes the organization and the war's centrality to its legitimacy and identity.

Chapter 3 then begins the analysis of the IRGC's history of the Iran–Iraq War. It examines how the IRGC authors explain the war's outbreak and the lead-up to the Iraqi invasion. It also introduces one of the book's main themes, the connections between the war and the Iranian Revolution that preceded it. According to the Guards, the success of the revolution was the most important catalyst for the Iraqi invasion. Iraq made the strategic decision to strike while the revolution was still hot – to attack the Islamic Republic in the midst of its revolutionary transition, when the new regime's power was tenuous and its readiness for war diminished.

The examination of how the IRGC analyzes the war's early stages is continued in Chapter 4, which turns to Iran's response to the Iraqi invasion. That response, according to the Guards, was characterized by a combination of willingness and inability. Though many Iranians scrambled to repulse the attack on their territory, their nation, and their Islamic Revolution, they generally proved unable to do so. That dynamic exposes another of the connections between the Iran–Iraq War and the Iranian Revolution. One of the central arguments the IRGC authors make in their publications is that Iran's ability to prosecute the war depended in large part on whether the revolutionary conditions in the country helped or hindered that effort. In this initial stage of the fighting, the disorder left in the revolution's wake debilitated the Islamic Republic, rendering it unable to prevent Iraq's occupation of parts of its territory.

Chapter 5 presents the story of how Iran finally turned the tide, of how the revolution progressed to the point that it could help instead of hinder the war effort. What the IRGC authors term "the epic of Khorramshahr" – Iran's retaking of that city after months of Iraqi occupation – marked the culmination of the reversal. For the Guards, the liberation of Khorramshahr represents a case in which faith could be used effectively against firepower. Though the Iraqi forces retained their advantage in firepower, the Iranians' faithful determination gave them the ultimate edge in their fight to retake the city. The liberation of Khorramshahr signified a turning point both in the war and for the Revolutionary Guards. The campaign marked the IRGC's most substantial participation in the war to that point and initiated its transformation into the powerful and professional military that experience has allowed it to become.

The Iran–Iraq War's second critical reversal, Iran's shift from defense to offense, is examined in Chapter 6. Decades later, the Islamic Republic's decision to continue the war and invade Iraq following the liberation of most of its territory remains a point of contention and misunderstanding. While for most outside analysts the decision exemplifies the aggression, irrationality, and ideological zeal that make the Islamic Republic so dangerous, for the IRGC the invasion was an act not of aggression but of defense. According to the IRGC authors, Iran's decision to pursue the war's original aggressors into their own territory was made carefully and rationally and only after the invasion was deemed necessary for restoring Iran's national security. Dreams of marching straight through Iraq and onward to Jerusalem, though useful rhetorically to rally the troops, played no role in the decision-making process. For too long, however, such rhetoric has been taken literally. Instead of relying on the hyperbole of slogans and battle cries, this chapter utilizes the internal accounts included in the IRGC sources to rewrite the story of how and why Iran decided to invade Iraq.

Chapter 7 examines the numerous difficulties Iran faced following that invasion. In its last six years, the Iran–Iraq War became more and more difficult for the Islamic Republic to prosecute, forcing Iranian political and military leaders to come up with ways to keep the war going. The liberation of Khorramshahr had greatly bolstered morale and popular support and had generated enough initiative to drive the war into Iraq. But that initiative began to run dry after the invasion, as successive Iranian operations failed to produce the desired results – a decisive victory that would force the acceptance of Iran's ceasefire terms and ensure the security of the country. In addition to these military challenges, in the later stages of the conflict Iran was forced to confront the war's pluralization as the parties to and the scope of the conflict expanded.

Chapter 8 completes the chronological analysis of the IRGC's history of the Iran–Iraq War by examining how the Revolutionary

Guards assess the conflict's conclusion. As the indelible declaration from Supreme Leader Khomeini made clear, deciding to end the war was agonizing for Iran, akin to drinking from a poisoned chalice. The assessment of the IRGC sources presented in this chapter reveals why that was so and why the decision was finally made. Understanding the disquiet that surrounds Iran's acceptance of the ceasefire also reveals the IRGC's view of the conflict as unfinished, a view that represents one of the ways the Iran–Iraq War continues to have a profound impact on the Islamic Republic.

In Chapter 9, we take a closer look at one of the book's overarching themes, the relationship between faith and firepower. In the existing literature and the news media alike, much weight is given to the rhetoric Iranian leaders used during (and since) the Iran–Iraq War and to the importance of faith and revolutionary fervor in understanding the Islamic Republic and its prosecution of the conflict. As this chapter demonstrates, the IRGC sources and the Islamic Republic's actions reveal a different story. By taking those as the basis of analysis and by casting aside a literalized interpretation of the regime's rhetoric, here the book illustrates that Iran prosecuted the war by relying on all the tools at its disposal, which included both faith and firepower.

Chapter 10 examines some of the most important ways the Iran–Iraq War and its history impact the IRGC and the Islamic Republic today. These include efforts to derive political and strategic lessons from the conflict and how Iran's experience in the war gave rise to a security doctrine that seeks above all to establish effective deterrence and ensure Iran's independence, in part by integrating Iran into the wider region and utilizing asymmetric and soft power. Running through these and many other aspects of the war's ongoing significance is the conception that the conflict has not ended, and therefore that the Holy Defense continues.

Chapter 11 examines the ongoing processes of how the war has continued to shape the IRGC and how the IRGC has continued to shape the history of the war. The former is discussed in the first half of the chapter, which assesses how the war transformed the IRGC into a more complete and professional military and how the organization has used its contributions to the war effort to justify its growing power in the years since; and the latter is discussed in the chapter's second half, which examines how the Holy Defense Research and Documentation Center has expanded and promoted its projects.

Finally, Chapter 12 ties together the book's central themes and highlights its main contributions. It argues that the Revolutionary Guards have endeavored to write the history of the Iran–Iraq War because of the way the Guards view the importance and meaning of the conflict in Iran today, the way they understand the nature and dynamism of history, and their commitment to what they view as the historical imperative of keeping the war alive.

1 | Guards

The Establishment of the IRGC

This chapter introduces the book's main protagonists, the Islamic Revolutionary Guards Corps (IRGC) or Sepah, Corps, how the IRGC often refers to itself in its own publications. It traces how the Sepah formed from groups brought together by the shared goal of protecting what they saw as the Islamic Revolution's most important principles. The Sepah emerged in the days after Ayatollah Khomeini's return to Iran on February 1, 1979 and in the midst of the revolution's turbulent and precarious transitory phase, which was characterized by political and violent struggles over the character of the new regime. A particularly contentious issue, and one especially critical in the Sepah's formation, was the fate of the Artesh, Iran's regular military, and the nature of military power in the post-revolutionary state.

The Birth of the Armed Forces of the Revolution

The Sepah's formation is examined in the first volume of the *Chronology of the Iran–Iraq War* (*Chronology* or *War Chronology*), the major work produced by the IRGC's Holy Defense Research and Documentation Center (HDRDC), which it defines as the "birth of the armed forces of the revolution."[1] Understanding that process, according to this volume, requires assessing in more general terms the importance of the control of military power in determining a revolution's fate. The emphasis on armed force is apparent in the way the IRGC authors outline the stages through which "political revolutions generally pass." The "conclusive fall of the [old] government and the victory of the revolution," they state, occur when all of the *ancien régime*'s "military-strategic centers" have been conquered.[2] In discussing the Iranian case, the authors pay particular attention to the struggles over and involving armed force. They highlight the clash

---

[1] *Chronology of the Iran–Iraq War 1* (HDRDC, 1997), 28, 31.   [2] Ibid., 28.

between the shah's Imperial Guard and pro-revolutionary members of the Iranian air force (technicians known as *humafaran*) at the Doshan Tappeh training camp in Tehran on February 9–11, 1979 as "the final stage in the collapse of the monarchical regime."[3] They argue similarly that "the beginning of the political life of the new system raised by the Islamic Revolution in Iran was the inevitable appearance of fundamental transformations in the structure of the armed forces."[4]

Such transformations, however, take time, during which an incipient revolutionary regime finds itself dangerously vulnerable. According to this volume, because a revolution "does not lead to the immediate establishment of a new system," it is followed by "a period in which the previous system and its pillars have been destroyed but the new system and its institutions have still not been completely established." Accordingly, "the rule of the revolutionary state over the country is very weak because the tools it needs to exert power do not exist." Of all of these missing tools, the IRGC authors assert that the "lack of centralized armed power with the necessary and sufficient strength and legitimacy for the complete establishment of the new government" had the most serious consequences in Iran, because it "made for fertile ground for the mobilization and expansion of opponents of the new system."[5]

It was in that context that the Sepah was born. Groups calling themselves "Guards of the Islamic Revolution" first began operating a few days before the monarchy's collapse on February 11.[6] Several such "religious-revolutionary groups" were brought together over the next several months to form what became the "Corps of Guards of the Islamic Revolution" by the end of April. Each of these groups, though established independently of one another, emerged because of the perceived "need to establish as quickly as possible a military-revolutionary force that both had the support of the political power of the new system and that could thwart [various] kinds of possible plots" against the revolution.[7]

In this period the Sepah gradually formed from the coalescence of sundry revolutionary vagabonds. It integrated people who had participated in the revolution and who sought a group with which they could "continue to guard."[8] It also absorbed some of the various revolutionary committees that had formed in the revolution's wake.[9] Given the

---

[3] Ibid., 29, 39–42. [4] Ibid., 30. [5] Ibid., 28, 31. [6] Ibid., 871–72.
[7] Ibid., 880–81. [8] Ibid., 178, 186. [9] Ibid., 264, 325, 347.

disorder and insecurity that accompanied the fall of the monarchical regime, the Sepah was immediately useful in taking on some of the functions that had been carried out by the police and other security forces – by collecting the mass of free-floating weapons, distinguishing between the political prisoners and the criminals who had together been released from the jails and apprehending the latter, and arresting those responsible for the "nightly shooting in Tehran."[10]

From the start the Guards found themselves at the center of the post-revolutionary power struggle between the Provisional Government headed by Prime Minister Bazargan and the Council of the Islamic Revolution headed by Khomeini. The initial formation of the Sepah was announced on February 21, both in the daily press conference of the Provisional Government's deputy prime minister and spokesman Abbas Amir-Entezam and in a statement signed by the "central head-quarters" of the "Corps of the Guards of the Islamic Revolution."[11] On February 24, a "gathering of Guards of the Islamic Revolution was held to deliberate and select members of the Corps of Guards." This meeting was attended by Hassan Lahouti, Khomeini's representative in the new organization, whom Khomeini had authorized "to supervise the establishment of this Sepah," which had "also been approved by the Provisional Government."[12]

The overall extent of the Sepah's mission was likewise murky in this initial period. Deputy Prime Minister Ebrahim Yazdi said at the February 24 gathering that the Sepah "will not have an extensive organization." It would be limited to "a central coordinating committee and a command headquarters, at the head of which will be a commander-in-chief" who was yet to be appointed. The Sepah's organization, however, would be extensive enough to include a "regional network" and to have both active and reserve members. Yazdi's statements on the balance between faith and firepower in the Sepah were similarly confusing. The Sepah, he said, "will not be an armed force but a revolutionary battalion that will be armed." An armed revolutionary battalion would have to know how to use the weapons with which it would be armed, so the members of the Sepah would need to be trained in the "functioning of weapons"; but they would also have to "have faith in the Islamic revolution," which

[10] Ibid., 226–27, 325, 347, 354.   [11] Ibid., 178–79.   [12] Ibid., 201.

would require "political and ideological training alongside military training."[13]

In a newspaper interview on March 4, portions of which are quoted in the *Chronology*, Lahouti put emphasis on the Sepah's revolutionary and religious identity and explained its military functions as stemming from its mission to defend the revolution. The Sepah, he stated, was envisioned and established as "a force of fighters faithful to the revolution." It would function as "the pillar and protector of the revolution in order to protect the revolution from attacks of anti-revolutionaries and destructive agents." When asked about who was eligible to join the force, Lahouti said the Sepah was open to "all forces with faith and Muslims who believe in the holy Islamic movement under the leadership of Imam Khomeini." Would Marxists and other leftist groups be welcome? "No!" Lahouti declared in response. "Faith in Islam" was "the most important" qualification. "How can you be a Guard of the Islamic Revolution when you don't believe in Islam?" He did stipulate, however, that members of the Artesh who met that standard would be accepted.[14]

The primacy of the ideology of Islamic revolution, including relative to armed power, reflected the efficacy of inspired action and the success it had just had in bringing down a highly militarized regime. Their conviction that in Islam they had finally found agency and a vector for change galvanized the Guards and fueled their commitment to remain at the revolution's helm. That creed of Islamic revolution came to the fore in the "first statement of the Corps of Guards of the Islamic Revolution," which was published in the press on April 9:

As the glorious revolution of the people of Iran surprised the world, disrupted all theories, forced the experts to reconsider, and doomed strategies to failure, all speak of the depth of the genuine and profound ideology of our people. We are now persuaded to enshrine this ideology more than ever, ... [as] the reason for our stagnation and paralysis and indifference was only our separation from Islam. Many of our intellectuals, experts, and leaders consciously or unconsciously were effective in establishing, spreading, and continuing this separation that was requested by imperialism, ... so that day by day we became more disappointed, more pessimistic, more dejected, and more identity-less, while imperialism ... was watching and laughing at us from afar![15]

---

[13] Ibid., 202–03.   [14] Ibid., 274.   [15] Ibid., 667.

Islam, then, had to be reckoned with. If its marginalization was the cause of degradation and decay, then its revitalization could very well hold the keys to redemption and recovery. But only, the statement continued, if the Islamic revolutionary movement did in fact succeed:

> Our human and Islamic duty is to support and guard this holy achievement, otherwise it will not take long for our sensational revolution to have a similar fate as the constitutional movement, and after a while there will be no trace of the results of so much sacrifice and purity.[16]

This conviction, apparent in the Sepah in its earliest days of existence, anticipates some of the primary tenets of its philosophy of history and its work to record the history of the Iran–Iraq War. Already we see the Guards invoking history to guide the future, to learn from the promise and perils of the 1905–11 Constitutional Revolution to ensure that the goals of their Islamic Revolution would be realized more fully. And we see a restlessness to guard both the lived and recorded reality of the revolution from the impermanence that only history prevents.

According to the IRGC sources, the formal establishment of the Sepah at the end of April 1979 was, in two ways, the definitive development in the establishment of the Islamic Republic. First, it was the turning point in the confrontation with the militant groups outside the government fighting the new regime. After the Sepah's formation,

> The armed organizations opposing the Islamic Revolution confronted ... an armed revolutionary organization [the Sepah] that had the advantages of "revolutionarism," organizational flexibility, and the support of the religious masses. .... Therefore, the establishment of the Sepah was the most important change in the balance of power in the ruling system [and] the most acute change in the balance of power in favor of the Islamic Revolution in its confrontation with the groups opposing [it].[17]

Second, the establishment of the Sepah was the turning point in the struggle between the "two official poles of power" within the post-revolutionary government itself – the Provisional Government and the Council of the Islamic Revolution. "Meanwhile, alongside these two official and established poles," the volume continues, the Sepah and an "alliance of radical and religious-revolutionary forces" emerged as "a third pole" that "disturbed the existing balance between the two trends

---

[16] Ibid., 668.   [17] Ibid., 35–36.

in the new government in favor of the revolutionary and radical current." From that point, "the Provisional Government encountered more and more problems in implementing a conservative line of policy and [only] incrementally reforming and correcting the former regime (including the armed forces)." The Sepah and this third pole gradually "became the most important and most serious critic of the policies of the Provisional Government" and earned the support of Ayatollah Khomeini.[18]

The contest between the Provisional Government and the Council of the Revolution for control of this new force and the revolution as a whole was protracted.[19] According to the IRGC authors, while the passage of the statute establishing the Sepah on April 25, 1979 marked the formal and legal creation of the IRGC, the official announcement of the statute on May 6 firmly settled the Sepah's position in the new regime. As the *Chronology* states, "after the formation of several distinct Sepahs," the May 6 declaration by the Council of the Revolution recognized the IRGC as "the sole legally acceptable Sepah." That Sepah, which "is and will not be under the authority of the Provisional Government or other institutions," was the Sepah "whose Council of Commanders was selected and approved by the Council of the Revolution and [that] is commanded only by the Imam [Khomeini]." The formation of the IRGC is once again portrayed as a turning point in the revolution. The establishment of the Sepah under the Council of the Revolution, the volume concludes, "resolved one of the conceptual and political conflicts between the two existing trends in the government" in a manner that was "completely in the favor of the revolutionary trend."[20]

In this way, and especially as set out by the Revolutionary Guards in this volume, the story of the armed forces in the revolution encapsulates the story of the revolution as a whole, and the Sepah emerges as the quintessence of the Islamic Republic. While it may not be surprising that the IRGC portrays itself in this manner, it is important to note the responsibility that comes with that role, meaning that the Guards, as their title suggests, assume responsibility for guarding the Islamic Republic, for ensuring its survival for the long term, which is a mission that influenced their prosecution of the Iran–Iraq War and that influences their policies and positions today. Further, the IRGC authors'

---

[18] Ibid., 34–35.   [19] Ibid., 686, 701.   [20] Ibid., 871, 874.

analysis of the Iranian Revolution implicitly validates the emphasis social scientists have placed on the control of armed force in revolutionary transitions.[21]

Formal Establishment and Mission

The Sepah was formally established by the statute issued by the Council of the Revolution on April 25, 1979. The statute contains nine main articles, which set out the Sepah's mission and duties, its organization and decision-making structure, and guidelines for the recruitment and conduct of its members.[22] The Sepah's primary mission, according to the statute's first article, is "guarding the Islamic Revolution in Iran and propagating it based on the ideology of authentic Islam and carrying out the aims of the Islamic Republic."[23]

To accomplish that mission, the statute assigns the Sepah eleven duties in article two. As these duties represent the official, statutory basis of the IRGC's activities, and because they shed light on the origins of its power, they are paraphrased here nearly in full:

1. Defending against attacks and occupation by foreign agents or forces.
2. Cooperating with the state in matters of law enforcement and security and in combatting armed anti-revolutionary groups.
3. Establishing effective cooperation and coordination with the regular armed forces.
4. Protecting public property; collecting weapons from unauthorized individuals and transferring them to officials.
5. Collecting intelligence, within the limit of its responsibilities.

---

[21] See Jonathan Adelman, *Revolution, Armies, and War* (Lynn Rienner, 1985); Katharine Chorley, *Armies and the Art of Revolution* (Beacon Press, 1973); John Ellis, *Armies in Revolution* (Croom Helm, 1973); Samuel Huntington, *Political Order in Changing Societies* (Yale University Press, 1968); Theda Skocpol, "Social Revolutions and Mass Military Mobilization," *World Politics* 40.2 (1988); Theda Skocpol, *States and Social Revolutions* (Cambridge University Press, 1979).

[22] *Chronology 1*, 783. The *Chronology* summarizes those nine articles as follows: "1 – Mission; 2 – Duties; 3 – Formations; 4 – Recruitment; 5 – Informed participation of all Guards in decisions; 6 – Use of state facilities; 7 – Need for discipline; 8 – Guards' dress; 9 – Guards' budget."

[23] Ibid., 783–88.

6. Training the Corps' permanent Guards in ideological, political, and military matters.
7. Training the Corps' reserve Guards in military and political-ideological matters.
8. Aiding the implementation of court orders.
9. Maintaining order in protests and assemblies in order to prevent the violation of law and the infringement of community rights, and likewise to prevent the violation of the rights of the protesters.
10. Supporting liberation and justice-seeking movements of the oppressed under the supervision of the Council of the Revolution and with the permission of the state.
11. Aiding in disaster recovery and development in order to utilize the Guard Corps to the fullest extent possible.[24]

These duties demonstrate well the breadth of the Sepah's mission, which encompasses both internal and external security as well as certain judicial, executive, and societal functions. Some of them – particularly the fourth calling on the Sepah to collect weapons and transfer them to state officials – clearly reflect the revolutionary circumstances in which the Sepah was established and its central role in helping certain factions (the Council of the Revolution) establish a monopoly on the legitimate use of force and with it control of the nascent state.[25] At the same time, the duties reveal that the Council of the Revolution and the Sepah's founders were looking beyond these particular circumstances and to a future in which the Sepah's responsibilities would expand. Therefore, although it has been widely noted that the Revolutionary Guards have become more powerful in recent years, the statutory basis for their expansive role is as long-standing as the organization itself.

The second volume of the *Chronology* reports that the Sepah had a "wide scope for implementing its diverse missions" very shortly after its formation in practice as well. Often these missions varied from city to city. For example, while in Tehran "the Sepah was responsible for security and discipline in rallies against America," in Shiraz it "supported the disadvantaged" and worked against "profiteers and narcotics distributors." It notes, seemingly defensively, that the Sepah's broad

---

[24] Ibid., 786.
[25] Max Weber, "Politics as a Vocation" (1918), in *From Max Weber*, trans. and eds. H. H. Gerth and C. Wright Mills (Oxford University Press, 1946), 78.

responsibility "did not seem irregular or problematic; rather, it was considered advisable and necessary."[26]

Of the duties listed above, the one that usually receives the most attention is the tenth, which calls on the Sepah to "support liberation and justice-seeking movements of the oppressed." Although the statute does not include the term, this duty is often identified as the "export of the revolution." According to the foreign press reports the IRGC authors include in the *Chronology*, this was the mission that garnered the most concern at the time, as it has since.[27] In contrast, in their sources the Guards do not highlight or emphasize the primacy of those activities. Their discussion indicates that the goal of supporting movements of the oppressed was far less pressing than guarding the revolution within Iran, especially in the Islamic Republic's precarious first year, and that doing so remained a "hope [for] the future." According to one Sepah official, "the Sepah's duties are to guard and preserve the movement that has arisen [inside Iran]. ... Our activity is currently limited to within the country, but we hope in the future to be able to expand and to aid the Muslims of the world."[28] Notably, though, the Sepah's duty in this regard is not limited to only Shi'i, or Muslim, or revolutionary groups, as the secular and anti-colonial language of the statute is inclusive of all those seeking justice and liberation from oppression.

The prominence of the Sepah's national security mission in the statute is also noteworthy. Throughout their sources the Guards characterize their original and primary mission as "protecting the revolution and its achievements" and "combatting the counter-revolution." One volume states that in the view of its founders the Sepah "was organized in order to confront anti-revolution[ary] movements in various regions" of the country.[29] Yet, according to the statute, the very first of the Sepah's duties is "defending against attacks and occupation by foreign agents or forces." Therefore, while protecting the revolution from internal opponents was the main motivation for the Sepah's establishment, its statute indicates that protecting the country, and not just the revolution, was part of the IRGC's mission from its founding. The conferral of that charge evinces Iran's long history of

---

[26] *Chronology of the Iran–Iraq War 2* (HDRDC, 1999), 33.
[27] *Chronology 1*, 872–73.   [28] *Chronology 2*, 33. Ellipsis included in the text.
[29] *Survey of the Iran–Iraq War 1*, 4th ed. (HDRDC, 1998), 59.

foreign invasion and anticipates the opposition to the revolution that was manifest so clearly in the Iran–Iraq War.

The basic structure of the Sepah is also outlined in its founding statute. According to the third article, the main "pillars" of the Sepah consisted of the Coordinating Council, its "highest advisory and decision-making authority," responsible for "establishing coordination among the Sepah and government organizations"; the General Command Council, charged with overseeing the six main Sepah units responsible for operations, intelligence, training, procurements, public relations, and administration and finance; and the Command Council for each Iranian province.[30]

While the Coordinating and General Command Councils represented the highest levels of decision-making and were responsible for issuing commands to subordinate and regional units, much of the Sepah's activity in its first year was carried out in the provinces and was focused on expanding the Guards' membership. In this period, therefore, "the most important Sepah units were the regional coordination units, which were responsible for forming and organizing Sepah forces in various provinces of the country."[31] That characterization is reflected in the statute's provision that the Sepah's "organizational structure ... will be based on the principle of decentralization." In practice, this meant that while "general principles and policy" were determined by the General Command and Coordinating Councils and had to be respected by Sepah units, "operations in each province could be carried out independently in conjunction with the center."[32]

The Sepah's decentralized structure mirrors the way in which the organization developed in practice. Both before and after its statutory establishment by the Council of the Revolution, the Sepah formed as a collection of revolutionary forces with little overall conformity or subordination to a central authority. According to another IRGC source, "revolutionary Sepah forces, with the mission of protecting the revolution and its achievements, appeared in various fields of the country," which "gradually formed the main nucleus of the Sepah."[33] Throughout the months following the declaration of the Sepah's formation, there were "announcement[s] of existence" and

---

[30] *Chronology 1*, 786–87.
[31] *Analysis of the Iran–Iraq War 1*, 2nd ed. (HDRDC, 2001), 98–99.
[32] *Chronology 1*, 786. [33] *Survey 1*, 59.

"announcement[s] of positions" of Sepah branches in various Iranian cities and provinces, as well as the first efforts to recruit members and resources, establish ranks, and carry out organized operations.[34] Indeed, in its initial stage the Sepah consisted not of one Sepah but of "several parallel Sepahs," which eventually became "a centralized, permanent, and legitimate force."[35]

This method for expanding the Sepah reflected the decentralized structure of the organization and its involvement in post-revolutionary conflicts across the country, but it also hindered the Sepah's institutionalization. The Guards classify that issue as one of their first organizational challenges, and their discussion of how it played out sheds light on one of the critical problems that is intrinsic to a revolutionary transition. In the second volume of the *War Chronology*, the IRGC authors focus on this "defining issue[]" of the Sepah's institutionalization by examining how the nascent force dealt with members "who in the course of the revolution had been placed in one of the Sepah divisions but [who] lacked the traits and characteristics desired" for Guards. Further, many of these members "were not prepared to accept the ground rules of the centralized Sepah organizations, but also did not agree to renounce the Sepah." The Sepah's struggle to deal "properly and ethically" with its share of the revolution's flotsam "was among the mental and behavioral preoccupations of the first months of the Sepah's establishment and formation" and generated "sit-ins and strikes" that were indicative of the "discontent with the structure, leadership, and stated ground rules of the newly organized centralized Sepah."[36]

According to this volume, some Sepah officials – including Javad Mansouri, the first Sepah commander, and Abu Sharif (Abbas Zamani), the first Sepah operations commander – tried "to explain the necessity of rule-making and the inevitability of some refinements in line with the formation of a faithful and informed revolutionary armed force" to the Guards' cadres. While enforcing rules and standards had not been practicable in the first months of the revolution, after the Sepah's formal establishment, the recruitment of Guards "was

---

[34] *Chronology* 2, 17, 21, 32.   [35] Ibid., 32.

[36] Ibid. On the IRGC's institutionalization, see Maryam Alemzadeh, "The Islamic Revolutionary Guards Corps in the Iran–Iraq War," *British Journal of Middle Eastern Studies* 46.4 (2019); Kenneth Katzman, *Warriors of Islam* (Westview Press, 1993).

converted into a merit-based procedure with accepted organizational norms." In concluding their discussion, the IRGC authors point to a key paradox of revolutionary transition. The "same revolutionary and ideological policies and methods that had been the main factor in attracting excellent cadres" during and immediately after the revolution "were afterwards a main part of the problems concerning the cadres and elites of the newly established Islamic system, whether within or outside the Sepah."[37]

In the period between its formal establishment at the end of April 1979 and the beginning of the Iran–Iraq War in September 1980, the Sepah's development was uneven. The organization did grow in size: According to sources quoted in the IRGC publications, the Sepah included only 6,000 Guards at the beginning of that period and somewhere under 30,000 at the end.[38] The Guards argue that the number could have been higher, but the "lack of facilities, supplies, [and] sufficient budget, and disagreement over the fate of the Sepah among the country's political [leaders] hindered [its] quick and comprehensive growth."[39] The Sepah also remained disorganized. According to the same source, "despite [its] determinative role in ending the conflicts" in various regions of the country, Sepah forces were identified "only by the title 'members of the Revolution Guards'" rather than as members of battalions or brigades, which remained the case "even in the first years of the [Iran–Iraq] War." Further, the Sepah's underdevelopment meant that it remained secondary to the Artesh for several years after the revolution.[40]

One of the factors contributing to the Sepah's numerical growth was the formation of the Basij (the Organization for the Mobilization of the Oppressed) in November 1979, after the seizure of the US Embassy in Tehran when tensions with the United States threatened to boil over into full-blown conflict.[41] Although the Basij was not fully integrated into the IRGC until after the war, the Sepah oversaw much of the Basij's activities beginning shortly after its establishment.[42] As was the case with the Islamic Republic's other armed forces, the Basij became the subject of factional dispute, which left it in an ambiguous position and impeded its development. The IRGC sources assert that while

---

[37] *Chronology 2*, 32–33.   [38] *Chronology 1*, 871.
[39] *Analysis 1*, 99; *Chronology 1*, 861.   [40] *Analysis 1*, 99.
[41] Ibid., 100; *Chronology of the Iran–Iraq War 7-1* (HDRDC, 2006), 975–78.
[42] *Survey 1*, 60; *Chronology 7-1*, 16, 54.

there were "various forces committed to training the Basij" in "every corner of the country," the Provisional Government and then the Islamic Republic's first president, Bani-Sadr, impeded those efforts. The Basij remained without an "independent organization or facilities" and its training "did not go beyond M1 and G3 rifles!" Therefore, the force was "prevented from developing the desired quality and quantity."[43]

Sepah and Artesh

As was discussed in the beginning of this chapter, the IRGC authors emphasize that the transition of military power was one of the distinctive and most consequential features of the Islamic Revolution. They recount the deep disagreements among the revolutionaries about the fate of the shah's military, the nature of armed power under the Islamic Republic, and the relationship between the two, which resulted in a protracted and acrimonious transition. While the monarchy's political institutions were largely destroyed in the initial stages of the revolution, they argue, the old system's "military structure did not undergo destruction, dispersion, or dissolution." Some important changes, like the dismissal of commanders of ranks higher than colonel, had begun, but the military's "body and foundations suffered only small [and] reparable wounds," which contributed to calls among some factions for the complete dissolution of the Artesh.[44]

Despite these concerns, the Sepah is not portrayed as among the anti-Artesh factions, and in this and other volumes the Revolutionary Guards refer to those who called for the Artesh's dissolution as "opponents of the new system." They argue that the effort to eliminate the Artesh stemmed from anxiety over its possible counter-revolutionary tendencies (which turned out not to be unfounded), as well as from an inaccurate view of its incompatibility with the revolution.[45] To illustrate that position, the *War Chronology* describes the opposition to the Artesh on the part of the People's Mujahidin, one of the most prominent revolutionary groups and also one of the most reviled among the religious-revolutionary faction that came to dominate the new regime. In a speech at the University of Tehran on February 24, 1979, the group's leader, Massoud Rajavi, issued what the IRGC

[43] *Analysis 1*, 100.   [44] *Chronology 1*, 29.   [45] Ibid.; *Survey 1*, 59.

authors call a "severe and unprecedented attack on the Provisional Government," claiming that its legitimacy was contingent on the dissolution of the Artesh. "The revolution must begin by dissolving the Artesh," Rajavi declared, "otherwise you're not talking about a revolution." Although the Sepah was not usually the first to defend the Provisional Government, doing so in this instance was likely easier given that Rajavi also "attacked the formation of the Sepah" and compared it to a secular and only nominally revolutionary "national guard" of the kind found in Arab states.[46]

In contrast to groups like the People's Mujahidin, the Sepah is presented as supporting the Artesh's preservation. In one volume the IRGC authors praise Khomeini's "foresight and understanding of the need to preserve the Artesh [and] his all-out support for this force."[47] The Guards go even further in the *War Chronology*, portraying themselves as among the Artesh's foremost supporters and as having "a determinative role in implementing the commands and judgments of Imam Khomeini regarding protecting the Artesh and in preventing its disintegration and dissolution." In "guarding the military centers and equipment" and in working against "the currents that were earnestly seeking the dissolution of the Artesh, [the Sepah's] role was important and determinative."[48]

Instead of disbanding the Artesh, the Guards argue that it was necessary to "reconstruct and rehabilitate" the military and allow it to "adapt to the new culture and ideology" of the revolution.[49] The *War Chronology* asserts that "the religious-revolutionary forces [like] the Sepah ... were serious supporters of the Artesh ... and endeavored to preserve and transform it into the Artesh of the Islamic Republic."[50] That position was articulated by Khomeini's representative in the Sepah. In his March 4 interview, when asked whether the "monarchical Artesh can be converted into a revolutionary Artesh," Lahouti objected to the question itself as indicating that "there must be someone here who explicitly attacks the Artesh and speaks ill of it with ugly words like these." He argued that in establishing their new government the revolutionaries must understand that "although the Artesh of Iran received bad training, its individual [members] attained the greatest

---

[46] *Chronology 1*, 209.   [47] *Survey 1*, 59–60; *Chronology 1*, 669, 687–88.
[48] *Chronology 1*, 36, 179–80.   [49] Ibid., 30; *Survey 1*, 59–60.
[50] *Chronology 2*, 36–37.

victory with the victory of the Islamic Revolution, because they were liberated, they were not guilty." Accordingly, he concluded, "we must preserve this Artesh."[51]

The Guards' support for the maintenance of the Artesh relates to their broader analysis of the relationship between the Islamic Republic's two armed forces, which consistently emphasizes their compatibility. That characterization, which will be discussed further in later chapters, diverges from the image presented in the secondary literature of the Guards invariably opposing and competing with the Artesh. However, the Sepah's role in reforming the Artesh did add a degree of unease to what the IRGC authors generally describe as a cooperative relationship.

Converting the Artesh into a force that represented and was loyal to the Islamic Republic involved purges, "detentions, and confrontations that were naturally carried out by the revolutionary armed forces," meaning the Sepah. Although in this volume of the *War Chronology* the IRGC authors state that the Artesh was amenable to and cooperated in its own reformation, the manner of implementing reforms caused resistance among the "general Artesh soldiery." Therefore, "several months after the victory of the revolution and [following] the identification of the faithful and competent Artesh forces and the passage of the acute revolutionary period, steps to change the manner of implementation of these [reforms] were carried out." These steps included the greater involvement of Artesh officials in implementing changes to the force, improved oversight, and the regularization of the process, which together represented "a sign of progress in . . . reconstructing the Artesh."[52]

The Guards assert that the process of revolutionizing the Artesh would be a slow one. According to the second volume of the *War Chronology*, this transition "from the shah's American Artesh to an Islamic and national Artesh" was "naturally not possible in several weeks or several months."[53] The volume goes on to argue that after "Imam Khomeini and revolutionary and religious forces" defeated the effort to dissolve the Artesh, the attempts of political groups to influence and infiltrate the military, and the efforts of officials to prevent that, became the prevailing issue related to the armed forces, which made the reconstruction of the military even more problematic and

[51] *Chronology 1*, 275.   [52] *Chronology 2*, 36–37.   [53] Ibid., 33–34.

drawn out.[54] As a result, the revolution within the Artesh was still ongoing when the Iran–Iraq War began over a year later, which naturally hindered the military's ability to confront the Iraqi invasion, as will be discussed in coming chapters. In addition to the political disputes about the fate and control of the military, the fourth volume of the *War Chronology* argues that the purging and replacing of anti-revolutionary officers, the conflicts with anti-revolutionary groups, and the elimination of the Artesh's American identity (which, it says, "had been ingrained in [its] bone marrow"), further "prevented the opportunity to implement essential changes" in the military before the outbreak of the war.[55]

Combatting the Counter-Revolution

Before the beginning of the conflict with Iraq, the Sepah's activities centered around countering armed anti-revolutionary groups, particularly those formed among Iran's ethnic minorities in the southwestern province of Khuzistan and the northwestern province of Kurdistan. Doing so engaged the Guards in their first military confrontations and gave them experience in guerilla, urban, and mountain warfare, on which they drew in the war with Iraq. In some of those conflicts, the Guards also had their first encounters with Iraqi forces, who were supporting Iran's anti-revolutionary and separatist groups. Confronting the armed movements was the Sepah's primary mission before the war, and carrying it out had a formative impact on both the IRGC and the Islamic Republic.[56]

In their analysis of the conflicts in both Khuzistan and Kurdistan, the Guards argue that the use of force against the armed groups resisting the rule of the Islamic Republic was necessary and essential in protecting the new regime. Indeed, the most significant feature of the Guards' analysis of those conflicts is their assertion that Iran's Arab and Kurdish populations were invariably opposed to the Islamic Republic, and therefore that the regime was forced to use violence to extend its sovereignty to those regions. The weak hold of the Iranian state over its extensive territories is, of course, not unique to the post-

---

[54] Ibid., 34–38; *Chronology 1*, 225.
[55] *Chronology of the Iran–Iraq War 4* (HDRDC, 1993), 29 (the fourth volume was republished as the tenth).
[56] Ibid., 99; *Chronology 1*, 36.

revolutionary regime, and preceding governments also relied on armed force to control Iran's diverse and far-flung populations.[57]

The conflicts over the Islamic Republic's rule that emerged among Arabs and Kurds did have different sources. In Khuzistan, resistance came primarily from the Arab People (*Khalq-i ʿArab*) group, which received support from Iraq and which the Guards accordingly viewed as foreign and illegitimate. At the same time, the confrontation between the Sepah and the Arab People group stemmed from ongoing conflict between competing revolutionary forces and thus had local origins.[58] In Khuzistan, the formal establishment of the Sepah came in the midst of "increasing confrontation [between] ethnic and religious-revolutionary currents." The formation of the Sepah of Khorramshahr, the IRGC sources assert, broke the stalemate in that city, again in favor of the religious-revolutionary forces. According to the second volume of the *Chronology*, the Sepah's "emergence and presence [as] a nation-wide revolutionary armed force ... was able to strengthen exponentially [the local] revolutionary-religious forces," to "operate as a deterrent force, and to have a determinative role in operating against [anti-revolutionary] currents."[59]

According to this volume, the critical juncture in the conflict came in the middle of May 1979, when Arab "anti-revolutionaries" attacked a mosque in Khorramshahr during a ceremony marking the third day after the martyrdom of a Sepah leader and attended by pro-regime forces, killing several people. That incident, the volume states, "was the event underlying the decisive actions of the revolutionary forces

---

[57] Shaul Bakhash, "Center–Periphery Relations in Nineteenth-Century Iran," *Iranian Studies* 14.1–2 (1981); Lois Beck, "Tribes and the State in Nineteenth- and Twentieth-Century Iran," in *Tribes and State Formation in the Middle East*, eds. Philip S. Khoury and Joseph Kostiner (University of California Press, 1990); Stephanie Cronin, "Riza Shah and the Disintegration of Bakhtiyari Power in Iran, 1921–1934," *Iranian Studies* 33.3–4 (2000); Leonard M. Helfgott, "The Structural Foundations of the National Minority Problem in Revolutionary Iran," *Iranian Studies* 13.1–4 (1980); Philip C. Salzman, "National Integration of the Tribes in Modern Iran," *Middle East Journal* 25.3 (1971).

[58] *Chronology* 2, 16–17; *Chronology* 1, 189–90, 305, 360, 673.

[59] *Chronology* 2, 17; UPI, "Iran Orders Disarming of Arab Nationalist Groups," *Los Angeles Times*, May 16, 1979; AP, "17 Arrested in Iran in Attack on Police," *The Sun*, May 20, 1979; UPI, "Southern Iranian Militia Won't Give Up Arms," *The Hartford Courant*, May 20, 1979; "Fighting Rages Between Iran Troops, Arabs," *Los Angeles Times*, May 30, 1979; AP, "Khomeini's Forces Check Arab Uprising in Oil Port," *Chicago Tribune*, May 31, 1979.

and government officials" against the Arab groups in Khuzistan, which involved the execution of the alleged perpetrators within a day after the attack and the forced removal of one of the important Arab leaders from the province.[60] The Islamic Republic's decision to act swiftly and fatally, according to the Guards, was key to the eventual suppression of the uprising, as the regime's response "transformed the crisis in Khuzistan" by "demonstrating that the Islamic Revolution was capable" of defeating such plots.[61] In this volume the IRGC authors also argue that the Sepah was able to have a definitive role in the city of Khorramshahr in part because the operations included both local Guards and expeditionary Guards sent from other parts of the country, which demonstrated the "need for partnership" among Sepah forces in such armed conflicts at a time when the Sepah was still "consolidating [its] organizational identity."[62]

In their sources, the Guards stress that the Arab People group was unlike and less successful than other movements that emerged during the revolutionary period, and they provide two reasons to support that assertion. First, the group was closely connected to and supported by Iraq and was thus in the Guards' view essentially a foreign faction; and second, it was based on ethnic rather than religious identity and could thus only hope to represent a small and localized portion of Iranians. According to the IRGC's *Guide Atlas*, the group had not been successful in opposing the monarchy prior to the revolution "because it relied on ethnic motivations and lacked ideological homogeneity with the nationwide movement of the Muslim people of Iran, and because it was ideologically and organizationally dependent on Iraq."[63] The *War Chronology* describes how those same two features continued to characterize the Arab People group after the fall of the monarchy. The group, it states, was "not related to other political conflicts or groups opposed to the system because [its] armed actions had their source from outside the borders, [it] lacked any legitimacy or popular support

---

[60] *Chronology 2*, 18–19; Youssef M. Ibrahim, "Iranian Oil Pipeline Is Cut, Reportedly by Arab Group," *The New York Times*, July 12, 1979; Tony Allaway, "Iran's Arabs Getting Angrier; Arms from Iraq Make More Trouble Likely in Oilfields," *The Christian Science Monitor*, July 13, 1979; Nicholas Cumming-Bruce, "Attack on Iranian Mosque Sparks Anti-Arab Conflict," *The Washington Post*, July 15, 1979.

[61] *Chronology 2*, 19.   [62] Ibid., 33.

[63] *Guide Atlas 2* (HDRDC, 2001), 22–23.

from Iranian Arabs in the region, and [it was] clearly an anti-national and anti-Islamic conspiracy."[64]

This characterization overstates the illegitimacy of the Arab and other ethnic-based opposition to the Islamic Republic. At the same time, these perspectives do reflect the uneasy relationship between religion and ethnicity that has long characterized conceptions of the Iranian nation. Iran is a country that is far more ethnically than it is religiously diverse, and ethnic splintering has persistently threatened its territorial integrity. Making religion the cornerstone of Iranian national identity, at least from the perspective of the ruling regime, would therefore seem to make sense. That is especially true when we understand the Islamic Revolution as a reaction to the rule of the monarchy. During his reign, the shah worked to define national identity in terms of Iran's Persian majority, which represents about 60 percent of the population.[65] Yet in many instances, and especially in the beginning of their rule, the leaders of the Islamic Republic found ethnic opposition to the new regime to be highly problematic and were only able to quiet it with force.[66]

In contrast to the resistance in Khuzistan, in Iran's Kurdish regions the resistance to the Islamic Republic's rule came primarily from local Kurdish groups that had a long history of fighting for autonomy from the central government.[67] Therefore, the Revolutionary Guards do not view them as foreign or illegitimate, even though the Kurdish groups, like the Arab groups, were fighting against the Islamic Republic and were based on an ethnic identity. Also in contrast to the situation in Khuzistan, the Kurdish opposition to the new regime began right after the fall of the monarchy and did not stem from localized clashes between Sepah and Kurdish forces. As the seventh volume of the

---

[64] *Chronology 2*, 16.   [65] *CIA World Factbook: Iran.*

[66] On ethnic minorities and the state in Iran, see Alireza Asgharzadeh, *Iran and the Challenge of Diversity* (Palgrave Macmillan, 2007); Ali Banuazizi and Myron Weiner, eds., *The State, Religion, and Ethnic Politics* (Syracuse University Press, 1986); Alam Saleh, *Ethnic Identity and the State in Iran* (Palgrave Macmillan, 2013).

[67] *Chronology 7-1*, 54. See also Nader Entessar, "The Kurds in Post-Revolutionary Iran and Iraq," *Third World Quarterly* 6.4 (1984); Denise Natali, *The Kurds and the State* (Syracuse University Press, 2005); Peyman Vahabzadeh, "Secularism and the Iranian Militant Left," *Comparative Studies of South Asia, Africa and the Middle East* 31.1 (2011); Abbas Vali, *Kurds and the State in Iran* (I.B. Tauris, 2011).

War Chronology states, "less than ten days after the victory of the Islamic Revolution and despite the repeated declarations of its leader, Imam Khomeini, not to attack military centers," members of the Kurdish Democrat Party (*Hizb-i Dimukrat*) occupied a garrison in the predominantly Kurdish city of Mahabad.[68] The unrest in Kurdistan escalated over the next several months and prompted Khomeini to issue a decree in August 1979 establishing "an extraordinary and unprecedented mobilization" to confront the Kurdish opposition. The decree further "enabled the Sepah to organize and guide extensive popular volunteer forces in the region" and supplied it with the resources it needed to do so, which "completely changed the balance in the Kurdish regions in favor of the system and the Muslim forces."[69]

Although under the Sepah's leadership "the rule of the state was established," Kurdish opposition groups continued to be active and were again able to undermine the Islamic Republic's control of the northwestern regions. The main reason for that, according to the *War Chronology*, was that the Sepah forces sent to the Kurdish areas did not view their efforts as part of an "organized and institutionalized operation." They lacked a "centralized decision-making" body and a program to perpetuate government authority, and as a result the local Kurdish groups viewed the Guards as "unreliable, temporary, volunteer governmental forces" whom they had a chance of defeating.[70]

Yet the determination of the Kurdish groups to continue the fight helped convince the pro-regime forces that "a peaceful solution to the ethnic crisis in Kurdistan" was little more than an overly optimistic hope. According to the same volume of the *War Chronology*, the violent suppression of the opposition was therefore the only solution. Also contributing to that conviction was the nature of the Kurdish opposition itself. In that volume the IRGC authors argue that the goals and claims of the opposition groups were fundamentally incompatible with the Islamic Republic because those groups sought full autonomy or independence from the Iranian state. Accordingly, the Guards assert that the complete suppression of the Kurdish movement was the only way to resolve the crisis, as the "cycle of armed conflicts

---

[68] *Chronology 7-1*, 53; "Kurds Attack Iranian Army," *The Irish Times*, February 20, 1979; "Secession Groups Worry Khomeini," *The Irish Times*, February 21, 1979; William Branigin, "Iran Confronts Separatism Among Tribal Minorities," *The Washington Post*, February 21, 1979.

[69] *Chronology 7-1*, 54.   [70] Ibid.

in opposition to the establishment and enforcement of the rule of the Islamic Republic system in Kurdistan" meant that "it was necessary for the Sepah to take the initiative from the armed groups as quickly as possible."[71]

Another noteworthy feature of the Guards' discussion of the conflict in Kurdistan is the way they portray the role of President Bani-Sadr in the Islamic Republic's efforts to establish its rule there. Though Bani-Sadr is most often the target of some of the Guards' most acerbic criticisms, in this case the Guards actually praise his actions. In the *War Chronology* the IRGC authors call Bani-Sadr's leadership "one of the important factors bringing an end to the period [of acute conflict in Kurdistan] and beginning the period in which the system moved to establish suitable and definite accountability over the armed and violent movements." In contrast to other leaders, he "spoke strongly and explicitly of the system's non-surrender to the armed groups."[72] According to this volume, Bani-Sadr rightly "emphasized that the government of the Islamic Revolution would not tolerate the remoteness of Islam and Muslims in Kurdistan and ... would not remain quiet against ... the threat to internal security."[73] Any kind of approval of Bani-Sadr is hard to find in the IRGC sources, and the fact that the authors praise him here may reflect the importance they attach to the stance he took in support of the Islamic Republic and against the opposition groups.

***

From this review of the Sepah's early history, we can identify several important themes that will reemerge throughout this study. First is the Sepah's commitment to maintaining Iran's territorial integrity and national sovereignty from both internal and external threats, which is apparent in its founding statute and in the way it conceived of its work to bring the country under the control of the central government. Second is the way that history and historical thinking shaped the Sepah's mission from its earliest days. The importance the organization attached to armed power in revolutions derived at least in part from its attempts to learn from the past and to use the lessons of history to

---

[71] Ibid., 55, 60–61.   [72] Ibid., 56–57; *Chronology 1*, 363–64.
[73] *Chronology 7-1*, 58.

more effectively guard Iran's independence and revolution from the exploitation the country has historically suffered. Finally is the combination of faith and firepower in the Sepah's institutional identity and mode of operation. From the start, the Sepah's espousal of the ideology of the Islamic Revolution was shaped by an appreciation of the power of inspired action and of how mighty a weapon faith could be.

2 | Historians

The IRGC's History of the Iran–Iraq War

This chapter traces the development of the IRGC's efforts to document the Iran–Iraq War, including the people, activities, and publications that make up that enterprise. It focuses on the project's origins and foundations, the work undertaken to record the history of the war as the conflict was ongoing, the methodology and approach applied to those efforts, and the publications that have resulted therefrom and on which the present book is based. In doing so, it demonstrates that the development of the IRGC's documentation of the war mirrors the evolution of both the Iran–Iraq War and the IRGC as a whole, which highlights how the project emblematizes the organization and the war's centrality to its legitimacy and identity. It argues, in other words, that in order to understand the IRGC, we must understand its members not just as Guards but also as historians.

For both the IRGC and the Islamic Republic, the Iran–Iraq War stands out as the most impactful episode in their relatively short history. One of the clearest indications of the importance the Guards attach to the war is the vast amount of material they have published on the conflict, which represents their efforts to record, shape, and learn from its history. The core and most important element of that project is the IRGC's Holy Defense Research and Documentation Center (*Markaz-i Asnad va Tahqiqat-i Difa'-i Muqaddas*) (HDRDC or Center), formerly named the Center for War Studies and Research, which is responsible for the vast majority of the IRGC publications on the war.[1]

---

[1] The HDRDC website was accessed at www.defamoghaddas.ir. Despite the HDRDC's similarity to centers associated with the militaries of other countries, the Guards do not state that they modeled their center on others.

A Particular Awareness of the Need to Preserve the History of the War

The information on the establishment of the HDRDC and on how the Guards came to play such an active role in recording the war's history – which can be found in its publications, on its website (when available), and elsewhere online (in Persian) – is of unparalleled value in understanding the IRGC and the significance it attaches to the war. The origins of the project are outlined in an appendix included in the fourth volume of the HDRDC's major work, the *Chronology of the Iran–Iraq War* (*Chronology* or *War Chronology*), which was published in 1993 and was the first volume of the series to be completed and released.[2] "Several months after the start of the ... Iran–Iraq War," it states, "the Sepah Political Bureau, which at that time was part of the Sepah Command Council, sought to form a division named 'History of the War (*Bakhsh-i Tarikh-i Jang*).'"[3] That volume credits the "considerable commitment, efforts, and motivation" of several individual IRGC members – Guards who possessed a "particular awareness of the need to preserve the identity and truth of the war" – for driving that project. Two individuals – Ibrahim Haji Mohammadzadeh, one of the founders of the IRGC and the first head of the Political Bureau, and Mohsen Rezaee, the commander-in-chief of the IRGC during the war – had particularly important roles in promoting the project of recording the war's history.[4]

According to Mohammad Doroodian, himself an early member of the IRGC Political Bureau and one of the central war researchers, the "plan of recording the history of the war within the Sepah" was proposed by Mohammadzadeh in a meeting of IRGC commanders at the very beginning of the conflict. In addition to Rezaee and Mohammadzadeh (and himself), Doroodian points to the significant involvement of several other Revolutionary Guards in promoting and carrying out that plan, including Gholam-Ali Rashid (G. Rashid), one of the top IRGC commanders during the war; Mohsen Rashid (M. Rashid), another founder of the Political Bureau; and Hadi Nakhai, who joined the Political Bureau shortly after its formation

---

[2] *Chronology of the Iran–Iraq War 4* (HDRDC, 1993), 590.   [3] Ibid., 586.
[4] The "About Us" pages on the HDRDC website included very similar information.

and played an instrumental role in establishing and leading the war research project.[5]

The work of recording the history of the war began right away, in the spring of 1981. Over the course of the next year IRGC researchers, known as war narrators, were sent to either the southern or northern warfronts. Each front had its own field bureau and was divided into three axes or areas of operation. This manner of dividing the research reflected the way in which the war was prosecuted during that period, with sporadic and initially unsuccessful Iranian attempts to expel the Iraqi forces.[6]

A new research system was inaugurated in the *Fath-ul-Mubin* (Undeniable Victory) Operation carried out in March 1982, which resulted in a critical Iranian victory that helped turn the tide of the war. In addition to a number of tactical and organizational changes that made the campaign successful, "a significant development also emerged in the matter of researching the war." From that point on, the Sepah's "narrators were organized according to the operation's combat, command, and guidance organization ... and were deployed in various chains of command" at every stage of the operation with the goal of "directly establish[ing] and record[ing] the events of the war."[7] In other words, the Guards' research on the war expanded in parallel with and in a manner that mirrored both the expansion of the IRGC and the changing circumstances of the war.[8]

The IRGC narrators and officials managing the research remained part of the organization's Political Bureau until the first months of 1985, when they formed the Holy Defense Research and Documentation Center (then called the Center for War Studies and Research) as an independent institution under the authority of the Sepah General Command. With that development, "the presence of the Center's narrators in the war became fixed and continuous" and they "became an integral element of the war's command system."[9] Following

---

[5] "Note from Mohammad Doroodian," *Defa Press*, May 31, 2014 (Persian); "Interview with Book News Agency," Blog of Mohammad Doroodian, May 14, 2014 (Persian).

[6] HDRDC "About Us" pages.

[7] *Chronology 4*, 586–87; *Chronology of the Iran–Iraq War 1* (HDRDC, 1997), 18–19.

[8] *Survey of the Iran–Iraq War 1*, 4th ed. (HDRDC, 1998), 13.

[9] *Chronology 4*, 589.

Supreme Leader Khomeini's order establishing the three separate ground, naval, and air forces within the Sepah in September 1985, "bureaus of war researchers were also launched" in each one of the forces, "which were dissolved and re-absorbed into the Center at the war's end."[10] The narrators carried on their work for the remaining years of the war and even for a period after the establishment of the ceasefire in August 1988.

Throughout the course of the conflict, the HDRDC was engaged primarily in collecting and recording the war's history, which involved training and overseeing the work of the narrators, dispatching them to the fronts, coordinating their activities, and establishing bureaus in the various operational areas.[11] Given the extent of their presence in the war, recruiting and training narrators was a fundamental part of the HDRDC's work in its early years.[12] As noted above, the first narrators came from the Sepah Political Bureau, who before the *Fath-ul-Mubin* Operation "were released from working in various sections of the bureau" in Tehran in order to be stationed on the warfronts. The narrator's duty was being "present in their assigned region" to "investigate what was actually happening" and "to obtain precise information" about the conflict "in order to reach a determined conclusion about the development of the war."[13]

Though the narrators' presence on the warfronts was the essence of their job, they were "ordered to avoid participating in combat operations" so as not to put themselves at further risk. Despite that order, the killing and wounding of narrators took a toll on the work. Of the approximately 200 narrators present on the fronts during the course of the conflict, "a considerable number" were wounded and up to seventeen were martyred.[14] The *War Chronology* states that attracting Iranians willing to assume the risks of researching the war was difficult, as was quickly replacing those who were injured. The training the

---

[10] Ibid., 588, 605–06.   [11] Ibid.

[12] "Overview of the Research Activities of the Center for War Studies and Research," Resource Center for Holy Defense Sciences and Education, May 26, 2010 (Persian).

[13] *Chronology 4*, 587–88.

[14] Ibid., 588, 591, 603–05. This volume provides the names and positions of fourteen martyred narrators (pp. 604–05). M. Rashid put that number at sixteen, and on its website the Center reported that there were seventeen martyrs among the 206 narrators. "IBNA Interview with Mohsen Rashid About the First War Writers," *IBNA*, April 20, 2009 (Persian); HDRDC "About Us" pages.

HDRDC gave the narrators included efforts to minimize risks and stipulated that the narrators must be able to have a say in when and where the research was conducted in order to protect themselves and the quality of their work.[15]

In discussing that training, this volume cites passages from one of the "educational pamphlets used by the Center in [1984], which was prepared as a special educational instruction for the researchers." According to the pamphlet, narrators should have a number of particular "characteristics" that would allow them to carry out their difficult work. Among these was an understanding of and a commitment to "the serious duty of preserving for history what [they have been] trusted with." Another was "patience and perseverance" in dealing with the strains of war and with an environment "where the issue of death and blood is [part of] the work and that differs from the environment of research in a library." Narrators had to keep in mind that during operations they might be required to interview someone who had just "witnessed the most horrific scenes" or who had even seen a "brother or friend lost before their eyes." In other words, the narrators "had to represent a dual cultural and military identity, meaning they had to have the necessary intellectual qualities of a researcher on the one hand and the motivations and qualities of a [soldier] on the other, so they could endure the particular operational conditions."[16]

Developing the "intellectual qualities of a researcher" was an important element of the HDRDC's instruction for the war narrators. In the educational pamphlet they received during their training, the researchers were instructed not to rely on information obtained only from one person and to verify what they heard by consulting a number of sources, to acknowledge that complete objectivity was not possible while also refraining from imposing themselves on their work, and to write down what they had observed as soon as possible.[17] It also emphasized the "serious duty of preserving [the narrators'] integrity for history" so they could focus on "discovering the facts and obtaining information."[18]

That task was accomplished in a variety of ways. The narrators collected a wide range of information – news, reports, statistics, and other documents – from the "planning, guidance, and operations

---

[15] *Chronology 4*, 591–92, 600, 603.   [16] Ibid., 590–94.
[17] Ibid., 594–95, 600–01.   [18] Ibid., 593, 597.

command centers," the "central and subsidiary bases and the units under their command," and the "combat forces present in the battle-fields." They did so while also "observing and recording and register-ing" the goings on of the war, which they kept track of primarily in their notebooks and by recording audio and video tapes.[19] The Guards emphasize the pervasive and continuous nature of their presence. The IRGC researchers "covered the war . . . from the highest levels of policy-making and decision-making to the operational levels and frontlines, in all [of] the . . . various stages of planning . . . and implementing oper-ations." They maintained a "full-time presence beside the commanders, recording their conversations and activities, . . . conducting [] interviews with various [participants], [and] collecting written documents from each unit."[20]

The narrators were given instructions regarding the three methods they should employ in their research – questionnaire, interview, and observation. As discussed in the pamphlet, there were pluses and minuses to each. Questionnaires could be used to obtain a variety of information from many different people, but the responses might be ambiguous or of variable quality. Interviews, on the other hand, were often time-consuming and laborious but were the more "complete and comprehensive research method and the one that has great documen-tary value because the information is collected from the history makers in their own voices." In order to conduct successful interviews, the pamphlet suggests that the narrator spend some time getting to know the interviewee before beginning to ask questions, especially if they are meeting for the first time. Interviewees should also be provided with information about the project so they understand the purpose for which their answers would be used. To protect their safety, narrators were instructed to avoid conducting interviews late at night, in a car or in transit, or at the frontline when it could be avoided.[21]

The third method, observation, was in practice "the very first step of research," and the one that allowed the narrators to themselves incar-nate the history of the war. By carefully observing the events of the conflict, "the narrator gradually becomes part of the knowers and experts of the war, and what they report as a collection of observations will itself become a document with historical value." Observation also

[19] HDRDC "About Us" pages; *Chronology* 4, 589.   [20] *Chronology* 4, 588–89.
[21] Ibid., 594–95, 597, 600–01.

has a high degree of accuracy because no intermediaries have been used. In some instances, information can be obtained only through observation, since "because of the narrators' direct presence on the scene, events are tangible for them and they can present the spirit of the subject very well."[22]

As with the other research methods, there were cons to observation as well, including the inability of the narrator to be present in certain locations (such as the frontlines), to record all the events that occur simultaneously in many different places, and to predict when and where things will happen and accordingly to be there when they do. The results of observation are also highly personal, as "two people with the same instruction might present differing conclusions about a single subject." Further, observation can accurately reflect qualities but not quantities. So, for example, with observation the narrator can report the morale among soldiers in the barracks or the feelings of victory and defeat, but not the exact number of forces present at a base or lost in a battle. Given the pros and cons of each of the research methods, the HDRDC encouraged its narrators to combine them all, "so that with full integrity and in the most accurate manner possible, the moments of the war can be collected, registered, and recorded."[23]

According to the Guards, the creation of an interlinked network of researchers produced "a multifaceted exchange of information that flowed among" them. The holistic nature of the research system involved "strict and active control" of the work "in which the possibility of the emergence of errors and mistakes has been minimized" and that "ensured the accuracy and health of the research." It likewise helped prevent the events of the war from being "distorted" or "concealed," as "fewer subjects and matters were hidden from their view."[24] The result of "the narrators' continuous [and] direct presence throughout the Imposed [Iran–Iraq] War" was their ability to develop "a high [degree of] expertise" and to "accumulate rich and comprehensive sources."[25]

The idea that the Revolutionary Guards would be both the makers and writers of history was a very early consideration. In their training narrators were told that one of the goals of their work was "the greatest possible involvement of the history makers in the writing of

[22] Ibid., 595.   [23] Ibid., 588, 597–600.
[24] Ibid., 589; HDRDC "About Us" pages.   [25] *Chronology 4*, 588–89.

history" in order to achieve "the greatest possible authenticity of the history."[26] The assimilation of the IRGC narrators into the Iran–Iraq War, and the war's assimilation into them, is thus one of the defining features of the Guards' research on the conflict. According to the same volume, "the cohesive group of war narrators was [like] a living organism that encompassed all the dimensions of the war. … The war's various ranks and units and modules were linked together as one by the extensive network of narrators."[27] Essentially, then, the IRGC narrators are portrayed as the war incarnate, as constituting a being through which the war is kept alive.

The Guards assert that, altogether, the combination of research methods, the quality of the narrators, the extent of their presence in the war, and their integration with the conflict at numerous levels allowed them to record history in a comprehensive and authoritative manner. But despite those advantages and the "high performance" of the research system, the *Chronology* contends that there was also a "major problem" with it: it "was only able to form in particular conditions." The HDRDC's success is attributed to "the existence of several opportune factors particular to the time period," the first of which was "the particular space that the Sepah was granted in the first years [after its] formation." In its formative years the Sepah "arose not only as a revolutionary-military force," but also as a political and cultural organization that allowed it to take on a number of different roles.[28] Another volume of the *Chronology* extends that point to the sources collected during the war and now housed in the HDRDC. These, it states, "are the fruit of unique field research that was made possible by the particular historical conditions" in which it was carried out and which therefore "cannot be repeated."[29]

As will be discussed in later chapters, the Sepah's identity as a fledgling and amorphous revolutionary organization was instrumental to its expansion and successes in the war, in part because it had few preestablished structures constraining its ability to develop and adapt. In a statement that is as applicable to the Guards as a whole as it is to their roles as the war's historians, the IRGC authors assert that the enterprise of recording the history of the war "began from nothing like other [instances of] revolutionary spontaneity," but "quickly proliferated in terms of quantity and quality and was changed along with the developments of the war" that proceeded "in an unparalleled and perhaps

[26] Ibid., 592.   [27] Ibid., 589.   [28] Ibid., 589–90.   [29] *Chronology 1*, 25.

unique manner."[30] As vanguards of a revolution, the Guards were attentive to what was unparalleled and unique about themselves, which helped inspire the conviction that the war they were fighting was different and revolutionary and that it therefore needed to be preserved.

The Sepah's revolutionary identity thus shaped its approach not only to prosecuting the war but also to recording its history. The first lines of one of the "educational handouts" the HDRDC prepared for its researchers illustrates that point:

> Like all the dimensions of the revolution [in] which we [the Guards] have had superior achievements in spontaneously moving far from classic formats and systems, in the matter of writing history, if the work is befitting the revolution, then all the classic formats and methods are set aside and we discover methods and plans that shoot forth from the Islamic Revolution.[31]

My analysis of the IRGC's histories and of the way those histories portray the Guards' roles in the conflict reveals that the above statement is simultaneously true and false. In both prosecuting and writing the history of the war, the Guards have approached their work in ways that reflect their revolutionary identity and mission, but they certainly have not shunned more traditional methods. Despite this and a few other statements to the contrary, there is a great deal about the IRGC that can be defined as traditional or typical. The Guards' own discussions of their activities make that abundantly clear. Indeed, the quality of the IRGC that is so essential to its identity is its integration of the revolutionary and the traditional, the spiritual and the mundane. In most cases, the former is used in the service of the latter; revolutionary or spiritual approaches are used to achieve and justify ordinary and worldly aims. That does not mean, however, that revolution, religion, and ideology are hollow for the Guards. Rather, it means that it is those things that give the Guards meaning, that give purpose to their mission.

The Pen for the Sword

From Fighting to Writing

After the conclusion of the Iran–Iraq War, the HDRDC "took on a new form," becoming part of the Sepah Joint Staff.[32] The conflict's end

---

[30] *Chronology* 4, 587.   [31] Ibid., 591–92.   [32] Ibid., 588, 605–06.

allowed "those involved in the Center [to] enter[] new fields free of the difficulties and worries of the battle scenes."[33] The HDRDC underwent a major shift in its activities, moving from field research and acquiring primary sources to organizing (and continuing to supplement) those sources and to publishing studies. Both elements of that project are considerable undertakings requiring deliberate planning. Accordingly, in 1989, the HDRDC prepared an "outlook document" and a series of five-year plans as a "roadmap" for its future endeavors.[34]

The first of those new fields involved cataloging the records it collected during the conflict, which is an immense task. According to its publications and website, the HDRDC possesses a massive amount of raw historical data: millions of written records, including narrators' journals and research reports, political and military files, operational plans, maps, bulletins, and press reports; tens of thousands of hours of audio recordings, including meetings and cellular conversations between commanders and interviews conducted on the battlefield and at various bases; and tens of thousands of photos and images.[35]

None of this data, however, could be effectively referenced or used unless it was preserved and organized. To that end, the HDRDC took the following steps: 33,000 cassette tapes were "dismounted" and the audio recorded thereon was compiled into its own data bank; the narrators' notebooks were catalogued, edited, transcribed, and bound; a "main part of the documents was scanned and made computer-usable"; "specialized software" was procured that allowed the HDRDC to store "a mass of informational data," including sources like images, films, and maps; and "more than 1,700 books of 'selected documents'" were prepared in order to make the HDRDC sources available to researchers right away, while the data processing measures were still underway.[36]

Acquiring the substantial and in some cases costly means to do all that took time. One of the earliest volumes published in 1993 reports that the HDRDC had limited resources and facilities; it was working on an informatics system and had endeavored unsuccessfully to obtain

---

[33] HDRDC "About Us" pages.　　[34] Ibid.

[35] *Chronology 4*, 606–07; *Chronology 1*, 25; HDRDC "About Us" pages; "Holding of Friendly Meeting with More Than 100 Holy Defense Researchers," *Mehr News*, December 9, 2019 (Persian).

[36] HDRDC "About Us" pages.

computers. "Of course," it states, "proper and efficient utilization of these documents requires them to be organized in a computerized system, which the Center's officials have sought to procure for several years, but these efforts have still not reached the desired result."[37] Yet by 2010 the HDRDC had obtained both an informatics system and computers, and in 2020 its website actually touted how much progress it had made in that regard.[38]

The second field in which the HDRDC has been engaged entails serving as a research center and disseminating the information it has obtained. This "resource information" stage began around 1991–92, after the work of processing, preserving, and storing the sources had advanced "in a relatively satisfactory manner." Since that time the HDRDC has consulted with and made (parts of) its archive available to "trusted researchers, authors, and writers ... working in the field of Holy Defense" to "prepare works and cultural products" and to "make their contents available to the general and specialized users of the community."[39]

The IRGC publications note that the HDRDC's efforts to collect additional documents still continue, and so its archive has grown even larger.[40] Several appeal directly to their readers for help supplementing the HDRDC records.[41] "Despite the extensiveness ... of the research and the extraordinary effort" that has gone in to building the archive, the authors of the thirty-third volume of the *Chronology* state, the HDRDC "accepts the presence of deficiencies in various areas, which is natural in such a major enterprise." They would be grateful, therefore, "to anyone who is able to help the Center rectify and complete the history of the war, whether by offering an opinion or by presenting documents and pictures."[42]

In its published works, the HDRDC makes these primary sources an important part of the story. As one volume states, the IRGC publications are based almost entirely on "the sources obtained first-hand

[37] *Chronology 4*, 606–07.
[38] "Overview of the Research Activities"; HDRDC "About Us" pages.
[39] HDRDC "About Us" pages.
[40] "Overview of the Research Activities"; *Chronology 4*, 607.
[41] *Chronology 4*, 586; *Chronology of the Iran–Iraq War 5* (HDRDC, 1994), 15 (the fifth volume was republished as the eleventh); *Chronology of the Iran–Iraq War 50* (HDRDC, 1999), 7; *Khorramshahr in the Long War*, 2nd ed. (HDRDC, 1998), 26.
[42] *Chronology of the Iran–Iraq War 33* (HDRDC, 2000), 12.

[and] without intermediaries" as the result of "the direct presence of the Center in the course of events."[43] In contrast, IRGC wartime commander-in-chief Rezaee explains in his forward to the first volume of the HDRDC's *Analysis of the Iran–Iraq War* series, authors of other studies of the conflict "were not present on the scene of the war." They "were not familiar with the war's main participants and decisions" and were therefore unable to "present an accurate and comprehensive" assessment of the conflict.[44]

Although having access to sources is important for historians of all subjects, the Guards argue that it is particularly significant and problematic for those studying war. "During battle keeping issues secret is common practice, as the smallest indiscretion can lead the enemy to [your] secrets and have a serious effect on the fate of the war," while after the conflict most of the relevant records remain classified.[45] But the difficulty of obtaining sources does not change the fact that "in order to understand the special features and characteristics of any war it is necessary to have access to information on various levels of decision-making and implementation." Unlike many researchers, the HDRDC "has had much success in this regard because of its particular position" in the war and the Islamic Republic.[46] Proximity to the relevant sources is additionally important because facts themselves are often the first casualties of war.[47] As the Guards note, "in defeats all consider themselves innocent and in victories a partner." Therefore, "it is when researchers [have] direct [access] to the scenes of decision-making and involvement that the value of their analysis is higher."[48]

That contention is valid, but more so when taken in isolation. Access to sources and the insight that comes from experiencing events are important components of historical expertise and knowledge, but their value is greater when they are accompanied by transparency, when they can be scrutinized and verified by third parties. The Guards' tendency to champion the value of proximity and access over that of transparency must accordingly be seen at least in part as a strategy for

---

[43] *Chronology 4*, 13.
[44] *Analysis of the Iran–Iraq War 1*, 2nd ed. (HDRDC, 2001), 15–16.
[45] *Chronology 1*, 24.　　[46] Ibid., 25.
[47] The quote "the first casualty when war comes is truth" is most often attributed to American progressive politician Hiram Johnson (1866–1945).
[48] *Chronology 1*, 24.

promoting their own rendering of history on terms favorable to themselves.

However, the limited extent to which the IRGC makes the contents of its sources available to outsiders does not mean that they are untruthful or fabricated. The research conducted for this book in fact indicates that the Guards are not in the business of presenting contrivance and falsification as history. Their publications actually emphasize the importance of making the information the HDRDC collected available to those outside the organization and how they therefore serve as a vehicle for making the exclusive primary sources housed in its archive available to the public.[49] One states that after the ceasefire the Guards "felt the need to compile and depict what the Center's researchers and narrators had collected" during the war, a need that resulted in its publications.[50] According to the *War Chronology*, the HDRDC researchers have "taken significant steps to ... compile and present the results of [their] research," and their efforts have resulted in the publication of "writings about various dimensions and subjects of the war, which now form a considerable volume of reference books and texts of war research."[51]

The prominence of primary and other sources is a notable feature of the HDRDC histories. Citations are prevalent and proper.[52] Photos, maps, images, and other graphics are integrated throughout the text and are often featured prominently and sometimes in color. Quotes from documents are included as part of the narrative, longer excerpts are amended as appendices, and images of originals sometimes appear as well. In many cases the HDRDC sources are supplemented by others, like confidential Iranian sources from civilian and military bodies, other official sources (e.g., from the United Nations), and both domestic and foreign publications (newspapers, books, etc.).[53] Explanatory notes serve to clarify pieces of evidence and the arguments

---

[49] "Overview of the Research Activities"; *Chronology 1*, 23, 25; *Chronology 4*, 13–14, 579, 587–95, 610; *Chronology 5*, preface, 14; *Chronology of the Iran–Iraq War 53-1* (HDRDC, 2019), 19; *Chronology of the Iran–Iraq War 54* (HDRDC, 2013), 14, 49–50; *Khorramshahr in the Long War*, 25; *Analysis 1*, 13–14; *Survey 1*, 13–14; "Holding of Friendly Meeting."
[50] *Guide Atlas 2* (HDRDC, 2001), 7.   [51] *Chronology 4*, 607.
[52] The IRGC authors emphasize that their publications include citations and information on their sources in part to help the reader judge the history. *Chronology 1*, 25, 27; *Chronology of the Iran–Iraq War 2* (HDRDC, 1999), 38.
[53] *Chronology 54*, 49–50.

they are being used to make. More recent volumes of the *War Chronology* include especially explicit discussions of the particular sources utilized.[54]

Publications

The work of publishing books and articles on the war has thus proceeded alongside the efforts to complete and organize the archive and forms the second area on which the HDRDC has focused since the end of the war. By far the largest and most important of the HDRDC publications is the *Chronology of the Iran–Iraq War*. Once complete, the series will cover the nine-and-a-half-year period from the victory of the revolution in February 1979 to the end of the war in August 1988. It is intended to be a comprehensive, analytical, and documented reference work for researchers, scholars, and others interested in the war.[55] As one volume states, HDRDC officials "prepared this immense and documented series" in the hope that "it will be the most important 'reference and source of information on the Imposed War' for domestic and foreign researchers of current and especially of future generations."[56] The volumes of the *Chronology* published thus far fit that description well. They are certainly immense, with each volume containing between 600 and 1,400 pages (about 900 on average), and are also well documented.

According to the fourth volume, which was the first of the series to be released, the plan for publishing the IRGC's history in the form of a large chronology was developed in 1987–88, and the compilation stage began in 1990–91. As part of that latter stage, "the general plan of the *War Chronology*" was prepared, according to which the series would be divided into twenty books or war logs, each of which could include between one and three volumes depending on the magnitude of the subjects.[57] However, after four volumes of the series were published, the HDRDC overhauled this original plan in order to reduce its unnecessary complexity and to rectify "other problems" that arose after the publication of the first volumes. This led to a "review of the titling and periodization and the adoption of a brief[er] and [more]

[54] *Chronology 53-1*, 19; *Chronology 54*, 14, 49–50.
[55] *Chronology 4*, 585–86; *Chronology 1*, 16, 23–24; *Chronology 33*, 13, 40; *Chronology of the Iran–Iraq War 43* (HDRDC, 1999), 33.
[56] *Chronology 50*, 7.   [57] *Chronology 4*, cover pages, 579–84.

useful plan." In that revised plan, the series was divided into fifty-seven individual volumes (sometimes called books), each with one unique title and number.[58] Despite that reorganization, the events of some periods still ended up being too considerable to present in a single book, and so in those cases the books were divided further into two separate volumes.

Volumes of the *War Chronology* have been steadily published according to the 57-volume plan and have continued to appear out of order. The IRGC authors state that they originally intended to publish the books according to the chronological order of the series, but they decided instead to publish each volume as soon as it was ready. Given the magnitude of the project, they felt that it was preferable not to delay the release of the books that had been completed and designed each volume so that it could be used independently of the others.[59]

The series has become increasingly standardized over time, and most of the volumes published since the reorganization include similar introductions and prefaces. All explain to the reader that the book is divided into chapters, each of which corresponds to one day of the specific period covered; that each chapter includes numbered reports from a variety of sources on the important events and issues that arose on that day; that reference information for those sources, as well as additional reports that did not fit neatly into the main part of the chapter, are included at the end of each day; and that an index and a summary of all the reports appear at the end of the book under the title "Report of the *Chronology*." Each introduction is also preceded by a list of all the books in the series, which is updated with the latest information on their current status.[60]

The reports that make up each chapter or day consist largely of accounts of the warfront – including meetings of commanders, operational plans, and descriptions of battles – recorded by the HDRDC narrators; and annotated press reports from a variety of Iranian and international sources about important developments relating to the war. Though the reports, especially those based on the accounts of

---

[58] *Chronology 50*, 6–7.
[59] *Chronology 4*, 12, 580; *Chronology 1*, 36; *Chronology 5*, 22–23; *Chronology 33*, 11, 40–41.
[60] For example, *Chronology of the Iran–Iraq War 20* (HDRDC, 2002), 13–14; *Chronology of the Iran–Iraq War 47* (HDRDC, 2002), 15.

the HDRDC narrators and that are available to the public only in these volumes, contain much useful information, the voice and analysis of the IRGC authors can be found primarily in the introduction to each volume. These lengthy introductions contain not only excerpts of the most important reports from the body of the volume and descriptions of the key events from the particular period, but also the bulk of the authors' analysis of the reports and events.[61]

The HDRDC has published several other series that analyze the war in a variety of ways, all of which are much shorter than the volumes of the *Chronology*. Two series – the six-volume *Survey of the Iran–Iraq War* and the five-volume *Analysis of the Iran–Iraq War* – are organized chronologically and examine the important issues and progression of the war in different periods. There are several series of atlases that focus on particular geographical regions, battles, and military divisions. The series entitled *Critique and Review of the Iran–Iraq War* includes five volumes on the critical questions of the conflict, such as whether it was unavoidable and why it continued for as long as it did. A recent series presents the oral history of the war as told by its commanders in conversation with HDRDC researchers.

In addition to these series, the HDRDC has published monographs that deal with a variety of subjects related to the war. One category includes studies that analyze the war's history from the perspectives of the IRGC's own commanders. In some cases, the HDRDC asked IRGC commanders to work with a research team and to oversee the composition of a study on a specific operation, while in others the studies were based primarily on what the HDRDC narrators recorded as they accompanied the commanders during the war.[62] Other monographs examine, for example, Iraq's military strategy, the involvement of the Kurds, the War of the Cities, particular battles and operations, individual martyrs, and the leadership of Ayatollah Khomeini. The HDRDC has also published collections of articles and a few works of fiction.

[61] The authors state this explicitly in many of the introductions or prefaces. *Chronology 2*, 16; *Chronology of the Iran–Iraq War 7-1* (HDRDC, 2006), 15; *Chronology 33*, 13; *Chronology of the Iran–Iraq War 37* (HDRDC, 2004), 15; *Chronology 47*, 17; *Chronology of the Iran–Iraq War 51* (HDRDC, 2008), 15.
[62] *Battles on the East of the Karun* (HDRDC, 2000), 13–14; *The Sepah Pasdaran's First Naval Operations in the Persian Gulf* (HDRDC, 1996), 17–18.

Although the HDRDC is by far the most important and prolific IRGC institution researching and producing publications on the Iran–Iraq War, it is not the only one. During the war, the IRGC published several periodicals and monographs under the auspices of its various branches, including its political, education, and propaganda departments. The IRGC's Imam Hossein University publishes a journal on defense policy that often includes articles about the conflict, and the Guards have convened a number of conferences to commemorate the war, which have resulted in series of publications.[63] Finally, several IRGC leaders have published memoirs that include their experiences in the war.[64]

These non-HDRDC sources were examined as part of the research conducted for this study and some are referenced in the coming chapters. They do not, however, figure anywhere nearly as prominently as do the HDRDC sources. There are several reasons for this. First, the HDRDC has produced far more publications than has any other IRGC branch. Second, it is responsible for the vast majority of the historical and analytical sources on the war, which are the focus of the present examination. Various sources that do not fit that description have been included, but it was not possible to undertake a full or comparative analysis of both the historical and nonhistorical (or more propagandistic) sources published mainly during the war. Similarly, the volumes of fiction and poetry produced by the IRGC are not part of the examination.

Authors

As was described in the beginning of the chapter, several Revolutionary Guards were responsible for the initial establishment of the IRGC War History Division in the first months of the war, specifically IRGC founder and Political Bureau head Mohammadzadeh and wartime commander-in-chief Rezaee. In addition to these two, the other key players who undertook and managed the project included historians and

---

[63] The conferences are often held in honor of the martyrs of particular areas or IRGC divisions. The related publications usually consist of memoirs or personal narratives, biographies, short stories, and poetry.

[64] For example, Mohsen Rezaee, http://rezaee.ir/fa/archive (Persian); Yahya Rahim Safavi, www.yahyasafavi.com/index.php/fa/ (Persian); Mohammad Ali Jafari, *Dusty Overlays* (Soore Mehr, 2016) (Persian).

Political Bureau members Doroodian, M. Rashid, and Nakhai and IRGC commander G. Rashid.[65]

Most of those individuals – Rezaee, G. Rashid, Doroodian, M. Rashid, and Nakhai – have been at the heart of the history project since the beginning. They have been intimately and extensively involved in the HDRDC for several decades and their names appear on many of its publications. Rezaee and G. Rashid, whose main roles in the war were as military commanders rather than as researchers, have been involved in the HDRDC primarily as advisors rather than writers but have still played an important role over the course of many years. Rezaee is acknowledged in several IRGC volumes and had an important role in supervising one of the HDRDC's series. G. Rashid reviewed several volumes of the *War Chronology*, has written articles in Imam Hossein University's *Journal of Defense Policy*, helped prepare the HDRDC's monograph on Khorramshahr, and is acknowledged in the *Survey* and *Analysis* series.

Doroodian is one of the war's most prolific researchers and has made significant contributions to the HDRDC's research and publications during and after the war. His involvement in the conflict forced him to delay his studies, but he earned a B.A. in history from Shahid Beheshti University in 1992.[66] He has actively maintained a blog for the better part of a decade, which he has updated regularly with posts and links to books, reviews, articles, and interviews. The blog's homepage defines its goal as sharing "views and comments about the political, social, and military dimensions of the Iran–Iraq War, and likewise rethinking and revising views and published works."[67]

Nakhai, in addition to helping establish the HDRDC, remained actively involved in its work during and after the war. He served as a narrator and was involved in many of its publications and in most volumes of the *War Chronology*. He was on the faculty of Amir Kabir University and is sometimes given the title of "doctor." He continued working with the HDRDC until his death at the end of 2016.[68] M. Rashid

---

[65] "Note from Mohammad Doroodian"; "Interview with Book News Agency."

[66] "The Issue-Oriented and Documented Approach to the Holy Defense," *Tasnim News*, May 13, 2013 (Persian); "Journey to the Depths of War," *IBNA*, January 31, 2006 (Persian).

[67] www.m-doroodian.ir/ (Persian).

[68] "Hadi Nakhai Passed Away," *Feydus*, December 10, 2016 (Persian); "A Memoir for Hadi Nakhai," *ISNA*, December 13, 2018 (Persian).

has likewise remained active in the HDRDC's work, including by over-seeing the *War Chronology*.[69]

In addition to those who helped establish the HDRDC, the other individuals who have been most active in its activities and publications are Hossein Ardestani, a narrator during the war and the HDRDC director until his death in March 2017; Mehdi Ansari, a manager of the HDRDC who was also a narrator during the war; and Alireza Lotfallah-Zadegan, a writer and researcher with the HDRDC. Ansari and Lotfallah-Zadegan, along with Nakhai and M. Rashid, have been part of the Council for Compiling and Publishing the *War Chronology*, which manages the production of that series. There have been many other individuals who have worked on the HDRDC publications as narrators, researchers, writers, editors, and advisors. Although some have contributed to more than one publication, none have been involved to the same degree as those discussed above.

The role of HDRDC director was taken over by Ali-Mohammad Naini in October 2017, and since that time he has done much to expand its activities (as will be discussed in Chapter 11). According to Iranian news reports, Dr. Naini holds a bachelor's degree in educational sciences, a master's in defense management, and a doctorate in strategic management. He has done research on subjects including cultural management, soft war, and human resources, and has published tens of articles on his work. During the war he worked with the Sepah as a cultural deputy in several regions and units. Prior to becoming head of the HDRDC, Naini worked in cultural affairs, research, and policy for the city of Tehran, Imam Hossein University, and various branches of the armed forces.[70]

While it is possible to identify these individuals and the extent of their contributions to the HDRDC's work, gathering this information is not as easy as it should be. A directory of HDRDC leaders and researchers, and the nature and size of any permanent staff it maintains, are not readily available. Determining the HDRDC's leadership and organizational

---

[69] M. Rashid maintained a blog for several years. http://mohsenrashid.persianblog.ir/ (Persian).

[70] "A Look at Naini's Records," *Tasnim News*, August 2, 2014 (Persian); "Commander Naini Becomes Head of the Sepah Holy Defense Research and Documentation Center," *Tasnim News*, October 3, 2017 (Persian); "Visit of the Head of the Holy Defense Research and Documentation Center [with] the Holy Defense News Agency," *Defa Press*, September 15, 2019 (Persian).

structure is particularly difficult. However, some limited information can be gathered from various sources. The head of the HDRDC is appointed by the IRGC commander-in-chief and serves simultaneously as his "advisor." That was the case, at least, for its most recent head, Dr. Naini, who was appointed "by the order" of then IRGC commander-in-chief Mohammad Ali Jafari.[71] The IRGC commander is or can be involved in the HDRDC's work, as Naini has recognized Jafari's "support and guidance" as contributing to its achievements.[72] The IRGC commander, currently Hossein Salami, likewise serves as the "honorable head" of the board of directors that apparently oversees the HDRDC's work.[73]

***

One of the most important conclusions that can be drawn from the above review of the Holy Defense Research and Documentation Center is this: From the beginning of the war to the present, the IRGC's efforts to record the history of the war and the publications that have resulted from those efforts have been organized and guided by the highest levels of the IRGC and by some of the organization's founding members. This is not an informal attempt by individual or low-ranking Guards to write the history of the war in the organization's name. Far from it. The project of recording and publishing the history of the Iran–Iraq War is absolutely fundamental to the IRGC itself, and the fact that existing analyses of the organization have failed to consider that project exposes the deficiencies in our understanding of the Revolutionary Guards.

[71] "Commander Naini Becomes Head of the Sepah Holy Defense Research and Documentation Center," *Mehr News*, October 3, 2017 (Persian).
[72] "If the Names and Memories of the Martyrs Are Not Cherished, the Enemy Becomes Dangerous," *Mehr News*, September 25, 2019 (Persian).
[73] Ibid.

3 | Striking While the Revolution's Hot
The Causes of the Iran–Iraq War

The complexity that characterizes the IRGC's history of the Iran–Iraq War is readily apparent in the way the organization assesses the reasons for the war's outbreak. Like other historians of the conflict within and outside Iran, the IRGC authors strive to tease out the variety of causes that led to the war and, in particular, to understand the role of Iran's 1979 Islamic Revolution in the war's onset. These connections between the war and the revolution constitute both a prime concern for the Revolutionary Guards and a main theme of the present book. According to the Guards, the success of the revolution was the most important catalyst for the Iraqi invasion. Further, Iraq made the strategic decision to strike while the revolution was still hot – to attack the Islamic Republic in the midst of its revolutionary transition, when the new regime's power was tenuous and its readiness for war diminished.

The Success of the Revolution and the Outbreak of the War

The Iran–Iraq War began on September 22, 1980, nineteen months after the fall of the Iranian monarchy and while the processes of consolidating the revolution and establishing the Islamic Republic were still taking place. Although the relationship between the war and the revolution is complex and multifaceted, it is fundamentally tied to the temporal proximity of the two events. This is a point the Revolutionary Guards make throughout their sources. It is also a point that is often undervalued in much of the literature on the war.

The Guards conceive of the war as an attack on a country in the midst of a revolutionary transition. In their view, the fear of what the revolution might be or do was made perfectly clear in the timing of the war. It is those two things – the opposition to the revolution and the temporal proximity of the war to the revolution – that are responsible for the connection between the two phenomena. Making the connection was therefore not a matter of choice. The war and the revolution were necessarily connected because of the nature and timing of the war itself.

This does not mean that Iran contributed nothing to that outcome. Although they do not see the war itself as inevitable, the Guards understand it as a fundamental, violent encounter between the revolution and those whom it threatened. A volume of the HDRDC's *Survey of the Iran–Iraq War* (*Survey*) series states in the first lines of its introduction that the Islamic Revolution, "considering [its] intrinsic animosity and opposition to the goals and interests of global arrogance and also [its] rejection of any reconciliation and compromise, came under widespread and intense internal and external pressures."[1] Thus, because Iran's interests after the revolution were intrinsically opposed to those of other states, and especially to those of the "arrogant" powers like the United States that dominated the world system, some degree of confrontation was expected. But when opposition to the revolution became war to defeat the revolution, Iran could do nothing other than fight a war to defend the revolution.

On this general point of connecting the success of the revolution to the beginning of the war, the Guards' explanation aligns with that put forward in much of the secondary literature. Both agree that Iraq and other countries – particularly US partners in the region and those with monarchical or secular regimes – were threatened by the revolution, and that this sense of insecurity was one of the reasons Iraq invaded Iran. But there are important differences between the IRGC sources and the secondary accounts.

In the latter, presenting the Islamic Revolution as the reason for the war is sometimes offered as an alternative to blaming Iraq for initiating the conflict. Many of those accounts identify the Islamic Republic's threats to export its revolution as the source of the insecurity that precipitated the war. They see Saddam Hussein's decision to invade Iran as a predictable, if not justifiable, response to the threat the revolution presented to his rule.[2]

The IRGC sources offer a different interpretation. Tying the revolution to the beginning of the war is not intended to diminish Iraq's

---

[1] *Survey of the Iran–Iraq War 1*, 4th ed. (HDRDC, 1998), 20.
[2] Shahram Chubin, "Iran and the War," 13–15 and Efraim Karsh, "Introduction," 1–2, both in *The Iran–Iraq War*, ed. Efraim Karsh (Macmillan, 1989); Shahram Chubin and Charles Tripp, *Iran and Iraq at War* (I.B. Tauris, 1988), 6–7, 31–36.

responsibility for initiating it. The sources acknowledge that the success of the Islamic Revolution created enemies. They emphasize, however, that regional and world powers opposed the perceived threat to their interests embodied in the revolution itself, independent and regardless of any aggressive policies or forceful expansion of the revolution by Iranian agents. In this and other elements of the IRGC narrative we can identify an effort to downplay Iran's own contribution to the outbreak of hostilities. We can also detect a reluctance, still present today, to recognize that Iran's policies of challenging the status quo can only be seen as a threat to states that have an interest in maintaining the existing state of affairs.

Fear of the Revolution

Even though they reject the idea that Iran's active export of the revolution was the cause of the war, the IRGC sources do recognize that other states feared that the revolution would spread one way or another, and they see that fear as a primary reason for the war's outbreak. In the sources published after the conflict, the revolution's threat to the status quo is presented in economic and political terms, while its expansion is described in a nebulous manner, as something that might just happen and take off. For example, the first volume of the HDRDC's *Analysis of the Iran–Iraq War* (*Analysis*) series states that in the revolution "Iran clearly announced its opposition to the domination of the two great powers, particularly America." The "idea that the Islamic Revolution and its spread would endanger the interests of the West all over the world and especially in the Middle East deprived America and its allies of serenity."[3]

According to the HDRDC's *Guide Atlas* series, the revolution's enemies feared that "in the absence of multilateral opposition, the Islamic Revolution would become a phenomenon that would spread uncontrollably and endanger their interests."[4] The reference here to "multilateral opposition" reveals that the Guards view the war as the actualization of existing resistance to the revolution and as the tool to prevent the revolution from spreading and becoming more threatening. The fourth volume of the *War Chronology* makes a similar argument,

---

[3] *Analysis of the Iran–Iraq War 1*, 2nd ed. (HDRDC, 2001), 25.
[4] *Guide Atlas 1*, 5th ed. (HDRDC, 2002), 6.

again connecting the notion that the revolution could autonomously spin out of control to the resulting need to tame it. The continued success of the revolution, it asserts, "left no doubt for global arrogance that without comprehensive physical opposition, the appeal and influence of the Islamic Revolution as an uncontrollable and broadly expanding phenomenon would endanger the interests of the superpowers [and] especially of the West."[5]

While the Guards often describe the revolution as threatening to Western countries because it endangered their interests, to the states in closer proximity to Iran the revolution's challenge was more immediate. The *Analysis* series states that while after the revolution "the West saw its interests [become] increasingly threatened," the states of the region were "confronted with the danger of the export of Iran's Islamic Revolution."[6] The first volume of the *War Chronology* similarly explains how the revolution was more fundamentally destabilizing to Iran's neighbors. Middle Eastern states "aided Iraq['s war effort] in many ways [in order] to prevent the people of the region from welcoming the revolutionary Islam that had succeeded in Iran," it asserts.[7]

These passages demonstrate that the export of the revolution, and especially its forceful export by Iran, is an issue the Revolutionary Guards de-emphasize. Although much of the existing analysis has overemphasized that issue, it is notable that the IRGC sources move decidedly in the other direction. The de-emphasis on Iran's calls for the export of the revolution may have been prompted by the Guards' assessments of their own history and the realization that those calls were ultimately counter-productive. Nonetheless, the failure to analyze more directly how Iran's own actions precipitated the insecurity that led to the war produces an assessment of the conflict's causes that acquits Iran of its role without a full trial.

Fighting to Defeat the Revolution

For Iraq, defeating the revolution was one of several of its war aims. Iraq sought to "weaken or eliminate the Islamic Republic"; it "could not tolerate the region coming under the influence of the revolutionary Islam that had arisen in Iran, and [so] it pursued the opportunity to

---

[5] *Chronology of the Iran–Iraq War 4* (HDRDC, 1993), 17.   [6] *Analysis 1*, 31.
[7] *Chronology of the Iran–Iraq War 1* (HDRDC, 1997), 17, 595.

suppress it."[8] Another source notes that Iraqi leaders were especially concerned about this possible "ideological competition," which could have led to the "emergence of an Islamic revolution in Iraq."[9] But, according to the IRGC sources, both the war and the defeat of the revolution were essentially means to other ends for Iraq. Restraining the revolution and weakening Iran in war, the Guards argue, formed the strategy Iraq employed to attain those other goals, which will be discussed later in this chapter.[10]

The way Iraq conceived of the defeat of the revolution reflects its view of the emergence of the Islamic Republic as both a threat and an opportunity. The *War Chronology* describes the war as Iraq's "use of emerging opportunities ... to secure its unlawful territorial and national interests."[11] Indeed, while for several of Iraq's supporters, especially the United States, the revolution had replaced a close ally with a threatening enemy, for Iraq the revolution replaced a strong rival with a weak one.[12] This gave rise to circumstances in which Iraq faced a diminished adversary and enjoyed the backing of powerful allies. Since this situation was as temporary as it was tempting, Iraq moved against the Islamic Republic in order to take the power and territory Iran's weakness had made available.

For those supporting Iraq, on the other hand, the war was the means to the end of defeating the revolution. That was the primary goal.[13] The *War Chronology* asserts that even though the war appeared to be "between the states of Iran and Iraq, in truth it was between the Islamic Revolution on one side and its international enemies, meaning imperialists and regional reactionaries, under the cover of the Ba'th state on the other."[14] This volume further lessens the importance of defeating the revolution as a goal in itself for Iraq by arguing that Iraq trumpeted it as a war aim in order to gain the backing of other states whose opposition to the Islamic Republic was plain. According to this source, "ideological reasons" contributed to the Iraqi invasion, "but the more

---

[8] *Battles on the East of the Karun* (HDRDC, 2000), 19; *Chronology 1*, 17.
[9] *Analysis 1*, 24.
[10] Ibid., 13; *Chronology 1*, 16; *Chronology 4*, 22; *Survey 1*, 24–25.
[11] *Chronology 1*, 15.
[12] On the history of Iran–Iraq relations, see Shahram Chubin and Sepehr Zabih, *The Foreign Relations of Iran* (University of California Press, 1974); Rouhollah K. Ramazani, *Iran's Foreign Policy, 1941–1973* (University of Virginia Press, 1975); J. M. Abdulghani, *Iraq and Iran* (Johns Hopkins University Press, 1984).
[13] *Guide Atlas 1*, 6.   [14] *Chronology 4*, 30.

important" factor "was the hostile policy of the Western powers, especially America," and Iraq's need to secure their support.[15] In this and other IRGC sources, the United States is described as playing a particularly important role, as it was the country that had the most to lose from the success of the revolution given its support for the shah and its reliance on his government to protect US interests in the region. Another volume, for example, describes the United States as "the country most threatened by the revolution" because of its "apparent and declared sensitivity regarding its alleged vital interests in the Persian Gulf."[16]

Defeating the Revolution from Within

Although the Iran–Iraq War was the most significant attempt to neutralize the threat of the revolution, it was not the only one. According to the IRGC sources, the war was part of a larger effort against the Islamic Republic, one which was also carried out within Iran. It was the deficiency of those attempts to defeat the revolution from within, they argue, that made the full-scale invasion necessary.

The Revolutionary Guards assert that Iraq began working against the revolution shortly after the establishment of the Islamic Republic. At first, the fall of the shah appeared to present the prospect of improved relations between the neighboring states.[17] But as the incompatibility of the two systems became clearer, Iraq's leaders began taking action to prevent the new regime from becoming more of a threat. In addition to hosting Iranian opposition leaders and broadcasting anti-Islamic Republic propaganda, Iraq's main effort was aimed at destabilizing the post-revolutionary government by fomenting unrest and supporting the opposition movements that arose in the provinces populated by Iran's ethnic minorities.[18] The Guards acknowledge that these movements, and the "essential role" of "Iraq and its agents" therein, presented a significant challenge to the Islamic Republic.[19]

---

[15] Ibid., 20–22.
[16] *Guide Atlas 1*, 2; *Survey of the Iran–Iraq War 6* (HDRDC, 1997), 14–19.
[17] *Chronology 1*, 32, 129, 144, 628.
[18] *Chronology 1*, 32, 34, 320–21; *Chronology of the Iran–Iraq War 7-1* (HDRDC, 2006), 16, 48; *Guide Atlas 1*, 7; *Chronology 4*, 18.
[19] *Chronology 1*, 36.

Of the regions in which Iraq was active, the southwestern province of Khuzistan was the most significant.[20] As will be discussed below, separating Khuzistan from Iran was one of Iraq's main war aims, and so its activities in support of the large population of Iranian Arabs there served both to destabilize Iran's central government and to prepare for an invasion.[21] In the period prior to the outbreak of war, Iraq "trained, armed, and incited" Arab leaders in Khuzistan to carry out violent acts against the new regime and to "trigger regional conflicts" with the ultimate goal of "bringing about the grounds for the separation of Khuzistan" from Iran.[22] Even if it was not able to annex the province, Iraq could "at least [establish] a base of permanent influence [there] and impose a permanent ethnic Arab crisis in Iran."[23]

Iraq's principal activity in the province was supporting the Arab People group, which instigated a "political-security crisis" in the region through a campaign of violence and bombings.[24] The Sepah spent the first year-and-a-half after its formation forcefully quelling this and other ethnic uprisings, as described in Chapter 1. According to the reports sent to the Sepah commander in Tehran included in the second volume of the *War Chronology*, "the Arab People political organization, without official position, is trying to separate Khuzistan" from Iran and is using "contraband weapons sent from its supporters in Iraq to destabilize the region."[25] The Guards argue that their suppression of the group represented only a temporary victory, because it impelled Iraq to utilize other channels against Iran and ultimately to see full-scale war as the best option.[26]

---

[20] *Chronology 4*, 18; *Chronology 7-1*, 48.
[21] *Guide Atlas 1*, 7; *Chronology 1*, 32; *Chronology of the Iran–Iraq War 2* (HDRDC, 1999), 31.
[22] *Chronology 4*, 18.   [23] *Chronology 7-1*, 20–21.
[24] Ibid., 50, 120–21, 538; *Chronology 4*, 21; *Chronology 1*, 232–33, 277, 304–05, 333, 349; *Survey 1*, 31.
[25] *Chronology 2*, 16. Western press reports similarly describe Iraq's activities in support of Iranian Arab and Kurdish groups seeking autonomy or separation. Tony Allaway, "Iran's Arabs Getting Angrier," *The Christian Science Monitor*, July 13, 1979; Dana Adams Schmidt, "Iran and Iraq Stir Up Each Other's Dissident Ethnics," *The Sun*, August 29, 1979. Iranian Arabs were most commonly reported as seeking autonomy rather than the complete separation of Khuzistan.
[26] *Guide Atlas 2* (HDRDC, 2001), 27, 30; *Chronology 7-1*, 51.

Striking While the Revolution's Hot

The eventual weakening of opposition groups represented part of the process by which the new regime consolidated its power. By the time of the Iraqi invasion, several other steps had been taken along the road to the Islamic Republic's institutionalization. That process, however, was far from finished when the war began, and the Guards argue that the Iran–Iraq War must be seen as an attack on a revolutionary transition that was ongoing and incomplete.

Iran's Revolutionary Process

Throughout their sources the Guards emphasize that the Islamic Revolution was a process, one in which Iran was transitioning in fits and starts from one system to another. While it was not a brief and seamless metamorphosis, it was also not a permanent revolutionary posture. Rather, it was a protracted and difficult transition, but one that would eventually end. When describing Iran's revolution, the Guards depict it as a normal abnormal process, as an often illogical transition that logically follows such a major socio-political upheaval. There appears to be a concerted effort on the part of the IRGC authors to normalize the admittedly irregular revolutionary transition by asserting that it was particular to a specific period and that the irregularities that characterized the transition were unique to that time.

As the Guards discuss, Iran's conversion from monarchy to Islamic Republic was initiated not by a coherent and united Islamic Revolution, but by a conglomeration of revolutionary movements very much at war among themselves.[27] After those movements succeeded in toppling the shah, Iran became consumed by a war of revolutions, fought between many different groups with very different ideas about what the revolution was and should be. According to the Guards, this, too, was a normal part of revolutionary transition, because in revolution groups "naturally seize authority and power without the need for a coalition of rivals."[28] The incoherence to which the war of revolutions gave rise generated the anomalies of the transitional period, which the

---

[27] *Chronology 1*, 30; *Chronology 2*, 22–24, 33–34; *Chronology 7-1*, 20.
[28] *Chronology 1*, 30.

Guards see as being particularly evident in Iran's shifting foreign relations and the hostage crisis in the US Embassy.

In several sources the Guards describe how the revolution inevitably led to changes in Iran's foreign policy, but ones that were generally incoherent and sometimes histrionic. According to the *War Chronology*, "the state's new position in the context of politics and foreign relations [had new] forms and norms that predictably and naturally accompanied the emergence of the Islamic Revolution."[29] Yet, as it goes on to say, these new norms were far from normal:

The formation and announcement of a coherent foreign policy ... appeared far from existing realities and out of the reach of the new government; but the potential existing in the revolution, ... regardless of the positions of the new elites, automatically set Iran on a path where it would be accountable to the nature and character of the Islamic Revolution to the minimum necessary. It was for this reason that revolutionary and radical positions were often observed from moderate and even conservative elements in this period.[30]

That passage presents a chaotic picture of Iran's post-revolutionary politics, but one that is entirely reasonable from an analytical perspective. Here the Guards acknowledge that in its first stages the revolution took on a life and momentum of its own, radicalizing those in its path. Although the autonomous power of the revolution receded after the period of transition, the revolutionary "identity" of the Islamic Republic that had been "intertwined" with the new system gave rise to "'zigzags' in political behavior" and "caused the emergence of serious contradictions and even a 'crisis of legitimacy' within the regime."[31]

Such discussion of the internal conflicts that have plagued the Islamic Republic – as well as the conclusion that the conflicts stem from the system's revolutionary identity and the difficulty of adhering to it – represents the reflective rationalism that is apparent in the Guards' histories. In this source, the IRGC authors again exhibit their realist tendencies when they examine the relationship between national interests and national identity. They affirm that the Islamic Republic's national identity as a revolutionary and anti-imperialist state could not be easily negated for the sake of expediency. However, they also assert

[29] *Chronology 2*, 28; *Chronology 1*, 159–61, 169–70, 248.
[30] *Chronology 2*, 28.
[31] *Chronology of the Iran–Iraq War 33* (HDRDC, 2000), 33.

that in the case of "conflict between straightforward national interests and the obligations arising from national identity" in foreign policy, "it is possible for the first to be completely dominant."[32]

The complexity of balancing identity and interests in a revolutionary atmosphere was evident in the indeterminate path of relations between Iran and the United States. The change in Iran's view of the United States stemmed partly from the Islamic Republic's opposition to "the international system" as a whole, with its domination by Eastern and Western blocs.[33] Although the Guards describe the changes in Iran's foreign policy as inevitable, they do not see the enmity that developed between the US and Iranian governments as predetermined.[34] Instead, they portray the hostility as emerging and escalating gradually and as a result of actions and reactions on both sides.[35]

Before long, however, the repositioning created the basis for open and then sensational conflict, which erupted in the event that continues to bedevil American views of Iran and that exemplifies the excesses of the revolutionary period: The occupation of the US Embassy in Tehran by supporters of Ayatollah Khomeini beginning on November 4, 1979, during which they held hostage the Americans they found inside for 444 days. On the one hand, several IRGC sources present the event in a way that recalls the popular revolutionary discourse, as a symbol of the revolution's determination to confront the United States and expose the nefarious nature of US activities in Iran.[36] For example, the *Analysis* series states that Iran "clearly announced its opposition to the domination of the two major powers, particularly America, when students following the Line of the Imam [Khomeini] occupied the American Embassy."[37]

Yet on the other hand, the hostage crisis demonstrates how complicated it is to conduct relations both with and as a revolutionary government. Although the first theme of ardent opposition to the United States is the more prevalent trope, the aspect of the hostage crisis on which the Guards focus in the volume of the *Chronology* that deals with the incident is the tortuousness and heightened sensitivity that characterized the fledgling Islamic Republic. The below passages illustrate that point in a manner that is very telling for how residual

---

[32] Ibid.   [33] *Analysis* 1, 25; *Chronology* 2, 28.
[34] *Chronology* 1, 183–84, 190.
[35] Ibid., 619; *Chronology* 2, 29–30; *Chronology* 7-1, 255.   [36] *Survey* 1, 57.
[37] *Analysis* 1, 25.

revolutionarism and domestic politics more generally have impacted Iran's foreign-policy decision-making:

> In Iran, the state of public opinion was such that ... any kind of peaceful move was intensely rejected. ... The main reason for this ... was that political groups and currents [could] use this atmosphere to increase [their] public support; they therefore acted in a manner that emphasized only the intensification of the hostile environment. ... In the minds of most of the elites and in public opinion within Iran, the radical atmosphere was completely dominant, and in the [hostage crisis] nothing but Iran's resounding victory and America's clear submission would have been satisfactory.[38]

This account posits a conception of the post-revolutionary state in which the radicalism spawned by the revolution intoxicated the people and hung oppressively over the heads of their leaders. For the latter, the extremism created a noxious environment by constraining their ability to make decisions that in other circumstances would be much less contentious. That is why, according to the Guards, the release of the hostages did not initially happen, even though it was considered. In addition to the constraints created by the radical atmosphere, the formal and factional divisions within the Islamic Republic also inhibited that move.[39] The delay, however, generated a breaking point, as it was answered by the US decision to cut off relations with the Islamic Republic on April 7, 1980.[40]

In Iran, the reaction to the rupturing of relations reflected the extreme environment. As they have done in other instances, Iranian leaders used the intensification of external opposition to rally the population behind the regime in a conflict with newly raised stakes. They asserted that the diplomatic breach revealed the US government's fundamental opposition to the Islamic Revolution, and the IRGC authors argue that it "proved the validity of the view of those who were cautious and pessimistic and those who obstinately opposed appeasing America."[41] Yet a few pages later they make that statement less categorical. "Iran did not close the way for peaceful yet

---

[38] *Chronology 7-1*, 29, 33.
[39] Ibid., 35–36, 454–56, 482–83, 571–73, 577–78.
[40] Ibid., 573–74, 616–18; "Carter Severs Ties to Iran," *Chicago Tribune*, April 8, 1980; William Branigin, "Khomeini Bars Hostage Transfer Until Parliament Decides Issue," *The Washington Post*, April 8, 1980; "Text of Carter Executive Order on Transactions with Iran," *The New York Times*, April 8, 1980.
[41] *Chronology 7-1*, 37–38.

non-submissive steps," they state, and conclude that relations between the countries "do not have a certain future."[42]

Thus, here and elsewhere the IRGC authors advance a view of revolution as extraordinary and temporary.[43] In the context of both the Iran–Iraq War and Iran's foreign relations more generally, this view, like many others, is both critical and critically misunderstood. While the Guards are often depicted as operating in a state of perpetual and stringent revolutionarism, in their texts they assert that the radicalism that dominated the revolutionary period had to and did recede.[44] Although they acknowledge the difficulty of adopting policies that do not adhere to, or that seem to contradict, the regime's founding ideology, and that ideology's constraining influence on policy-making, the Guards conclude that national interests are paramount. Neither here nor in the IRGC sources is the argument being made that extreme, revolutionary, or ideological positions and policies disappeared completely after the revolution's transitory stage. Rather, the important point is that reality, interests, and time tend to temper the radicalism spawned by revolution and that they did so in Iran.

An Attack in Transition

The distinctiveness, incompletion, and impermanence of Iran's revolutionary period are also pivotal to understanding the way the Revolutionary Guards portray its connection to the Iran–Iraq War. The Guards assert, as discussed earlier, that the war stemmed in part from the ascendancy of the revolution and the fear that the revolution's success and strength generated. Yet, they also make the somewhat paradoxical assertion that it was the revolution's incompletion and weakness that produced the opportunity for the war.

The importance of that timing is evident in the introduction to the first volume of the *War Chronology*, in which the IRGC authors explain why it focuses primarily on the period preceding the conflict. The war, they state, "can only be correctly understood if it is studied in terms of the events that preceded Iraq's comprehensive invasion."[45] The unstable conditions in Iran in the months following the revolution

---

[42] Ibid., 41, 43, 694–97.
[43] *Chronology 1*, 184, 367, 616–17, 634–35, 655–56, 660, 831; *Chronology 2*, 25–26.
[44] *Chronology 2*, 26–27.   [45] *Chronology 1*, 27.

are thus essential to that understanding. The volume asserts that "the Iraqi regime undertook [its] invasion" of Iran "before the establishment of the new system and the formation of various sectors like the military sector." In other words, the invasion came during the "period of transition and the passage of the political and governmental system in Iran from the former state to the new state, as the Islamic Revolution had begun but not yet ended." This, it continues, was "a period in which the previous system ... had been overthrown but the new system and its institutions had still not been completely established." As a result, "the rule of the revolutionary state over the country was very weak because it did not have the tools it needed to exert power."[46]

The seventh volume of the *War Chronology*, which also deals with the period before the war, defines the Islamic Republic as being in "a binary condition" in this stage. On the one hand, several steps in the revolutionary transition – including the constitutional referendum in December 1979, election of the first president in January 1980, and convening of the Majlis midyear – had been completed. "But on the other hand," it continues, "the new system was still in a transition phase and had not reached the period of definitive establishment and natural and lawful stability." The "potential of the revolutionary situation was still powerful," and the country was still "operating in a revolutionary manner that had not been resolved in a single legal and rational cycle." This binary condition left Iran in a precarious position, as "powerful political demands existed that the system did not have the ability or authority to ... respond to appropriately," which led to political uncertainty and crisis.[47]

The authors of the first volume further describe the crises inherent to this period that made the Islamic Republic weak and susceptible to attack. At first they do so indirectly by discussing revolution in general and refrain from stating explicitly that they are characterizing the revolution in Iran. Yet it is nonetheless evident that their descriptions of revolutionary transition conform to the course of events in Iran. The authors also describe the revolution's cracks and weaknesses as "apparent" rather than actual, suggesting that what appeared to outsiders or enemies as critical deficiencies were in fact the manifestations of a successful yet incomplete transition.[48]

---

[46] Ibid., 27–28.   [47] *Chronology 7-1*, 19–20.   [48] *Chronology 1, 28.*

For example, they state that because the revolution had not yet ended and the rule of the state was weak, it "appeared" that there were "divisions" among the revolutionaries. Those circumstances "created space for the growth of currents that remained dismissive of the new authorities" and that "prepared to ... contest the new government and the revolutionary forces." The volume continues the discussion of revolution in theoretical terms, arguing that "if the territorial and ethnic conditions are favorable," the "result is the weakening of the central state's power and authority and the appearance of centrifugal currents and separatist forces that seek to break off an area or areas of the state or at the minimum to seize political privileges, which leads to armed conflict."[49]

Although stated as such, this is not a hypothetical account, for it describes precisely what happened in Iran. The "territorial and ethnic conditions" in Iran are indeed conducive to the rise of "centrifugal currents and separatist forces" that contest or seek autonomy from the state. That has been true for much of Iran's history and was the case in the Islamic Revolution.[50] Indeed, two pages later the authors introduce the "internal crises" generated by ethno-nationalist opposition that led to "the first pressures and crises and also the first military tests" of the new regime.[51]

The authors further explain away the revolution's weaknesses by attesting that they "concealed the revolutionary potential that existed in ... the new system." As the revolutionary transition progresses, they contend, "the revolutionary forces repair all the weak spots in the new system and prepare for the opportunity to bring about its ... strengthening and consolidation." Similarly, the authors argue that "the threats and weakness were confronted by the abundant revolutionary potential of the supporters of the new system and the strength and power of the legitimacy of the revolution," which "resolved the numerous problems afflicting the government."[52] While it is true that the ethnic separatist movements were suppressed not too long after the establishment of the Islamic Republic, their defeat had more to do with the revolution's brute force than it did with its legitimacy.[53]

The campaign against the opposition movements was partly responsible for the unpreparedness of the Iranian armed forces when they

---

[49] Ibid.   [50] Nikki R. Keddie, *Modern Iran* (Yale University Press, 2006), 244.
[51] *Chronology 1*, 28, 30.   [52] Ibid.   [53] Keddie, *Modern Iran*, 245.

were confronted with the Iraqi invasion. Also responsible was the ongoing revolutionary transition, which was taking place as much in the military as it was in other parts of the government and society. Iran's regular military (Artesh) "was in transition from one stage to another," while combatting opposition forces "prevented the opportunity to implement essential changes" in the military. Similarly, the Sepah, "because of the continuous conflicts with anti-revolutionaries, did not have sufficient opportunity to establish a proper military organization to confront major plots like the Imposed War," while the "popular and Basij forces ... remained in an ambiguous position." Altogether, at the time of the Iraqi invasion, "the essential and fundamental work to transform the dominant organization and culture in the military had not yet taken place."[54] Defending against an invasion while putting down an internal insurrection would be problematic even for fully formed armed forces. For the Islamic Republic's pulverized military, the mission was nearly impossible to carry out.

And that, the Guards contend, was precisely the plan. The Iraqi invasion was launched when Iran was "in the worst [possible] condition of military and political preparation."[55] The unsettled state of affairs in Iran and the dilapidated state of its armed forces were readily apparent to Iraqi leaders and were significant factors encouraging them to undertake the invasion. "From Iraq's perspective," the *Chronology*'s fourth volume states, "the internal conditions in Iran were stricken by dissolution and disintegration."[56] According to another publication, the Islamic Republic was "twisting and vulnerable and unable to manage serious foreign crises and pressures."[57] It was a regime, in other words, that was manifestly susceptible.

As the *Chronology* explains, "Iraq's strategists were convinced that the army of the Islamic Republic did not have the capability necessary to enter into a broad war, and likewise that the political disputes among officials would be an obstacle to a united popular presence."[58] Iraqi leaders concluded, therefore, that "a significant and organized force would not exist to stand up against the Iraqi force," and that "the political-military balance ... was in Iraq's favor."[59] In the areas where Arab and Kurdish opposition movements were fighting the regime with

[54] *Chronology 4*, 29.   [55] *Chronology 1*, 17.   [56] *Chronology 4*, 17.
[57] *Battles on the East of the Karun*, 19.   [58] *Chronology 4*, 22–23.
[59] Ibid., 23, 17.

their support, Iraqi leaders "thought not only that significant popular resistance would not arise, but that [they] would be welcomed and supported by the residents of the border towns." It was such calculations, the volume concludes, that convinced Iraqi leaders "that it was possible to quickly secure their aims."[60] That did not turn out to be the case, and the Iraqi forces were not greeted by the warm reception they had anticipated.

As will be discussed in the next chapter, the Guards assert that just as the chaos of the revolutionary transition created the opportunity for the Iraqi invasion, it also prevented Iran from preparing to defend itself against it. The incompleteness and "normal abnormality" of the revolutionary process are once again key. "Every state raised by revolution," the Guards assert, must confront "various crises that are the natural outcome of this period of transition that necessarily must be resolved gradually. But revolutionary Iran, in addition to this, had to confront very formidable foreign crises."[61] In other words, instead of having the opportunity to deal with the conflicts that are an inherent part of every revolutionary process, the Islamic Republic was consumed by the more immediate and grave threat of the Iran–Iraq War. Iran's transition, therefore, was stunted and distorted by war, and the war was necessarily intertwined with its revolution.

Roots of Invasion

The revolution therefore contributed significantly to the outbreak of the war by creating both a threat that Iraq decided it must confront and the circumstances that made it possible to do so. Defeating the revolution, however, was not the only goal of the Iraqi invasion, and the IRGC sources describe the beginning of the war as the result of a number of factors. *Roots of Invasion*, published as part of the *Analysis* series, focuses on the beginning of the war. The first chapter states that two kinds of factors led to the invasion. The first comprises "the underlying causes and variables," including "the policies and positions of the great powers, the encouraging and supportive role of the states in the region, [Iraq's] favorable internal situation, and the intentions of Iraq's leader," Saddam Hussein. The second comprises "Saddam's ultimate reasons and goals in starting the war," including

---

[60] Ibid., 35.   [61] *Chronology 7-1*, 20.

his desire to revise the terms of the 1975 Algiers Agreement that settled the border between Iran and Iraq, "become the successor to the shah [as] the gendarme of the region, prove the power of the [Iraqi] Ba'th Party against the Islamic Revolution, eliminate his ideological competition, [and] acquire the oil-rich areas in the south of Iran."[62]

One of Iraq's primary goals in the war with Iran was attaining sovereignty over the Arvand Rud (or Shatt al-Arab), the river that forms part of the border between the two countries and empties into the Persian Gulf. Control over the river, and the location of the border more broadly, had been a source of contention in the preceding decades.[63] On the eve of the war, the status of the river was governed by the 1975 Algiers Agreement, negotiated by the Iranian shah and then Iraqi Vice President Saddam Hussein.[64] According to the agreement, the water border between the countries followed the river's centerline, or thalweg. This arrangement fell short of the full sovereignty over the river Iraq had sought and that it tried to attain by invading Iran in 1980.

When describing Iraq's war aims, several IRGC sources list attaining "sovereignty over the Arvand" first, as "Iraq's definite and immediate goal."[65] As one volume notes, securing control over the river ensured Iraq "free and secure access to the waters of the Persian Gulf."[66] The sources interpret that goal as being grounded in the geopolitics of the Iraqi state and as largely independent of the policies and ideologies of its (or Iran's) particular regime. According to the first volume of the *War Chronology*, "the geopolitics of Iraq has meant that sovereignty over the Arvand Rud has been important for every ruler of that territory, because [Iraq] has no other way to access the Persian Gulf. Whenever it has the opportunity, Iraq will try to solve [this] problem" by establishing control over either the Arvand Rud or Kuwait.[67]

---

[62] *Analysis 1*, 24.
[63] Richard N. Schofield, "Evolution of the Shatt al-'Arab Boundary Dispute," Menas Studies in Continuity & Change in the Middle East and North Africa (Middle East & North African Studies, 1986); Efraim Karsh, "Geopolitical Determinism," *Middle East Journal* 44.2 (1980); Efraim Karsh, "Military Power and Foreign Policy Goals," *International Affairs* 64.1 (1987–88).
[64] "No. 14903 Iran and Iraq," *Treaty Series: Treaties and International Agreements Registered or Filed and Recorded with the Secretariat of the United Nations, Volume 1017* (United Nations, 1986).
[65] *Chronology 4*, 20; *Survey 1*, 24–25.   [66] *Battles on the East of the Karun*, 19.
[67] *Chronology 1*, 16.

Indeed, after trying and failing the first way by invading Iran, Iraq tried and failed the second way when its occupation of Kuwait was ended by Operation Desert Storm in 1991.

The fourth volume of the *Chronology* similarly emphasizes the geostrategic importance of the waterway for Iraq, as well as how historical grievances can infuse such issues with greater intensity. Iraq "consistently claimed" that the 1975 agreement "benefitted Iran and that Iraq signed it under pressure," it states. These claims served to amplify Iraqi demands for sovereignty over the river, which was one of Iraq's "deep-rooted desires." The IRGC authors depict the underlying reasons for that desire as logical. Iraq's limited coastline and its reliance on oil exports meant that "accessing and moving in and out of the Persian Gulf" was of "abundant importance" and "a vital issue for Iraq's economy." For Iraq, "the possibility of [securing] complete freedom in the Arvand Rud" has "critical strategic significance."[68] Notably, in these passages the Guards characterize the goals of controlling the Arvand Rud and securing access to the Gulf as the most understandable and nearly legitimate of Iraq's war aims. Absent is outright condemnation of these goals, even though they contributed to the beginning of a costly conflict and are naturally at odds with Iran's own interests.

Another of Iraq's goals in the war was occupying and seizing control of Khuzistan Province, the southwestern region of Iran that borders Iraq, the Arvand Rud, and the Persian Gulf. Khuzistan also contains a number of important Iranian cities – such as Khorramshahr, Abadan, Ahvaz, and Dezful – as well as a significant portion of Iran's oil and gas fields and a large Arab population.[69] Because taking over Khuzistan was one of Iraq's main goals, and because of the geographic factors mentioned above, much of the war was fought in this province.

The Guards argue that the aim of taking Khuzistan was connected in two significant ways to the aim of attaining sovereignty over the

[68] *Chronology 4*, 20.
[69] "In 1986 there were an estimated 530,000 Arabs in Iran. A majority lived in Khuzistan, where they constituted a significant ethnic minority." Helen Chapin Metz, ed., *Iran: A Country Study* (GPO for the Library of Congress, 1987). On Iran's oil and gas industry and reserves, see Fareed Mohamedi, "The Oil and Gas Industry," *The Iran Primer* (United States Institute of Peace, 2010); "Khuzestan: Iran's Achilles Tendon" (CIA, Undated).

Arvand Rud and access to the Persian Gulf.[70] First, both concerned geopolitics and Iraq's attempt to improve its admittedly vulnerable geostrategic condition.[71] Iraq's first two aims were also connected because the second, controlling Khuzistan, would automatically achieve the first, access to the Persian Gulf. But because taking Khuzistan would achieve much more than that, it was "Iraq's ideal goal" as opposed to its "definite and immediate goal" of dominating the Arvand Rud; it was "on a higher level and a broader horizon" and was thus "the most important aim" in terms of Iraq's "military, political, and economic motives."[72] The idea of Khuzistan as the loftier of the two goals was important militarily. Even if "Iraq's main goal in invading ... Iran was occupying Khuzistan," doing so was much more difficult and costly than controlling the Arvand Rud, which Iraqi forces discovered soon after the invasion as their advance into Khuzistan slowed. When that happened, "all of [Iraq's] efforts revolved around ... acquiring sovereignty of the Arvand Rud."[73]

Iraq's third goal in beginning the war moves farther away from what the Guards deem legitimate or understandable in terms of Iraq's geostrategic interests. In several texts, the IRGC authors include good-old power in the list of things Iraq sought to gain in the war. "Iraq's goals in the invasion," according to a volume of the *Survey*, included "the expansionist desires of the Ba'th regime."[74] Its ultimate goal, according to another source, was "transforming [Iraq] into a dominant regional power and the leader of the Arab world."[75]

Iraq's preparations for the war included efforts to expand its influence, particularly by championing the popular Arab position condemning Iran's occupation of three disputed islands in the Persian Gulf that Iran had (re)asserted control of in 1971.[76] Saddam

---

[70] *Guide Atlas 1*, 6.   [71] *Chronology 4*, 20–21.   [72] Ibid.

[73] *Guide Atlas 1*, 64.   [74] *Survey 1*, 24–25.

[75] *Battles on the East of the Karun*, 19. See also *Analysis 1*, 24; *Chronology 7-1*, 20–21.

[76] *Guide Atlas 1*, 4–5. The shah seized or reclaimed the three islands of Abu Musa and Greater and Lesser Tunb, which are situated in a strategic location in the Persian Gulf near the Strait of Hormuz, in 1971. The Emirate of Sharjah, now part of the United Arab Emirates, also claims ownership of the islands. Kourosh Ahmadi, *Islands and International Politics in the Persian Gulf* (Routledge, 2008); Farhang Mehr, *A Colonial Legacy* (University Press of America, 1997).

demanded that Iran relinquish control of the islands in a speech in April 1980.[77] In the view of the IRGC authors, Saddam propagated this position as a way to convince Arab states that they needed to stand behind Iraq so it could reclaim these territories. The Iraqi president later expanded that campaign by claiming that he was also "determined to liberate ... the Arabs" in Khuzistan, and by announcing that "if there was a need for confrontation [with Iran], Iraq would not refrain from engaging in ... war and would thus defend the honor of the Arab and Iraqi nation."[78]

A related element that several IRGC sources identify as leading to the outbreak of the war was "the individual characters of Iraq's leaders," which was "also an important factor in [their] pugnacity."[79] Here we complete our descent from what the Guards understand as Iraq's rational geostrategic interests to what they brand as the displaced desires of its rulers. "From a psychological perspective," one source states, Saddam "endeavored to construe his carnal desires as the national will and to impose them as the collective interest on Iraqi society and the Arab world."[80] According to a volume of the *Analysis* series, "Saddam brutally and mercilessly consolidated the bases of his power" in order to launch a war that was "intended to satisfy his limitless ambitions."[81] While Saddam's zeal elicits some colorful descriptions, of the factors contributing to the war discussed by the Guards this last one receives the least attention.

A final factor that contributed to Iraq's decision to invade, the Guards argue, was Iraq's confidence in the likelihood of third-party support for its opposition to Iran. In the lead-up to the war, Iraq began moving away from its former anti-Western positions in order to secure whatever political and military support it could from Western states and their allies in the region.[82] When the IRGC sources assess Iraq's combination of goals, they describe the international environment as an enabling factor – one that facilitated the decision to invade, but not one that dictated it completely.[83] According to the *Chronology,*

---

[77] "Iraq Ready to Do Battle with Iran, Leader Says," *Los Angeles Times*, April 9, 1980; Helena Cobban, "Iraq Bids for Arab Leadership," *The Christian Science Monitor*, April 10, 1980.
[78] *Chronology 7-1*, 50–51.   [79] *Chronology 4*, 17.
[80] *Battles on the East of the Karun*, 19.   [81] *Analysis 1*, 31.
[82] *Chronology 2*, 31–32; *Chronology 1*, 638; *Chronology 7-1*, 1010–11.
[83] *Analysis 1*, 24.

"the international conditions were highly favorable as the imperialist world was strongly stimulated and mobilized against the Islamic Revolution."[84] Another text similarly describes external support as a factor enabling the invasion but puts greater emphasis on its positive role. Iraq initiated the war "with confidence [in] and reliance on the political, economic, and military support of regional and extra-regional powers" and "with assurances that all regional and global powers and international institutions would support its aggression," it asserts.[85]

This is an instance in which the Guards overstate their case. Saddam rightfully had confidence that other states would support him in the war. However, the claim that "all" powers "assured" Saddam that they would actively support the invasion does not reflect the historical record, which includes a very muddy picture of who assured Iraq of what.[86] The *Analysis* series does a better job of acknowledging that ambiguity by defining the American position as "either support [for] Iraq or impartiality," but states that either way the US posture was one of the factors encouraging Iraq's aggression.[87]

* * *

From this examination of the IRGC's analysis of the causes of the Iran–Iraq War, we can make several important conclusions, both about how the Revolutionary Guards understand the war and about how they approach history. As historians, the IRGC authors embrace complexity. The conflict between Iran and Iraq, they contend, was caused by a variety of factors. In addition to trying to comprehend the geostrategic, political, and personal causes of the war on the Iraqi side, they also turn their analytical lens inward and attempt to discern the conditions within Iran that prompted the Iraqi invasion. Their investigation leads them to a conclusion similar to the one reached by other analysts, that the nature, ideology, and policies of the Islamic Republic generated fear that contributed to the outbreak of war.

[84] *Chronology 4*, 17.   [85] *Battles on the East of the Karun*, 19.
[86] Hal Brands and David Palkki, "'Conspiring Bastards': Saddam Hussein's Strategic View of the United States," *Diplomatic History* 36.3 (2012); F. Gregory Gause III, "Iraq's Decisions to Go to War, 1980 and 1990," *The Middle East Journal* 56.1 (2002); Kevin M. Woods, David D. Palkki, and Mark E. Stout, *The Saddam Tapes* (Cambridge University Press, 2011).
[87] *Analysis 1*, 24–25.

The IRGC authors approach several of these issues in a reflective and dispassionate manner, but in some cases their histories betray a reluctance to come fully to terms with the substance and subtleties of the historical record, or at least to do so publicly. Yet the particular combination of reflection and reticence that characterizes their analysis reveals much about the IRGC and the Islamic Republic both during the Iran–Iraq War and today. The idea of Iran as isolated and of other powers conspiring against it was and remains an important part of Iran's strategic outlook. Although the Guards overstate their case in their descriptions of the Iraqi invasion and of world politics more recently, the importance of this self-conception means that it cannot be ignored in any attempt to understand Iran's policies and actions.

Similarly, the disquietude that imbues the discussion of Iran's revolution and revolutionary character exposes the apparent blind spots in the Islamic Republic's views of itself and the world. Since the revolution Iran has embraced its role as an anti-status quo power. Given the interests, ideology, and search for independence that have driven the regime, that stance makes sense. However, the IRGC authors, and Iranian leaders today, often fail to appreciate that the countries that have been empowered by the existing status quo will view the Islamic Republic's attempts to alter it as a threat and will respond accordingly. That challenge presented by the nature and locus of power, which is fundamental to revolution and international politics alike, has consistently led to conflict in some form. In September 1980, it led to war.

4 | *Willing and Unable*
Iran Confronts the Iraqi Invasion

Just as Iran's Islamic Revolution provided the underlying catalyst and opportunity for the Iran–Iraq War, it also had a definitive impact on the war's early stages. The Iranian response to the Iraqi invasion, according to the Revolutionary Guards, was characterized by a combination of willingness and inability. Although many Iranians scrambled to repulse the Iraqi attack on their territory, their nation, and their revolution, they generally proved unable to do so. That dynamic exposes another of the connections between the war and the revolution. One of the central arguments the IRGC authors make in their publications is that Iran's ability to prosecute the war depended in large part on whether the revolutionary conditions in the country helped or hindered that effort. In this initial stage of the fighting, the disorder left in the revolution's wake debilitated the Islamic Republic, rendering it unable to prevent Iraq's conquest and occupation of parts of its territory.

"Iraq Beats the War Drum"[1]

Like the Guards' assessments of the reasons for the beginning of the war, their descriptions of Iraq's preparations for the invasion are detailed and developed.[2] The IRGC sources emphasize the extent and sophistication of Iraq's military mobilization.[3] Activity along the border heated up in the weeks prior to the invasion as Iraqi forces prepared for the war and launched limited attacks on Iranian targets.[4]

---

[1] *Chronology of the Iran–Iraq War 7-1* (HDRDC, 2006), 47. "Iraq beats the war drum" is how this volume describes Iraq's preparations for the war.

[2] *Chronology of the Iran–Iraq War 4* (HDRDC, 1993), 28; *Guide Atlas 1*, 5th ed. (HDRDC, 2002), 4–5.

[3] *Chronology 4*, 19–20.

[4] *Chronology of the Iran–Iraq War 1* (HDRDC, 1997), 232–33, 277, 304–05, 333; *Chronology of the Iran–Iraq War 2* (HDRDC, 1999), 31; *Chronology 4*,

The sources contain numerous reports of these activities and of the resulting insecurity in Iranian border cities, which forced residents to move, and of the Iranians who were involved in these early conflicts.[5] One text sums up Iraq's military preparations by emphasizing that, "considering Iraq's long and extensive planning, it was appropriately militarily prepared" for the coming conflict.[6] The focus on Iraq's military preparedness relates to a larger theme that runs throughout the IRGC sources, namely, the glaring discrepancy between Iran and Iraq in terms of their readiness for and ability to wage war.

Both Iraq's political positioning and its military preparations accelerated and became increasingly hostile in the days prior to the war. In the second week of September 1980, Iraq announced that it had begun "liberating" pieces of Iranian territory.[7] On September 17, Saddam Hussein tore up and declared the abrogation of the 1975 Algiers Agreement, thereby modifying the status of the border and relations between Iran and Iraq more broadly.[8] Armed conflicts continued to escalate in the following days, and on September 22, 1980, Iraq invaded Iran and launched an aerial campaign against Iranian targets.

In these early stages of the war, Iraq was able to use the revolutionary conditions in Iran to its advantage by working with antirevolutionary forces to facilitate the invasion. As discussed in the previous chapter, supporting opposition movements was an important part of Iraq's plans in Khuzistan, the control of which was one of its main war aims.[9] In that province the Iraqis, "with the guidance of internal anti-revolution elements, extended their infiltration [into the city of Khorramshahr] in the dark of night."[10] Iraq also worked with Iranian opposition forces in the Kurdish areas in the northwest. During Iraq's initial invasion of that region, "because of the presence of anti-revolutionary forces and their domination of points along the border, the main movements of the Iraqi army were practically not seen" by

18–19; *Chronology 7-1*, 48, 75–76, 104, 142–43, 210–11, 244–46, 262–65, 308–09, 579–80, 704–05, 809–11, 927; *Guide Atlas 1*, 1–6; *Guide Atlas 2* (HDRDC, 2001), 30–35.

[5] *Chronology 7-1*, 48, 160–61, 434–35; *Guide Atlas 2*, 30–35.

[6] *Chronology 4*, 27.

[7] Ibid., 20; "Revolutionary Council Gives Way to Iran's Cabinet," *The Washington Post*, September 11, 1980.

[8] *Chronology 4*, 20; *Guide Atlas 2*, 33; Ned Temko, "Iraq Tears Up Pact with Iran, Risks Area Unrest," *The Christian Science Monitor*, September 18, 1980.

[9] *Chronology 4*, 21.   [10] *Guide Atlas 2*, 66.

Iranian defenders.[11] When the pace of the advance began to slow unexpectedly, the "efforts of anti-revolution groups" helped convince Iraq to "reinforce its positions" and continue the fight.[12]

And so went the Iraqi invasion. While the revolution-induced weaknesses did enfeeble Iran's defense and made considerable Iraqi gains possible, neither the enfeeblement nor the gains were as significant as Iraq had anticipated. On various points along the front, the "invasion became stagnant after a week. In most areas Iraqi forces did not succeed in occupying their targets and fully carrying out their missions."[13] Another source states similarly that "despite occupying a vast area of Islamic lands in the south of the country, the enemy did not obtain its main goals and was practically crippled behind the walls of Khorramshahr."[14]

What, according to the Guards, explains Iraq's mixed or partial success? Their sources argue that the impasse that followed the first week of the war was the result of a combination of factors on both the Iranian and Iraqi sides.

Iran's Defenders: Willing and Unable

Iran's response to the Iraqi invasion can best be described as willing and unable. Iranian military and popular forces demonstrated a determined willingness to confront the invading Iraqis, which slowed the advance. In many cases, they did so despite the absence of commanders giving the order to attack. But they also proved unable to prevent the Iraqis from occupying Iranian territories and to drive them out once they had, the result of the attenuated and unprepared state of the armed forces and the ongoing political and military disputes within and against the Islamic Republic. The combination of willingness and inability produced a chaotic situation that eventually settled into stalemate.

Willing

When Iraq began its invasion, many Iranians proved willing to defend the country. The *War Chronology* contrasts Iran's response in sparsely populated regions, where there were no defenses or potential

---

[11] *Chronology 4*, 35.
[12] *Survey of the Iran–Iraq War 1*, 4th ed. (HDRDC, 1998), 55.
[13] Ibid., 49–50.   [14] *Chronology 4*, 34.

defenders, to the reaction in cities, where Iranians mobilized when they realized they were at war and effectively stalled the Iraqi march. These first defenders consisted both of members of the military and of volunteer or popular forces, especially those who resided near the western border and who confronted Iraqi forces just by happening to reside in their warpath. The IRGC sources depict the early resistance as stemming in large part from the revolution – both in terms of the perception that the war was an attack on the revolution as well as the country, and in terms of the revolution's continued ability to mobilize the population.[15]

The inability of the armed forces to lead the defense, also because of the revolution, generated the need for popular resistance. "In this period," the same volume states, Iran's "military establishment could not play an effective role because of the lack of necessary preparation, and [so] the people in various capacities, including the Guards Corps, confronted ... the Iraqi units."[16] Evident in this description is the characterization of the Revolutionary Guards operating as part of the popular forces rather than as part of the military establishment. Still, other sources do characterize the Guards as part of the military forces, including in the early stages of the war.[17] The conflicting depictions reflect the fact that the Sepah was in a period of transition when the war began, that it played a key role in the initial resistance, and that its position as part of the military establishment was a change that occurred in and as a result of the war.

Several IRGC sources describe specific instances in which the Guards took the initiative in confronting the Iraqi forces. They recount, for example, the celebrated "nocturnal raid" led by Ali Ghayur Asli in the first weeks of the war. Asli, a member of the Sepah forces in the city of Ahvaz, commanded several dozen lightly armed Guards and Basijis in an attack on Iraqi forces and tanks. The ambush took the Iraqis by surprise and caused them to fall back and away from an important road near that city.[18]

---

[15] Ibid., 31, 35. [16] Ibid., 36.
[17] *Chronology of the Iran–Iraq War 5* (HDRDC, 1994), 21–22.
[18] *Survey 1*, 28–29; *Guide Atlas 1*, 25. On Asli see "How the Operation of Martyr Ghayur Asli Was Carried Out," *Fars News*, October 2, 2008 (Persian); "The Commander Who Drove Saddam Back Behind Bostan with 40 People," *Tabnak*, October 12, 2011 (Persian).

In Susangerd, an Iranian city north of Khorramshahr and close to the border with Iraq, individual members of the Islamic Republic's various military forces – including the Sepah, Artesh, and gendarmerie – "prepared a plan to prevent the occupation of the city," which successfully drove back the enemy troops.[19] The Guards describe sporadic cooperation between these Iranian forces as common in this stage of the war, and many in the Artesh and gendarmerie, like those in the Sepah, were ready and willing to defend the country.[20] They typically classify these early defenders as forming a "popular," "guerilla," and "sporadic" "resistance" that was comprised of both members of the armed forces and civilians. Where Iraqi forces were confronted with such resisters, as they were in Khorramshahr, their movement was slowed and in some places halted before they could attain their goals.[21]

Unable

Willing though they were, the Islamic Republic's first defenders were largely unable to fight the Iraqis in anything but a chaotic, ad-hoc manner. Overall, the Guards are critical of Iran's response to the invasion. Their sources include numerous accounts of Iranian forces retreating because they were surprised by the invasion, as well as by its extent and initial speed. Some forces fell back because they did not have a plan for defense, were inexperienced, lacked equipment and weaponry, or were not deployed in favorable positions.[22] In such conditions, therefore, the Iraqi army was able to occupy large pieces of territory without facing formidable resistance.[23]

According to the IRGC sources, both the overall unpreparedness and the inexperience and disarray of the armed forces were responsible for Iran's inability to prosecute the war more effectively than it did. The *Analysis* series states that Iran "in no way had the necessary readiness to confront a classical, extensive, and comprehensive war. On the macro level, there were many variations in the country's national security policy-making and defensive policy," while the country's armed forces were rife with "inconsistency and

---

[19] *Guide Atlas 1*, 26–27.   [20] *Survey 1*, 49; *Guide Atlas 1*, 41–42.
[21] *Chronology 4*, 31–34; *Guide Atlas 2*, 41–42; Drew Middleton, "Iraq Offensive in Slowdown?," *The New York Times*, September 29, 1980.
[22] *Survey 1*, 28; *Guide Atlas 1*, 14; *Guide Atlas 2*, 39; *Chronology 4*, 32–34.
[23] *Chronology 4*, 31; *Guide Atlas 1*, 7.

disorganization."[24] The *War Chronology* describes how that unpreparedness played out on the border when the invasion began. The few
ill-prepared units of the Artesh ground forces that were stationed at the
border posts were unable to operate effectively, it reports. The Sepah,
"which did not have the necessary soldiers, formations, or equipment,
was also defeated. As a result, the border posts . . . fell and immediately
Iraqi divisions moved deep into the Islamic Republic's territory."[25]

All of Iran's armed forces suffered from various problems and were
altogether wholly unprepared. The Guards had little or no experience
"confronting an organized army" or with large-scale interstate warfare. Iran's regular army had been purged and weakened in the wake of
the revolution and was still "passing from an old to a new stage."[26]
The *Analysis* notes that although the Artesh "had been equipped
with the newest armaments throughout the 1970s, the military
skill of the Artesh forces had not grown at the same rate."
Accordingly, "the military forces did not have adequate ability to
utilize the new weapons."[27]

Yet if Iraq, as the Guards recount, undertook such extensive and
visible preparations for the war, why did Iran not prepare accordingly?
There were two main reasons, according to the texts. First, Iranian
officials were not cognizant of the certainty and scope of the invasion
before it happened; that became clear only once the war began and
with the help of hindsight. According to the *Guide Atlas*, "the reports
and evidence" available at the time related the extent and readiness of
the Iraqi attack in September 1980, "but before the Iranian forces
realized the certainty of this evidence of an extensive invasion, and
before they were able to prepare and reinforce themselves, the Iraqi
army's comprehensive and large-scale attack began."[28] Second, in the
period prior to the invasion (and for a period thereafter), Iran remained
in a state of general disorder produced by the continued unfolding of
the revolutionary process, which contributed to the failure on the part
of Iranian leaders to recognize the definite imminence of the invasion
and to take action to defend the country.[29]

The seventh volume of the *War Chronology* explicates Iran's incapacity by contrasting the positions of the belligerents on the eve of the

---

[24] *Analysis of the Iran–Iraq War 1*, 2nd ed. (HDRDC, 2001), 100.
[25] *Chronology 4*, 30–31.   [26] *Guide Atlas 1*, 14–15.   [27] *Analysis 1*, 97–98.
[28] *Guide Atlas 2*, 33.   [29] Ibid.

conflict. While Iraq undertook "a coherent series of steps to comprehensively prepare" for the war, in Iran "the intensity of political
conflicts between internal groups and the government, which in [some]
regions were accompanied by armed conflict," combined with "the
conflict among the governing factions, ... did not leave the opportunity or possibility to prepare reciprocally."[30] The Guards suggest in the
fourth volume of the series that in these circumstances Iranian leaders
could not have done more to prepare than they did: "The system of the
Islamic Republic of Iran, which had still not passed through its period
of establishment, was wrestling with major political, economic, and
military crises." Therefore, "despite the cognizance of officials of the
possibility of an Iraqi invasion, they could not make the necessary
preparations in order to confront that possible action."[31]

Although the Guards are critical of Iran's response to the invasion
and do not exculpate themselves or other Iranian leaders for their
inability to defend the country, they do not assess more explicitly and
thoroughly whether Iran could or should have done a better job
preparing than it did. Their implicit argument is that it could not.
The Guards' position on that issue is not out of line with other
assessments of the war, some of which also attribute Iran's unpreparedness to the tumultuous postrevolutionary conditions, though
others argue that Iran should have been better prepared for the invasion given its apparent imminence.[32] The Guards may also have
undertaken a more critical assessment of their performance in texts
that have not been made publicly available, the existence of which they
do mention.[33]

One way to understand the Guards' somewhat self-critical analysis
is as a response to those within and outside Iran who castigated the
Islamic Republic's poor performance in the beginning of the war. By
acknowledging that Iranian forces made mistakes, the IRGC aims to
insert itself into the discourse on the war as a credible and objective

---

[30] *Chronology 7-1*, 52.   [31] *Chronology 4*, 28.

[32] Shahram Chubin, "The Last Phase of the Iran–Iraq War," *Third World Quarterly* 11.2 (1989), 2; Shahram Chubin and Charles Tripp, *Iran and Iraq at War* (I.B. Tauris, 1988), 35, 37, 41; William F. Hickman, "How the Iranian Military Expelled the Iraqis," *Brookings Review* 1.3 (1983), 21–23; Edgar O'Ballance, *The Gulf War* (Brassey's Defence, 1988), 35–40, 58.

[33] *Chronology 4*, 610–11; *The Sepah Pasdaran's First Naval Operations in the Persian Gulf* (HDRDC, 1996), 17.

interpreter, thereby giving weight to its own representations of the conflict. Further, it is in the IRGC's interest to provide reasons for its mistakes, like a learning curve and disorganization, that are potentially less damaging to the organization than the reasons that have been provided by others, which include misguided revolutionary fervor and a belief in the force of faith over firepower. The fault-finding may also reflect an effort on the part of IRGC leaders to improve their ability to defend the country by learning from their past deficiencies. Self-assessment, review, and critical examination are practices in which military organizations commonly engage. Iran's failures in the first stage of the war were blatant and costly. Trying to argue otherwise would therefore be both illogical and deleterious to the IRGC's credibility and effectiveness.

Iraq's Mistakes

Despite the efforts of the country's early defenders, the IRGC sources argue that Iran's resistance was not by itself sufficient to halt the Iraqi advance and that Iraq's own mistakes contributed to its inability to attain its goals. The Guards put much of the blame on Iraq's flawed war plan, as do other assessments.[34] Saddam's strategists erred in their confidence that the invasion would not confront organized or formidable resistance and would therefore progress quickly and successfully. They were only partially correct: Although Iran's resistance was certainly not organized, it still managed to be formidable. Most significantly for the Iraqis, the resistance was formidable enough to stymie the plan on which they were relying.

According to the *Survey* series, Iraqi commanders did have largely accurate information about the chaotic conditions within Iran and especially within its armed forces. They concluded accordingly that the invasion would not face significant resistance. Apparently they reached that conclusion even after accounting for the "morale and power from the victory of the Islamic Revolution." Their error, according to this source, was that they failed to appreciate the full "extent of popular resistance," which was one of Iraq's major

---

[34] Middleton, "Iraq Offensive in Slowdown?"; Stephen C. Pelletiere, *The Iran–Iraq War* (Praeger, 1992), 35–38; Stephen C. Pelletiere and Douglas V. Johnson II, *Lessons Learned: The Iran–Iraq War* (US Army War College, 1991), 27–29, 32.

"miscalculations in assessing Iran's internal conditions."[35] The first battle for the city of Khorramshahr in the war's first week illustrates that point. The Iraqi forces who were charged with the "mission of occupying and clearing Khorramshahr ... assumed that the city's defenders were few and lacked morale," and so the Iraqis "believed that the mission ... would last several hours at most and would end in success."[36] Resistance did take form in Khorramshahr and prevented, at least for a time, the Iraqi forces from occupying the city.

The appearance of unexpectedly formidable resistance was doubly problematic because it undermined Iraq's principal plan. The *War Chronology* relates that Iraq's planning and preparations had been intended "for the purpose of obtaining goals that had to be realized over the course of several days." Accordingly, "the emergence of any factor ... that led to the prolongation of the war was automatically accompanied by the defeat of the initial strategy."[37] The Guards argue, as will be discussed in later chapters, that the failure of Iraq's strategy set the stage for the expansion and prolongation of the war, which emerged as one of the conflict's defining features.

The unanticipated Iranian resistance was not the only factor that impeded Iraq's invasion. The maladroitness of the Iraqi armed forces contributed to that result as well. Iraq's military deficiency was manifest on several levels, with the discounting of Iranian resistance and the failure to prepare for that contingency at the top. Below that was the misalignment of Iraqi forces on the various axes of the invasion, which stretched along the border on three fronts in the south, center, and north. Iraq's most important military aims were in the south, in Khuzistan, but "excessive optimism toward the ease of advancing on the southern front persuaded Iraq's military planners" to spread out their forces along the fronts, "despite the primary objectives in the

---

[35] *Survey 1*, 51–52. See also *Chronology 4*, 35–36; Henry Tanner, "Iran Vows to Press War Despite Losses; Iraqi Drive Goes On," *The New York Times*, September 29, 1980; Doyle McManus, "Willingness to Die: Young Fanatics Pose Major Problem for Iraqis," *Los Angeles Times*, October 3, 1980.

[36] *Survey 1*, 32–35.

[37] *Chronology 4*, 23, 35. See also *Survey 1*, 26; "Two Ports Defy Iraqi Drives," *Chicago Tribune*, October 1, 1980; Doyle McManus, "Long Standoff Expected If New Iraqi Drive Fails," *Los Angeles Times*, October 13, 1980; Stuart Auerbach, "With Its Strategy a Failure, Iraq Improvises," *The Washington Post*, October 30, 1980; James MacManus, "Iraq Army Humiliation Complete," *The Guardian*, May 26, 1982.

south." This volume of the *War Chronology* acknowledges that the northern and central fronts did have their own military, political, and economic importance, but still less than the south. "Therefore, the initial lack of concentration of all or a major part of its force toward the main aims, and the diffusion and disintegration of its military force on a wide latitude and the expending of most of the forces in the first stage, were other factors preventing the enemy from obtaining success."[38]

To those major errors, this volume adds the failure of Iraq's leaders to prepare adequate plans for the actual occupation of Iranian territories, which resulted in their forces taking up defensive positions in unfavorable conditions, and for overcoming the natural obstacles (mountains and rivers) that were bound to hinder the advance.[39] The Iraqi military also had difficulty executing the plans it did have. The Guards describe the Iraqi soldiers' "disharmonious movement," their "unfocused and illogical" defensive formations, the "lack of unity among the units," and the overall "weakness of the tactics and maneuvers" as further complicating their progress.[40] Although in the beginning of the war Iran's own armed forces could easily be described in the same way, as they are in the IRGC texts, one thing the Iraqi military lacked but from which the Iranian resistance benefited was morale. The dearth of commitment on the part of the Iraqi soldiers had tangible effects on the battlefield because it made them unwilling to accept casualties in the pursuit of their aims, especially when they were confronted with "the revolutionary and martyrdom-seeking spirit" that animated the Iranian resistors.[41] The Guards note this discrepancy in commitment and morale and its impact on many points of the war and describe it as one of Iran's most important weapons in the conflict.

---

[38] *Chronology 4*, 31, 33, 36. See also Helena Cobban, "In Iraq, Emphasis Is on Slackening the Fighting," *The Christian Science Monitor*, October 3, 1980. It is clear that Iraq's offensive in the south was insufficient to achieve its aims, but it is not clear the extent to which a more balanced alignment of forces would have improved that situation.

[39] *Chronology 4*, 35–37; *Survey 1*, 27. See also Auerbach, "With Its Strategy a Failure"; William Tuohy, "Iraq Strategy Seen as Causing a Stalemate," *Los Angeles Times*, October 5, 1980; Robert Johnson, *The Iran–Iraq War* (Palgrave Macmillan, 2011), 26–66.

[40] *Chronology 4*, 36; *Survey 1*, 27.

[41] *Chronology 4*, 32, 36–37. See also Tuohy, "Iraq Strategy Seen as Causing a Stalemate"; MacManus, "Iraq Army Humiliation Complete."

Altogether, Iraq's failures and mistakes in planning and executing the invasion added up to what the Guards classify as its "most important weakness": the "incongruity of [Iraq's] vast aims with [its] military ability and with its national power generally." Iraq simply did not have the "necessary capacity to secure the goals" it had set out to attain. The Guards indicate that, essentially, Iraq gave too much weight to one discrepancy and not enough to another. By inflating the disparity between itself and Iran in terms of readiness to wage war, Iraq disproportionately narrowed the gap between its goals and its own capabilities.[42]

The Guards' concern with the concordance of means and ends sheds light on the IRGC's strategic thinking. In much of the existing literature, Iran and especially groups like the IRGC are described as making the same error, the foolhardy pursuit of goals they lacked the ability to attain. The IRGC sources, however, are colored by the opposite tone, one of balanced pessimism. There are no delusions of goals that can be achieved with a prayer. Rather, the volumes are filled with solemn deliberation of the persistent and exacting struggle to reach what were perceived as vital objectives.

The Guards' focus on Iraq's missteps is also indicative of the IRGC's willingness to acknowledge Iran's own failures in the war. By conceding that Iraq's mistakes played a substantial role in frustrating the invasion, the Guards are also conceding, *ipso facto*, that Iran's new leaders, the Guards themselves, were incapable of defending the country. The obvious counterfactual is that had the Iraqi military done a better job planning and executing the invasion, Iran would have lost the war in a matter of days or weeks and that its resistance would have been readily overcome.

Impasse

As a result of the factors discussed above, the war reached an impasse after its first week. Iraq's military movement slowed and its forces tried to regroup with the hope of continuing the advance, yet "the signs of the defeat of Iraq's strategy also became apparent."[43] At the time, the important Iranian cities of Khorramshahr, Ahvaz, Dezful, and Abadan had been heavily attacked and surrounded by Iraqi forces, but not fully

---

[42] *Chronology 4*, 23, 36; *Survey 1*, 50, 52–53.   [43] *Chronology 4*, 30–31, 37.

captured. The disappointing results of the first week led Iraq to the conclusion that it was not capable of attaining anything close to its desired objectives, and that absent political pressure the stagnation on the battlefield would give way to Iran taking the initiative and dissipating the gains it had made.[44]

According to the *War Chronology*, at this point the military activities on the fronts "were overshadowed" by Iraq's diplomatic initiatives, which were intended to secure control of the territories it had occupied by inducing Iran to negotiate from an inferior position.[45] Iraq realized that "should there be diplomatic help, the military victories it had obtained could be transformed into considerable advantages; otherwise, in addition to the certainty of the defeat of its strategy, the initiative would transfer to the opponent." Iraq therefore began "protecting the occupied areas" and, from "a superior position, ... resorted to political tools" and "a peace-seeking policy" to end the war. Its "diplomatic officials became active," and Iraqi leaders "announced [that] they were ready to enter into negotiations with the Islamic Republic through international organizations and to declare a unilateral ceasefire."[46]

This represents the first stage of the war's political internationalization, which was a key part of Iraq's strategy to secure its territorial gains. Iran, however, was not ready to negotiate. It was clear to Iranian leaders that "in the case of the acceptance of negotiations by the Islamic Republic, Iraq would have been able to obtain substantial concessions because of its occupation of pieces of Iranian land [and] could have the final word in the negotiations." Iran's officials "understood well that accepting any negotiations while Iraq was inside Iranian territory, considering Iraq's past record, would result only in giving that state and the arrogant [countries] the levers of power."[47] They were not ruling out a negotiated settlement to the war but were maintaining the position that they "would not be prepared for negotiations so long as one Iraqi soldier remained on Islamic Republic soil."[48]

Iran's rejection of United Nations Security Council (UNSC) Resolution 479 calling for an end to the hostilities, which was adopted on September 28, 1980, and accepted by Iraq, was the result of that

---

[44] Ibid., 30–31, 37–38; *Guide Atlas 1*, 48; *Survey 1*, 50.   [45] *Chronology 4*, 30.
[46] Ibid., 30–31, 37–38.   [47] Ibid., 38.   [48] Ibid.

policy.[49] According to the *War Chronology*, Resolution 479 was unacceptable because it "did not mention Iraq's aggression or its violation of Iran's territorial integrity," and it did not call on Iraqi forces "to withdraw from the occupied territories." Instead, the "resolution only requested that Iran and Iraq avoid further use of force." Therefore, "the implication was that Iraq's aggressor army could hold the occupied areas and Iranian forces could not carry out operations to recover [their] own occupied territory!" Iran also objected to the language used in the resolution, which termed the war a "situation between Iran and Iraq" and which indicated that the UNSC "deemed [the conflict] a case that might lead to international friction or discord, not one where international friction and discord [already] existed. Therefore, existing realities were ignored."[50] A sense of outrage characterizes the way the Guards portray the international pressure for peace, especially from the UNSC, which they argue was consistently and unjustly applied to Iran but that failed to deal justly with the "realities" of the war and its initiation by Iraq. According to the Guards, the UNSC's positions in the beginning of the war, including as articulated in Resolution 479, generated a profound distrust of the organization among Iranian officials that they carried throughout the war and that has made them wary of entrusting it with their country's security ever since.

Iran's reluctance to accept an "imposed" peace also reveals how the Islamic Revolution influenced Iran's prosecution of the war. Most often in their sources, the Guards discuss Iran's decision-making as being guided by national security considerations. At times, however, they describe how revolutionary considerations tended to heighten Iran's obstinacy. When we consider the way the Guards define the relationship between the war and the revolution, that tendency makes sense. As discussed in the previous chapter, the Guards portray the war as an attack on both the country and the revolution, and Iranians as

---

[49] UNSC, "Resolution 479 (1980) of 28 September 1980"; Henry Tanner, "Iraq's Leader Calls for Talks with Iran to Settle Conflict," *The New York Times*, September 28, 1980; Bernard D. Nossiter, "Iraq to Accept U.N. Call If Iran Does," *The New York Times*, September 29, 1980; Henry Tanner, "Khomeini Dismisses Truce Offer, Vowing a Fight 'To the End,'" *The New York Times*, September 30, 1980.

[50] *Chronology of the Iran–Iraq War 20* (HDRDC, 2002), 21. See also "Text of Bani-Sadr's Letter to Waldheim on Pleas for End of Fighting," *The New York Times*, October 1, 1980.

accordingly defending both those things. Therefore, the path for ending the war could not endanger the security of either the country or the revolution.

In contrast to their discussions of what security for the Iranian nation-state must entail, which will be examined in coming chapters, the Guards are less explicit when defining what it means to provide security for the revolution. Still, we can discern from their sources that ensuring the security of the revolution entailed eschewing actions and decisions that could fundamentally and irrevocably undermine the principles the revolution claimed to represent and thus the basic legitimacy of the Islamic Republic. The *Survey* describes in general terms how this dynamic affected Iran's refusal to accept a ceasefire in the beginning of the war: "On the one hand, Iran lacked the necessary power to recover the occupied areas," and "the continuation of this situation" was "fundamentally damaging to the Islamic Republic of Iran." On the other hand, however, "accepting an imposed peace was contrary to the goals of the revolution and the basic necessities of preserving its political-military existence."[51]

This passage depicts the precarious position Iran was in during the first year of the war, when both accepting an imposed peace and trying to fight an imposed war were seen as endangering the Islamic Revolution and Republic. Subsequent events – specifically the decision to tolerate the Iraqi occupation until Iran could end it on its own accord and not to accept a ceasefire while Iraqi forces remained – reveal that Iranian leaders viewed the latter scenario as more dangerous than the former. According to one volume, the determination Iranians showed in resisting the Iraqis demonstrated that the population also preferred fighting, even if costly, to compromise, and that ignoring the will of the people would be even more costly for those who did so. Iran's determined resistance, it argues, "showed that any kind of doubt or weakness in dealing with the enemy ... was unacceptable and would mean [its leaders'] loss of legitimacy."[52] Iran's ability to eventually drive out the Iraqi forces seemed to vindicate the choice to fight rather than compromise, and contributed to the decision to continue the war in the summer of 1982.

---

[51] *Survey 1*, 169.
[52] *Khorramshahr in the Long War*, 2nd ed. (HDRDC, 1998), 15.

And so with Iran's "assertive stance," and "considering the grounding of the Iraqi army, the war entered a new stage." After Iran refused to negotiate, "continuing the war was the only path" for Iraq, because its "retreat without a logical and appropriate justification could have dangerous consequences for the Iraqi system."[53] This pattern of Iraq welcoming the political internationalization of the war and Iran refusing to negotiate from an inferior position, thus leading to the continuation of the war, was repeated over the course of the conflict and is viewed by the Guards as a critical aspect of Iraq's strategy. Since success in a quick war was no longer feasible, Iraq adopted a new strategy and prepared for a war of attrition. The aim of occupying the whole of Khuzistan was scaled down to the occupation of certain strategic points in the south. The focus shifted to the establishment of suitable defensive lines in order to protect the occupied areas with the hope of still coming out of the war with control over the Arvand Rud.[54]

As it unfolded, this second stage that began in the war's second week proceeded in a manner similar to the first, but on a more dramatic scale. Like the initial Iraqi invasion, the second effort combined victories and defeats on both sides. But in the second stage, Iraq's advances, especially its siege of Abadan and its occupation of Khorramshahr, were more substantial and more permanent, even while Iran's resistance was more tenacious. And like the initial effort, the second stage ended in stalemate, but one that lasted longer and turned the tide of the war far more profoundly.

The Occupation of Khorramshahr

Iraq's occupation of Khorramshahr came at the end of October 1980 and represented its most substantial gain. The major city was one of Iraq's primary targets because of its strategic location on the banks of the Arvand Rud touching the border with Iraq. The significance of Khorramshahr, however, extends far beyond its strategic value for either Iran or Iraq.

For the Revolutionary Guards, the "epic of Khorramshahr" – the heroic but ultimately unsuccessful defense of the city in 1980 and its triumphant liberation in May 1982 – can be understood as

---

[53] *Chronology 4*, 38.   [54] Ibid., 38–39.

exceptionally historical, as its significance extends beyond the events themselves to the course and history of the war as a whole. Discussions of the city come up in nearly all the important subjects under examination, including the war's major turning points, how the revolution affected the conflict, and how the Guards and other Iranian leaders commanded the war. In many cases, the events that make up the epic of Khorramshahr take on an elevated place in the war's history and effectively encapsulate the broader themes that characterize the IRGC histories.

The IRGC's focus on Khorramshahr begins with the onset of the war, with the first battle for the city exemplifying the overall progress of the conflict in this early stage. The Guards' descriptions of the invasion of Khorramshahr are strikingly vivid. The *Guide Atlas* recounts how on the first day of the war "Khorramshahr came under heavy fire from the Iraqi army. ... The city burned under enemy fire; the noise of explosions did not stop for a moment. ... Hospital rooms were full of martyred and wounded."[55]

The residents of the city were unprepared for the attack, but by the third day of the war "Khorramshahr gradually assumed a military formation and prepared for an epic and fateful resistance." Although "some families left the city, a number of residents and the military forces thought only of defense. Popular forces came from various parts of the country to Khorramshahr and joined the cores of the resistance." When they arrived, they went to the mosque where the Sepah had established a command center and was organizing soldiers and supplies. As the Iraqis fired on and attempted to besiege the city, the Sepah, Artesh, and gendarmerie forces from this and other cities, along with the people of Khorramshahr, "deployed on several axes from which the enemy was likely to come and began their vital resistance."[56]

In this first attempt to occupy Khorramshahr Iraq relied heavily on intense aerial, artillery, and tank fire. That was not enough, however, to take the city, largely because its defenders deterred Iraqi commanders from using infantry to force their way in, which would have exposed them to heavy casualties.[57] The result was that "the Iraqi army, which had sought to occupy Khuzistan in three days, after six days had not only failed to occupy this province, but had been forced to stop behind the gates of Khorramshahr." Iraq's failure, this volume

[55] *Guide Atlas* 2, 38. [56] Ibid., 38, 42. [57] Ibid., 39–41.

continues, was the result of "the devotion of the fighters and of many people along the border."[58]

In one sense, then, Iraq's initial failure represented the inability of firepower alone to overcome lightly armed but committed forces. Using faith against firepower contributed to Iran's few early successes, which stopped the Iraqis after the war's first week and forced them to reevaluate their strategy. The defeat of Iraq's original plan prompted it to come up with a new one that took account of Iran's fiercer-than-expected resistance.[59]

After a brief pause, the Iraqis redoubled their efforts and concentrated on taking Khorramshahr as part of the new scaled-down strategy.[60] They had uneven success for a time, and through October 8 "the Iraqis frenetically beat the walls of the city and struggled to enter." But on the following day the "invasion began and the city came under heavy fire" and in most areas the Iraqis were able to advance despite the Iranian resistance.[61]

As the IRGC sources describe, Iraq's second and ultimately successful campaign against Khorramshahr represented a case in which firepower was able to overcome faith. In contrast to the battle in the first week of the war, the fight for Khorramshahr over the course of the subsequent weeks was characterized by greater Iraqi firepower, including both heavier weapons and better planning, which was ultimately able to wear down the determination of the Iranian defenders. "The main feature of this stage of the invasion," according to the *Survey*, "was the enemy's extensive use of fire support," which "inflicted many losses."[62]

On October 11 the Iraqi forces took control of several major roads around Khorramshahr, cutting it off from its surroundings and "tightening the noose" around the city.[63] Two days later they attacked one of the important defense bases in "the darkness of night" and "took [their first] footsteps into the city, ... making it susceptible to complete collapse." The "epic resistance" of the Iranian defenders forestalled its fall, but only for a time, as Iraqi forces began fanning out into the city.[64]

---

[58] Ibid., 48. See also *Chronology* 4, 32, 39–40; *Survey* 1, 32–40; *Guide Atlas* 2, 52.
[59] Ibid., 50; *Chronology* 4, 38–39.
[60] *Chronology* 4, 39; *Guide Atlas* 2, 53–57.
[61] *Chronology* 4, 40; *Guide Atlas* 2, 58.   [62] *Survey* 1, 40.
[63] *Guide Atlas* 2, 58–59.
[64] *Chronology* 4, 40; *Survey* 1, 45; *Guide Atlas* 2, 60–62.

What followed over the course of the next several days was one of the war's most determined and bloody engagements, as "the defending forces, without sufficient and proper weapons but with steadfast will, were determined to confront the enemy's attack."[65] The *Guide Atlas* vividly describes the scene in the final days of the battle:

The number of invading units, the numerous paths for infiltration, the small number of defenders, the lack of unified command, [and] the lack of necessary organization and discipline all contributed to the heavy pressures incurred by the defenders of the city, so if someone was not wounded by the enemy's bullets and shrapnel they would surely be knocked out from intense fatigue and a lack of water and food, or, because of the lack of coordination, it was possible that in the dark of night our fighters would be set against one another. . . . [But] with all this, the fighters did not allow the aggressors to easily infiltrate, so that with every step forward the enemy suffered heavy casualties and losses.[66]

The *War Chronology* describes the scene in a similar fashion. Even as "the fall of the city [became] certain," and as some Iranian officials urged the remaining forces to evacuate, the defenders refused "to hand over the city to the enemy," and so they continued to fight until they could fight no more.[67]

Ultimately, however, none of this was enough to prevent the well-armed Iraqi forces from occupying Khorramshahr.[68] On the Iranian side, "the overwhelming fatigue of the struggle ... overcame the spirits and lives of the fighters," whose ranks were diminished by martyrdom and casualties and the paucity of reinforcements.[69] The depletion of soldiers ready to give their lives in the war proved to be fatal not only for the resistance of Khorramshahr but also for Iran's prosecution of the conflict as it dragged on. That was especially true given the Islamic Republic's consistent shortage of materiel with which to fight the war. In the case of Khorramshahr, the *Guide Atlas* describes how in the final days of resistance the city's defenders were not only few and fatigued, but their "supplies had [also] run out and they did not have bullets to confront the [enemy] tanks. ... One of the [defenders] shot the last RPG [rocket-propelled grenade] rounds toward the enemy's forward tank and set it on fire. But the enemy continued its advance," and then the city fell.[70]

---

[65] *Guide Atlas* 2, 50.   [66] Ibid., 66.   [67] *Chronology* 4, 41.
[68] *Guide Atlas* 2, 64; *Survey* 1, 46.   [69] *Chronology* 4, 40.
[70] *Guide Atlas* 2, 69.

Although they acknowledge that the battle represented a victory for firepower, the Revolutionary Guards assert that faith was vindicated in Khorramshahr as well. The significance of the resistance, according to *Khorramshahr in the Long War*, derives from the lesson it conveyed to both belligerents that the war would not be easily won:

The resistance of Khorramshahr established the tradition of unequal struggle, of struggle with facilities close to zero and with the likelihood of victory approaching zero, and taught the fighters who afterwards forged eight years of war that they must engage the enemy at every inch of [its] advance and they must fight for every inch of [their own] advance and [that] this was the only way to fight an enemy whom nearly all the world powers were comprehensively equipping and providing for financially, morally, politically, and militarily.[71]

This is a lesson that goes to the heart of the potency of faith in battle, as the willingness to suffer losses in order to advance the objectives of war can indeed be a powerful weapon.

Yet the significance of the resistance extends further, to the history of the war and the country. "The defenders of Khorramshahr," relates the *Survey*, "fought with the enemy until the final moments, and with their resistance, sacrifice, and zeal they wrote an epic and revolutionary yet tragic and victimized tradition and left behind an honorable and illustrious history in their place."[72] The *Guide Atlas* depicts the extraordinary historical value of the battle as follows:

Without a doubt, the admirable sacrifices and persistence of the defenders of Khuninshahr (Khorramshahr) against the aggressing army equipped with varieties of weapons will remain eternal in history and in the memory of rightful and oppressed people. [October 26, 1980] is the day of the occupation of a city whose defenders endeavored, with round-the-clock battle and struggle [and] with the performance of divine duty, to deter the enemy from extending its aggression into Islamic Iran. Khorramshahr was occupied, but the epics, resistance, and heroism created [there] inscribed a major honor in the history of this land.[73]

As this and other IRGC sources recount, the transformative nature of the battle was manifest in the adoption of alternative locution. The fight for Khorramshahr was so fierce that the "joyful (*khurram*) city

---

[71] *Khorramshahr in the Long War*, 15.   [72] *Survey 1*, 48.
[73] *Guide Atlas 2*, 71.

(*shahr*)" was renamed the "bloody (*khūnīn*) city (*shahr*)" to sanctify all that was poured out in its defense.[74]

Thus, although ultimately the Iranians were not able to prevent the Iraqi occupation, the Guards assert that the resistance of Khorramshahr was one of the single most important events of the war. The authors of the *Survey* explain that they consider "the occupation of Khorramshahr and the resistance of its defenders a brilliant and outstanding chapter in the history of the Islamic Revolution and the Holy Defense."[75] While the vanquished are prone to fabricate victory from the scraps of defeat, the argument for the battle's significance is well supported.[76] Further, Iran's successful campaign to recover the city in the spring of 1982 reduces the incentive to do so, making the Guards' attention to the unsuccessful resistance particularly notable. To the Revolutionary Guards, the defense of Khorramshahr is so significant because it reified the ideology of the Islamic Revolution as it was resurrected in the Holy Defense; it actualized the principle of fighting so persistently and against such unfavorable odds because the cause was that worthy. More important than the fall of the city, therefore, was how fiercely it and the Islamic Republic were defended.[77]

---

[74] *Chronology 4*, 40–41; *Survey 1*, 46; *Guide Atlas 2*, 64. *Khūnīnshahr* can also be translated as "city of blood."

[75] *Survey 1*, 31.

[76] R.D. McLaurin, "Technical Memorandum 13-82, Military Operations in the Gulf War: The Battle of Khorramshahr" (US Army Human Engineering Laboratory, 1982). Casualties in the battle are estimated at 7,000–12,000 on each side, with Iran likely suffering more losses than Iraq. Anthony Cordesman, *The Lessons of Modern War, Vol. II: The Iran–Iraq War* (Westview Press, 1991), IV–19.

[77] *Khorramshahr in the Long War*, 12, 15–16.

5 | *The Epic of Khorramshahr*
Iran in the War from Occupation to Liberation

The first and ultimately failed resistance of Khorramshahr in October 1980 represents only the first half of the epic of Khorramshahr. The second half of the saga played out in Iran's retaking of the city in May 1982 after over a year of Iraqi occupation. The developments during the interlude compose the story of how Iran finally turned the tide, of how the revolution progressed to the point that it could help instead of hinder the war effort. The liberation of Khorramshahr marked the culmination of the reversal and, according to the Guards, represents a case in which faith could be used effectively to overcome firepower. Although the Iraqi occupying forces retained their advantage in firepower, the Iranians' faithful determination gave them the ultimate edge in their fight to retake the city. The liberation of Khorramshahr signified a turning point both in the war and for the Revolutionary Guards. The campaign marked the Sepah's most substantial participation in the war to that point and the beginning of its transformation into the powerful and professional military that participation has enabled it to become.

From Occupation to Liberation

According to the Guards, the resistance of Khorramshahr, although ending in the city's occupation by Iraqi forces, set the stage for its eventual liberation, which further reveals its significance in the war. The fifth volume of the *War Chronology* asserts that "the effects of the ... resistance in Khorramshahr did not let go of the occupier's collar" throughout "the period of the occupation of Iran. The resistance in Khorramshahr made Iraq's defensive lines clumsy and vulnerable," while "the will of the occupying troops shattered against the popular resistance."[1] The first volume of the *Survey* similarly argues

---

[1] *Chronology of the Iran–Iraq War 5* (HDRDC, 1994), 18.

that "Khorramshahr, whether in our view or that of the enemy, was the most important [battleground] of the war through the end of the period of occupation."[2]

During this period Iraq was in possession of significant pieces of Iranian territory, of which Khorramshahr was the most important. The war overall had reached an impasse: both sides had run out of steam, with Iraq unable to expand its occupation and Iran unable to end it. Iraq was not prepared to relinquish the advances it had made and hoped it could use them to induce Iran to negotiate, which Iran was not in the slightest inclined to do precisely because of the presence of Iraqi forces on its territory. Several factors had nevertheless persuaded Iraq of the potential success of its policy. These included the continuing instability within Iran, the dilapidated state of Iran's armed forces, and the political and military support Iraq enjoyed from a number of countries. Together those circumstances produced stagnation on the warfronts as Iraq dug in and Iran tried to find a way to dig out.[3]

The process of digging out took about a year and was closely tied to the unfolding of the revolution. The outbreak of the war in the middle of Iran's revolutionary transition meant that the Islamic Republic would have to complete that transition at the same time as it prosecuted the war. Naturally, then, the process of completing and consolidating the revolution impacted Iran's ability to prosecute the war, as well as how Iran approached that task.

As discussed in the previous chapters, the chaos in Iran to which the revolution gave rise generated the opportunity for Iraq to invade and allowed its invasion to proceed with relative success.[4] Although the revolution contributed greatly to the initial mobilization against the attack, in the first year of the conflict the weaknesses that accompanied the revolution had a much greater impact on Iran's prosecution of the war than did its strengths. In other words, this was a period in which the revolution was working against the war.

This situation was readily apparent in Iraq's occupation of Iranian territory and the resulting stalemate in the war. That impasse, according to the *Survey*, stemmed from "the Islamic Republic's inability to recover the occupied areas, considering the internal political

---

[2] *Survey of the Iran–Iraq War 1*, 4th ed. (HDRDC, 1998), 16.   [3] Ibid., 54–56.
[4] *Guide Atlas 1*, 5th ed. (HDRDC, 2002), 9; *Chronology of the Iran–Iraq War 4* (HDRDC, 1993), 29.

problems" with which it was struggling.[5] For a period of about three months after Iraq's occupation of Khorramshahr at the end of October 1980, Iran "took no [military] action whatsoever, and complete stagnation dominated the fronts. In this period, political conflicts within the country intensified in an unfavorable manner."[6] The Islamic Republic remained "in an inactive condition. ... 'Instability on the internal front' and 'the lack of the military capability' needed to retake the occupied areas were the two evident features of the Islamic Republic's situation in this period," which "deprived the military forces of any possibility for extensive movement or action."[7]

That conclusion was reinforced by an unsuccessful attempt to retake territory in Khuzistan in January 1981, which revealed that the mistakes and failures that had incapacitated the Iranian forces remained unresolved. Although advances were made in the first stage of the operation, they were lost in part "because well thought-out tactics to secure the gains and continue the operation had not been considered," and so the units "returned to their previous positions."[8] Iranian forces made another go of it in the subsequent days, the second volume of the *Guide Atlas* reports, but once again the initial successes were lost because "the disunion of the units with one another and the failure to anticipate [Iraq's] defensive tactics compelled the forces to withdraw."[9]

The IRGC authors contrast Iran's initial, somewhat successful, defense against the invasion with its complete impotence in the following months. "With the beginning of the enemy aggression and the emergence of the new situation in the country," the *Survey* states, "internal conditions improved to an extent, and all sights were focused on confronting the enemy." But after the invasion stalled, "internal conflicts again intensified and appeared in new forms."[10] The main axis of political conflict in this period was between the liberal and Line of the Imam factions, led respectively by President Bani-Sadr and Ayatollah Khomeini, and it was the resolution of that conflict that paved the way for the shift on the battlefield.

In *Passage of Two Years of War*, published in 1982 by the IRGC Political Department, Bani-Sadr and the liberals are depicted as being closely connected to the revolution's external enemies. That portrayal

---

[5] *Survey* 1, 56.   [6] Ibid., 62.   [7] Ibid., 167–68.
[8] *Guide Atlas* 2 (HDRDC, 2001), 78.   [9] Ibid.   [10] *Survey* 1, 58.

exposes how Khomeini and his allies in organizations like the Sepah used the external enmity manifest in the war to eliminate their political rivals and ensure their ascendancy in the new regime. According to this source, through the war "our nation ... is not only suppressing the external aggressor but is also successful in dissociating from the liberals [inside Iran], who, like hyena[s], await the death of the revolution." The war created the circumstances in which both sets of enemies could be defeated. In "the storms of the Imposed War," this source contines, "whoever is not saved on the ship of Imam Khomeini, the Noah of the time, will be sentenced to destruction in the floods."[11]

In contrast to that depiction, the texts published after the war focus on the internal sources of the Islamic Republic's insecurity and discord. After outlining the foreign policy challenges with which Iran was wrestling, the *War Chronology* states that "despite ... the external problems," the "main problem was internal, in Iran." The divisions among the ruling factions "overshadowed nearly all areas of political [and] governmental activity" and "deprived the war of a united, coherent, and powerful high command."[12] In contrast to the wartime source quoted above, here the IRGC authors do not accuse the liberals of acting as agents of the revolution's external enemies, which effectively transforms an internal problem into an external one. The absence in this postwar source of an attempt to make that shift signals a greater willingness to claim ownership of the internal conflicts that afflicted the Islamic Republic and hindered its war effort.

Indeed, external issues had very little to do with changing the situation. Those adjustments, too, happened within Iran and included two sets of developments. The first involved the relative stabilization of Iran's postrevolutionary politics and conflicts: the consolidation of power by the Line of the Imam faction; the suppression of the groups and leaders who opposed that faction; the impeachment of Bani-Sadr in June 1981; and the reorganization and strengthening of the armed forces, including greater cooperation between the Sepah and Artesh and the inauguration of a more coherent system of planning and command.[13] According to the first volume of the *Analysis* series, those developments constituted "the most fateful period of the

---

[11] *Passage of Two Years of War* (IRGC Political Department, 1982), 23.
[12] *Chronology 5*, 19–20.
[13] *Survey 1*, 16, 66–70, 169; *Battles on the East of the Karun* (HDRDC, 2000), 21; *Guide Atlas 2*, 78.

Islamic Revolution" that in turn had a "substantial impact on the [war]front."[14]

The second set of developments involved the series of military operations made possible by the first. The military campaign began at the end of September 1981 with the Eighth Imam (*Samin-ul-A'immih*) Operation that broke the siege of Abadan. In explaining the success of that and the subsequent operations, the Guards focus on two of the changes mentioned above, the ousting of Bani-Sadr and the Sepah's greater involvement in prosecuting the war. Overall, the consolidation of the revolution within Iran minimized the effects of the revolution's weaknesses on the war effort and allowed its strengths to make more of an impact.[15]

Bani-Sadr Out, Sepah In

Bani-Sadr Out

According to the IRGC sources, the first development that allowed Iran to break the siege of Abadan and gain the momentum on the battlefield was the impeachment of Bani-Sadr and his flight out of the country. As a general matter, the Revolutionary Guards are highly critical of Bani-Sadr's leadership. One source references succeeding president Ali Khamenei's incisive stricture on Bani-Sadr's management of the war.[16] According to Khamenei, "Bani-Sadr fundamentally did not know a thing about matters of war." The subsequent exchange illustrates the profound divide between the way the two revolutionaries, neither of whom could boast of his military experience, conceptualized the substance and orientation of their fragmented revolution. His expertise, Bani-Sadr asserted, came from his "knowledge of the 2,500-year history of the Iranian army," to which Khamenei retorted "the present situation of the army differs from that of the past," but Bani-Sadr apparently refused to concede the point.[17]

In their critique, the Guards focus on Bani-Sadr's mismanagement of Iran's own armed forces. They frequently blame him for preventing the

---

[14] *Analysis of the Iran–Iraq War 1*, 2nd ed. (HDRDC, 2001), 82.
[15] *Survey 1*, 54, 66.
[16] Mohammad-Ali Rajai served very briefly as president after Bani-Sadr and before Khamenei.
[17] *Battles on the East of the Karun*, 17.

Sepah from developing in ways that would allow it to prosecute the war more effectively.[18] They also denigrate what they brand as his "insidious efforts to block the full cooperation" of the Sepah and Artesh.[19] The characterization of the forces' relationship found in the IRGC sources contrasts sharply with the picture provided in many Western studies, which assert that it was defined by dogged antagonism.[20] The IRGC sources, however, provide numerous examples of the forces' cooperation and consistently assert that they had complementary roles and that their coordination was critical to Iran's success in the war.[21]

When conflict between the forces existed, as the Guards acknowledge it did, the sources attribute the disunion to internal political disputes, not to inexorable animosity between them. The IRGC authors report that collaboration increased over the course of the war, and especially after Bani-Sadr's removal. With that development, "opportunities for joint cooperation between the Sepah and Artesh became possible."[22] The "establishment of coordination between the Artesh and Sepah commanders" led in turn to "the planning of a new strategy in the war with the goal of liberating the occupied areas."[23]

What was really new about the changed situation, however, was the presence of any strategy at all, not the development of a new one, a fact that the Guards acknowledge by recounting the chaos and "foggy conditions" that clouded the war's initial stages. Since the grounding of the Iraqi invasion, Iran's goal had invariably been the liberation of the occupied territories, but the political and military disunion that dominated the period of stalemate forestalled the development of a plan to achieve that goal. The greater harmony that followed Bani-Sadr's removal, according to the Guards, allowed Iranian leaders to

[18] Gholam-Ali Rashid, "Conditions and Exigencies of the Birth, Development, Consolidation, and Expansion of the Sepah in the War," *Journal of Defense Policy* 7.19 (Imam Hossein University, 1997), 3–4, 27; *Analysis 1*, 99–100; *Survey 1*, 67; *Battles on the East of the Karun*, 16.
[19] *Survey 1*, 61.
[20] Shahram Chubin, *Iran's National Security Policy* (The Carnegie Endowment for International Peace, 1994), 30; Dilip Hiro, *The Longest War* (Grafton, 1989), 95–96, 207; Stephen C. Pelletiere, *The Iran–Iraq War* (Praeger, 1992), 64, 75, 79–80; Stephen C. Pelletiere and Douglas V. Johnson II, *Lessons Learned: The Iran–Iraq War* (US Army War College, 1991), 32–34, 44–45.
[21] *Guide Atlas 1*, 15, 26–28; *Guide Atlas 2*, 55.
[22] *Guide Atlas 1*, 44; *Survey 1*, 67.   [23] *Guide Atlas 1*, 29.

devise a coordinated strategy and gave rise to the first semblances of a coherent structure of command.[24]

The other significant changes in the command of the war that accompanied Bani-Sadr's removal were the appointment of Ali Sayad Shirazi as commander of the Artesh ground forces, which facilitated coordination between the two militaries, and the service of Majlis Speaker Akbar Hashemi Rafsanjani as de facto commander-in-chief and Khomeini's representative on the Supreme Defense Council (SDC).[25] In addition to his central roles in formulating, executing, and communicating policies, Rafsanjani was also involved in planning and implementing Iran's military strategy.[26] According to the Guards, "he was in fact the supreme commander of the war, and after the Imam he was considered the second individual determining and outlining" Iranian policy and strategy.[27]

In their discussions of the operation to break the siege of Abadan, the first major campaign of the post-Bani-Sadr era, the IRGC authors provide information on how the Islamic Republic commanded the war for the first time. In this case, the operation was designed jointly by Sepah and Artesh commanders (led by deputy Sepah commander Yusuf Kulahduz and Artesh army colonel Mousa Namjoo) and submitted for approval to the SDC.[28] Although the SDC, the constitutionally established body in charge of national defense, led the command of the war throughout its duration, the Guards only discuss the council in detail in the period after Bani-Sadr's removal as SDC chairman, which is indicative of their overall characterization of the war as lacking real command under his leadership.[29] One source published during the war

---

[24] News accounts and secondary sources support this analysis: John Kifner, "Iranian Progress in Gulf War Raises New Fears in Area," *The New York Times*, April 3, 1982; "Khorramshahr Is 'Liberated,'" *The Sun*, May 25, 1982; William F. Hickman, "How the Iranian Military Expelled the Iraqis," *Brookings Review* 1.3 (1983), 21–23; Robert Johnson, *The Iran–Iraq War* (Palgrave Macmillan, 2011), 61–62; Sepehr Zabih, *The Iranian Military in Revolution and War* (Routledge, 1988), 17, 153–54, 174.

[25] *Guide Atlas 1*, 29.

[26] The Guards consistently refer to Rafsanjani as the supreme commander of the war (*farmāndih-yi 'ālī-i jang*). Khomeini formally appointed Rafsanjani as commander-in-chief on June 2, 1988, just before Iran accepted a ceasefire. Rafsanjani joined the SDC in October 1981 to replace Mostafa Chamran, who had been killed in the war that June.

[27] *Chronology of the Iran–Iraq War 37* (HDRDC, 2004), 45.

[28] *Survey 1*, 67; *Guide Atlas 1*, 44.   [29] *Survey 1*, 71.

asserts that after "the collapse of the liberal line from positions of power and the issuance of the resounding order from the Imam regarding the ouster of Bani-Sadr," the siege of Abadan was broken in "a coordinated attack that was accomplished jointly by the Sepah and Artesh."[30]

The Guards contend that the success of the operation proved the importance and efficacy of cooperation between the two forces, as well as the concordance of classical and revolutionary militaries.[31] It also inaugurated a new chapter in the command of the war and in the Sepah-Artesh relationship. According to the *Survey*, after the victory in Abadan, "a new method for integrating the forces" was initiated and "a new operational strategy" adopted. "The mutual cooperation of the Sepah and Artesh in an atmosphere of ample rapport" helped overcome the conception of the forces as incompatible and mutually antagonistic.[32] Thereafter, Sepah and Artesh commanders regularly convened joint meetings to plan military strategy, which culminated in the series of operations that liberated the rest of Iranian territory.[33]

In addition to the changes at the command level, the shared experience of fighting the war brought the Sepah and Artesh closer together. In some cases, it was the communal exposure to loss. As the *Survey* states, "the martyrdom of high-ranking Sepah and Artesh commanders, despite the heavy shadow their absence" cast, "engendered a deep spiritual connection among the armed forces." In other cases, the experience they gained helped commanders appreciate what each force could contribute to the fight and how to integrate their strengths effectively. Once they began working together, "the martyrdom-seeking spirit of the revolutionary forces" combined with "the proficiency and equipment of the Artesh" to "transform the conditions on the battlefields."[34] That passage exemplifies not only the Guards' view of the Sepah and Artesh as complementary but also how they view faith and firepower in the same way. The Sepah and Artesh, like faith and firepower, were better together.

---

[30] *Toward Karbala* (Islamic Revolution Guards Corps, 1981), 18.
[31] *Survey 1*, 71–72.   [32] Ibid., 67.
[33] Ibid., 72; *Guide Atlas 2*, 78; *Chronology of the Iran–Iraq War 19* (HDRDC, 2018), 18.
[34] *Survey 1*, 68.

Sepah In

The second major change in the Islamic Republic's military posture
was the Sepah's augmented role in the war, particularly in command
and leadership. That change, according to the IRGC sources, had a
significant impact on the course of the conflict.[35] In an article for the
Journal of Defense Policy, which is published by the IRGC's Imam
Hossein University, IRGC commander Gholam-Ali Rashid argued that
the Sepah's approaches to the war became increasingly dominant,
particularly after they had been proven in battle in the spring and
summer of 1981 and then in the liberation of Abadan that
September.[36] Thereafter, the *Survey* states, "a new stage began in
which principally the popular and Sepah forces used methods and
tactics based on revolutionary spirit and with limited facilities to
organize and plan a series of new operations" to liberate the territories
occupied by Iraq.[37]

That development is the focus of the monograph *Battles on the East
of the Karun*, which examines "the reasons for the Sepah's presence in
the direction and command system of the war."[38] The introduction to
that volume explains that "answering the question of why and how the
Sepah was set in a position of planning, decision-making, and guidance
in the Imposed War has special importance," especially "considering
the Sepah's dearth of suitable war equipment and lack of high levels of
military training." Answering that question, it continues, is particularly important because it "can aid in better understanding the organizational development of the Sepah and the future developments of the
war," and because "it opens an appropriate window for researchers to
analyze" those subjects.[39]

The authors caution, however, that the window will not be opened
fully. "In this writing we are not in a position to fully answer and
examine this subject," they concede, and so they have addressed its
"strategic aspects" and "the Sepah's first extensive presence in the
command field of the war" in the Abadan operation to shed light on
the issue.[40] Such comments explaining the process through which the
IRGC authors have composed and presented their published works

[35] Ibid., 67, 114; *Battles on the East of the Karun*, 116.
[36] Rashid, "Conditions and Exigencies," 9.   [37] *Survey 1*, 64.
[38] *Battles on the East of the Karun*, 116.   [39] Ibid., 120.   [40] Ibid., 116.

help us understand the Revolutionary Guards and their approach to history. In this case, the authors acknowledge the presence of certain restrictions on what they are able to discuss publicly, although without specifying what exactly those restrictions are. Nevertheless, doing so allows the reader to better judge the argument that is being made and the people who are making it.

In proceeding to the discussion of the Sepah's involvement in the command of the war, the authors state that "many factors contributed" to that development, though they focus on three major ones.[41] First was "the Sepah's insight [into] and scope of combat with the aggressor," which derived from the Guards' experiences fighting counterrevolutionary forces, including Iraqi soldiers, in Khuzistan prior to the war. According to IRGC wartime commander-in-chief Mohsen Rezaee, that experience gave the Guards a "superior understanding of the land and its obstacles and a very good understanding of the enemy and the weakness in its defensive system," which were both "primary factors in successful planning."[42]

The second factor enabling the Guards to become war planners was what they term "thinking about organized combat." This, too, derived from their past experiences, particularly from their involvement in "the conflicts in Kurdistan." The volume again quotes Rezaee, who explains that "the result of this thinking" was the Sepah's "formation of an operational center named the Southern Operational Headquarters." That headquarters instituted a system of collecting and analyzing intelligence from the various axes of the warfront, which the Guards used to formulate "strategies for confronting the aggressor and which ultimately became the basis for the creation of a planning system by this headquarters." Rezaee concludes that "if organized combat thinking had not prevailed on the battlefield, the Guards Corps would never have obtained the cohesion necessary for planning."[43] Another of the key commanders in the Southern Operational Headquarters, Gholam-Ali Rashid, provided further insight into that development in his *Journal of Defense Policy* article. According to Rashid, the Sepah's appreciation of "organized combat" had a substantial impact on both the war and the IRGC, leading to, among other things, the formation of the Southern Operational Headquarters.[44]

---

[41] Ibid.   [42] Ibid., 116–17.   [43] Ibid., 117.
[44] Rashid, "Conditions and Exigencies," 9.

The third and final factor driving the Sepah's involvement in the war's command was the Guards' determination and initiative on the battlefield, which the IRGC sources consistently present as characterizing their performance in the war. *Battles on the East of the Karun* states that the Guards' "repeated requests ... to carry out operations against the aggressor enemy" put "intense pressure" on the officials running the war, ultimately convincing them to grant the Sepah a greater role and to expedite the pace of operations. For the Guards, "the presence of Iraqi forces on the territory of Islamic Iran tormented the brave men in the field of jihad like a dagger to the heart. They could not tolerate the presence of these forces or remain quiet in their trenches as spectators," and so their faith in the cause compelled them to act.[45]

The dedication described in that quote was especially evident in the youth who joined the Sepah and who in some cases became leading commanders. One of the young men who made a name for himself in the war was Hassan Baqeri, whose commitment to the fight could not hide his youthful stature when it was set against the vast dimensions of war. As this volume recounts, when Baqeri drove to a meeting and emerged from a Chevy Blazer, another Sepah member declared, "this car is too big to give to a child!"[46] Baqeri, like Rashid, was among the Sepah commanders involved in the Southern Operational Headquarters and who pushed for the Sepah's greater involvement in the command of the war. According to the IRGC authors, "the personal characteristics of Sepah officials" like Baqeri and Rashid were additional factors in those developments. These commanders, "understanding the capabilities of the country" and "the strength of the popular forces," "very much endeavored to guide the Sepah in that direction."[47]

Together, the three factors driving the Sepah's ascendancy reveal how its revolutionary identity led to its adoption of a military identity, and accordingly that the Guards view these attributes as concordant. In the case of the first two factors, the Guards' experiences fighting anti-revolutionaries provided them with military training that they used in the war and that facilitated their transformation into a military

---

[45] *Battles on the East of the Karun*, 119.   [46] Ibid., 117–18.

[47] Ibid., 116. The volume also discusses the roles of Khamenei, Yahya Rahim Safavi, Rezaee, and Mustafa Radani-Pur in launching the IRGC's command role. Ibid., 117–21.

organization. Yet it is in the third factor that we find the essential revolutionary foundation on which the military organization rested. The Sepah was composed of young and energetic individuals, deeply committed to the Islamic Revolution and the Iranian nation, and galvanized by a potent blend of faith and patriotism. They were therefore often the ones to take the initiative against the forces fighting the Islamic Republic, whether armed anti-revolutionary movements or the Iraqi military, which in turn gave them battle experience and an understanding of how adopting the characteristics of a military organization augmented their power and ability to fulfill their mission.

Continuing its discussion of these developments, *Battles on the East of the Karun* explains that the Guards began taking on command roles in the spring of 1981, after "acquiring valuable experience from [their] limited operations in the first six months of the war" and with an "understanding of the situation on the warfront and [of] their duty at this sensitive juncture."[48] Quoting Rashid, the volume states that Sepah commanders "in the Southern Operational Headquarters began to discuss" how the Sepah "could have a presence in the traditional system of war command." Planning the operation to break the siege of Abadan, Rashid continued, helped "prove the Sepah's capability to the country's military officials" and made "them understand that if they were not able to deal with the problem of the occupation, there were other individuals who could assume [that] responsibility."[49]

Those efforts appear to have gotten the message across. The victory in Abadan represented "the first extensive presence of the Sepah in the command field of the war" and "vindicated the Sepah and the popular forces' capabilities." That outcome was itself an important development. The Sepah's involvement in "planning [and] implementing large operations, and generally the Sepah's entrance into the command system, is one of the important intersections and developments of the war." After the operation in Abadan, "the Sepah was set in a position of planning, decision-making, and guidance in the Imposed War."[50]

The Liberation of Khorramshahr

Additionally significant about the retaking of Abadan in September 1981 was that it gave Iranian forces the initiative for the first time,

---

[48] Ibid., 120–21. [49] Ibid., 120. [50] Ibid., 116, 120.

which they relayed into a string of operations that resulted in substantial gains. After that operation, Iranian commanders held "extensive and considerable discussions about selecting the operational areas" for the upcoming maneuvers. This, according to the *Survey*, was "the first time" they had done so.[51] The result was the major operations carried out in December 1981 and March 1982, which gradually drove the Iraqi forces out of many of their positions in southwestern Iran.[52] The union and cooperation of the Sepah and Artesh, the authors of this volume argue, contributed significantly to that outcome.[53]

The victories further galvanized the Iranians and alarmed the Iraqis (and their allies). Iraq again issued "requests to establish peace (!)," which Iran was still not prepared to entertain and which years later the Guards clearly still find exasperating.[54] In a continuation of its earlier position, Iran refused to take part in negotiations while Iraq remained in control of pieces of its territory. Although Iranian forces had made impressive gains, they had not yet managed to retake Khorramshahr, and so "immediately after the completion" of the March 1982 operation, the commanders began planning the maneuver that would achieve that goal.[55]

The liberation of Khorramshahr on May 24, 1982 in the *Bayt al-Muqaddas* (Jerusalem, literally the Holy Temple) Operation represents a turning point in the conflict. It was the result of the best-planned and most coherent Iranian operation to that point, and it likewise established the model for subsequent operations in terms of planning, command, Sepah-Artesh relations, and the organization of forces. Its two most notable features were the extensive and integrated coordination of the Sepah and Artesh in both preparing and carrying out the operation and the tactic of attacking the city by crossing the Karun River.[56]

At the end of April 1982, "a joint meeting of Sepah and Artesh commanders was convened" to formulate the plans for liberating

---

[51] *Survey 1*, 96–97.

[52] In Operation *Tariq al-Quds* (Toward Jerusalem), of November 29–December 7, 1981, Iran retook the city of Bostan. In Operation *Fath-ul-Mubin* (Undeniable Victory), on March 22, 1982, Iran retook the cities of Shush, Dezful, and Ahvaz.

[53] *Survey 1*, 81.

[54] Ibid., 87; Geoffrey Godsell, "Shaken Iraq Looks for Way to End Its War with Iran," *The Christian Science Monitor*, April 1, 1982; "Saddam Ready to Quit Iran If It Will Guarantee Peace," *The Guardian*, April 13, 1982.

[55] *Survey 1*, 106.   [56] Ibid., 142.

Khorramshahr. Those plans centered on the three areas of combat organization, mission, and maneuver and were carried out over the course of the next two weeks alongside preparations like conducting "reconnaissance of the area and the enemy positions" and "equipping and preparing the fighters."[57] One of the most significant advancements that came out of that meeting was the creation of the Karbala Central Base and with it the system of combat organization that was employed in the remaining years of the war. The Karbala and later incarnations of the central base represented the highest operational level of management and command: it was run by the top commanders involved in the operation, in this case Sepah commander Rezaee and Artesh ground force commander Shirazi; designed and managed the campaign; and organized and oversaw the subsidiary bases executing the attack.[58] The composition of the subsidiary bases in the *Bayt al-Muqaddas* Operation also represented an important development in the command of the war. Based on the commanders' "previous experiences," each of the three main bases (Quds, Fath, and Nasr) under the command of the Karbala Central Base consisted of a mix of Sepah and Artesh divisions and brigades, just as the central base was itself composed of both Sepah and Artesh commanders.[59]

According to the *Survey*, "following numerous discussions and examinations, finally the Karbala Central Base announced the mission" of the operation:

The armed forces of the Islamic Republic of Iran, consisting of the Islamic Revolution Guards Corps and the Ground Force of the Islamic Republic Artesh, have the mission of attacking in the general area south of the Karkheh River and west of the Karun River at (H) hour on (D) day and, by destroying the enemy forces present [there] and liberating the cities of Khorramshahr and Hoveyzeh, of securing the international border line and preventing another possible attack on the Islamic country.[60]

While the command and combat organization of the forces reflected the importance of combining Sepah and Artesh units, the process of designing the maneuver for the operation revealed the tension that persisted alongside their cooperation. According to the same volume,

---

[57] Ibid., 106; *Chronology 19*, 19.   [58] Ibid.
[59] On the composition and charges of these bases, see *Survey 1*, 107–15; *Guide Atlas 1*, 79–80.
[60] *Survey 1*, 107. See map at https://sites.google.com/view/unfinished-history/images.

two different strategies for the operation were examined in the joint meetings of Artesh and Sepah commanders.[61] The first, designed and proposed by the Artesh, involved "attacking the enemy" in Khorramshahr "by relying on the Ahvaz-Khorramshahr road" that led to the city from the north. The IRGC authors state that although there were certain benefits of the proposed strategy, it also had disadvantages that stemmed from "the classical thinking of the Artesh brothers." Namely, because of the conventional principles on which it was based, the Iraqi forces would likely anticipate the maneuver and would therefore be able to defend Khorramshahr and inflict heavy losses on the advancing units.[62]

The second strategy, designed and proposed by the Sepah, called for attacking the enemy by "crossing the Karun River," which flows from the north into and around the city. This plan, too, had its drawbacks, including the "complications" of erecting an extensive series of bridgeheads that would enable Iranian forces to access the city. Reports also indicated that an Iraqi division had taken up a position that "could have ruled out" the river crossing and that necessitated "accelerating the implementation" of the operation. But the IRGC authors explain that even with those impediments, the second was the better strategy: It "was very far removed from the enemy's classical thinking because it was based on the creativity and innovation of the revolutionary and popular forces, [and so] the factor of 'surprising' the enemy was greatly increased."[63] In addition to the sophistication of the second strategy, the authors argue that its complexity augmented the chances of surprising and overcoming the Iraqis because the maneuver was thought to be beyond the capabilities of the Iranian forces.[64] Thus, while crossing the river presented a formidable challenge to the Iranian fighters, it was also "incongruous with the enemy's classical thinking and assessments of the capabilities of the Islamic Republic's armed forces." The plan would succeed, in other words, because neither side thought it could, and after much discussion the Sepah and Artesh commanders agreed to move forward by traversing the river.[65]

In comparing the river crossing to the road not taken, the IRGC authors conclude that the selection of the amphibious strategy "was

[61] Ibid., 108.   [62] Ibid., 109.   [63] Ibid., 109–10.   [64] Ibid., 142.
[65] Ibid., 120. See also Edgar O'Ballance, *The Gulf War* (Brassey's Defence, 1988), 83–84; Steven R. Ward, *Immortal* (Georgetown University Press, 2009), 257–58.

the determinative factor in the victory of the operation."[66] While it is not surprising that the Revolutionary Guards come out in favor of their own plan, the reasons for their support are revealing. The Guards' justifications for their strategy are based on conventional military considerations, like surprising the enemy, even though they integrated the "creativity and innovation" that were essential to their success. Further, despite the descriptions of some Artesh commanders as reluctant to give up their classical thinking and adopt a more innovative approach, the Guards repeatedly endorse cooperation between the forces and characterize the tension that did exist as the result of healthy disagreements over strategy and tactics, not as the result of intrinsic incompatibility or squabbling over primacy.[67] Indeed, they argue that cooperation was the other determinative factor leading to the liberation of Khorramshahr. The victory, they assert, "was obtained with the absorption and organization of the popular forces, the expansion of the Guards Corps combat organization, the revival of the Artesh forces, and the cooperation and coordination of these forces."[68]

The Guards' descriptions of the liberation of Khorramshahr, like their descriptions of its occupation, are striking. One source recounts the "unutterable passion and excitement" that overcame the forces as they awaited the order to attack. When it finally came they rushed toward the enemy positions, "and in this way the decisive operation of the fighters of Islam began."[69] Not all junctures of the campaign felt so decisive, however. The first and second stages of the operation, beginning on April 30 and May 5, respectively, in which the Iranian forces had attacked the city by crossing the Karun River, surprised and unsettled the Iraqi troops. Despite Iraqi counterattacks, the opening of a breach between two of the Iranian bases, and the failure of some of the units to achieve their aims fully, on the whole these first two stages were completed successfully.[70] According to IRGC accounts, Iranian commanders began receiving reports "of the enemy's flight and retreat."[71] They accordingly decided to hasten the third stage "despite the extreme fatigue of the fighters."[72] The Guards indicate that they may have gotten ahead of themselves. The expedited third phase,

---

[66] *Survey 1*, 119.   [67] Ibid., 98.   [68] Ibid., 169.   [69] Ibid., 132.
[70] *Chronology 19*, 19.   [71] *Survey 1*, 146; *Chronology 19*, 19–20.
[72] *Guide Atlas 2*, 84; *Survey 1*, 146.

which began on May 9, ended unsuccessfully as a result of "the fighters' fatigue and the damage to the armed bases," the "intense resistance of the Iraqis," and "the lack of sufficient knowledge of the region and the positions of the enemy," and so the commanders decided to take time to reset before launching the fourth phase.[73]

When they did on May 22, they found that some enemy forces were prepared to continue their resistance inside the city.[74] In this stage of the battle, however, the remaining Iraqi defenders were not able to fend off the Iranian units, and when the Iraqis' commander was killed by a mine, they fell back and tried to decamp. "Not long" afterwards "the voice of the fighters of Islam was broadcast from speakers" inside the city, as the Iranians had finally completed their "pilgrimage to the tomb of the epic-makers of the resistance of Khorramshahr" on May 24.[75] With the retaking of the city, "the trauma that its occupation had inflicted on the soul and body of the Iranian nation was healed."[76] When the news of Khorramshahr's liberation was announced in other parts of Iran, "the country's cities drowned in happiness and joy ... comparable only to the people's happiness on the day of the shah's flight."[77]

The liberation of Khorramshahr, the IRGC authors argue repeat-edly, was one of the war's most significant turning points, if not its most significant. Their representations reveal clearly that the Guards regard the battle as having a fateful impact on the history of the war and the Islamic Republic and as accordingly possessing exceptional historical value. Iranian forces had "taken the initiative" and had "profoundly changed conditions to the benefit of the Islamic Republic of Iran."[78] As a result, "a new and fateful chapter" had begun and "the nature of the war changed."[79]

The monograph that focuses on Khorramshahr begins by recounting the many times the city was invaded over the course of several centur-ies, in all of which "the determinative element in liberating Khorramshahr was the agreement of the major powers and their

---

[73] *Chronology 19*, 19–20; *Guide Atlas 2*, 85–86; *Survey 1*, 146–50.
[74] *Guide Atlas 2*, 87; *Chronology 19*, 20.
[75] *Guide Atlas 2*, 87–88, back cover; *Chronology 19*, 20; "Historical Photos: 23 May 1981, Khorramshahr Liberation Day," *Payvand*, May 23, 2009; David Hirst, "Iran Victorious as Khorramshahr Falls to Advancing Troops," *The Guardian*, May 25, 1982; "The Routing of Saddam Hussein," *The Guardian*, May 26, 1982.
[76] *Chronology 19*, 17.   [77] *Survey 1*, 153.
[78] *Chronology 19*, 17; *Survey 1*, 168–69.   [79] *Survey 1*, 168–69.

friction and association of interests." Yet, unlike the previous regimes, the Islamic Republic liberated the city by relying on "Iran's internal and independent power."[80] Thus, according to the Guards, the revolution represents a new epoch in Iranian history, but one that is firmly connected to the past. This serves to illustrate that the Guards' commitment to writing the history of the war, then and now, is premised on a profound understanding of the past as essential in giving the present context and meaning.

[80] *Khorramshahr in the Long War*, 2nd ed. (HDRDC, 1998), 13–14.

6 | Pursuing the Aggressor
Iran's Invasion of Iraq

Iran's shift from defense to offense following the liberation of Khorramshahr represents the Iran–Iraq War's most critical reversal. Decades later, the Islamic Republic's decision to continue the war and invade Iraq following the liberation of most of its territory remains a point of contention and misunderstanding. For many outside analysts, it exemplifies the aggression, irrationality, and ideological zeal that make the Islamic Republic so dangerous.[1] For the Revolutionary Guards, on the other hand, the invasion was an act not of aggression but of defense. According to their histories, Iran's decision to pursue the war's original aggressors into their own territory was made carefully and rationally and only after the invasion was deemed necessary to restoring Iran's national security. Even while declaring "the road to Jerusalem passes through Karbala," dreams of marching straight through Iraq and onward to Jerusalem, though useful rhetorically to rally the troops, played no role in the decision-making process. Instead of relying on the hyperbole of slogans and battle cries, this chapter utilizes the internal accounts included in the IRGC sources to rewrite the story of why and how Iran decided to invade Iraq.

Why the War Continued

After the liberation of Khorramshahr at the end of May 1982, the concern stemming from Iran's apparent formidableness on the part of Iraq and its allies was coupled with the hope that the war could be ended.[2] As the first volume of the *Guide Atlas* states, after Iran's

---

[1] See Ali Alfoneh, *Iran Unveiled* (American Enterprise Institute, 2013), 215, 219–21; Shahram Chubin and Charles Tripp, *Iran and Iraq at War* (I.B. Tauris, 1988), 9–10; Kenneth Katzman, *The Warriors of Islam* (Westview Press, 1993), 19; Stephen C. Pelletiere, *The Iran–Iraq War* (Praeger, 1992), 60, 123–24; Steven R. Ward, *Immortal* (Georgetown University Press, 2009), 258.
[2] *Chronology of the Iran–Iraq War 19* (HDRDC, 2018), 27.

retaking of that city and "the withdrawal of the Iraqi army from most of the occupied areas, it was assumed that the end of the war had come."[3] There was a fair amount of scrambling to make that happen, and in the second week of June, Iraq announced that it was prepared to accept a ceasefire and complete the withdrawal of its troops from Iran.[4]

The United Nations also took up the cause with the Security Council's adoption of Resolution 514 on July 12.[5] The Guards describe this resolution as an improvement on the one the UNSC had adopted after the war's first week because it called for an immediate ceasefire and the withdrawal of forces to international borders. But given Iran's existing distrust of the Council and the fact that it had been reticent for nearly two years, the IRGC authors conclude that the resolution's "main goal" was "preventing Iranian forces from entering Iraqi territory," not the war's just conclusion.[6] Iranian leaders therefore remained resolute, rebuffing the various proposals for peace. Then, on July 14, 1982, Iran launched a major operation into Iraqi territory.

Iran's intransigence and its decision to continue the war by invading Iraq have been widely condemned by analysts, political leaders, and observers, both as and after it happened. The results of the invasion were deemed disastrous for both belligerents and for the other parties that were involved in the war's subsequent phases. The reasons for and the process through which Iran made that decision have also been the subjects of much discussion, with many analysts concluding that the decision was irrational and foolhardy, motivated by the Islamic Revolution and the desire to export it to Iraq, and embarked upon by leaders high on their recent successes. While they often characterize the IRGC as a strident proponent of that policy because of its commitment to the revolutionary cause, they do not examine the Guards' own sources on the matter.[7] The IRGC texts largely contradict those conclusions.

---

[3] *Guide Atlas 1*, 5th ed. (HDRDC, 2002), 48.
[4] Robin Wright, "Panic over Iran's Victory in Gulf," *The Times of India*, June 3, 1982; AP, "Iraq Declares Truce; Iran Turns It Down," *The Washington Post*, June 11, 1982.
[5] UNSC, "Resolution 514 (1982) of 12 July 1982"; "U.N. Call for Truce in Iran–Iraq War," *The Times of India*, July 13, 1982.
[6] *Chronology of the Iran–Iraq War 20* (HDRDC, 2002), 23.   [7] See Footnote 1.

The Guards examine the decision to invade Iraq in several of their publications, and particularly extensively in the twentieth volume of the *War Chronology*, entitled *Crossing the Border*. According to this text, the reasons for Iran's adoption of "the policy of pursuing the aggressor," as the invasion is often called, can be summed up as "disregard for the Islamic Republic's terms and rights." Iran insisted that it would only accept a ceasefire that guaranteed those rights, consisting of Iraq's complete withdrawal from Iranian territory, the formal recognition of Iraq as the aggressor in the war, and its punishment for that offense.[8] No such ceasefire had been proposed when Iran moved into Iraqi territory in July 1982; the only proposal that included those terms was UNSC Resolution 598, adopted five years later.[9]

In the IRGC sources, the invasion is tied particularly to the failure to recognize Iraq as initiating the war, despite Iran's diplomatic efforts and protestations. The *War Chronology* states that a critical issue in the period before the invasion "was the lack of cooperation of the international system in condemning Iraq's aggression and its disregard for Iran's requests to bring the war to an end."[10] The *Guide Atlas* similarly holds that, at the time of the invasion, "most international assemblies, along with Iraq's supporters, which had neglected Iran's rights, refrained from recognizing Iraq as the initiator of the war and were not prepared to compel [Iraq] to pay Iran for the damages" it had suffered in the conflict.[11]

Iranian leaders further contended that they could not end the war or even enter into formal ceasefire negotiations with Iraq because Iran was not safe from Iraqi aggression in either the immediate or short term. Despite the damage that Iran had inflicted while fighting the invasion, the main part of the Iraqi military was still intact and could be rebuilt fairly quickly.[12] Further, Iraq continued to occupy and threaten Iranian territory even after the liberation of Khorramshahr. Iran insisted that was the case at the time of its invasion of Iraq, despite Iraqi declarations to the contrary.[13] Contemporaneous news reports

---

[8] *Chronology* 20, 19.   [9] Ibid., 17, 19, 21.   [10] Ibid., 17.
[11] *Guide Atlas 1*, 96.   [12] *Chronology* 20, 24, 26–27.
[13] *Guide Atlas 2* (HDRDC, 2001), 96; *Guide Atlas 1*, 48, back cover; *Chronology* 20, 17, 24.

support the Iranian claims.[14] In addition to the ground Iraq continued to physically occupy and over which it had "total control," the IRGC authors state that several sites were still dominated or threatened by Iraqi forces, "meaning that from a military perspective the evacuated areas were still under [Iraqi] domination and that our forces could not deploy in those areas without [sustaining] casualties."[15]

Beyond the insecurity intrinsic to that situation, the IRGC sources contend that Iran could not agree to end the war because the "deceptive manner" of Iraq's withdrawal revealed that the retreat was designed to ensure its maintenance of its military advantage so it could attack again when it was ready to do so.[16] They note that in entertaining the ceasefire, Saddam had not committed to relinquishing his territorial claims or reinstituting the 1975 Algiers Agreement he had ripped up on the eve of the war.[17] Iraq, in other words, was interested not in peace but in the establishment of a ceasefire it could use to regroup from its defeats and then continue the war from a more propitious position. That was the argument Iranian leaders tried to present to the world. In a meeting with an envoy from the United Arab Emirates in the beginning of June, President Khamenei declared, "we consider an imposed peace, like the imposed war, [to be] distasteful and unbearable, and if the aggressor is not punished [then] the root of aggression ... will not be removed."[18] On another occasion he made the case that continuing the war was necessary to protect Iran not just against Iraqi aggression but against future aggression by other countries. "Today we punish Saddam so that no one else feels they can have the power to invade," he asserted.[19]

Iraq's partial withdrawal also gave it a political advantage and was a way to compensate for its military setbacks by employing international political pressure. Just as it had "imposed" the war on Iran, Iraq was now using diplomacy to "impose new political conditions" on the country. It was attempting to compensate for its "defeats by retreating from some areas of Iran" and by "presenting itself as the peace-seeker on the international political stage." Iraq "intended to withdraw from

---

[14] AP, "Iraqis Vow to Be Out of Iran Within 10 Days," *Los Angeles Times*, June 21, 1982; "Iraq Withdrawing in War with Iran," *The New York Times*, June 21, 1982.
[15] *Chronology* 20, 24.   [16] Ibid., 24, 26.   [17] Ibid., 19–20, 25.
[18] *Chronology* 19, 24.
[19] *Toward Karbala* (Islamic Revolution Guards Corps, 1981), 6–7.

some Iranian territory in order to draw the conflict from the battlefields into the political arenas and to create the image of peace-seeking in order to compel Iran to accept its new maneuver."[20]

Therefore, the Guards argue here that Iraq's turn to "peace-seeking" and its offers of a negotiated settlement were not about making peace or ending the war; they were about using political means in order to salvage a failed military strategy. Such an approach represents a crude inversion of Clausewitzian logic: While war is often seen as the "continuation of policy by other means," for Iraq, policy was the continuation of war by other means.[21] It is apparent throughout the IRGC sources that this view of Iraqi policies had enormous bearing on the war's fate. Iran's skepticism of international involvement in the war took root in Iraq's early peace-seeking endeavors and only grew more profound as the conflict continued. When Iranian leaders assessed these conditions, they concluded that agreeing to a ceasefire would place Iran in a highly disadvantageous and dangerously insecure position.[22]

The IRGC sources explain, however, that Iran was not opposed to peace, but to a ceasefire in the absence of peace. The *War Chronology* states that "a very important point" during this period of the war was that the ceasefire proposals that had been proffered did not include provisions for determining "the manner of the ceasefire and the rights of the two parties; their emphasis was only on the acceptance of the ceasefire!" The volume then explains that Iran was so reluctant to negotiate because no peace proposal "containing terms and steps and international guarantees for [its] implementation" had been presented. Iran could not accept a ceasefire when its method of implementation was uncertain and that "depended on factors like the wishes of the mediators, international conditions, [or] the actions of the countries supporting Iraq." Doing so would mean that "in any peace negotiations Iran's role in realizing its rights would be reduced to a negotiating party and a state under aggression."[23]

---

[20] *Chronology* 20, 25, 27, 31.
[21] Carl von Clausewitz, *On War*, trans. Michael Howard and Peter Paret (Oxford University Press, 2007), 28.
[22] See also *The Imposed War: Defense vs. Aggression* (Supreme Defense Council, 1983–87).
[23] *Chronology* 20, 20.

The importance of the distinction between peace and armistice was made clear by Iranian officials at the time. In a speech on June 20, Supreme Leader Khomeini announced his willingness to welcome the visit of an international peace council, saying "let the [council members] who both parties accepted come, and let them ... see whether we attack Iraq or Iraq us. Let them see the destruction that they inflicted." These remarks, according to the IRGC authors, "indicate well Iran's peace-seeking mentality and the acceptance of a compromise council," but despite that position Iran was still pressured to enter into formal negotiations with Iraq. As IRGC commander-in-chief Rezaee explained a few weeks later, "instead of taking action to recognize the aggressor, the council is recommending negotiations with the transgressing party, and it is clear that in negotiations like these there is no way the transgressing party will admit that it has encroached, especially when it is also supported by various political, military, and economic assistance."[24]

The IRGC authors thus argue that the decision to continue the war was made in the absence of an acceptable plan for establishing peace. They conclude that, in these conditions, Iranian officials "reached the consensus that a solution to the war was possible only militarily," and so they "adopted the policy of 'pursuing the aggressor.'"[25] As Khomeini declared on June 21, "the war with Iraq [will] continue until the realization of Iran's demands."[26]

The Guards' explication of the invasion is significant for both what they include and what they omit. In terms of the former, the motives for the decision are defined essentially as security and justice, in rather limited terms: national security, territorial integrity, some form of assurance against future Iraqi incursion, recognition of Iraq as the aggressor in the war, and the payment of reparations as part of its punishment for that crime – these were Iran's conditions for the acceptance of a ceasefire and the initiation of peace negotiations. They also essentially amount to a definition of Iran's war aims. In the first two years of the war, Iran's reasons for fighting could be summed up more simply as defense – defending against and then freeing itself from a foreign invasion and occupation – which does not necessarily demand further legitimation. Invading another country, in contrast,

---

[24] Ibid., 23–24. [25] *Guide Atlas 1*, 48; *Chronology 20*, 17.
[26] *Chronology 19*, 25.

decidedly does, and according to the Guards Iran continued the war in order to fulfill the conditions listed above and thereby establish security and justice.

The IRGC authors further emphasize that despite Iran's refusal to end the war through the imposition of a ceasefire, the country's policy beginning with the liberation of Khorramshahr was in fact centered on the goal of ending the war. As they recount, Iranian leaders reacted to that victory in a manner similar to other countries, with the hope that the war could be brought to an end. A volume of the HDRDC's *Critique and Review of the Iran–Iraq War* (*Critique*) series states that "the question of 'the manner of ending the war'" was "occasioned by the developments in the war after the victory of Khorramshahr," and that thereafter "Iran's will and effort" was "to bring an end to the war."[27] The nineteenth volume of the *War Chronology* states similarly that "the new and sensitive issue that was put forward for Iran after the end of this operation was the correct way to end the war," which led Khomeini to declare at the end of May, "we watch as the end of the war approaches."[28] The IRGC sources therefore assert that, in continuing the war, Iran was in fact attempting to end the war on terms it deemed essential to its national security.

In terms of the latter, of what they neglect to include, the Guards' discussions of the war's continuation are characterized by two important omissions. The first is the failure to discuss a goal that Iranian leaders stated explicitly and repeatedly during the war: the deposal of Saddam Hussein and/or the Ba'th regime. The exclusion of that motivation is striking, especially because some IRGC sources include quotes from Iranian leaders in which they call for Saddam's removal, and others note that Iran eventually softened that demand and began pushing instead for a commission that would condemn his aggression and determine his fate.[29] By sidestepping the goal of unseating Saddam, the Guards may be avoiding discussion of what they view in hindsight as an outcome Iran should not have insisted upon or tried to achieve (although in other instances they do discuss controversial issues and acknowledge mistakes).

[27] *Critique and Review of the Iran–Iraq War 4*, 4th ed. (HDRDC, 2015), 13–14.
[28] *Chronology 19*, 17, 24.
[29] *Chronology of the Iran–Iraq War 33* (HDRDC, 2000), 14.

The second is the exclusion of motives relating to the expansion of the Islamic Revolution. This stands in contrast to some of Iran's declarations during the conflict. It also contradicts much of the existing literature on the war, which claims that the Guards favored invading Iraq so they could export the revolution.[30] Still, the IRGC sources do attest that considerations relating to the revolution contributed to the rejection of the ceasefire. Their discussion intimates that when war follows and becomes intertwined with revolution, it tends to become more intractable. They argue in this context that the decision to continue the war stemmed in part from the need to safeguard the revolution internally.[31] Not only did the terms and circumstances of the ceasefire leave Iran vulnerable to aggression, they also degraded the principles – like independence and the power of faith – that the revolution claimed to champion. An imposed peace that utterly failed to vindicate those principles would have imperiled the regime's long-term survival and was therefore unacceptable.[32]

Inside the Decision to Invade

While the discussion in the previous section helps us understand the variety of reasons for Iran's decision to continue the war, we are still left with the question of how that conclusion was reached. In answering that question, the IRGC authors emphasize the weightiness of the verdict. "Decision-making for Iran's officials was very difficult and complicated," they state, as "every decision could be historic and [could] itself affect the fate of the country."[33]

The most informative examination of that issue comes in the twenti-eth volume of the *War Chronology*. The authors introduce the reasons for the decision and then get right to the heart of the matter. "The questions that have been raised regarding Iranian forces crossing the border and entering Iraqi territory have concerned the role of Imam Khomeini in the strategic decision-making" process, they state. "Although there are few first-hand sources, a partial answer to this question ... appears in the statements of IRGC commander-in-chief Mr. Mohsen Rezaee on July 12, 1982."[34]

---

[30] See Footnote 1.
[31] *Analysis of the Iran–Iraq War 3*, 2nd ed. (HDRDC, 2005), 11–12; *Toward Karbala*, 6–7.
[32] *Chronology 19*, 18.   [33] Ibid., 17.   [34] *Chronology 20*, 18.

There has indeed been much analysis and speculation regarding Khomeini's role in the decision to invade Iraq, and the Guards do proceed to provide exceptionally valuable information regarding that controversial issue. Yet they describe rather than explicate Rezaee's statements and present them, as they state, as a partial rather than complete answer. The comment regarding the scarcity of first-hand accounts is also curious, as we would assume that, in contrast to most analysts, the IRGC would actually have access to those sources to the extent that they exist.[35] Still, the fact that the authors do present a primary account of the decision reflects the Guards' intersecting roles in making, recording, and reporting the history of the Iran–Iraq War and the access to that history that the HDRDC publications provide.

The report included in this volume exemplifies that point. In it, Rezaee describes the conversation he had with Khomeini in late April 1982:

We went to see the Imam, and we said that in order to completely secure the country and drive away the aggressor it was necessary that, in addition to liberating the occupied areas and cities, we enter Iraqi territory and put pressure on the enemy. But the Imam commanded: "No, what need is there?" But, when we presented our reasons to the Imam, and we said that if we want to defend the country it was necessary that [in places] where we defend our forces not be anxious and uneasy every day of an enemy attack, the Imam commanded that "if this is the case, okay, that is correct, and insofar as it is necessary to be assured [of this] in order for us to defend, we will advance, and in this way any number we shall kill and any number we have killed is no matter and God has given his command and this is no matter. But my concern is that you not go somewhere that is not related to defense."[36]

This account of how Iranian leaders made the decision to continue the war casts sorely needed light on a matter that is of utmost significance for understanding the Islamic Republic and the Iran–Iraq War. Rezaee's statement supports the understanding of Khomeini as an arbiter rather than a commander in his leadership of the Islamic Republic and bears out the assessment that he was quite reluctant to

---

[35] Much of what has been written about the decision to continue the war is based on Rafsanjani's memoirs. See Ali Alfoneh, "Review of *The Twilight War*," *Middle East Quarterly* 20.3 (2013).

[36] *Chronology 20*, 18–19.

carry the war onto Iraqi soil. It also supports the view that IRGC leaders were advocates of the invasion and played an important role in making the case to Khomeini.

Furthermore, according to Rezaee, Khomeini was more than reluctant to continue the war; he was opposed to it, and it was Rezaee who changed his mind. (On this point of the IRGC's role in swaying Khomeini there still remains some disputation, even among the Revolutionary Guards, as will be discussed in Chapter 11.) Whereas other primary accounts have justified the invasion as a way to force recognition of Iran's conditions for a ceasefire, this statement reveals that Rezaee viewed it as necessary to defend the country, and that it was on the basis of defense that he made the case to Khomeini. As discussed, the IRGC sources describe the invasion as needed to ensure the punishment of Iraq as the aggressor, but what they emphasize equally, and what has received far less attention in the existing literature, is the necessity of continuing the war in order to ensure Iran's security and its ability to defend itself. That is a consideration that emerges as paramount in Rezaee's conversation with Khomeini, as it does throughout the IRGC sources.

A long note following Rezaee's account includes comments Khomeini made on July 25, 1982, shortly after Iran had launched its invasion into Iraq, about "the policy of 'security for peace,'" which further highlight the primacy of defense and security:

Defense is a matter that is both religiously and rationally indispensable for all. We have [been in] a defensive position and today too we are [in] a defensive position. Iraq's mercenary army has been in Iran for twenty-something months and has sensitive Iranian positions in hand and committed all those crimes – which history must record – and from countries that say "we are supporters of Islam" and human rights societies and similar organizations, there has been no talk, [and] if there has, they have condemned Iran! And today, in order to defend our country and [to] defend our oppressed nation, we enter Iraq, so that we do not allow [cities like] Abadan, Ahvaz, and other places to come under attack every day, to come under [Iraq's] long-range artillery and missile [fire], and we want to reach a point where [Iraq] cannot do this; this is an [act of] defense that we do.[37]

In his remarks to Sepah commanders, Rezaee similarly puts the emphasis on security and defense. Notably, he describes the invasion

[37] Ibid., 19.

as a continuation of rather than a change in Iranian strategy and, like Khomeini, as one that was fundamentally defensive:

> Iran's general strategic military principles from the beginning of the Iraqi aggression into Iran were based on the conviction that we must first destroy the enemy forces [and] liberate all occupied territories, and after that continue the offensive operations [and] attain a military advantage to establish an acceptable defensive position so that we can use our military advantage to punish the aggressor while defending our territory. ...
>
> Considering that parts of Iranian territory are still under Iraqi occupation, and [that] our cities and villages on the border are coming under [Iraqi] artillery fire, our country is not fully secure, and in practice our war has not been completed and Iran's military strategy will still continue on the basis of the same initial strategy.[38]

As discussed previously, the IRGC sources contend ardently that the Islamic Republic was in a defensive position even after it invaded Iraq because it was not and would not otherwise be secure in the future. The portrayal of how the decision to continue the war was made, particularly the argument that the invasion was the continuation of the defensive policy Iran had pursued since the beginning of the war, is indicative of that contention. The authors of this volume explain that, considering Iraq's abrogation of the 1975 Algiers Agreement and the accordant absence of a treaty governing the border, as well as Iraq's proximity to strategic Iranian cities, it was necessary for Iran to shift the "geostrategic balance" in its favor before it could safely agree to a ceasefire.[39]

They then demonstrate that the goal of obtaining the geostrategic and military balance was long-standing by noting that it was an aim of the Nasr Operation carried out in January 1981, several months into the war. The fact that Basra, the main target of the invasion, was one of the targets of the earlier operation "indicates the interest of the military forces in acquiring this balance." The Nasr Operation is particularly significant in demonstrating the continuity in Iranian policy, this volume continues, because it was planned not by the Sepah but by the Artesh and Bani-Sadr. According to the authors, "even Bani-Sadr made the destruction of the Iraqi army and entering the territory of that state one of his main aspirations." As the former president declared publicly before the operation, "let us be fully ready to

---

[38] Ibid., 18.   [39] Ibid., 25.

overwhelm the enemy forces in our territory and to cross into Iraqi territory."[40]

The assertion that the policy of pursuing the aggressor was part of Iran's long-standing strategy of ensuring its security by obtaining a military advantage is also suggested in the date of Rezaee's conversation with Khomeini, which itself is highly significant. According to the report quoted in the *Chronology*, that meeting took place during the planning of the *Bayt al-Muqaddas* Operation and roughly between April 21 and April 30, 1982. That means, according to the report, that Rezaee had convinced Khomeini of the necessity of continuing the war and invading Iraq *before* the operation to liberate Khorramshahr had even begun, which is earlier than what has been previously reported but which is congruent with the Guards' argument that the invasion was the continuation of a defensive policy.[41]

Pursuing the Aggressor

The Ramadan Operation and Its Aftermath

The invasion of Iraq was launched in the Ramadan (*Ramazan*) Operation on July 14, 1982. Although Iranian forces and fire had previously crossed into Iraq, this was the first major operation in which advancing into that country was the main and explicit objective. Basra, Iraq's strategic southern port city, was the central target. By taking the city, the Guards hoped, "the enemy would be compelled to accept Iran's conditions for peace and, if not, [Iran] would have created a stronger position for the possibility of continuing the war in the future."[42]

Iranian commanders anticipated that the advance would proceed without great difficulty. Before the liberation of Khorramshahr, Iraq had "regarded that city as the key to Basra and assumed that losing the city was not possible, so the positions in the east of Basra were not fortified." However, the "delay in implementing the Ramadan Operation," brought about in part by the diversion of Iran's attention to the Israeli invasion of Lebanon in the beginning of June, gave Iraq

---

[40] Ibid., 25.   [41] *Chronology* 19, 19.   [42] *Chronology* 20, 27–28.

the opportunity to reinforce its defenses, making the joint Sepah-Artesh advance much more difficult.[43]

Iran's work to support the resistance to the Israeli invasion, which gave rise to the formation of Hezbollah, is discussed in the nineteenth volume of the *War Chronology*. The description of the Iranian mission is notably dispassionate. According to this volume, Iran's military leaders met on June 6, 1982 "to discuss helping the people of Palestine and Lebanon, and ultimately decided to send a council to Syria to study how to extend help." The next day, following a meeting of the Supreme Defense Council, "the Sepah and Artesh announced in a joint communique that a number of their armed units would be dispatched to the south of Lebanon," and that afternoon "a top-level Iranian political and military council went to Syria." During the trip, the members of the council met with Syrian political and military officials and "obtained information about the latest conditions on the battlefronts in Southern Lebanon." Upon its return to Iran on June 10, the council "immediately reported on its 3-day trip by participating in a meeting of the Supreme Defense Council that was convened in the presence of Imam Khomeini." Five groups of Iranian forces and another council of officials traveled to Syria over the course of the next week, and on June 18 "the Guards Corps also established its Lebanon unit."[44]

In their sources the IRGC authors describe the mission to Lebanon with ambivalence: not as the triumphant export of the Islamic Revolution by its vanguard, not as proof that Iran could fight for the oppressed all over the world, and not as signaling the primacy of an Islamic or revolutionary duty to defeat Zionism over the imperative to fight for Iran in its war against Iraq. A sober assessment of Iran's actions and rhetoric also reveals that to be so. The second council returned to Iran after only a three-day visit, and on June 21, Ayatollah Khomeini made Iran's priorities clear. He described Israel's attack on Lebanon not as the opportunity for which the revolution had been waiting or as a conflict in which Iran had some duty to intervene, but as "an American trap for Iran" set to make "Iran forget its own war." Shifting the country's attention to fighting Zionism in Lebanon, thereby depleting its ability to fight its own war against Iraq, therefore meant falling right into that trap. Iran would not do so,

---

[43] Ibid., 28.   [44] *Chronology 19*, 30–31.

Khomeini decreed. "We must save Lebanon by defeating Iraq," he said. "We cannot save both Lebanon and Iran," so "we must pursue Lebanon by defeating Iraq."[45]

And that is the course of action Iran pursued. The military results of the Ramadan Operation, however, were mixed. The delay in executing the operation allowed Iraq to prepare for the attack by fortifying its positions in Basra and by laying landmines under the roads that led to the city. At one point, the Iranians came "so close to Basra that they could easily see the city lights," but they were subsequently driven back.[46] Iran was not able to take control of significant pieces of territory or maintain a presence near Basra.[47]

However, the operation was successful enough to generate renewed international concern. In invading Iraq, Iran had demonstrated both its intransigence and its ability to challenge Iraq militarily. According to the IRGC sources, that challenge was deemed unacceptable by those who feared an Iranian victory, something that now seemed possible. Therefore, they assert, Iraq's supporters "were persuaded to restore the military and political advantage in the war to Iraq" in order to block the threat that the Islamic Republic presented to Saddam's regime and possibly to the region.[48] Support for Iraq in various forms did increase after the Iranian invasion, and third-party involvement became more direct and substantial as the war went on.

What was additionally significant about the Ramadan Operation, according to the *War Chronology*, "was the offensive into Iraqi territory itself" and the message it conveyed: that the Islamic Republic "was determined to continue the battle until its claims were realized."[49] And that is what happened. From the invasion of Iraq onward, the Guards describe Iran's strategy in that manner, as pushing on to safeguard the full liberation and security of its territory and the recognition and punishment of Iraq as the aggressor. Iran's leaders,

---

[45] Ibid., 30–31, 1030–34. On Hezbollah and its relationship with the IRGC, see Marius Deeb, "Shia Movements in Lebanon," *Third World Quarterly* 10.2 (1988); A. Nizar Hamzeh, "Lebanon's Hizbullah," *Third World Quarterly* 14.2 (1993); Shireen T. Hunter, "Iran and the Spread of Revolutionary Islam," *Third World Quarterly* 10.2 (1988); Hala Jaber, *Hezbollah* (Columbia University Press, 1997).

[46] *Chronology 20*, 29.

[47] Ibid., 29–31. The operation ended on July 29, 1982. See also "Iran Reports Seizing 60 Square Miles of Iraqi Land," *The New York Times*, July 29, 1982.

[48] *Chronology 20*, 17.   [49] Ibid., 30.

therefore, resolved to fight until they achieved those goals, to continue the war in order to end the war.

The Swamp of Inaction

As it turned out, continuing the war in order to end the war resulted in the conflict's prolongation rather than its termination. Despite their ample determination, on the eve of the war's fifth year in September 1984, two years after the Ramadan Operation, Iranian leaders had very little to show for themselves. The third and fourth years of the Iran–Iraq War, from the autumn of 1982 to the autumn of 1984, consisted of repeated Iranian operations against the Iraqi defensive lines, with the hope of either breaking through or wearing them down to the point that Iraq could take no more. But at no point did they achieve either goal, let alone any substantial Iranian victory. The result was that the war carried on as a ferocious and costly stalemate.

In Iran, the anniversary of the Iraqi invasion was marked with "War Week" ceremonies, which are still held yearly as Holy Defense Week. The speeches that accompanied the events, according to the thirty-third volume of the *War Chronology*, were an opportunity for Iranian leaders to address the conditions of the war and Iran's strategy for prosecuting it in its fifth year. Majlis Speaker and de facto supreme war commander Rafsanjani explained that the war had not yet secured Iran's conditions for peace and that the Islamic Republic would continue to fight as long as that was the case:

Those who support Iraq do not want peace, they want a ceasefire because they want this bloody conflict between us and Iraq to continue. ... Only we really want peace. During War Week it is necessary to make clear that with the presence of the Ba'th Party, which is the agent of this crime and is responsible for all of the destruction and bloodshed, real peace will not exist. The road to real peace is through the full liberation of Iraq. ...

We want to reach a point where diplomacy will solve the problem, but this cannot be assured without decisive ... and victorious operations. Our desire is to solve the issue without bloodshed; but in my opinion one or two deep blows are still needed to achieve that result.[50]

Rafsanjani's statements sum up well Iran's position in the subsequent years. Iranian leaders continued to insist that they were the party

[50] *Chronology 33*, 14.

that sought peace, even though they were seeking that goal through war. Although the IRGC sources emphasize the necessity of achieving security and justice through the recognition and punishment of the aggressor (exacted as reparations rather than regime change), at the time Iranian leaders continued to call for Saddam's (or the Ba'th Party's) removal as the condition for "real peace," and they continued to send their soldiers into Iraq to force this peace into fruition on the battlefield. The heart of Iran's strategy was thus based on implementing major operations, which were envisioned as battles resulting in a decisive Iranian victory, ideally through the conquest of a significant Iraqi city like Basra, which would force the Iraqis to negotiate when Iran had the upper hand militarily. A tremendous amount of blood was poured into this endeavor, but, for various reasons described below and in the following chapters, the results were far short of what was anticipated in the auspicious summer days of 1982.

The inauspicious atmosphere that engulfed Iran as the war dragged on is portrayed lucidly in the *War Chronology*. In the fall of 1984, "the war's operational stagnation ... was palpable." Operations, "even on a limited scale, were not carried out, and aside from the exchange of fire and regular movements on the fronts, like the dispatch of reconnaissance forces and sometimes combat patrols, action was not taken." Perhaps to drive home that point, the authors actually go on to describe the actions that were not taken – the operations that were cancelled in various stages of consideration and planning. One of the reasons for this stagnation was strategic: the need to focus on preparing the "extensive" operations planned for the future and to reserve the forces needed to carry them out. The ground was further prepared for the coming "major" operations politically. "Iran announced that if its views were not provided for and its rights not respected, there would certainly be major operations in the future and that it was not faltering or hesitating," this volume states.[51]

An important part of preparing these decisive operations was figuring out how to compensate for Iran's continued disadvantage in firepower. "The attention of the Sepah command," the same volume relates, "was drawn to the marsh" – the wetlands north of Basra stretching across the southern border. In the view of Sepah commander-in-chief Rezaee, the marsh "was the only region where it was

---

[51] Ibid., 15–17.

possible for [Iran to take] the initiative and to overcome Iraq's egregious military superiority," and from there to "seriously threaten Basra ([which was] a strategic aim of the war)." The plan "was to break the stalemate in the war and get out of the swamp of inaction that every day devoured us more and more, while the enemy and its supporters became bolder in [refusing to] pay the costs of the aggression and [address] Iran's rights."[52]

Diplomatic Opening

Iranian leaders also sought to extricate themselves from the "swamp of inaction" by wading into the marshes of diplomacy. In the spring and summer of 1985, they embarked upon a "diplomatic opening." Led by Rafsanjani, the diplomatic opening was intended to improve Iran's relations with other countries – which had been rattled by the Islamic Revolution and the continuation of the war and had left Iran largely isolated – through a softening of rhetoric and the active cultivation of foreign ties. The initiative represented Iran's new strategy of improving its international standing in ways that would help it prosecute the war, such as securing diplomatic support and supplies of weapons and materiel, something it had failed to do up to that point. It likewise represented a recognition that Iran itself was at least partially to blame for its own plight and therefore that the onus was on Iran to adjust its positions if it sought to ingratiate itself with potential partners. According to the thirty-seventh volume of the *War Chronology*, the initiative "was designed to overcome Iran's relative isolation" and indicated an acceptance of "international norms and responsibility within the global [community]" through "dialogue" with the latter.[53]

That was no small feat. Iran's foreign policy has focused on what it views as the inherent unfairness of the international order and the system's domination by a select coterie of countries. As Iran is not part of that group, objecting to its power is in many cases a position that serves both Iran's national interests and its ideology. But at this point in the war that stance was clearly counter-productive. Some reconciliation, though somewhat out of step with its ideology, was therefore necessary, as in this case too pragmatism and national interest had to

---

[52] Ibid., 17–18.
[53] *Chronology of the Iran–Iraq War 37* (HDRDC, 2004), 18–19.

take precedence. In particular, the new foreign policy involved Rafsanjani's official trips to Syria, Libya, Japan, and China; diplomatic engagement with France and Saudi Arabia; and a tempering of hostile rhetoric toward the United States.[54]

When describing the last of those fronts, this volume relates that while it was pursued alongside the "continuation of anti-American positions," it was marked by "a kind of hopeful perspective (in the long term) delineated in the remarks of some officials." Rafsanjani's comments are used to demonstrate that point. When asked by an interviewer "Will America always be the 'Great Satan'?" he responded by saying that the query should be addressed to the United States. This answer, according to the Guards, was interpreted as having a "gentle tone" when compared with past positions, and as indicating that "the rupturing of diplomatic relations with America could be temporary."[55]

Rafsanjani made similar comments on his trip to Japan. "We are not determined that our diplomatic relations will always be ruptured, but resuming relations with the current American government will be difficult," he stated. "It was not Iran that cut off diplomatic relations with America; America must take the initiative in this matter and, because of the wrongdoings it has committed in the past, it must show remorse and regret."[56] But the United States, the IRGC authors concluded, "not only failed to show regret, it was actively hostile to Iran in all fields."[57] This amalgamated position – combining a willingness to resume relations and an insistence that the United States must be the one to seek mercy for its sins – has been repeated by Iranian officials with marked consistency over the past decades. Although it certainly puts the burden and blame on the United States, the position is typically associated with so-called pragmatists like Rafsanjani, so the fact that the Revolutionary Guards echo this equivocal stance again demonstrates their realist tendencies.

Even more central to the diplomatic opening was pursuing policies to bolster Iran's war effort. One of the primary aims was to find countries willing to sell Iran weapons, which was a way to "overcome the arms embargo" that had been imposed on Iran, thus securing its needs for the continuation of the war. As this volume of the *War Chronology* recognizes, "Iran was clearly anxious to emerge from its

---

[54] Ibid., passim.   [55] Ibid., 78.   [56] Ibid., 337–38.   [57] Ibid., 78.

present isolation and would find friends wherever possible; especially if these friends were willing to sell Iran weapons."[58] The trips to Libya and Syria were made in part for that purpose but were also intended to strengthen Iran's alliances with those two countries and to thereby prevent Iraq's efforts to establish "Arab solidarity" in the war against Iran.[59]

The most significant aspect of the diplomatic opening was the effort "to reduce tension with Iraq's supporters and especially to announce [Iran's] new positions regarding the issue of peace," which signaled its "propensity and readiness to end the war."[60] Specifically, Iran replaced Saddam's removal with the condemnation of his aggression as a condition for a ceasefire, a position which Rafsanjani communicated in several forums in the summer of 1985.[61] During an interview that aired on Japanese television, for example, Rafsanjani's "most important statements were about Iran's satisfaction with Saddam being tried as the aggressor and Iran's acceptance of whatever the result of the trial was." The meaning of this statement, according to the IRGC authors, was that Rafsanjani "replaced the condition of Saddam's removal with the condition of [his] trial."[62] Rafsanjani also held meetings in Iran with officials from other countries to explain Iran's new conditions for ending the war. He sent the foreign representatives home with an official message for their governments "expressing hatred for war and bloodshed and announcing Iran's readiness to cooperate in order to" secure the "conditions for the realization of justice" and the hope that an international tribunal would be established to try Iraq for its war of aggression.[63]

Despite "clearly demonstrating its flexibility in this manner," the *Chronology* concludes, Iran's new conditions were not met with a "suitable response," which seemed to confirm to Iranian leaders that they were the ones truly interested in peace.[64] Although the initiative received some positive responses, these were outmatched by the continued "pressures on Iran to accept peace," and "the prospect of obtaining peace with Iran's minimal rights did not emerge." The new initiative was not even met with universal approval within Iran. In a seminar with commanders, IRGC minister Mohsen Rafiqdust

---

[58] Ibid., 19, 263, 284.   [59] Ibid., 52.   [60] Ibid., 43–45.
[61] Ibid., 19, 43–45.   [62] Ibid., 95, 145–47.   [63] Ibid., 96, 172–74, 233.
[64] Ibid., 96–97.

addressed concerns that the diplomatic opening could have negative repercussions for the war effort and could hinder mobilization. "Saddam has not fallen with political action, but it is only with extensive military operations that the war will be ended victoriously and with Saddam's fall," he asserted. "The recent trips will not alter our [current] war policy. These trips have been about explaining our positions and policies."[65]

During this period of the conflict, however, Iran's war weariness was beginning to corrode its determination. In his meeting with foreign representatives, Rafsanjani acknowledged that even if the war continued to enjoy the support of the Iranian people, that might not always be the case, and Iran might reach a point where it was unable to continue down its current path:

If the people are not willing to continue the war, we will end the war at any price, but you have seen how the people have announced their support for the realization of Iran's terms. If we do not have sufficient power, we would not have this duty. If a reasonable solution is proposed . . ., we will consider it seriously, but we have no doubt that if a ceasefire was established in the current conditions the root of the existing hostility and enmity will be strengthened and its branches will grow in the future.[66]

Khomeini's words, also included in this volume, encapsulate that sentiment: "The people do not want war, but they [do want to] defend [themselves]."[67]

Along with the insistence that Iran was committed to finding a peaceful solution, what comes across in these depictions is the related but distinct insistence that Iran wanted to end the war. In the commentary and scholarship during (and after) the war, Iran is often portrayed as welcoming the conflict with open arms, as running into it head-on, which contributed to the belief at the time that Iran did not want peace.[68] The scenes and sounds of the war did provide some basis for that view, but also much to contradict it. The Revolutionary Guards,

---

[65] Ibid., 44.
[66] Ibid., 108–14. Rafsanjani refers to rallies Iranians held announcing support for the war.
[67] Ibid., 96.
[68] Chubin and Tripp, *Iran and Iraq at War*, 9–10; Katzman, *The Warriors of Islam*, 19, 49–50, 57; Pelletiere, *The Iran–Iraq War*, 60, 124; Ward, *Immortal*, 258.

who are usually seen as the most eager of the bunch, describe the war as unsought and unwelcome and depict themselves and other Iranian leaders as fighting to make their country secure by rooting out the source of the conflict. It was only the conclusion, reached in the war's eighth year, that they would not be able to do so that forced the war's inconclusive ending.

7 | *War for Peace*
The Iran–Iraq War, 1985–1987

Iran faced numerous difficulties after the invasion of Iraq, as the mixed results of the Ramadan Operation turned out to be a harbinger of how the war would proceed in the following years. As it dragged on, the Iran–Iraq War became more and more difficult for the Islamic Republic to prosecute, forcing Iranian leaders to come up with ways to keep the war going. The liberation of Khorramshahr had greatly bolstered morale and popular support and had generated the impetus to drive the war into Iraq.[1] But that momentum began to abate after the invasion, especially as the Ramadan and subsequent operations failed to produce the desired result – a decisive victory that would force the acceptance of Iran's ceasefire terms and ensure the security of the country. In its later stages, Iran was also forced to confront the war's pluralization, as the parties to and scope of the conflict expanded.

How to Keep Going

Limited Operations and the Taking of Faw

One way Iranian commanders sought to keep the war going was by working to replenish resolve on the battlefield. According to the thirty-seventh volume of the *War Chronology*, Sepah leaders viewed staging limited operations on a regular basis – which they termed "war drum and military march"– as one way to do that. This volume describes Sepah commanders discussing limited operations in a meeting held in June 1985, in which Sepah commander-in-chief Mohsen Rezaee emphasized: "Limited operations are the war trumpet and must be put in play regularly. . . . [They allow us to] keep the war hot, preserve our resistance," and shore up morale. When the armed forces "do not

---

[1] *Survey of the Iran–Iraq War 1*, 4th ed. (HDRDC, 1998), 153–54, 168–69; *Chronology of the Iran–Iraq War 20* (HDRDC, 2002), 17.

operate, their ability becomes rusty. It is on [the] battle[field] that we can raise our battle strength. So one of our [objectives] is carrying out limited operations."[2]

Sepah commanders also relied on limited operations for another reason, as a way to deceive the enemy. In the case described above, small-scale actions in mid-1985 were intended to prepare for an extensive operation in the southern Iraqi peninsula of Faw, in part by throwing the Iraqis off course.[3] In another meeting a few days later, Sepah commanders addressed their soldiers and discussed how diffuse, limited operations "force the enemy to operate along 1,000 kilometers of the border" but prevent the enemy from "acting because they wait for our main operation." When "the enemy sees you moving in thirty [different] areas [and] attacking thirty [different] areas, they will lose the position of your important operation [and] will think that [the major operation] is also a limited operation."[4]

Such actions were critical to the campaign in Faw because the extensive operation relied heavily on deception for its success. According to the Sepah plan, "succeeding in this highly complex and difficult operation ... was possible only if the enemy was utterly surprised." But ensuring stupefaction was just one of two critical problems that had to be resolved for the operation to succeed. The other was that a large number of units "had to be deployed to the area to prepare the ground for the operations," which involved undertaking "extensive engineering activities" that were sure to draw the attention of Iraqi forces and ruin the surprise. Staging limited operations was a way to get out of this bind. Sepah commanders understood that "these two urgent problems conflicted with each other, as the Sepah had to tactfully implement preparations ... in complete secrecy in order to maintain the surprise." However, "complete secrecy and camouflage were not possible, and therefore extensive 'deception' operations simulated in other areas had a determinative role in preventing the enemy from ... identifying the main operational area."[5] Alongside the diversionary operations, the commanders planned measures to prevent the Iraqis from anticipating their actions, including disguising the Guards deployed to the region as the gendarmerie forces who regularly

---

[2] *Chronology of the Iran–Iraq War 37* (HDRDC, 2004), 179–80.
[3] Ibid., 124–25, 180, 199, 216–18.   [4] Ibid., 216–17.
[5] Ibid., 32–33, 129–32, 151–52.

patrolled the area, using the date palms that lined the border to conceal their movements, and creating general ruckus by "broadcasting noise through speakers."[6]

Despite their preparations, the Sepah commanders confronted numerous problems in carrying out their plan, which delayed its implementation. As a result, the limited operations intended to be a diversion for the Iraqis ended up diverting the Iranian forces instead. In a meeting of the commanders charged with preparing the Faw operation in early July 1985, Yahya Rahim Safavi, head of the Sepah operations unit, chastised his colleagues for getting off course. "This issue is not a joke," he asseverated. His forces were forgetting that the "[limited] operations are primarily a cover for the operation in Faw. We are clinging to the branch but have let go of the root! ... We must not deceive ourselves of that! Our main job is in Faw and the limited operations are a deception for the main job."[7]

The preparations for Faw also suffered from a shortage of forces and resources, a problem that undermined the Iranian war effort more and more as the conflict went on. "To all the problems mentioned above," this volume continues, "must be added the lack of sufficient capability and the limitation[s] and underdevelopment of the [Sepah's] combat organization." This was an issue "the Sepah commanders had considered after the failure of the Badr Operation," which was launched outside Basra in March 1985, "and had begun to take actions to remedy, but the problem persisted." Therefore, in a meeting of Sepah commanders to formulate the Faw operation that summer, "the view of most [of those] present was that implementing extensive operations was not possible in the current conditions, and the capability of the Sepah had to be increased and [its] organization expanded," which contributed to delaying the operation for several more months.[8]

Despite the delay and frustrations, the extensive operations finally resulted in a major breakthrough. Iran's taking of Faw in February 1986 was an important military victory and the kind that Iranian leaders hoped would precipitate the end of the war on more favorable terms. The forty-seventh volume of the *War Chronology* describes the "fall of Faw" as "an intense shock for Iraq," while Iranian officials "indicated their readiness to examine the bases for ending the war,"

---

[6] Ibid., 33, 35, 169–70, 603–04, 649–50.   [7] Ibid., 290–91.
[8] Ibid., 32–33, 40, 179.

and "hoped that the realization of an important military goal would bring them closer to ending the war in the political realm."[9]

The fourth volume of the *Critique* series, which examines that very long process of ending the war, emphasizes the consonance of Iran's political and military strategies in this period. The Faw operation was the result of changes in Iran's operational strategy that were underway simultaneous with changes in Iran's foreign policy strategy that focused on "the expansion of international relations" through the diplomatic opening discussed in the previous chapter. "Thus it was expected that the new changes in the foreign policy arena and obtaining a victory in a region as important as Faw would change the balance of the war in Iran's favor," it states, "but this was not achieved."[10]

Indeed it was not. The major military victory did not bring the expected political advantage and did not result in Iran's conditions for ending the war being met. In fact, it had nearly the opposite result. As it turned out, Iraq was also reluctant to negotiate while foreign forces were on its soil, and the possibility of Iran's victory in the war again unsettled the region. The military achievement generated a hardening rather than a softening of positions regarding Iran's demands, and in March 1986 Iranian leaders found themselves at risk of sinking back into the swamp of inaction they had barely managed to escape.

The Decisive Operation

In order to maintain the momentum, Iran decided to stick with the strategy of using military means to achieve political ends. Despite the disappointing outcome of the conquest of Faw, the intensification of "overt diplomatic pressure" against Iran meant that, in the view of Iranian officials, they still had greater ability to affect the course of the war on the battlefield than they did in the political field.[11] That reading of the situation "strengthened the analysis ... that the successful execution of an important operation could facilitate the realization of Iran's claims." Iranian leaders therefore decided to again prepare "a

---

[9] *Chronology of the Iran–Iraq War 47* (HDRDC, 2002), 18.
[10] *Critique and Review of the Iran–Iraq War 4*, 4th ed. (HDRDC, 2015), 16.
[11] *Chronology 47*, 18.

major operation to bring the six-year war to a victorious end," declaring that the Iranian year beginning in March 1986 would be the war's "decisive year."[12]

Yet the same problems that beleaguered the preparations for Faw also debilitated Iran's decisive year. The forty-third volume of the *War Chronology* recounts that early in the year Sepah commanders discussed marshaling the resources for three major operations, but soon realized that doing so would require economic support, mobilization, manpower, and planning on a "massive" scale that was ultimately beyond Iran's capabilities.[13] As a result, the decisive year was reduced to one decisive operation, the planning of which still encountered numerous problems and delays.[14] The target of the major operation – like that of many of Iran's previous efforts – was Basra, or threatening it by advancing as close to the city as possible. Although actually reaching the city seemed like a possibility earlier in the war, at this stage the hope was that "a military victory in the strategic area of Basra could improve Iran's political position and its ability to end the war."[15] The difficulty of carrying out a victorious operation near Basra stemmed from its strategic significance and importance to both sides, and each Iranian attempt to take the city encountered more formidable Iraqi defenses than the last.[16]

Therefore, to "expand its combat organization" and "raise its combat power" in preparation for the decisive operation, the Sepah "launched a special initiative, the formation of Qa'im [Standing] Battalions." These battalions were to serve as "task forces" that would take over some of the defensive positions in order to "free the more effective forces" and allow them "to implement offensive operations." In the process, the Qa'im Battalions "would become more experienced and could then be elevated to the level of brigades."[17] Sepah commanders "planned to dispatch Basiji volunteers to secure the 500 battalions needed," and to use the Sepah's newly established Quds

[12] Ibid.; *Chronology of the Iran–Iraq War 43* (HDRDC, 1999), 17.
[13] *Chronology 43*, 16–17.
[14] Limited operations were still carried out throughout the year. *Chronology 43*, 18–19.
[15] *Chronology 47*, 18.
[16] *Chronology 43*, 18. The operations in the area of Basra included *Valfajr-i Muqaddamati* (Preliminary Dawn) in February 1983; *Valfajr* (Dawn) 1 in April 1983; Khaybar in February 1984; and Badr in March 1985.
[17] Ibid., 17.

Training Garrisons to prepare the Qa'im forces. But the initiative was not as successful as hoped, as "the difficulty of securing the amount of force needed, which was one of the basic problems of the battlefronts, remained."[18] Therefore, even though "planning a large and successful operation [on the southern front] had priority and the Sepah very much endeavored" to make that happen, "the problems stemming from the complicated plan for this operation, the shortage of needed forces . . ., and the lack of the necessary facilities" impeded progress.[19]

It ended up taking almost all of the decisive year, but finally Iran did launch the major Karbala 5 Operation toward Basra in January 1987. Like the previous efforts, Karbala 5 produced mixed, and far from decisive, results. During the battle, Iranian forces surmounted some of the Iraqi positions in the east of the city, but they were not able to consolidate their gains.[20] More than anything, the result of the battle was strategic stalemate on both sides. The operation demonstrated that "Iraq's defensive lines were vulnerable" and it "was not able to change the military balance." As a result, "Iraq's strategy confronted stalemate" because "the fate of the war would be determined on the land and Iraq did not have a suitable strategy to obtain victory on land." Iran's strategy was also "confronted with stalemate," because its military victories did not seem to bring a satisfactory end to the war any closer.[21]

The limited and transitory success on the battlefield produced analogous political results. The proximity of Iranian forces to Basra, combined with their continued presence in Faw, "did lead to multilateral diplomatic measures in which an effort was made to have some of Iran's rights taken into consideration," which will be discussed below and in the following chapter.[22] The change seemed to vindicate Iran's strategy of using military means to achieve political ends, and so Iranian forces continued their pressure on Basra (as well as their occupation of Faw and their operations in the northwest) with the expectation that "military action could improve Iran's position and affect the military and political balance" in its favor.[23]

---

[18] Ibid., 18.   [19] Ibid.; *Chronology* 37, 203, 471–72.

[20] *Chronology* 47, 82, 122–23. Operation Karbala 5 was carried out between January 9 and February 23, 1987.

[21] *Critique and Review* 4, 279–80.   [22] *Chronology* 47, 18, 195–96, 502–03.

[23] Ibid., 21.

But the fact remained that Iran had still not tipped the scales. The Karbala 5 Operation, which was supposed to be the decisive operation in the decisive year, hastened the war's indecisive end and revealed that Iran could not readily muster a critical juncture into being. While Iraq welcomed the end of that year with relief and celebration, Iranian leaders tried to manage the repercussions of the letdown and make the needed adjustments to their strategy.[24]

The quotes and discussion included in the IRGC sources reflect the tension in this period of pushing the war forward while also scaling it back, of still not being prepared to end the war while also beginning to prepare for its end. As the final month of the decisive year drew to a close, Prime Minister Mousavi proposed a very different vision for the Iranian year beginning in March 1987, calling for "more exact and less hasty planning."[25] Similarly, de facto supreme war commander Rafsanjani told members of the Sepah that in the coming year "the armed forces must bring the war to a point where the facilities of the state can be used for economic infrastructure and equipping the armed forces for the future."[26] Meaning, in other words, that it was time for the war to end.

But that realization did not make concluding the conflict more straightforward in practice. While asking commanders to work on ending the war, Rafsanjani was simultaneously leading the effort to explain why and how Iran intended to continue the war to both internal and external audiences. He exhorted Iranians to sustain the fight. Referring to the celebrations being held in Iraq to eulogize the demise of the Islamic Republic's strategy, Rafsanjani declared: "You will see our enemy fall in humiliation and defeat, so they celebrate with their remaining living days." He also reassured the armed forces, telling them: "Now you inflict the blow that will certainly disable the Iraqi war machine; this year is the conclusive year."[27] In a sermon delivered for Friday prayers in Tehran, Rafsanjani "addressed international assemblies [and] emphasized that Iran's ground attacks were meant to pave the way for achieving its requests." He clarified, though, that Iran was not acting hastily on the battlefield, "because it desires a just resolution with minimal bloodshed."[28]

---

[24] Ibid., 19, 346–48.   [25] Ibid., 19, 240.   [26] Ibid., 462–63.
[27] Ibid., 410–11, 451–52.   [28] Ibid., 19.

According to the IRGC sources, issues like those described in this section – declining morale and a dearth of forces and facilities – defined the Islamic Republic's war effort in the conflict's final years.[29] The Guards depict the lack of necessary resources and combat organization as a problem that was particularly serious for the Sepah. Whereas the Artesh was a professional military with a substantial amount of materiel and institutional infrastructure at its disposal long before the beginning of the Iran–Iraq War, the Sepah endeavored to acquire those things in the process of prosecuting the conflict. Their sources depict the Guards as unsatisfied in their attempts to expand and professionalize, a contention that partially contradicts the way the organization is often portrayed. In the existing secondary literature, the IRGC's efforts along those lines are usually characterized as being concerned with a quest for power and as subservient to its ideological dogmas.[30] Even though Sepah leaders were likely interested in increasing their power, and though they would not be expected to embrace that motivation publicly, it is the Sepah's commitment to professionalization and expansion for the explicit purpose of prosecuting the war more effectively that is emphasized throughout the IRGC sources.

Further giving credence to that commitment is the fact that the IRGC authors are just as critical of the Sepah and its shortcomings in the war as they are of the Artesh and others, if not more so. They do not obfuscate the Guards' failures or blame them on others. Rather, they portray Sepah commanders as frustrated with the circumstances as they were and as trying to keep fighting the war if they could. They do not argue that the war could or should have gone on longer if only the Guards had been given this or that. Their tone is not haughty or vindictive, but sober and pragmatic. That inflection is reflected in Rezaee's summation of the Sepah's operational strategy in the last year of the war. "We have limitations in various fields," he said, "so our plans must be consistent with realities."[31]

South to North

A major change the Sepah commanders made in order to prosecute the war, even with their limitations, was shifting the focus of their efforts

---

[29] *Chronology of the Iran–Iraq War 51* (HDRDC, 2008), 19–21.

[30] Ali Alfoneh, "Review of *The Twilight War*," *Middle East Quarterly* 20.3 (2013); Dilip Hiro, *The Longest War* (Grafton, 1989), 112; Kenneth Katzman, *The Warriors of Islam* (Westview Press, 1993), 19.

[31] *Chronology 51*, 630.

from the southern to the northern front. Targets in the north had already been part of the military plan when the shift occurred in the spring of 1987.[32] But in contrast to the primacy of the south in previous years, now "the goal of Iran's military strategy was implementing a major operation on the northwestern front."[33]

What is conspicuous in the Guards' discussion of the change is their assertion that it requires substantial justification, which they provide. As the authors of the *War Chronology* state, "the question arises that, considering the presence of strategic aims on the southern front and the lack of such aims on the northwestern front, why did the Sepah make such a choice?"[34] They acknowledge that the shift north reflected the war's dismal state. The conflict to that point had been fought in the south because that region contained almost all of the strategically important targets. But, after six years of war, the battle in the south had been beaten to death, in the process consuming so much of Iran's resources, that its continuation was perceived as futile.[35]

According to the *Chronology*, "the factor deterring Iran from continuing the war in the south, more than any other factor, was the lack of conformity of its combat power with the logistical and organizational needs of the war in this region against the fully armed Iraqi army."[36] Iranian commanders "recognized that continued operations in the south would face a stalemate," and that "a basic change and transformation was necessary" in order to obtain Iran's "strategic goals ... in the war."[37] They therefore believed that "different fields and initiatives and new tools were needed to untangle the knot of the war and bring it to the desired point."[38]

In further explaining the shift north, the IRGC authors note that "important factors caused the non-acceptance of and disbelief in this essential change" at the time. Those factors included "the proximity of primary targets in the south (like Basra) and the remoteness of accessing targets in the northwest (like Kirkuk), as well as problems with and shortages of needed materiel and deficiencies in training for battle in mountainous regions."[39] Indeed, "in previous years those same factors had prevented [Iran from] investing in operations" in the northwest. So

---

[32] Ibid., 18.   [33] *Chronology of the Iran–Iraq War 52* (HDRDC, 2003), 18.
[34] Ibid.   [35] *Chronology* 47, 24, 204–06, 495–96, 535–39.
[36] *Chronology* 52, 18–19.   [37] *Chronology* 51, 627.
[38] *Chronology* 47, 19–20.   [39] *Chronology* 51, 18.

too did the fact that "many commanders" were "not motivated" to go to work "on the snow-covered heights" that dominated the region.[40] Therefore, Sepah commander-in-chief Rezaee had to "explain the chosen line of policy" regarding the stalemate in the south and "persuade the commanders" of the need to go north.[41]

Despite these misgivings, the IRGC sources nonetheless argue that there were important military and political goals to pursue in the northwest that bolstered the decision to proceed with the plan.[42] In addition to threatening the northern Iraqi city of Kirkuk, other aims in the north included sabotaging Iraqi oil lines and obstructing its communications with Turkey.[43] One aspect of the strategy was, paradoxically, based on the negligible value of the targets in the region. Because of "the lesser importance of the northwestern front relative to the southern," it "promised positive outcomes because the enemy's forces were not centralized there."[44] When Iranian forces attacked, therefore, they would not be met with a formidable concentration of Iraqi defenders. It would take Iraqi units time to get to the area and, as Rezaee emphasized in a meeting with commanders, the mountainous region would prevent Iraq from employing the heavy armaments that often gave it an edge.[45]

Another stated reason for the shift was that it allowed Iranian forces to cooperate with Iraq's Kurdish opposition groups in the northwest to facilitate their operations and "open a new front in this region," just as Iraq had done with Iran's own Kurdish opposition.[46] As the IRGC authors explain, the "high importance" of the northwest was connected to "the strong and effective presence of Iraqi Kurdish opposition" actively working against the Ba'th regime.[47] Coordinating joint operations and overseeing those undertaken by the Kurdish groups was the primary responsibility of the Sepah's Ramazan Garrison, which specialized in irregular warfare. In addition to the Kurdish contingents, this garrison also supported operations carried out by forces affiliated with Shi'i opposition groups like the Badr Brigade, the military wing of the Supreme Council for the Islamic Revolution in

---

[40] *Chronology 52*, 20.
[41] *Chronology of the Iran–Iraq War 53-1* (HDRDC, 2019), 24.
[42] *Chronology 52*, 19.   [43] *Chronology 47*, 431–32; *Chronology 52*, 19–20.
[44] *Chronology 47*, 20, 310; *Chronology 52*, 19.
[45] *Chronology 51*, 21, 631; *Chronology 52*, 19.
[46] *Critique and Review 4*, 16–17, 280.   [47] *Chronology 53-1*, 29.

Iraq (SCIRI), and the Da'wa Party.[48] Working with these factions and distending "the guerilla wars in Iraqi Kurdistan," Rezaee argued, would force the enemy "to assemble its forces on a less regular war axis and to dispatch a number of its soldiers from the southern fronts to the north" to counter the Iranian cadre's operations. "As a result, Iraq's position on the southern fronts will weaken," Rezaee concluded.[49]

As those statements suggest, the shift to the northwest did not mean abandoning the south. Rather, one of its main aims was diverting Iraqi forces and attention from the south, thereby making it easier for Iranian forces to operate there and "creating the possibility for [further] operations on the southern front." The decision to fight in the northwest also derived from the need to keep stringing together successful operations in order to force Iraq's patrons to "accept that it was necessary to stop supporting Iraq and to submit to justice (punishing the aggressor)." Conversely, "unsuccessful operations disturbed" the pattern and "were negative for the strategy of 'pressure for peace.'"[50]

But before long the same problems that prompted Iranian leaders to move north arose on that front as well. Those old problems were also compounded by new ones. The operations were hindered by "the unfamiliarity of the units with the region, the difficulty of moving forces and transferring equipment inside Iraq, [and] uncertainty regarding the degree of loyalty of the [Kurdish groups]."[51] Iranian forces struggled to surprise the enemy and to procure sufficient resources, the same factors that had compelled them to shift away from the southern front.[52] Once again Iran lacked the capability to overcome Iraq militarily, and ultimately the move represented its desperation in a war it did not seem able to either win or end.

---

[48] Ibid., 33, 502, 576–77. On the Ramazan Garrison, see Said Mohammad-Pur, "The Impact of the Ramazan Garrison's Irregular Operations in the Imposed War," *Journal of Defense Policy* 12.47 (Imam Hossein University, 2004). On SCIRI and the Da'wa Party, see Nadejda K. Marinova, *Ask What You Can Do for Your (New) Country* (Oxford University Press, 2017), 236–59; "Supreme Council for Islamic Revolution in Iraq (SCIRI)," National Consortium for the Study of Terrorism and Responses to Terrorism, University of Maryland (June 2015); Rodger Shanahan, "Shi'a Political Development in Iraq," *Third World Quarterly* 25.5 (2004).

[49] *Chronology* 47, 20.   [50] *Chronology* 52, 19–20.

[51] *Chronology* 47, 380–81. The Kurdish forces mentioned here were part of the Patriotic Union of Kurdistan.

[52] *Chronology* 51, 24, 421–22, 608, 660.

The Pluralization of the War

Iran's inability to overpower Iraq, the Guards argue, was due in part to the extensive support Iraq received from third parties. The IRGC sources consistently define the war not as a battle only between Iran and Iraq, but as one between Iran and a powerful group of states that included Iraq, the United States, and various other allies and supporters. For example, the first volume of the *Chronology* introduces the war by comparing it to other conflicts in order to identify its "special features." According to the authors, "the main characteristic" of the war was Iran's "isolation ... in comparison with its opponent."[53] The fourth volume similarly describes the "terrible inequality of the two belligerent camps," with "Iran in isolation on one side and Iraq along with regional and world supporters on the other side."[54]

The Guards assert that the numerous patrons Iraq drew to its cause came not because of any particular affinity for or friendly relations with the Iraqi regime, but because of Iraq's "vindictive opposition to Iran."[55] But the line is not always drawn so starkly, as another volume notes that in the war "Arab states divided into two groups, one supporting Iraq and the other [supporting] Iran." In Iran's camp were Syria and Libya, which in several instances "took very effective positions in preventing the transformation of the war into an 'Arab-Persian' or 'Shi'i-Sunni' war," thereby saving Iran from even more outright isolation.[56]

The disparity between the camps was evident in several different areas, as "Iran's military power, economic situation, and international position were in no way comparable to Iraq's."[57] The imbalance also deepened in the conflict's second half, and the Guards term "the direct and practical political-military intervention of the major powers" the war's "main feature" in its concluding years.[58] In this period, Iraq sought to prevent Iran from gaining a military advantage by pluralizing the war – by expanding the number of parties involved in the conflict politically and militarily; by extending the battlefield from the land to the sea and air; and by augmenting its arsenal to include more

---

[53] *Chronology of the Iran–Iraq War 1* (HDRDC, 1997), 14.
[54] *Chronology of the Iran–Iraq War 4* (HDRDC, 1993), 608.
[55] *Chronology of the Iran–Iraq War 33* (HDRDC, 2000), 23.
[56] *Chronology 47*, 33.   [57] *Chronology 51*, 36.
[58] *Chronology of the Iran–Iraq War 50* (HDRDC, 1999), 3.

advanced and unconventional weapons, as well as economic, social, and political tools.

The Guards connect Iraq's new initiatives to Iran's gains in Faw and then near Basra, which "sounded the alarm" for Iraq and its supporters and generated the conclusion that more had to be done to "prevent Iran's victory and to end the war."[59] The pluralization of the war, the Guards argue, was thus the result of Iraq's own realization of its inability to end the conflict on its own. In the land war Iraq was essentially in a reactive and defensive position from the summer of 1982 onwards, but despite its success in preventing Iran from achieving a decisive victory, Iraq had not been able to do so decisively enough to force Iran to accept a ceasefire. Therefore, Iraqi leaders pluralized the war in order to "increase the pressure on the Islamic Republic to capitulate," and to compel Iran to acquiesce to "ending the war without a victorious party and without punishing the aggressor."[60]

The War of the Cities

One way in which Iraq pluralized the war was by taking advantage of one of its main assets: its superior air force. As the IRGC sources note, Iraq aimed to "use its air superiority in order to compensate for its defeats on land."[61] By expanding its aerial campaign, Iraq also sought to strike at morale within Iran, which was one of the few areas in which the Islamic Republic was stronger. To do so, Iraq focused its airstrikes on population centers, which went on throughout the war but which were particularly intense and reciprocal in certain periods known as the War of the Cities.[62]

The IRGC authors describe this campaign as "a psychological war" involving "an all-out incursion into residential areas" and the "continuous bombardment of cities." Iraq's "repeated threats to increase the extent" of the strikes and "to use far more destructive and dangerous weapons" were designed to "create panic in the minds of the people," to make them "exert pressure against the system," and "to draw the people and Iranian officials into inaction."[63] They were thus

---

[59] Ibid.; *Chronology 47*, 36.   [60] *Chronology 51*, 39.

[61] *Chronology 43*, 19–20; *Chronology 47*, 25.

[62] On Iraqi attacks on residential areas and the War of the Cities, see *Survey 1*, 102; *Chronology 37*, 21, 25–26; *Chronology 50*, 15; *Chronology 51*, 39–40.

[63] *Chronology 37*, 21–22.

intended "to destroy the strength of the Islamic Republic [and] establish fear," while the ultimate goal remained forcing Iran to accept a ceasefire.[64] The Guards acknowledge that this campaign inflicted heavy economic and human costs. Some cities along the border were so vulnerable to Iraqi airstrikes that most of their residents were forced to evacuate.[65]

Iran did what it could to defend itself from and confront Iraqi attacks. It retaliated on several occasions by striking targets in Iraq, although it was constrained by its lack of air power.[66] Iranian leaders also urged the United Nations to "take action to prevent the violation of international law," which prohibits the intentional targeting of civilians in war. In the summer of 1985, the UN did so by issuing a statement in which Secretary-General Javier Pérez de Cuéllar expressed concern regarding Iraq's announcement that it would resume attacks on Iranian residential areas and called for both sides to cooperate to end the war.[67] The IRGC authors suggest that such statements had minimal effect, in large part because Iraq had little reason to change course. "The backing of industrial powers for Iraq with the most advanced air equipment, the silence of international organizations, and the positions of the superpowers and especially America and other supporters of the Iraqi regime," they claim, "were among the incentives for Iraq to continue these aggressions."[68]

International War in the Persian Gulf

The primary axis of the pluralized war came as the result of the intertwining of oil and third parties. Iraq's strategy was based on the understanding "that the export of oil had vital importance" for Iran "because it funded the costs of the war." Iraq "also knew that oil had similar importance for the West," which was "prepared to pay a high price to protect" its "free flow" and "the passage of oil tankers in the Persian Gulf." Involving other states in the war in this way would also

---

[64] *Chronology 47*, 25. See also *Chronology 37*, 21–26; *Chronology 43*, 19–20; *Chronology 47*, 43–44.

[65] *Chronology 37*, 24; *Chronology 43*, 19–20.

[66] *Chronology 37*, 26; *Chronology 47*, 25; *Chronology 51*, 40–41.

[67] *Chronology 37*, 25; "Secretary-General Dismayed at Iraq's Intention to Resume Attacks on Iran's Civilian Areas," *UN Chronicle* 22.7 (July 1985).

[68] *Chronology 51*, 39.

increase pressure on Iran, as "the only way Iran could retaliate for Iraq's attacks on its shipping and oil centers was by attacking the shipping of Iraq's sponsors," who were ensuring that oil income continued to fuel Iraq's war machine.[69]

And so that is what Iran did. Iran adopted the "policy of responding in kind," of retaliating for Iraqi airstrikes on its oil tankers and facilities by targeting those belonging to Iraq's supporters. It did so in order to deter Iraq from continuing its campaign, despite the adverse repercussions, because it was seen as the only way to counter these attacks.[70] "Iran could not witness Iraqi airstrikes on its facilities and tankers in the Persian Gulf every day" while Kuwait and Saudi Arabia helped Iraq export its oil, the IRGC authors argue. Therefore, retaliating for Iraqi strikes was intended to compel those countries "to comply with the commitments of impartial states and to prevent Iraqi airstrikes in the Persian Gulf."[71]

In this way, as the Guards put it, "Iraq's one-sided attacks on Iranian shipping were transformed into the 'Tanker War.'"[72] The escalation of attacks and the initiation of the Tanker War generated the war's more complete internationalization, given the interest of third parties in protecting the flow of oil. "The spread and intensification of Iraq's airstrikes on oil centers and shipping lines in the Persian Gulf made ... the advanced industrialized countries aware of the dangers of the war," the *War Chronology* states, which led in turn to their "direct political-military intervention in the region."[73]

Together their fear of an Iranian victory and their fealty to oil compelled third parties to intervene in the war more directly.[74] US naval forces increased their presence in the Persian Gulf and Indian Ocean over the course of the conflict but did so appreciably in the spring of 1987 when the Reagan administration agreed to escort Kuwaiti oil tankers with the aim of shielding them from Iranian retaliation.[75] The IRGC authors assert that Kuwait's motivations mirrored

---

[69] *Chronology 47*, 26; *Chronology 51*, 26–27.   [70] *Chronology 50*, 15.
[71] Ibid., 11–12.   [72] *Chronology 33*, 20.   [73] *Chronology 50*, 3.
[74] *Chronology 43*, 19; *Chronology 47*, 25, 28, 356–58, 384–85, 403–04; *Chronology 50*, 3, 15; *Chronology 51*, 37; *Chronology 52*, 26, 28; Jim Muir, "Gulf Attack Could Spur New Efforts to Resolve Iran–Iraq War," *The Christian Science Monitor*, May 20, 1987.
[75] *Chronology 47*, 27, 114–15, 128, 350, 403–04, 425–26, 465–66, 520–21, 531–32.

those of its great power patrons, and that preventing an Iranian victory was just as important as protecting its tankers. Kuwait's request, they state, "was a vehicle for involving Iran with America and opening a new front for weakening the Islamic Republic's military power."[76]

The intensification of the reciprocal attacks and the swelling presence of international naval forces in the Persian Gulf led to direct confrontations between Iranian and American forces.[77] However, the United States' first major encounter in the Gulf was actually with Iraq rather than Iran. In May 1987, an Iraqi aircraft fired on the *USS Stark*, purportedly accidentally, killing members of its crew. Despite the fact that Iraq was the perpetrator of the attack, "America criticized Iran under the pretext of [Iran] not accepting a ceasefire."[78] There was criticism at the time of both the credulity of Iraq's claim that the strike was a mishap and the *Stark*'s reaction to the attack.[79] Two months later, the *USS Bridgeton*, which was serving as an escort for a Kuwaiti tanker, struck a mine likely laid by Iran, for which the United States retaliated that September by sinking the *Iran-Ajr* supply ship being used to lay mines.[80]

These incidents initiated "a more intense stage of face-to-face confrontation in the Persian Gulf" between Iranian and US forces and led to western European states sending naval forces to the region.[81] According to Rafsanjani, this was a war in which "America shot the first bullet" with its attack on the *Iran-Ajr*.[82] Although Iran insisted "that it would not begin [any] war in the Persian Gulf," it also affirmed that "it would decisively answer any attack" against it.[83]

Yet in this field, too, Iran was unable to achieve anything close to a decisive response to the US advances. In their sources the Revolutionary Guards present direct US military involvement in the

---

[76] *Chronology 50*, 10.   [77] Ibid., 3, 6; *Chronology 51*, 26.
[78] *Chronology 50*, 8. See also *Chronology 51*, 27.
[79] "The Attack on the Stark," *The New York Times*, May 19, 1987; Rudy Abramson and James Gerstenzang, "President Says Iran Is Chief Villain in Attack," *Los Angeles Times*, May 20, 1987; "A Dubious Explanation," *Los Angeles Times*, May 21, 1987; John Kifner, "US Move in the Gulf: More Firmly on Iraq's Side," *The New York Times*, June 11, 1987; US Navy, "Formal Investigation into the Circumstances Surrounding the Attack on the *USS Stark* (FFG 31) on May 17, 1987," June 12, 1987.
[80] *Chronology 50*, 7–10; *Chronology 51*, 27, 34–35, 117–18; *Chronology 52*, 23.
[81] *Chronology 50*, 13. See also *Chronology 51*, 27, 34–35, 858–59; *Chronology 52*, 23.
[82] *Chronology 51*, 205–06.   [83] *Chronology 50*, 13.

war as "a major threat" and one of the most significant and problematic features of the conflict's final year.[84] According to the *War Chronology*, "the active role of American naval forces in creating limitations for Iran and restoring Iraq's hand in attacking naval targets was important and determinative in the Persian Gulf" and in the war as a whole.[85] In addition to fighting Iraq, therefore, in this period Iran also "tried to defend its territory and national sovereignty" against "the extensive campaign of America and its allies in the Persian Gulf."[86] As a result, the Islamic Republic's attention and forces were divided. The resources that could be devoted to the land battle against Iraq were stretched even thinner, as "the pressures of the naval conflict ... negatively affected the ground war."[87]

Attacking Iran's ability to export oil was a doubly potent strategy for Iraq, because in addition to generating the war's internationalization, it also inflicted immense damage on Iran's economy. Denying Iran oil income eliminated its main source of government funding and made continuing the war nearly impossible.[88] Iraq and its supporters found numerous ways to undermine Iran's oil exports, including attacking tankers, refineries, depots, and other facilities; boycotting Iranian oil; and reducing the price of oil in the international market.[89] Overall, economic warfare proved to be very effective for Iraq. As will be described further in the next chapter, the damage inflicted upon the Iranian economy formed one of the main reasons for the conflict's termination.[90]

The War and the World

While third parties had a substantial effect on the Iran–Iraq War, the war also had a significant impact on international politics, one that

---

[84] *Chronology 51*, 19.   [85] *Chronology 52*, 23.   [86] *Chronology 51*, 36.

[87] Ibid., 36–37, 555–56, 575–76, 615–16.

[88] *Chronology 43*, 15, 19; *Chronology 47*, 26; *Chronology 50*, 15; *Chronology 51*, 26, 39; *Iran's Economy During the Imposed War* (HDRDC, 2008), 11.

[89] *Iran's Economy During the Imposed War*, 11; *Chronology 33*, 20–21; *Chronology 37*, 18, 27–31; *Chronology 43*, 20; *Chronology 47*, 25–26; *Chronology 51*, 40, 48–49.

[90] On economic conditions in Iran and their negative impact on the prosecution of the war, see *Chronology 43*, 19–20; *Chronology 47*, 32, 168–69, 175–76, 212–14, 239–40, 322–23, 334–35; *Chronology 51*, 42. On the decrease in the price of oil specifically, see *Chronology 33*, 21; *Chronology 43*, 24–26; *Chronology 47*, 38. Although the Guards assert that Iraq's economic situation was far better than Iran's, they acknowledge that Iraq had problems too. See *Chronology 47*, 164, 412, 422–23; *Chronology 51*, 48–50, 56–57.

often led to bizarre alliances and alignments. The first example of this trend was the renewal of relations between Iraq and the United States at the end of November 1984. As the Guards emphasize, those two countries – which had been estranged since the 1967 Arab–Israeli War when Baghdad severed relations with Washington – were not natural allies. Although the IRGC sources include US statements asserting that the renewal of ties with Iraq would not alter US neutrality in the Iran–Iraq War, the development was certainly not unrelated to that conflict. Despite the importance the Guards attach to the rapprochement, they take a rather dispassionate view of the matter, stating that "Iran naturally expressed discomfort about the renewal of relations," as "the greater closeness of two enemies could not be welcomed by Iran."[91]

Another set of unlikely bedfellows were the United States and the Soviet Union. Cold War competition was still apparent at many points during the conflict. For instance, the United States was ultimately persuaded to escort Kuwaiti tankers by the Soviet Union's offer to do so, and each superpower continued to be concerned by the other's influence in the Middle East.[92] Yet the cooperation that did emerge was reflective of both the conditions of the Iran–Iraq War and the Cold War's denouement. The former's seeming interminableness, combined with the perceived threat of the Islamic Republic, gave rise to such unusual alignments. In the war, the IRGC authors note, "three competing systems and ideologies – communism in the USSR, capitalism in the West, and traditional monarchism in the regional states" – were brought closer together because "they were [all] alarmed by the Islamic Revolution and its spread."[93]

The Iran–Iraq War also shuffled regional politics, as the attention of Arab states was drawn away from Israel and toward Iran. This was a circumstance that Iranian leaders met with much chagrin. The Islamic Revolution and the continuation of the war had already compounded Iran's intrinsic isolation as a Shi'i and Persian state in the majority Sunni and Arab Middle East, which obstructed its search for allies and supporters (and which continues to be a concern for Iranian leaders today). This condition has led Iran to pursue strategies to ingratiate

---

[91] *Chronology 33*, 27.   [92] *Chronology 47*, 27–28, 30, 36, 284–85, 401–03.

[93] *Chronology 51*, 35–36. See also *Chronology 47*, 36–37; *Chronology 50*, 3–4, 9–10; *Chronology 52*, 28; *Passage of Two Years of War* (IRGC Political Department, 1982), 38–39.

itself with the wider Middle East, of which pointing to Israel as the regional outcast has proven particularly appealing. According to the Guards, "the struggle against Zionism and opposition to the existence of the usurper state Israel – which the Islamic Republic of Iran calls 'the regime occupying Quds (Jerusalem)' – has been one of the important parameters of Iran's foreign policy" since the 1979 revolution.[94] However, as "the Iran–Iraq War became the absolute priority for the Arab world [and] enmity toward Israel was relegated," Iran's isolation was also reinforced.[95]

In some ways, these passages mask the true face of Iran's foreign policy. Even though the Guards express consternation that the Arab world was focused on the Iran–Iraq War instead of on Israel, they openly acknowledge that they very much were too. Despite asserting that the struggle against Zionism was an important aspect of Iran's foreign policy, and that Israel should be called "the regime occupying Quds," neither is borne out in the sources. Throughout its duration the Iran–Iraq War took absolute precedence over opposition to Israel, which is also the name the Guards usually use to refer to the country in their sources. One example of that disposition can be found in the *War Chronology*'s description of Quds Day in June 1985, an annual event that is nominally and sometimes actually about support for the Palestinians. That year, however, the day "concerned more the issue of the war than the issue of Israel" and provided an opportunity to rally popular support, especially in a period of intense Iraqi airstrikes on residential areas.[96]

Understanding the war's priority in all matters, and thus over Israel, allows us to consider some of the rhetoric used during the war in a different light. In fact, it reveals that much of the Western analysis on the war has got it backward. Declaring that "the road to Jerusalem passes through Karbala" was not a way of saying that the Iran–Iraq War was somehow subjugated to or part of the war to liberate Jerusalem, that the Holy Defense was more about defending Palestinians than it was about defending Iranians. Quite the contrary. It was a declaration of the predominance of the Iran–Iraq War over all else. The Guards state this unequivocally when they explain that "Iran understood that the Iran–Iraq War was the first priority of its actions

---

[94] *Chronology 33*, 33. [95] *Chronology 51*, 50, 96, 103, 219.
[96] *Chronology 37*, 21.

and plans, based on the directive of the Imam [Khomeini] that 'the road to Jerusalem passes through Karbala.'"[97] This does not mean that the idea of liberating Jerusalem was not desirable on some level, but it was not the primary goal for which Iranians were fighting. Thus, much of the existing scholarship inverts the rhetoric, viewing actions as being at the service of slogans instead of slogans at the service of actions. One author, for example, argued that the struggle with Iraq was really "part of another: to liberate Jerusalem from its Zionist occupiers and oppressors," as Iranians "saw the march . . . [to] Iraq . . . as part of the advance to Jerusalem."[98]

Such inversions are one of the most problematic shortcomings of the scholarship on the Islamic Republic and especially on the Revolutionary Guards, and one which this book seeks to correct.[99] Although the idiom of battle was often inspired by Islam and the revolution, those were not what the fight was really about. Assessing Iran's prosecution of the Iran–Iraq War only in terms of a literal rendering of shibboleths does much to explain the cognitive dissonance that has too often characterized analysis of the Islamic Republic. Therefore, viewing the slogan "the road to Jerusalem passes through Karbala" as if it was literally about forgetting Iraq and marching straight to Jerusalem is just as nonsensical as asserting that Operation Desert Fox was literally about chasing a fox in the desert.[100]

---

[97] *Chronology 47*, 34.   [98] Hiro, *The Longest War*, 106.

[99] See Hiro, *The Longest War*, 177; Edgar O'Ballance, *The Gulf War* (Brassey's Defence, 1988), 81–82, 120; Stephen C. Pelletiere, *The Iran–Iraq War* (Praeger, 1992), 58.

[100] Operation Desert Fox was a US bombing campaign in Iraq in 1998.

8 | *An End to a War Without End*
The Iran–Iraq War, 1987–1988

This chapter completes the chronological analysis of the IRGC's history of the Iran–Iraq War by examining how the Revolutionary Guards assess the conflict's conclusion. As Supreme Leader Khomeini's indelible declaration on July 21, 1988, made clear, deciding to end the war was agonizing for Iran, akin to drinking from a poisoned chalice.[1] The assessment of the IRGC sources presented in this chapter reveals why that was so and why the decision was finally made. Understanding the disquiet that surrounds Iran's acceptance of the ceasefire also reveals the IRGC's view of the conflict as unfinished, which represents one of the ways the Iran–Iraq War continues to have a profound impact on the Islamic Republic today.

American Involvement: Problem and Opportunity

As discussed in the previous chapter, one of the central aspects of the pluralization of the Iran–Iraq War was the conflict's internationalization, which was most dramatic in the multi-party naval war in the Persian Gulf. According to the IRGC sources, Iranian leaders viewed US involvement as a formidable challenge that they struggled to confront effectively. At the same time, the entrance of the United States into the conflict presented the Islamic Republic with an opportunity to rejuvenate the flagging war effort. For most of the war's previous years, a divided Iranian population had come together to confront an external aggressor. But popular unity and support for the war began to dissipate as the conflict dragged on and the fight appeared increasingly hopeless.

---

[1] "Full Text of the Imam's Letter on the Acceptance of Resolution 598," *Fars News*, July 20, 2007 (Persian); Robert Pear, "Khomeini Accepts 'Poison' of Ending the War with Iraq," *The New York Times*, July 21, 1988.

The embroilment of the United States in the naval war gave the Islamic Republic a new external aggressor around which it could rally the war-weary population. The stakes of the conflict had clearly been raised. Throughout the war Iranian leaders had been making the case that Iran was confronting a number of enemies in addition to Iraq. Although there was some truth to their assertions, there was also considerable distance between their rhetoric and the reality. The US vessels cruising into the Persian Gulf to protect Iraq's allies, and then the direct engagements between Iranian and US forces, gave credence to the case Iranian leaders had been making all along and lent verifiable urgency to their appeals for mobilization.

The *War Chronology* describes the dichotomous effects of US involvement in the naval war, which "opened a new front on Iran's southern borders." Although that new front "absorbed a main portion of the country's military capabilities, [it also] sweetened the confrontation with America as the 'Great Satan' [and] inspired passion among the people." That dedication was manifest in the "expeditionary caravans named 'Defenders of the Persian Gulf' [that] set out from various cities of the country," and in "the increase in the number of popular volunteers being sent to the warfronts" in the south and north.[2] These mobilization drives were part of the "effort to increase support for the war" and a response to the dwindling reserves of manpower that plagued the later years of the conflict.[3]

Spearheading the effort was the Supreme Council for War Support (SCWS), established by Khomeini in 1986 to assist the Supreme Defense Council in procuring the forces and resources needed for the war.[4] The SCWS took action in early November 1987 by announcing the beginning of "readiness week to confront America's aggression."[5] Rafsanjani put out the call to the Iranian people at the November 4 rally marking the anniversary of the takeover of the US Embassy in Tehran. He contended that the full force of the state and the people must be brought to bear. "The government, news media, armed forces, ... and all our facilities must be mobilized in the course of this week," he declared, "so that America will know the major error it has committed, that the place for saber-rattling is not along the coast of

---

[2] *Chronology of the Iran–Iraq War 50* (HDRDC, 1999), 13.
[3] *Chronology of the Iran–Iraq War 51* (HDRDC, 2008), 42.   [4] Ibid., 43.
[5] Ibid., 43, 731, 741.

this revolutionary nation."[6] Prime Minister Mousavi stressed the gravity of the situation: "The announcement of this week must not be regarded as a political or propaganda move. We are in critical conditions and the total mobilization of [our] forces to confront the Great Satan is a serious necessity."[7]

Mobilization efforts continued throughout the week. On November 7, the Sepah presented the SCWS with a plan "to equip the people to confront America and secure the needs of the front."[8] Two days later, Iranian officials participated in an "extraordinary seminar [entitled] 'At Your Service Imam'... to examine the situation on the fronts and in the Persian Gulf and how to secure force and capabilities." In his opening remarks to the seminar participants, Rafsanjani urged Iranian leaders to stick with the strategy they had clung to since they invaded Iraq but that had yet to deliver the desired result. "Only our military power can dictate political victory," he proclaimed. "The enemy will only submit to our political victory in order to prevent a military catastrophe." Rafsanjani asserted further that "the lack of force" was "the main agent of stagnation on the fronts," a problem which could be solved by relying on "extraordinary encouragement to secure manpower."[9]

At the end of preparedness week to confront American aggression, Iranian officials proceeded to put Rafsanjani's artlessly sanguine plan into action. The SCWS began by submitting a letter to Khomeini "asking him to issue a decree for the increased provision of the fronts." His simple response evokes both the magnitude of the war and the imperativeness of its termination. According to the text included in the *War Chronology*, Khomeini decreed:

It is clear and it has frequently been said that this Imposed War is at the top of all matters and it is necessary that all classes of the country endeavor for victory to be achieved as quickly as possible, with the grace of god. Therefore, what the Supreme Council for War Support and the military professionals have determined must be acted upon and [must] not be spared.[10]

---

[6] *Chronology 51*, 721. See also Loren Jenkins, "Iran Rallies Nation for New Drive," *The Washington Post*, November 13, 1987.

[7] *Chronology 51*, 43, 731.

[8] Ibid., 43–44, 741–42. The plan was refined later that day in meetings with the SCWS, heads of the armed forces, and prime minister.

[9] *Chronology 51*, 44, 770–71.   [10] Ibid., 802–03.

With that directive, the SCWS issued "a message to the Iranian nation to support the war" that included a "ten-provision instruction with general duties that were entrusted to various classes of people." The directive called on "every person, to the extent capable," to support the war in one way or another. For those who were physically able, support should come "in the form of direct presence on or behind the front," but for "artists and speakers," support could be shown with "their art and speech." Government agencies should likewise "give priority to the use of facilities on the front."[11]

Both the Sepah and the Artesh declared their readiness to "attract, train, organize, and deploy volunteer forces."[12] The Supreme Defense Council and the SCWS held a joint session with political and military leaders a few days after the issuance of the ten-provision instruction to "examine the country's critical position regarding organizing popular forces, securing facilities for successive operations, dispatching forces nationwide, and reinforcing military preparedness in the Persian Gulf."[13] The Sepah organized Basij forces to rally the nation and recruit volunteers, while the SCWS launched campaigns to encourage "financial jihad."[14]

Overall, the Guards' assessments of these final mobilization efforts reflect the difficulty Iran faced in continuing the war in its last years, as well as its determination to fight until the difficulty became impossibility. The IRGC sources indicate that the mobilization called for in the SCWS's ten-provision instruction was the result of the Islamic Republic's recognition that it was time for the war to end. Yet it could not just capitulate, especially after so many years. The *War Chronology*'s characterization of US involvement in the war reflects that situation and, more broadly, the way Iranian leaders have very reluctantly recognized the downsides of the external adversity upon which they have often relied to legitimize their rule. Ultimately, it concludes, "with their presence in the region, America and the West were able to achieve their goal of intensifying pressure on Iran, but they were not able to force Iran to capitulate."[15]

---

[11] Ibid., 44, 809–10.   [12] Ibid., 44–45, 821–22.   [13] Ibid., 45.
[14] *Chronology of the Iran–Iraq War 52* (HDRDC, 2003), 24–25; *Chronology 51*, 45, 846–47.
[15] *Chronology 51*, 38.

Toward a Resolution

The Iran–Iraq War thus continued to grow in both duration and scope, even as both belligerents asserted that they were fighting to bring the war to an end and that the other side's intransigence was to blame for the conflict's continuation. In the view of Iraq and its supporters, Iran's refusal to accept the UN-proposed ceasefire was certainly the reason for the war's prolongation. For Saddam Hussein, Iran's obstinacy had become the punchline of a bad joke. "The Iranian regime cannot get the result [it wants] from this war, but Iranian officials do not see reality," he charged. To better illustrate his point, he compared Iranian leaders to "beautiful, proud women who lack the desired dignity so they establish impossible standards; they want a man of such a color and such a shape and with so much money, and most of these kinds of women remain without husbands." Iran's refusal to understand that its war aims were unattainable, he concluded, meant that its continuation of the fight was akin to a guarantee of spinsterhood.[16]

In contrast to that characterization, the Guards maintain that Iran wanted peace, even though it was continuing the war by refusing to accept a ceasefire without attaining its demands. They acknowledge, however, that other parties were not in agreement, and that trying to convince them of the rightfulness of Iran's position proved difficult. According to the *War Chronology*, despite "the logical position of the Islamic Republic and the terms that it had announced for a truce, a peace was never proposed that guaranteed the fulfillment of Iran's primary requests." This proved to be doubly problematic, because "Iran's refusal to accept the terms periodically proposed by international assemblies and major powers became a pretext for never ceasing the numerous pressures on the Islamic Republic."[17] Iran also came to realize that Iraq refused to concede any of its positions "even when Iran had a relative military victory and was present on Iraqi soil." Iraq chose instead to adopt a "pretension of peace-seeking" in order to secure "a truce that maintained the factors that caused the war. Therefore, both parties continued the war as the [only] way to resolve their disputes."[18]

---

[16] *Chronology of the Iran–Iraq War 37* (HDRDC, 2004), 749.
[17] *Chronology of the Iran–Iraq War 43* (HDRDC, 1999), 23–24.
[18] *Chronology of the Iran–Iraq War 1* (HDRDC, 1997), 17.

These descriptions expose what the Guards recognize as the ultimate futility of the fight. Even though Iranian leaders "perceived that Iraq would not give up," they continued the war because it was the only way to settle the conflict.[19] The galling frustration and hollowness inherent in that situation can be discerned throughout the sources. What is less clear is the extent to which Iranian leaders understood the war in that manner at the time, or if this is a conclusion the Guards accepted only after it ended. The quotes and analysis they include in their texts suggest that Iranian officials did become increasingly cognizant of the war's inefficacy as it went on, and that ultimately their acceptance of their inability to transform the situation formed the basis for its termination.

The IRGC sources maintain that the most important issue of the war for almost its entire duration, and the issue that was responsible for its protraction, was the failure of international assemblies and ceasefire proposals to acknowledge Iraq as the aggressor in the war and to thereby provide Iran with at least some sense of security. Bringing about a change in that situation was the desired outcome of Iran's military operations in the "decisive" year, as well as its diplomatic opening. In the war's final years, and in response to the diplomatic pressure on Iran to end the conflict, Iran engaged in its own diplomacy in order to encourage international assemblies to "work to end the Iran–Iraq War by finding a just solution," one that "must fulfill Iran's primary demands to punish Iraq as the aggressor and [include] the payment of war reparations."[20] Although the results of both the military and political campaigns consistently fell short of Iran's aims, and though they often did little to mitigate the pressure on Iran to accept a truce, eventually the efforts produced a shift in Iran's favor.

This shift consisted of the "multilateral diplomatic measures in which an effort was made to have some of Iran's rights taken into consideration," the most significant of which was the UNSC's adoption of Resolution 598 in July 1987.[21] As noted in the previous chapter, the Guards view the achievement as the product of Iran's military successes in Faw and then near Basra in the Karbala 5 Operation.[22] The *Guide Atlas* presents that argument in a graphic

---

[19] Ibid.   [20] *Chronology of the Iran–Iraq War 47* (HDRDC, 2002), 281–82.
[21] Ibid., 18; UNSC, "Resolution 598 (1987) of 20 July 1987."
[22] *Chronology 47*, 18; *Chronology 52*, 28; *Guide Atlas 1*, 5th ed. (HDRDC, 2002), 54, 60.

and striking fashion. The final page of its second volume displays a large picture of a young Iranian soldier. He sits awkwardly, using the wall of a dusty trench or alley to support his head and rifle, his eyes closed. To the right of the picture is a box with white text set against a dark green background, several words bolded for emphasis, which reads:

The importance of victory in the Karbala 5 Operation, which entailed the presence of Iranian forces in the area of Basra, [was that] it caused the United Nations Security Council, with the adoption of Resolution 598 – which for **the first time considered Iran's claims** – to bring about the basis to end the war. In other words, with the victory in the Karbala 5 Operation, the countdown to the end of the war began.[23]

This text's characterization of the war's concluding years attests to how the Revolutionary Guards and other Iranian leaders have sought to render Iran's limited successes as definitive victories. Faced with a reality that failed to live up to their rhetoric and a war they could no longer fight, they accepted a political shift in Iran's favor as the basis for ending the conflict and portrayed it as a vindication of a military strategy that they had promised would produce much more.

Specifically, UNSCR 598 was "the first resolution that set forth the responsibility and determination of the aggressor."[24] It did so in paragraphs 6 and 7, in which the Security Council "6. *Request*[ed] the Secretary-General to explore ... the question of entrusting an impartial body with inquiring into responsibility for the conflict"; and "7. *Recognize*[ed] the magnitude of the damage inflicted during the conflict and the need for reconstruction efforts, with appropriate international assistance, ... [and] request[ed] the Secretary-General to assign a team of experts to study th[is] question." Iranian leaders regarded the inclusion of these paragraphs as an important victory and a step toward resolving the conflict. They asserted, however, that the resolution did not do enough to satisfy Iran's requests. As a result, while Iraq welcomed Resolution 598, Iran's formal response was to neither accept nor reject it, which reflected its ambivalence.[25] The

---

[23] *Guide Atlas 2* (HDRDC, 2001), 107. See image at https://sites.google.com/view/unfinished-history/images.

[24] *Chronology 50*, 4.

[25] *Guide Atlas 1*, 54; *Chronology 50*, 5–6; *Chronology 51*, 45–46; *Critique and Review of the Iran–Iraq War 4*, 4th ed. (HDRDC, 2015), 16; Neil A. Lewis,

position also represented a break from Iran's previous policy, as to that point Iran had rejected all UNSC ceasefire proposals outright. The goal of its new, equivocal position was to demonstrate the change in policy, to signal its willingness to work with the UN and consider the resolution as the basis for ending the war, and to prevent Iraq from appearing as the only party interested in peace, while at the same time indicating its dissatisfaction with certain parts of the resolution.[26]

The IRGC sources note that the resolution, even while prompted in part by Iran's military and diplomatic advances, was still passed in the context of political and military pressure on Iran to end the war.[27] As the *War Chronology* recounts, the initial text of the resolution did not contain language acknowledging Iran's rights, but Iranian leaders successfully lobbied members of the Security Council to have them included "so that Iran would be willing to accept it."[28] Furthermore, Iran withheld its full approval to ensure the adoption of a certain method for the resolution's implementation. Iranian officials insisted, as they had throughout the war, that they would not agree to a ceasefire without the granting of their demands. In the case of Resolution 598, this meant that the establishment of the "immediate cease-fire" called for in the first paragraph "as a first step towards a negotiated settlement" not be implemented before the formation of a commission to identify the aggressor called for in the sixth.[29] "Iran believed that Resolution 598 was an integrated series and that the implementation of all of its provisions must begin simultaneously," the IRGC authors state, "but Iraq emphasized its 'sequential' implementation."[30]

This insistence, according to the Guards, was based on Iran's experience in the war and the role the United Nations had played in the conflict to that point. Iranian officials "did not have very much

"Security Council Demands a Truce in Iran–Iraq War," *The New York Times*, July 20, 1987; Marian Houk, "Iranians Hint at Cooperation with UN on Cease-Fire," *The Christian Science Monitor*, July 24, 1987.

[26] *Chronology 50*, 5–6; *Chronology 51*, 45–46.

[27] *Chronology 50*, 3–4; *Chronology 52*, 28; *Guide Atlas 1*, 60.

[28] *Chronology 50*, 4. See also *Guide Atlas 2*, 60; Hella Pick, "Split in Security Council Hinders Ceasefire Moves," *The Guardian*, October 7, 1987; Marian Houk, "UN Considers Iranian Demand in Cease-Fire," *The Christian Science Monitor*, October 9, 1987.

[29] *Guide Atlas 1*, 60; *Chronology 51*, 45–47.

[30] *Chronology 51*, 47; *Chronology 50*, 5.

confidence in international organizations" as a result of "the function-ing of the Security Council in the beginning of Iraq's aggression," they relate. When it came to "the manner of implementing Resolution 598," Iran's position reflected its enduring "pessimism regarding inter-national organizations."[31] The IRGC authors define the "obstacle preventing [Iran's] acceptance of Resolution 598" as "Iran's concern about stopping the war before determining the aggressor, which was based on the Security Council's long record of partiality for the aggressor."[32]

Iran's distrust of the UN and especially of the Security Council notwithstanding, the Guards note as "a significant point" the Islamic Republic's "considerable confidence in the UN Secretary-General [Javier Pérez de Cuéllar] and his ability to play an important role in the peace process."[33] The IRGC sources describe Iran working with the secretary-general in particular to have its position on the imple-mentation of the resolution accepted.[34] Making progress in that regard meant that "the subject of the end of the Iran–Iraq War was raised on a large scale."[35]

Iranian officials worked simultaneously to diffuse the continuing pressure on Iran to accept Resolution 598 immediately as is, which took form conspicuously in Iraq's own diplomatic initiatives, the effort to impose an arms embargo on Iran, and the continuation of the internationalized war in the Persian Gulf.[36] According to the Guards, the fact that such pressure continued and increased served to "intensify Iran's pessimism" regarding its ability to have confidence in the UN and its fear that accepting a ceasefire without or before the recognition of the aggressor would leave Iran vulnerable.[37] Iran's deputy foreign minister Mohammad Javad Larijani similarly emphasized this fear that the resolution lacked "a guarantee for the future" that would provide Iran with security in the case that Saddam remained in power. If

---

[31] Ibid.   [32] *Chronology 52*, 29.   [33] *Chronology 51*, 47.
[34] *Chronology of the Iran–Iraq War 53-1* (HDRDC, 2019), 39–41, 44;
    Chronology of the Iran–Iraq War 54 (HDRDC, 2013), 36–39; *Chronology 50*,
    5–6; *Chronology 51*, 45–47; *Guide Atlas 1*, 54.
[35] *Chronology 53-1*, 40.
[36] *Chronology 50*, 11; *Chronology 51*, 45–47, 51–52; *Chronology 52*, 27–29;
    Chronology 53-1, 40; *Guide Atlas 1*, 60.
[37] *Chronology 51*, 47.

"today the war ends and this [Ba'th] regime stands," he asked, then "who guarantees that Iraq will not attack us again?"[38]

Pluralized Pressure

Despite the fact that international pressure made Iran pessimistic about accepting the ceasefire resolution, ultimately that pressure induced it to do so. As the war dragged on, Iran found itself confronted by a growing number of opponents who were becoming increasingly impatient to end the war. "Most Arab states" had maintained their "steadfast support for Iraq" throughout the conflict, the *War Chronology* relates, but in the last year of the war "their threats against Iran intensified and occasionally assumed a militant flavor."[39]Additionally, the expansion of the war in the Persian Gulf inflicted severe damage on Iran's economy by "raising the cost for Iran to export oil and limiting the volume" it exported. The overall result was a substantial reduction in government income, which relied overwhelmingly on oil revenues.[40]

Iran's difficulty in procuring weapons also became more problematic in the war's later years, especially as Iraq's ability to import armaments amplified the military imbalance between the countries.[41] The continuation of the war and specifically Iran's refusal to accept a ceasefire led to more active measures to deny Iran materiel.[42] Although efforts in the UNSC to impose an arms embargo on Iran were not successful, those outside the UN progressed.[43] In particular, the Reagan administration's program to prevent Iran from accessing military materiel, known as Operation Staunch, inaugurated in the spring of 1983, "caused Iran to face more problems, and procuring its required equipment [took] a longer time, [was] more expensive, and sometimes [resulted in equipment of a] lower quality."[44] After the summer of 1987, "the actions of [the United States] and its allies to deprive Iran access to supplies and military armaments needed in the war intensified," and included not only "official tools like diplomatic pressure,"

---

[38] *Chronology 54*, 38–39.   [39] *Chronology 51*, 50.   [40] Ibid., 42.
[41] Ibid., 48; *Chronology of the Iran–Iraq War 33* (HDRDC, 2000), 37–39.
[42] *Chronology 43*, 23–24.
[43] *Chronology 51*, 48; *Chronology 52*, 27–28; *Chronology 53-1*, 41–43; *Chronology 54*, 35, 43.
[44] *Chronology 37*, 69.

but also "unofficial channels like the media." The Guards emphasize the scrupulousness of the campaign by noting that the Reagan administration went so far as "prohibiting the export of diving equipment to Iran, claiming it would be used for military purposes."[45]

In stark contrast to Iran, Iraq had easy access to weapons, which the Guards often describe in great detail. In addition to being sold weapons and spare parts directly, Iraq received loans and other financial support to subsidize its purchases, aid in transporting the materiel, and assistance training its forces.[46] Iraq, the Guards proclaim, was awash with weapons: "As an inexhaustible river crashes into a dam, the flood of materiel and weapons entered Iraq from the four corners of the world."[47] The reason for this, the Guards claim, was that "Iraq's supporters could not accept its defeat." They provided Iraq with "unprecedented support, equipment, and arms to the extent that it became a threatening regional power" and ensured that Iraq's losses "were quickly recovered."[48]

The impact of Iraq's material advantage was felt particularly in the air war. Iraq had "the support of France and the USSR" and the use of advanced airplanes, so "it bombed important targets in Iran without limitations."[49] Upon acquiring "Mirage 1 planes and Super Etendards armed with Exocet missiles" from France, by the fall of 1987 "the Iraqi air force's offensive operations capability against floats and other naval targets was extended to intermediate ranges in the Persian Gulf," putting Iranian sites like oil installations and ports at risk of attack.[50] In contrast, "Iran was deprived of weapons support as a result of the embargo by Western states, so it tried with a limited number of airplanes to play a deterrent role, though using the existing airplanes was also problematic because of the severe shortage of parts."[51]

---

[45] *Chronology 51*, 48; Stuart Auerbach, "Reagan Bans Scuba Gear Sales to Iran," *The Washington Post*, September 26, 1987.

[46] *Chronology of the Iran–Iraq War 4* (HDRDC, 1993), 19; *Chronology 33*, 27; *Chronology 47*, 31–33, 37; *Chronology 51*, 40, 49–51.

[47] *Chronology 33*, 37.   [48] *Chronology 1*, 17.

[49] *Chronology 52*, 23. See also *Chronology 54*, 30.

[50] *Chronology 53-1*, 35. See also Edward Cody, "France Fails to Woo Both Iran, Iraq," *The Washington Post*, July 24, 1987; AP, "Iraq, Iran Launch New Ship Attacks," *Toronto Star*, October 3, 1987; Michel Zlotowski, "France to Sell 20 Mirages to Iraq," *The Jerusalem Post*, October 18, 1987; "Iraq Hits World's Largest Tanker at Iranian Depot," *The Gazette*, December 23, 1987; AP, "Iraq Hits Tanker with Exocet," *Orlando Sentinel*, January 28, 1988.

[51] *Chronology 52*, 23.

Further evidence of the imbalance can be found when comparing the two belligerents' arsenals directly.[52] Rather than crunch the numbers themselves, the Guards rely on the data collected by Anthony Cordesman, the undisputed champion of military balances in the Persian Gulf. Even though Iraq lost more arms than Iran in the war, Cordesman found, it also had more opportunities to replace them. Iraq, for example, actually had more tanks at the end of the war than it did at the beginning (while Iran had fewer).[53] In the final period of the war, Iraq's military advantage allowed it to "change its strategy from defense to offense with the aim of determining the fate of the war."[54] The IRGC authors accordingly contend that "the egregious discrepancy that existed between the two military camps in procuring materiel and weapons" was one of the most consistent and consequential features of the war, impacting tactical and strategic capabilities and choices and ultimately the war's outcome.[55]

Foreign intervention was thus responsible for much of the desperation and powerlessness Iran increasingly experienced and that finally forced the war to end. As noted previously, the IRGC sources emphasize that Iraq had internationalized the war for precisely that reason and that its strategy was ultimately successful.[56] The pluralization of the war "divided Iran's military power and completely threatened the state's currency and economic revenue. Iran's military power, economic conditions, and international position were in no way comparable to Iraq's." This situation "ultimately resulted in new decisions in the manner of continuing and ending the war."[57] The *Critique* series puts even more weight on the impact of foreign intervention. Whereas the *Guide Atlas* marked the beginning of "the countdown to the end of the war" with Iran's partial successes in the Karbala 5 Operation, this volume attributes it to "the intensification of international pressure on Iran to accept Resolution 598," as well as "the increased military pressure on Iran with the opening of a new front in the Persian

---

[52] *Chronology 43*, 24; *Chronology 47*, 32; *Chronology 51*, 48–49.

[53] *Chronology 47*, 421. Cordesman is the Burke Chair on Military Balance at the Center for Strategic and International Studies and has published prolifically on that subject in the Middle East and Persian Gulf.

[54] *Critique and Review 4*, 16.

[55] *Chronology 33*, 37. See also *Chronology 43*, 24; *Chronology 47*, 32; *Chronology 51*, 48–49.

[56] *Chronology 53-1*, 36; *Chronology 54*, 28–29.   [57] *Chronology 51*, 35–36.

Gulf and Iran's confrontation with America." "Indeed," the IRGC authors assert, the outcome of the war was itself largely determined by that external pressure, as "the balance of power prevented Iran's victory."[58]

The *War Chronology* depicts expressively how the economic hardship was experienced in Iran, and how the privations "became increasingly manifest day to day in the operational units." Fighters learned to subsist on "dry bread or bread with jam for two or three days," and to make do without warm clothes. Units still being supplied with flour, rice, and meat saw their rations reduced by 50 or 75 percent due to nationwide shortages. "Considering the emptying of the depots, the meager imports of equipment and armaments were quickly sent from the ports for use on the warfronts, [and] units encountered problems in obtaining minimal equipment to carry out their missions." Attempts by "domestic military industries and factories" to make up the difference "also encountered financial problems and shortages of parts for the design and production of equipment needed for the war."[59]

The difficulty and mixed results of the *Bayt al-Muqaddas* 2 Operation, Iran's major operation in January 1988 on the northwestern front, epitomized the mounting problems that soon proved insurmountable. During the various stages of the operation, in addition to confronting "heavy Iraqi counter-attacks," the Iranian forces failed to secure many of their objectives because of their "lack of time to adequately prepare, the lack of mobility on the road, the lack of fortifications and shelter," and the lack of appropriate weapons and other materiel.[60] The insufficient shelter was a serious problem in the snow and bitter cold of winter in the mountains. A report included in the *War Chronology* describes how the freezing weather forced some of the units to retreat. One commander explained that members of his brigade returned to their tent for that very reason. When asked by Rezaee whether the forces had found relief and if "their place in the tent is good?," the commander replied "No, ... the tent is like an umbrella."[61] "Over time," this volume concludes, "the wearing out of the strength of the units made the possibility of continuing the operation harder and gradually impossible."[62]

---

[58] *Critique and Review* 4, 16.   [59] *Chronology* 51, 42.
[60] *Chronology* 53-1, 27–28.   [61] Ibid., 157.   [62] Ibid., 28.

That conclusion forced Iranian commanders to shift their operational focus to Halabja, the city in Iraqi Kurdistan close to the border with Iran. The IRGC sources indicate that Rafsanjani and "some commanders" were "initially opposed" to the change, but that "with the insistence of the Sepah commander-in-chief" and with his explanation of "the political and military advantages of the operation in Halabja," they were convinced to give primacy to that area.[63] The operation that was launched in the middle of March by the Sepah and Iraqi Kurdish forces, *Valfajr* (Dawn) 10, did have some initial successes, but those were quickly overshadowed.[64] On March 16, 1988, a few days into the operation, the Iraqi air force attacked the city with poison gas, killing thousands of people, mostly civilians. Even in the context of a war as atrocious as this, the attack stands out for its depravity.[65]

Indeed, Iraq's deployment of chemical weapons was another issue that epitomized Iran's unwillingness to continue to expose itself to the heinousness of war. That, of course, was precisely the point of their use. According to the IRGC sources, the ability to deploy chemical weapons with impunity gave Iraq an important advantage on the battlefield. It likewise proved highly costly to Iran both in terms of its ability to carry out operations successfully and in the lives lost.[66] Chemical attacks on Iranian positions east of Basra in April 1987 induced Iran to see new initiatives on the southern front as hopeless.[67] In the north, Iraq's use of poison gas in Halabja and against Iranian forces in operations in the spring of 1988 helped convince Iran that here too the costs of continuing the war were simply too high.[68]

In addition to its actual use of chemical weapons, the Guards describe how Iraq employed the threat of their use to deter Iran from acting.[69] The IRGC authors emphasize the effectiveness of those threats, pointing to the fear that chemical weapons would be used to attack Iranian cities – especially after they were deployed to push Iranian forces out of Faw in April 1988 – as one of the factors that convinced Iran to accept a ceasefire and end the war.[70] The authors

---

[63] Ibid., 29–31.   [64] *Chronology 54*, 17–20.
[65] Joost R. Hiltermann, *A Poisonous Affair* (Cambridge University Press, 2007); *Genocide in Iraq* (Human Rights Watch, 1993); Alan Cowell, "Iran Charges Iraq with Gas Attack," *The New York Times*, March 24, 1988.
[66] *Chronology 43*, 19, 21.   [67] *Chronology 47*, 24.
[68] *Chronology 53-1*, 21, 34; *Chronology 54*, 24–25.   [69] *Chronology 33*, 22.
[70] *Guide Atlas 1*, 61–62.

explain Iraq's reliance on these weapons as stemming from its inefficient use of its plentiful resources, its inability to defeat Iran decisively, and its conclusion that extraordinary measures were the only way to force Iran to give up the fight.[71]

At the same time, the Guards are highly critical of the failure of the international community to condemn Iraq's deployment of chemical weapons, which they say abetted its misconduct.[72] One source states that "Iraq's supporters not only did not object to Iraq's use of chemical weapons, but also encouraged" the use of such weapons with their inaction.[73] The IRGC authors find the US Government's mild response to Iraq's behavior similarly galling, noting that "while Iraq had complete freedom to aggressively use this kind of weapon, Iran was prohibited from procuring tools to defend [itself] against such weapons!"[74]

The Guards describe Iran's own efforts to defend itself against chemical attacks and to prevent them from occurring. These included Iran's attempts to lobby international organizations to condemn Iraq for using the weapons, which were often led by the Islamic Republic's representative to the United Nations, Saeed Rajaee Khorasani.[75] At a meeting of the Non-Aligned Movement (the international organization of developing countries promoting independence and formal nonalignment) in September 1986, Iran tried to persuade member states to denounce Iraq for beginning the war and for using chemical weapons, "but a number of countries supporting Iraq blocked [the effort]." It was reported "that most of the leaders present at this meeting, in conversations with [Iran's] president, confirmed Iraq's aggression and its use of chemical weapons, but the Islamic Republic's proposal to condemn Iraq was [still] not voted on (!)."[76]

---

[71] *Chronology 37*, 91.
[72] *Chronology 43*, 21. See also G. H. Jansen, "Iraqis Defy World on Use of Poison Gas," *Los Angeles Times*, March 23, 1986; "Iraq Rejects Security Council Criticism," *The Irish Times*, March 24, 1986.
[73] *Chronology 37*, 91.
[74] Ibid., 92. See also AP, "Four Are Indicted in Plot to Export Warfare Outfits," *The New York Times*, August 31, 1984; "Exporter Found Guilty in Plot to Supply Equipment to Iran," *San Francisco Chronicle*, May 18, 1985; "Man Convicted over Exports to Iran," *The Globe and Mail*, May 18, 1985; "Two-Year Prison Term Assessed in Iran Smuggling Operation," *Houston Chronicle*, June 27, 1985.
[75] *Chronology 33*, 22; *Chronology 37*, 91, 147.   [76] *Chronology 43*, 28–29.

Iranian leaders also took steps to care for those who had been exposed to chemical weapons. The Sepah established special "C.M.R. defense" units devoted to defending against chemical, microbial, and reactive weapons attacks.[77] On the whole, however, the Guards argue that Iran did not have the means to deal with the effects of these weapons. At the same time, the sources note that the resultant suffering bolstered Iran's efforts to galvanize world opinion against Iraq. Because Iran could not treat victims domestically, sending them outside the country for treatment "automatically revealed in a definite and effective manner the war crimes of the Iraqi government that [Iran] was not capable of combatting."[78]

An End to a War Without End

Iran's inability to continue the war was ultimately the result of the coalescence of external pressures with internal ones. The Guards describe the most important of these as declining morale and the decrease in forces to send to the fronts, which essentially amounted to diminished support for the war among the Iranian people.[79] In their analysis, the Guards point to several different, yet interconnected, reasons for this.

First, as described above, was the "decline in support for the fronts caused by the decline in state revenue and the problems encountered in procuring the minimum food, clothing, and equipment for individual fighters," which made fighting in the war an even greater sacrifice.[80] Iran's "greatly diminished economic power" as a result of the decline in oil revenue was felt throughout the country.[81] In turn, the widespread deprivations "weakened the government and people's support" for the war.[82] So too did Iraq's continued missile attacks on Iranian population centers, and their intensification in the fifth and final War of the Cities in the first months of 1988, which exposed an even larger

---

[77] *Chronology 33*, 22. The abbreviation in Persian is "Sh.M.R.," as the word for chemical begins with the letter that is transliterated as "sh."

[78] *Chronology 37*, 91.

[79] *Chronology 33*, 39; *Chronology 51*, 55; *Chronology 53-1*, 32; *Chronology 54*, 34–35.

[80] *Chronology 51*, 42–43.   [81] *Chronology 43*, 17, 26; *Chronology 47*, 38.

[82] *Chronology 50*, 15; *Critique and Review 4*, 279.

segment of the population to the horrors of the war.[83] The threat that "Iran's major cities including Tehran would be attacked with chemical missiles" should the war continue, even with the concerted efforts by Iranian leaders to prepare for such a scenario, proved to be too much to countenance.[84]

A second cause of the diminished support was what the Guards describe as the view among Iranians that their leaders were preparing to end the war. For the first seven years of the conflict Iran "had immediately rejected every resolution the UNSC had issued about the war because none considered Iran's rights." When Iran changed course and did not reject Resolution 598, it "created the atmosphere that peace was close, which had a negative impact on the dispatch of force" to the fronts. That atmosphere was exacerbated by the first problem, as the "decline in support for the fronts ... reinforced the view that support had decreased because a ceasefire was nearing."[85]

This dynamic reveals the dilemma intrinsic to ending the war for Iran: as soon as that decision was considered seriously, it became a foregone conclusion. If Iranian leaders were aware or fearful of that outcome at the time, then it helps explain their intransigence in refusing to consider or negotiate a ceasefire until they were confident that their claims would be acknowledged. The Guards suggest that they were and are critical of how the situation was handled. In the *War Chronology* they describe a meeting Sepah chief Rezaee held with the force's commanders, several of whom expressed concern about "the effect of political issues on military power." The sense was that "when there was talk of peace and reconciliation, the people do not send their children to the front, officials become weak, and there is doubt among the people." In his response Rezaee put the blame squarely on those he was addressing, including, it appears, himself. The reason for the weakness and doubt, he said, "is because of our own lack of confidence; meaning it is because of this same thinking that exists in us now."[86] The same conclusion is echoed later in the volume by the IRGC authors:

People wanted seriousness from the authorities. People did not have a problem [becoming] motivated for the war, it was only necessary that they

---

[83] *Critique and Review* 4, 280; *Chronology* 54, 26–27.
[84] *Chronology* 54, 26–27; *Guide Atlas* 1, 61–62.
[85] *Chronology* 51, 42–43, 608–09.   [86] Ibid., 629.

see seriousness in the state and authorities for them to come, meaning they see that it is worth them giving their children and their time. If they understand it is serious, they come.[87]

A third reason provided by the Guards for the diminished support was the uneven contribution of different sectors of the population to the war effort, what the Guards call the unequal "division of labor." As it became increasingly apparent that "some [people] were pursuing life, education, [and] income" while others "were working on the fronts, fighting, and becoming martyrs," those inclined to join the second group decreased.[88] The division of labor widened in the years after Iran's invasion of Iraq. Although "issues related to the war were [Iran's] top priorities" throughout the conflict, they plainly could not have the same momentousness after Iran's invasion of Iraq as they did when Iran was fighting to expel Iraqi forces from its own territory. After the invasion, the perception among Iranians was that their country "was not in danger of destruction," and so in this period the uneven commitment was even more "evident and clear." While "one class of people led the war, the other class led regular and natural lives as if the country was not at war!"[89] While the burden borne by soldiers is decidedly inordinate, wars by necessity involve some sectors of society more than others. Calling attention to this divide can therefore serve to elevate the worth and power of those, like the Guards, who sacrificed more in these particular instances.

Altogether, the Guards conclude that these "reasons diminished the seriousness that had previously existed" for continuing the war.[90] And for Iran, that seriousness was crucial. In the same way that faith proved to be decisive in Iran's ability to turn the tide of the war, the dissipation of morale toward the end of the conflict proved faith to be a weapon Iran could not prosecute the war without. Fighting primarily with faith and commitment and a dearth of weapons was difficult but possible for a time; fighting with neither faith nor firepower was simply futile.

The fifty-second volume of the *War Chronology* indicates that it was just time for the war to end. "With the passage of seven years of war," it states, "it appeared that the temporal and historical duration of the war was ending and the country was not able to sustain the state of war for a longer period."[91] The leaders of the Islamic Republic

---

[87] Ibid., 43, 608–09.   [88] Ibid.   [89] *Chronology* 52, 25–26.
[90] *Chronology* 51, 43, 608–09.   [91] *Chronology* 52, 24.

certainly endeavored to shore up morale and keep up the fight until they were satisfied Resolution 598 would be implemented in the manner they deemed necessary to ensure justice and security, but ultimately this short passage encapsulates why the war ended: it had gone on long enough and could not go on any longer.

In its final months, "the international political-military pressure on Iran," including the "conflict with America in the Persian Gulf," was a "determinative variable" tipping the balance in the war. "Iraq used the opportunity and by increasing its military capability ... changed its strategy from defense to offense."[92] In the spring of 1988, Iraqi forces began to retake the territories the Iranians had occupied. Its success in doing so, according to the Guards, was "tantamount to a military shock."[93] So too was the Iraqi operation to retake the Faw peninsula in April, which had been held by Iranian forces for two years. The Iraqis had prepared for the attack over the course of the previous months, which prevented Iranian forces from undertaking operations of their own in the area of the peninsula.[94]

The reports of Iraq's preparations, however, failed to convince Iranian leaders of the imminence of the attack. Some reports from the Iranian units stationed in the south "indicated Iraq's possible immobility" there, while others reported that Iraqi forces were moving toward and focused on the northern fronts. Those developments "caused the possibility of Iraqi military action on one of the southern fronts to fade ... to some extent." The "disbelief regarding the possibility of an Iraqi attack on Faw," according to the IRGC sources, was maintained "despite some evidence" that signaled that possibility. None of that evidence – the failure of Iranian forces to "strike a determinative blow on the Iraqi army" in the operations in the north, "Iraq's increasing movements, especially in Faw," the "statements of some [Iraqi] refugees about an imminent attack of the Iraqi army on Faw," Saddam's meetings with military commanders that had been reported in the news as concerning the "liberation of Iraq's lost territories," the "intelligence obtained from non-military channels [that] also confirmed the possibility of an Iraqi attack" – shook that disbelief.

---

[92] *Critique and Review 4*, 280; *Chronology 54*, 26–27.
[93] *Critique and Review 4*, 280.
[94] *Chronology 53-1*, 161–64, 275, 575; *Chronology 54*, 30–31.

Therefore, "suitable and effective action to strengthen the defensive lines ... was not carried out."[95]

Eventually, though, as the evidence of Iraq's impending campaign in Faw continued to build, "the possibility ... of an enemy attack was taken seriously" by Iranian leaders. Their attempts to ready a response, however, came too late. The "units deployed on the Faw line were given the [order to] be 100% ready" on April 14, just three days before the Iraqi onslaught began. At this stage in the war, the shortage and fatigue of Iranian forces made quickly mobilizing and deploying them to the area difficult. Many of the units had been sent to rebuild, and some had been permitted to go on vacation. Therefore Iraq, "with information on the major reduction in the strength of the units and the unlikelihood of the implementation of another operation by Iran, ... quickly prepared itself for the invasion of Faw."[96]

In the final assessment, according to the *War Chronology*, "Iranian forces were in [a state of] more fundamental neglect, and for the same reason were not able to prevent the enemy's taking of Faw."[97] During that operation, launched on April 17, the Iraqis used chemical weapons on a wide scale to drive the Iranians out of their last significant position in Iraq.[98] In doing so, Iraq "changed the military-political and psychological balance in its favor," essentially "determining the fate of the war on the ground."[99] Then, according to the *Guide Atlas*, the continuation of Iraqi offensives and the shooting down of an Iranian passenger airplane by the United States, killing the 290 people onboard, "placed the Islamic Republic in a difficult position for which it had no appropriate measures to overcome."[100]

These developments forced Iran to announce its agreement with Resolution 598 on July 18 and to "withdraw from the Iraqi areas under its possession." The withdrawal was also motivated by the need to "free its forces to confront the coming attacks" of the Iraqi forces, as hostilities continued surrounding and after Iran's retreat and acceptance of the ceasefire.[101] These included air attacks by both countries, Iraqi incursions into Iranian territory, and an operation launched by

---

[95] *Chronology 54*, 30–32.   [96] Ibid., 32–33.   [97] Ibid., 33.
[98] Ibid., 15–16.   [99] *Critique and Review 4*, 280, 16.
[100] *Guide Atlas 1*, 61–62.   [101] Ibid.; *Critique and Review 4*, 16.

members of the People's Mujahidin, the Iranian opposition group that had found refuge in Iraq.[102]

The *Guide Atlas* goes on to describe how, "like in the first days of the war," a "mass of people's forces" rose to confront the Iraqis and push them back over the border. They then heard the "unbelievable" news of Iran's acceptance of the ceasefire resolution. "After reaching the border, the Iranian forces announced their readiness to pursue the enemy." However, "they did not agree on this matter with Imam Khomeini and were reminded of [Iran's] acceptance of Resolution [598]."[103]

This description of the disquiet that surrounded these decisions indicates that the Guards regard the end of the war with unease. Any achievements that had been gained could not obscure the bitterness of Iran's ultimate failure at the war's end. As another volume concedes, "it was expected that the war would end with Iran's military victory and the fall of Saddam, but that is not what happened." Instead, Iran's "weakness in protecting the captured areas in the final months of the war changed the war's fate, and Iran ended the war by accepting the ceasefire." Although "various factors" affected "the final determination" of the war, Iraq's victories in the conflict's final months "had a definitive and ultimate impact on Iran's decision-making." The conclusion the IRGC authors are accordingly forced to reach is that Iran's "military victories were insufficient to support the political efforts."[104] The implications of that assessment, like the war itself, have not yet been fully or satisfactorily resolved.

The Guards, however, stop short of equating Iran's failures with its defeat, or Iraq's victory. They portray the war as a loss for Iraq because it failed to achieve its goals in attacking Iran.[105] Iran's defense of its territory was one of the war's outstanding features. According to the *Guide Atlas*, the war "was the first time . . . Iran defended itself from an aggressor without foreign aid."[106] A volume of the *Analysis* series

[102] Youssef M. Ibrahim, "Iraq Mounts New Drive on Border to Gain Edge in Talks with Iran," *The New York Times*, July 23, 1988; Charles P. Wallace, "Iraqi Forces Push Deep into Iran," *Los Angeles Times*, July 24, 1988; Warren Richey, "Anti-Khomeini Rebels Attack as Iran and Iraq Prepare to Talk," *The Christian Science Monitor*, July 27, 1988.
[103] *Guide Atlas 1*, 62–63.   [104] *Critique and Review 4*, 277–79.
[105] *Guide Atlas 1*, 64.   [106] Ibid., back cover.

similarly puts the Iran–Iraq War in historical perspective to characterize the conflict's outcome. It says:

> In the wake of every war throughout Iran's contemporary history, we have
> always witnessed the separation of parts of this vast territory in the hands of
> foreigners. ... But in the Iran–Iraq War, despite the backing of the great
> powers for the aggressor, not one span of Iranian land remained in the hands
> of Iraqi forces.[107]

To that achievement, this source continues, were later added two
others – Iraq's reacceptance of the 1975 Algiers Agreement and with
it the antebellum border between the countries, and UN Secretary-
General Pérez de Cuéllar's formal censure of Iraq for initiating the
war – that helped vindicate the "rightfulness" of the Iranian effort.[108]

Thus, the war is portrayed as a victory for Iran, primarily because it
survived intact. The emphasis the Revolutionary Guards place on the
Islamic Republic's ability to withstand foreign aggression and on how
that success distinguished it from previous Iranian regimes is a prominent feature of the IRGC narrative. While that accomplishment was
undoubtedly impressive, characterizing Iran's experience in the war as
a victory in those terms narrows greatly the expansive way the war had
initially been defined, especially rhetorically. The focus on its effective
resistance against external aggression does much to substantiate the
Islamic Republic's rule, and shifts the focus from the offensive failures
to the defensive accomplishments. The contemporary priority the
Guards give to Iran's security and territorial integrity may thus be seen
as a reflection of its most significant achievements during the Iran–Iraq
War. Much is made of the grandiloquence Iranian leaders sometimes
use to communicate their policies. But the Guards' emphasis on survival as success reveals the importance of contextualizing such rhetoric
and understanding its place within the Guards' overarching narrative.

---

[107] *Analysis of the Iran–Iraq War 1*, 2nd ed. (HDRDC, 2001), 15.
[108] Ibid. Secretary-General Pérez de Cuéllar formally blamed Iraq for beginning the
war in December 1991. The decision was related to the release of Western
hostages held by Hezbollah in Lebanon, which Iran helped arrange.

9 | Faith and Firepower
Iran's Prosecution of the Iran–Iraq War

This chapter takes a closer look at one of the book's overarching themes, the relationship between faith and firepower. In the existing literature and the news media alike, much weight has been given to the rhetoric Iranian leaders used during (and since) the Iran–Iraq War and to the importance of faith and revolutionary fervor in understanding the Islamic Republic. As this chapter demonstrates, the IRGC sources and Iran's actions reveal a different story. By taking those as the basis of analysis, here the book illustrates that Iranian leaders prosecuted the war by relying on all the tools at their disposal, which included both faith – religious commitment, revolutionary ideology, and popular morale – and firepower – military professionalism, strategy, and weapons. In this context, it is important to distinguish between rhetoric – declarations made during the war intended to mobilize the population and give meaning to the fight – and historical analysis – the documented narrative the IRGC authors have composed in their publications. In the second half of the chapter, the theme of faith and firepower is utilized in another way, to examine how the Guards conceptualized the war in relation to Islam and the Iranian Revolution, and to demonstrate that they did so in order to expound the significance of the conflict.

Faith and Firepower

Faith Against Firepower

The first way to examine faith and firepower in the Iran–Iraq War is to analyze how the Islamic Republic tried to use faith against Iraq's firepower. As noted in the introduction, the concept of faith and firepower derives from a wartime declaration attributed to de facto supreme war commander Rafsanjani that "the faith of the Islamic troops is stronger than the superior firepower of Iraq's troops."[1] In many cases, the IRGC sources explore the balance between the belligerents in terms of those two factors. They generally conclude, like Rafsanjani did, that Iran was stronger in faith – its forces' commitment to the war effort, their belief in the righteousness of their fight, and the ability of Islamic and revolutionary ideology to mobilize the population and give the war greater meaning – and that Iraq was stronger in firepower – it had superior weaponry and greater ease of access to the materiel it needed to prosecute the war.

But the Guards readily acknowledge that in many cases Iran's faith could not overcome Iraq's firepower. They give no indication that this was a shocking revelation that hit them at some point in the midst of or after the war, and there is no reason to conclude that Rafsanjani viewed the matter differently. Still, in other cases, faith was an effective weapon against Iraq, and this is exactly how the role of faith should be understood: as a weapon, a tool, a means to an end. In contrast to how the relationship is usually construed, far more important than the idea of the war strengthening the revolution was the strategy of using the revolution to get through the war. This was not a naively sanguine fantasy about massive violent conflict in the service of a revolutionary dream. It was a strategy of using whatever means were available to prosecute a war.

Faith, of course, is not merely a weapon or tool, and I am not arguing that religious belief is not incredibly meaningful for many Iranians, as it is for many people. Rather, the argument here is that in their sources the Revolutionary Guards often depict faith as something that could be used effectively in the war against Iraq. That was especially true given their lack of other means, like firepower, which is also critical to understanding the relationship between the two. Iranian leaders were, quite simply, working with what they had. In contrast to the clichéd caricature of turbaned "mullahs" shunning firepower in disgust because they reckoned they could win the war just fine with faith, the Guards argue throughout their sources that firepower is of utmost importance to the prosecution of any war.[2]

---

[1] Quoted in Sayyed-Hossein Yahyavi, "War of the Cities," *Negin Iran* 10.36 (HDRDC, 2011), 31.

[2] Shahram Chubin, "Iran and the War," in *The Iran–Iraq War*, ed. Efraim Karsh (Macmillan, 1989), 13–15, 17; Shahram Chubin, "The Last Phase of the Iran–Iraq War," *Third World Quarterly* 11.2 (1989), 3–4; Dilip Hiro, *The Longest*

One aspect of faith that was critical to the Islamic Republic's ability to prosecute the war was the morale of its armed forces and population. According to the IRGC authors, morale is a significant factor in the prosecution of war in general, one, as argued above, that is analogous to other tools. "'Morale' is one of the most important 'principles of war,'" the *War Chronology* asserts. "The presence or absence and also the extent of morale is [equivalent to] the success of the continued resistance and the motivation to continue the war." Morale can "even determine the role of [other] tools and equipment and [can] alter military tactics and strategies."[3]

The importance and necessity of relying on morale was particularly important in the beginning of the Iran–Iraq War, when the firepower discrepancy between the belligerents was considerable. Several IRGC sources outline in great detail the extent and preparedness of Iraq's armed forces, carefully delineating its military formations and the materiel they had at the ready.[4] Iran, on the other hand, lacked any military organization worthy of the name, the result of the reconstitution of the armed forces during the revolution. Although the leaders of the Islamic Republic inherited a sizeable and modern arsenal from the shah, they encountered many problems in attempting to make use of it.[5]

Iran had equally little ability to design a strategy or execute well-planned operations. The Guards consistently describe Iran's initial reaction to the invasion as chaotic, with no command and control and very little sense of direction. The response was dominated by "popular forces" – individuals in little or no organized capacity – rushing to confront the Iraqi army. In such circumstances, when no commander was present to give the order to attack, it was those who were most "faithful" to the revolution and the nation who resolved to attack anyway. As the *Survey* states, "because of ... the absence of centralized command and [of] the ability to deploy forces, the essential resistance against the aggressor ... relied on the popular and

War (Grafton, 1989), 95–96, 106; Edgar O'Ballance, *The Gulf War* (Brassey's Defence, 1988), 40, 47; Sepehr Zabih, *The Iranian Military in Revolution and War* (Routledge, 1988), 183–84.

[3] *Chronology of the Iran–Iraq War 33* (HDRDC, 2000), 39.

[4] *Survey of the Iran–Iraq War 1*, 4th ed. (HDRDC, 1998), 24; *Chronology of the Iran–Iraq War 1* (HDRDC, 1997), 19–20.

[5] *Analysis of the Iran–Iraq War 1*, 2nd ed. (HDRDC, 2001), 100.

revolution[ary] forces."[6] Similarly, the *War Chronology* describes the unpreparedness of Iran's armed forces and states, "in these conditions, only the presence of popular forces … [could] compensate to an extent for the absence of regular military forces." It was therefore "the popular and revolutionary forces, with reliance on faith, under the guidance of the Imam, [who] played the primary role in slowing and ultimately stopping Iraq's military machine."[7] As these passages demonstrate, Iran relied on popular, less-capable forces not by choice, but because the professional military was not in a position to respond quickly or effectively.

In some cases, however, forces who were highly committed had an edge on the battlefield. The same volume describes how "the Iraqi army's encounter with [the Iranian] resistance and its unpreparedness to confront the diffuse and irregular movements of the Islamic fighters increased the percentage of Iraqi losses and influenced the movement of the Iraqi units." The "revolutionary and martyrdom-seeking spirit" of the Iranian fighters was even more fearsome to the Iraqis given "the lack of sufficient morale among the Iraqi soldiers, especially [among] some of the commanders."[8] In this conception, morale contributed materially to the Islamic Republic's ability to fight the Iraqi invasion with some degree of success, especially when this was one of the few areas in which it had the advantage.

One of the main sources of popular commitment to the battle against Iraq was the Islamic Revolution. According to the Guards, the revolution bolstered the war effort in two important and complementary ways. The first stemmed from the fact that "the battlefield with Iraq was considered [part] of the arena of the revolution." That conception of the war derived from "the temporal proximity of the outbreak of the war to the victory of the Islamic Revolution," which "was an important factor in transferring the legitimacy of the revolution to the warfronts." Because the war began in the midst of Iran's revolutionary transition, "the powerful revolutionary potential raised in the revolution, before subsiding … in the system, were transferred to the fields of the 'War of Holy Defense.'"[9] In other words, the revolution contributed to the mobilization for the war because people were already mobilized by the revolution. Instead of being channeled into the

---

[6] *Survey 1*, 61.   [7] *Chronology of the Iran–Iraq War 4* (HDRDC, 1993), 31.
[8] Ibid., 37, 43.   [9] *Chronology of the Iran–Iraq War 5* (HDRDC, 1994), 21.

construction of the new regime and then abating, which it likely would have done in the absence of the war, the popular mobilization generated by the revolution was directed toward confronting the Iraqi invasion.

The second way the revolution bolstered the war effort was the result of "the people's understanding of the nature of the enemy's aggression and its consequences for the fate of the revolution and the country," which "generated resistance by popular forces and prevented the enemy from fully realizing its political and military goals."[10] In this case, the revolution buttressed the war effort because it broadened the conception of what was being assailed and what was at stake. As discussed in Chapter 3, Iranians saw the attack as one on the revolution and the country alike and believed that both would be overrun unless popular forces contributed to their defense.

The revolution thus helped mobilize Iranians for the war by giving value to the fight on both the socio-political and individual levels. For many, the defense of country and revolution was a cause for which they were prepared to give their lives. For others, the sacrifice is portrayed as an inherent feature of the Islamic revolutionary spirit. The "revolutionary fighter who was born with the Islamic Revolution and introduced to the world with the Imposed War essentially did not calculate whether their participation in the war would achieve something worth dying for or not," the IRGC authors state. "Essentially for them it was not dying but martyrdom and joining those who [as a result of their sacrifice] were 'alive with their lord.'" The presence of these fighters was so important because in the wake of the Iraqi invasion "not only the prospect of victory but also the conditions of managing the war were foggy."[11] The revolution's strength thus helped compensate for its weakness. As there was such a foggy sense of what was going on, Iran needed the people who were willing to fight through the fog and become martyrs to secure even the chance for victory. And it was because of them, the Guards state triumphantly, that "Iraq paid a heavy price for ignoring the revolutionary spirit of the Muslim nation of Iran."[12]

While Iran's spirit of revolutionary resistance was an important factor in slowing and then stopping the Iraqi advance, Iraq's occupation of parts of Iranian territory proved disastrous for morale. During that period the Iranian armed forces were in a dejected state, first from

---

[10] *Survey 1*, 56.   [11] *Chronology 5*, 21–22.   [12] *Survey 1*, 52.

their transfiguration during the revolution and then from the clobber-
ing they received from the Iraqi military. According to the Guards,
overcoming this dejection was a necessary factor in Iran's recovery of
its occupied territories.

The Guards describe, for example, the success of a limited operation
in March 1981, launched after several weeks of failed Iranian counter-
offensives against Iraqi positions, as stemming less from "its material
results" and more from its "spiritual and mental consequences" and
the "genesis of belief and faith in breaking the political and military
stalemate of the war."[13] According to the *Survey*, this "spiritual and
mental change in the people" helped initiate a new strategy to liberate
Iranian territory.[14] That campaign allowed for "initiative and creativity on the battlefields" and ultimately "changed the military balance to
the advantage of the Islamic Republic." The revival of faith and the
effective use of firepower were together responsible for turning the tide,
as "the martyrdom-seeking spirit of the revolutionary forces" worked
"alongside the proficiency and equipment of the Islamic Republic
Artesh" to "transform the conditions on the battlefields."[15]

The lesson that should be drawn from these changes, the Guards
assert, is that the same revolutionary spirit and civic engagement that
gave rise to the Islamic Revolution had to be tapped in the war with
Iraq, as Iran's victories "demonstrated that the solution to the revolution's problems was possible only with revolutionary tools."[16] In the
War Chronology, the Guards note that abandoning traditional pre-
cepts in favor of creative or revolutionary approaches is itself a well-
established principle of war, one that was particularly important for
the Islamic Republic in the beginning of its conflict with Iraq:

Carl von Clausewitz, the most reputable philosopher of war, has said: 'No
skilled commander should forget recognized military principles; but every
skilled commander must be ready in cases of necessity to disregard even the
most important military principles.' It is very likely that none of the revolutionaries who formed the resistance in the first months of the war had read any of
the works of Clausewitz, but not only were they ready to ignore the prevalent
principles of war, which dictated their defeat, but they were also ready to
illustrate and defend the principles of revolutionary war in practice.[17]

---

[13] Ibid., 63.   [14] Ibid., 64–66.   [15] Ibid., 68.   [16] Ibid., 64.
[17] *Chronology 5*, 22. The passage appears to be a paraphrasing of sections from
Book 1, Chapter 3, of *On War*.

In that statement the IRGC authors encapsulate one of the main points being made here, that the Guards' prosecution and understanding of war is far more rational than it is fanatical, more familiar than it is foreign. Even if, as they acknowledge, the Islamic Republic's early defenders were not actively modeling their behavior on Clausewitzian principles, their actions can and should be understood as aligning with the most well-established traditions of warfare.

Faith in Islam and the revolution continued to help Iran prosecute the war in the years after Iran's invasion of Iraq in the summer of 1982. This was particularly important because Iran still relied heavily on "volunteer forces who were present on the fronts with strong religious and revolutionary motivation." In this context the Guards point to "Imam Khomeini and his spiritual influence, and the mutual heartfelt and sincere devotion of the fighters to him," as having "a pivotal and determinative role" in sustaining the mobilization for the war. They note that the connection Khomeini was able to establish with the Iranian people was one that the Western media had difficulty understanding. One foreign reporter quoted in the *War Chronology*, for example, remarked that "one of the greatest inconsistencies in Iran is that the 82-year-old Khomeini can completely establish an intellectual relationship with Iranians who are one quarter of his age."[18]

In the final years of the war, when morale was sinking, Iranian leaders used religious tradition and practice to revitalize flagging support for the conflict. Toward the end of 1987, the Supreme Council for War Support launched a "nationwide propaganda" campaign to mobilize the population and began organizing Basij forces as "Soldiers of Muhammad" to be sent to the warfronts from various parts of the country. The process of assembling and dispatching these forces provided the opportunity for "the country to witness the passion and expression of the human and faithful emotions of the people as holy warriors in the way of God." The grievous task of sending soldiers to war was transformed into an opportunity for communities to come together and celebrate those who were making that sacrifice:

Smoking harmala and sprinkling rosewater over the heads and faces of the fighters, sacrificing many cattle and sheep before their feet, and escorting children and spouses and brothers by grandparents and newly married

---

[18] *Chronology* 33, 39.

brides, and bidding farewell to the fighters under Qurans, created beautiful scenes that prevailed over the spirit of sorrow and the saga of the society.[19]

To more widely distribute the burdens of war, Iranian leaders launched the Helpers of the Mujahidin project to provide assistance to "families whose members had gone to jihad in the way of God" and requested the population to engage in "financial jihad" to support the war effort. The IRGC authors note that using "the word jihad [in conjunction with] financial help for the front generated more motivation among the people and especially religious people."[20] The degree of callousness in that remark demonstrates well how the Guards view faith as a weapon, as not just a complement to firepower but practically as an element of firepower itself.

One IRGC source uses the words of Ayatollah Khomeini to make precisely that point. While Khomeini emphasizes the role of Islam for the Iranian fighters, he does so in a way that speaks directly to the way Iran "weaponized" faith in the war. "You now must act as the soldiers at the forefront of Islam," the Supreme Leader declared in a message to "the nation and army of Iran" that appears in a volume published during the war entitled *Toward Karbala*. "Our forces are armed with the force of God, mighty God is their weapon and no weapon in the world is equivalent to this weapon."[21] In a letter also included in this volume, Khomeini congratulates Iranian commanders for a victory over "the satanic forces [with] brains empty of faith. [Those who] relied on machine guns and tanks and neglected mighty God were brought to the abyss of perdition and opprobrium."[22]

These quotes evoke the Islam-inflected oratory that was so prominent in Iran at this time, yet they do not disparage the importance of weapons to the extent that they might appear to at first. Khomeini does not assert that machine guns and tanks are useless in war, nor does he suggest that the force of God is the only weapon that should be brandished by Iranian fighters. Rather, he emphasizes the importance of faith by arguing that Iranian forces are made stronger by having it and that Iraqi forces are made weaker by lacking it.

That combination of elements is conspicuous in another of the wartime slogans that appears in an IRGC source from the same period. Iranian soldiers, Khomeini commanded, must march "with the Quran

[19] *Chronology of the Iran–Iraq War 52* (HDRDC, 2003), 25.   [20] Ibid.
[21] *Toward Karbala* (Islamic Revolution Guards Corps, 1981), 3.   [22] Ibid., 21.

in one hand and a weapon in the other."[23] That statement demonstrates quite plainly that the Islamic Republic relied on both faith and firepower in prosecuting the war, not just one or the other, and that the combination of the two is what the Guards and Khomeini see as making Iran powerful.

Ultimately, however, when they take faith and firepower together, the Revolutionary Guards conclude that the advantage was with Iraq.[24] Iraq was able to replenish its firepower relatively easily from a variety of sources, but Iran could neither readily access weapons nor simply restock its supply of faith. Accordingly, the abatement of morale within Iran spelled the ruin of its war effort.

The Importance of Firepower and the Iran–Contra Affair

While Iran's fight against Iraq was characterized by the use of faith against firepower, the Guards consistently describe the Islamic Republic as relying on both faith and firepower in prosecuting the war. "One of the main factors determining the fate of wars is the amount and kind of arms in the possession of the two parties in the war," the *Chronology* affirms. "In the Iran–Iraq War, despite the fact that Iran's strategy was based on the steadfast will and martyrdom-seeking of the faithful, the role of weapons in victory and preventing losses must not be neglected."[25]

One of the clearest indications of the importance the Islamic Republic attached to weapons is the lengths to which it was willing to go to get them. Iran's military system was based overwhelmingly on American-made weapons to which it had hardly any access after the revolution.[26] Meeting its supply needs proved to be incredibly difficult, and given "Iran's level of advancement, it was not possible to furnish them domestically." Iran had almost as little success finding states that would sell it weapons and spare parts for its American-made systems. But the sources state that Iran needed access to military materiel and

---

[23] *Passage of Two Years of War* (IRGC Political Department, 1982), 42.
[24] *Chronology 4*, 608; *Chronology 33*, 39; *Chronology 52*, 18–19; *Analysis of the Iran–Iraq War 3*, 2nd ed. (HDRDC, 2005), 12; *Survey 1*, 14–15.
[25] *Chronology of the Iran–Iraq War 47* (HDRDC, 2002), 30.
[26] Ibid.; *Chronology 1*, 32, 339–40, 495–96, 584, 592; *Chronology 33*, 19; *Chronology of the Iran–Iraq War 37* (HDRDC, 2004), 69; *Chronology 52*, 18; *Analysis 1*, 100.

was going to find one way or another to get it. The Guards explain this as an inevitability. As Rafsanjani asserted in April 1987, "replacing the military system for a state like ours that is wrestling with both super-powers is not possible, [and] therefore it is completely natural that we are trying to preserve and supply our existing military system." The IRGC authors express their approval of that statement, adding, "it was inevitable that Iran would somehow purchase these weapons and materiel from the West, with or without an intermediary, more or less expensive."[27]

The most infamous example of Iran's convoluted weapons procurement process was the Iran–Contra Affair (or Irangate), which became public in November 1986.[28] The affair, in a nutshell, was a plan hatched by members of the Reagan administration to secretly sell weapons to Iran in the hope that the gesture would expedite the release of American hostages being held by Hezbollah in Lebanon and improve relations with the Islamic Republic in the process, and then to siphon off profits from the weapons sales to fund pro-American guerillas, known as Contras, fighting the Communist government in Nicaragua. In Iran, the episode is often dubbed "McFarlane's Adventure" in honor of US National Security Advisor Robert "Bud" McFarlane's expedition to Iran in May 1986 to facilitate the exchange.

When discussing McFarlane's Adventure, the IRGC sources characterize it as "a 'completely secret' connection between Iran and America" that "culminated in a strange and unusual clandestine agreement between these two enemy governments."[29] The agreement derived from mutual interest; each side needed something the other could offer. For Iran, the goal was securing needed weapons, even if that meant doing business with its bitter rival, because doing so was necessary to prosecuting the war.

This definition of Iran's aim is presented in a way that makes the contrast with the United States' goals – consisting of "opening the door of strategic relations [with Iran] as the main goal, then using Iran to free the American hostages in Lebanon as the secondary

---

[27] *Chronology* 47, 30–31, 499–501.
[28] "Report of the President's Special Review Board (Tower Commission)," February 26, 1987; Peter Kornbluh and Malcolm Byrne, eds., *The Iran–Contra Scandal* (The New Press, 1993).
[29] *Chronology* 37, 69, 80, 318–19.

goal" – clear.[30] In other words, the Guards emphasize that Iran's goal in the deal was only to get what it needed to fight the war; it was not to improve its relationship with the United States, even if that was the US objective. Although such an emphasis could be construed as indicating the IRGC's dogged opposition to the United States, it can also be interpreted as revealing that the Revolutionary Guards are open to dealings with the United States should they see both a need to do so and a way to justify that need.

Another element of the deal – the involvement of Israel – was potentially even more damaging to Iran's credibility and even more difficult for it to justify. The detachment that characterizes the Guards' discussions of that issue reflects its controversial nature. One volume of the *War Chronology* states matter-of-factly that "the Americans some-how involved Israel in the sending of arms to Iran."[31] Another volume focuses on how and why the United States was responsible for bringing in the Israelis. "An important point" in the US plan to transfer the weapons to Iran, it states, "was that it was necessary that the weapons be sent to Iran via Israel." In a lengthy footnote, the authors argue that involving Israel, and emphasizing its role after the affair was revealed, was in the United States' interest because it deflected some of the blame and controversy away from itself. They also go on to describe Rafsanjani's address at Friday prayers in Tehran in the beginning of November 1986, just after the adventure was first disclosed, and his insistence that Iran "did not agree to the presence of [even] the smallest Israeli footstep."[32]

The Guards' discussion of Israel's involvement reflects their conclusions regarding the repercussions of the affair more generally. Because Rafsanjani's statement was made upon Khomeini's instruction and confronted the scandal head-on, they assert it effectively "transferred the crisis arising from the disclosure of the adventure to America."[33] The Guards argue that Iran ended up benefitting more from the deal, as it achieved its goal of procuring weapons, while the United States did not achieve its primary goal of improving relations with Iran, and most of the hostages being held in Lebanon were not freed (some were). Overall, the negotiations "were a sign of [Iran's] tact and capability in political games."[34]

---

[30] *Chronology of the Iran–Iraq War 43* (HDRDC, 1999), 31.   [31] Ibid., 32.
[32] *Chronology 37*, 84–85.   [33] *Chronology 43*, 32–33.   [34] Ibid., 31–32.

The blowback from the adventure, however, still ended up negatively affecting Iran's war effort. The revelation of the affair caused
"America's position among the states of the region [to] become highly
precarious," in part because "Iraq initiated an extensive propaganda
[campaign] about the effects of American weapons on the battlefronts." Arab states, especially Kuwait and Saudi Arabia, "saw their
position endangered and expressed concern about America's commitments in the region."[35] Such negative reactions motivated the United
States to take a more active role in the war on the side of Iraq and the
other states directly supporting it. One part of the effort was the
escorting of Kuwaiti tankers in the Persian Gulf, discussed earlier,
which led to the intensification of the Tanker War in the later years
of the conflict. The United States also tried to compensate for any
advantage the weapons might give the Islamic Republic by reinvigor-
ating efforts to curb arms sales to Iran, and worked to reassure
Baghdad of its support.[36]

The adventure ended badly in terms of relations between the United
States and the Islamic Republic. It "increas[ed] the enmity" between
the countries, the Guards conclude, especially because its disclosure
coincided with Reagan's naming Iran as a member of a "criminal
confederation" of enemy states.[37] In their texts, the Guards highlight
the contradictory behavior that characterized the US approach to Iran
in this period. The duality was especially apparent in the contrast
between the attempts to reach out to Iran and explore the possibility
of improved relations as was manifest in the arms deal, on the one
hand, and the effort to promote the image of Iran as a terrorist state,
on the other.

Of course, this duplicity was partly responsible for the scandal the
adventure's disclosure generated, and the Guards join the many others
who have commented on the sheer hypocrisy of the imbroglio.
"America, while claiming to combat terrorism, was implicated in a

[35] *Chronology 47*, 26.
[36] Ibid., 31–32, 36–37, 172. According to Cordesman, the arms sent to Iran as
part of the deal "had only a limited effect on the fighting." Anthony Cordesman,
The Lessons of Modern War, Vol. II: The Iran–Iraq War (Westview Press,
1991), VIII.8.
[37] *Chronology 37*, 69, 80. The "criminal confederation" or "confederation of
terrorist states" included Iran, Cuba, Libya, North Korea, and Nicaragua.
George de Lama, "Reagan Condemns Five 'Outlaw Nations,'" *Chicago
Tribune*, July 9, 1985.

covert transaction with a country that was called the embodiment of terrorism; and ... the subject of the transaction was also something that America designated as terrorism: exchanging American prisoners for weapons!"[38] The IRGC authors note that the dissonance in foreign policy stemmed in part from disagreements within the US government, which indicates the Guards' attentiveness to domestic political conditions within the United States. They further explain the contradictory behavior as resulting from the United States' ambivalent recognition of the need to deal with Iran because of its important role in the region, which existed uncomfortably alongside the "deep and serious enmity" with which Americans viewed the Islamic Republic.[39]

In contrast to their detailed discussions of the duality in US foreign policy and the ways American leaders tried to justify their positions, the Guards express little concern for how the affair represented a contradiction in the Islamic Republic's declared policy. As noted above, they argue that the potentially negative repercussions of the incident were palliated when Iranian leaders dealt with the issue directly, but the Guards do not explore the inconsistency intrinsic to dealing with a declared enemy of the revolution. The IRGC authors may be avoiding an uncomfortable issue, but their sources suggest an additional explanation. Their analysis indicates that while the deal was ostensibly inconsistent with the Islamic Republic's policy, it was in fact consistent with the overarching mission of defending the country and the revolution. Indeed, McFarlane's Adventure exemplifies how the pursuit of material interests, like securing weapons, trumps adherence to revolutionary considerations, like obstinate opposition to the United States, when it is deemed in the overall interests of the Islamic Republic.

Altogether, the most important conclusion that must be drawn about how the Revolutionary Guards discuss faith and firepower is this: They present both as effective tools in prosecuting the Iran–Iraq War and argue accordingly that utilizing both tools together was better than using just one or the other. At no point do they suggest that they could prosecute the war with faith alone. The combination of faith and firepower is especially significant because it mirrors the compound nature of the IRGC itself and the way its revolutionary and military missions are intertwined.

---

[38] *Chronology 43*, 31.   [39] *Chronology 37*, 77, 79–82, 86; *Chronology 43*, 31.

A War of Faith and Firepower

Faith and Firepower in Victory and Defeat

In addition to understanding how Iran prosecuted the Iran–Iraq War, the combination of faith and firepower is also evident in how the Revolutionary Guards characterize the war as a whole, including in how they describe Iran's victories and defeats. The IRGC sources consistently attribute Iranian successes in the war to worldly causes – careful planning, cooperation between the armed forces, and exploiting the enemies' weaknesses. Descriptions of the outcomes of operations focus on whether the predetermined goals were achieved and are often recounted in a dispassionate manner. Operational successes are measured in kilometers liberated and equipment seized or destroyed. Particular achievements are not directly ascribed to the triumph of Islam, and certainly not to religious factors as the operative causal mechanism.[40]

References to religion, revolution, and other elements of faith serve to magnify the significance of victories and are combined with references to firepower in striking ways. In *Toward Karbala*, the Guards recount how one operation pitted the "militant fighters of Islam" against the forces of "Ba'th blasphemy." The operation was victorious because it "struck a hard blow against the rotten body of the aggressing Ba'thists" and because it "liberated two important and strategic roads."[41] Several pages later the text discusses another operation in which the "heroes of Islam" captured "170 tanks and armored vehicles, 120 loaders and bulldozers, 250 light and heavy vehicles, and a number of cartridges" from the Ba'th blasphemers.[42]

The *War Chronology* describes the outcomes of the first stage of the Ramadan Operation, Iran's first major incursion into Iraqi territory in the summer of 1982, in a similar manner. In that campaign, the Iranians

Were able to destroy all the positions of the enemy forces with admirable speed and to advance their [own] positions to a depth of 30 kilometers and to reach the Katiban River on the east of the Arvand [Rud] and Fish Lake. From

---

[40] *Guide Atlas 1*, 5th ed. (HDRDC, 2002), 15–19, 26–31, 33, 43–44, 47, 49, 51, 55.
[41] *Toward Karbala*, 18.   [42] Ibid., 27.

there our forces attacked the command headquarters of the enemy's 9th armored division and, after destroying it, they took the commander of the post's [Mercedes] Benz as a trophy and performed ablution in the water of Fish Lake and the Katiban River.[43]

The material and the metaphysical could not be combined more seamlessly or matter-of-factly. It is as if there is nothing exceptional or incongruous about a celebration that combines the humility of worship with the extravagance of a luxury car, just as there is nothing incompatible about faith and firepower.

A Battlefield of the Revolution

The meaning of faith and firepower can also be understood by examining the relationship between the war and the Islamic Revolution as the Guards define it in their sources. During the conflict, tying the war to the revolution served to heighten the stakes. *Passage of Two Years of War*, published in 1983 by the IRGC Political Department, illustrates that point. It characterizes "Saddam's Imposed War against our revolution, which occurred with the funding and management of America, [as] a sign of the power of this revolution. [The war] is presenting a new way to confront all those who share the hope of defeating the Islamic Revolution."[44] In this and other wartime sources, the impulse to augment the magnitude of the war, and with it the potential momentousness of any victory, often produced an exaggerated account of US involvement in the conflict.

A source published after the war presents a much soberer picture of the revolution's confrontation with the United States, especially as it escalated in the last years of the conflict, after the source quoted above was published. The fifty-first volume of the *War Chronology* includes a statement by Sepah commander-in-chief Rezaee in which he also describes the war as an attack on the revolution, and Iran as accordingly fighting to defend the revolution, but in his statement the triumphant tone apparent above is replaced with an apprehensive one:

The Americans [have] come to the region and threatened us in order to defeat the dignity of the Islamic Republic and to prevent us from becoming a

---

[43] *Chronology of the Iran–Iraq War 20* (HDRDC, 2002), 29.
[44] *Passage of Two Years of War*, 22, 26.

pattern. The whole world has mobilized to defend its identity against us. We too are opposing the world and are defending our identity. . . . We seek to overcome two hundred years of industrial and scientific investment. We have settled on such a major goal and we must perform consistently.[45]

On the whole, the sources published after the war describe the conflict in a similar manner, as stemming from a clash of identities and the revolution's intrinsic opposition to the interests and power of certain countries. According to the *Survey*, "the prospect of conflict with global arrogance stemmed from the essence of the Islamic Revolution."[46] Prosecuting the war was accordingly viewed as part of Iran's greater religious and revolutionary struggle.

Publications issued during the conflict devote more time to defending the war and depicting it as a blessing that will ensure the revolution's success than do the postwar publications. One describes the war in positive terms as an important step in consolidating the revolution's Islamic identity and eliminating its enemies. The concern appears to be with justifying the war as it was being fought, in part by claiming that it was inevitable:

The divine blessings of the Imposed War are thanks to the divine blessings of the Islamic Revolution, because defending our victorious Islamic Revolution against worldwide arrogance of East and West . . . is unavoidable. . . . The Imposed War [represents] a special stage in the growth of the healthy tree of the Islamic Republic.[47]

In later pages that source further explains those "divine blessings" by arguing that the example of the Islamic Republic, an independent country that was neither Eastern nor Western and that was fighting the superpowers in an unequal war, would allow for the "continuation of the revolution" and would show the "oppressed of the world" the "way to be liberated."[48] In contrast to that characterization, a more recent source mentions briefly that the war "allowed Iran to achieve comprehensive development," though it also caused "many human and financial losses."[49]

The subtler version of the assertion that the war was a positive development can also be found in the first volume of the *War*

[45] *Chronology of the Iran–Iraq War 51* (HDRDC, 2008), 19, 43.
[46] *Survey 1*, 60.   [47] *Passage of Two Years of War*, 21–22.
[48] Ibid., 34, 37, 47–49.   [49] *Analysis 1*, 13.

Chronology. On its first page appear two verses from the Quran, the first of which reads, "War is something that has been prescribed upon you while it is horrible and abhorrent to you. But perhaps that which is horrible and disagreeable to you is in fact that which is good for you."[50] The effect of the passage is not only to place the war in an Islamic context, but also to imply that the Iran–Iraq War, like war in general, is an elemental feature of human existence and that it can, at least, lead to positive outcomes.

The other noteworthy feature of the passage is what it leaves out. The verse as it appears in the *Chronology* is incomplete. In the Quran, the section quoted above is followed immediately by the verse's concluding line, "And Allah knows, while you know not." The omission of that phrase is significant because it suggests that the authors believe there is room for human judgment in understanding the consequences of war, which not coincidentally is a space the Guards are occupying.

The IRGC authors expand on the message contained in the verse in the very beginning of the volume's introduction. They assert that "war is one of the permanent elements of history"; although war "has always been hated and will always be hated by all people and all societies," it cannot be averted. The task of historians and analysts, they conclude, "is to consider that in every war the fighters are pursuing an objective and [to consider] what the war is against, what the war is for, and what its results are."[51] That assessment reveals that the Guards attach paramount importance to the ultimate and righteous purposes that sometimes drive wars and their belligerents. By conceding that war is universally abhorrent and focusing on the goals that drive people to take up arms, the Guards elevate those ends to a realm above and apart from the brutality of war itself and present them as the bases on which combatants and conflicts should be judged. In other words, the Guards believe that what is important is not that there is fighting, but what it is people are fighting for.

The Islamic Nation

Although the Guards characterize the war as a Holy Defense and as a battlefield of the Islamic Revolution, they define it also as a war fought to defend the Iranian nation. Despite Islam's centrality in postrevolutionary Iran, nationalism remained a driving force in the Islamic

---

[50] *Chronology 1*, 13. Surat al-Baqarah 2:216.   [51] Ibid., 14.

Republic, an outcome to which the Iraqi invasion contributed considerably. In the IRGC sources, concepts and terms traditionally associated with nationalism – including the nation, territory and Iran's territorial integrity and borders, patriotism, the international system and relations between nation-states, a secular reading of history – figure prominently in the way the Guards describe the war and the Islamic Republic more generally. In many cases, nationalist terms are interwoven with references to Islam and revolution, which demonstrates that the relationship between nationalist and Islamic ideologies in postrevolutionary Iran is less discordant than would appear at first.[52] Further, it sheds light on the complexities and multifaceted nature of Iranian nationalism and the strategies Iranian leaders have adopted to define and redefine it.

Territory, a key feature of nationalism in general and of Iranian nationalism as it had long been defined, plays an important role in the ways the Guards describe the war. The goals and outcomes of Iran's military operations are almost always described in territorial terms, and securing Iran's territorial integrity was a paramount consideration in the decision to invade Iraq.[53] As noted at the end of the previous chapter, the IRGC authors argue that the successful defense of Iranian territory was one of the most significant outcomes of the war, and they portray it as legitimizing the Islamic Republic's rule.[54] They accordingly make Iran's territorial integrity and the defense of the Iranian nation-state central to their understanding of the nature of the Islamic Republic and its war with Iraq.

The epic of Khorramshahr provides a fitting example. In their analyses of the resistance and liberation of the city, the Guards present a conception of the Islamic Republic that places it firmly in the tradition of Iranian national history and that demonstrates the synthesis of nationalism with Islamic-revolutionary ideology. The source that

---

[52] *Analysis 1*, 18, 25; *Guide Atlas 1*, 2; *Survey of the Iran–Iraq War 6* (HDRDC, 1997), 14–19; *Toward Karbala*, 3, 11, 16. On nationalism in Iran, see Mehrzad Boroujerdi, "Contesting Nationalist Constructions of Iranian Identity," *Critique: Critical Middle Eastern Studies* 12 (1998); Farideh Farhi, "Crafting a National Identity Amidst Contentious Politics in Contemporary Iran," *Iranian Studies* 38.1 (2005); David Menashri, "Iran's Revolutionary Politics," in *Ethnic Conflict and International Politics in the Middle East*, ed. Leonard Binder (University of Florida Press, 1999).

[53] *Guide Atlas 1*, 15–16, 48, back cover; *Analysis 1*, 15; *Analysis 3*, 11.

[54] *Guide Atlas 1*, back cover; *Analysis 1*, 15.

focuses on the battles for Khorramshahr recounts the several times the city was occupied over the course of Iranian history and states:

In the Imposed War Khorramshahr was again occupied and liberated, but this time Khorramshahr was a turning point not only in the Imposed War but in Iran's history. After centuries, this declaration of national existence, [which] relied purely on our own power against an aggressor who had the support of nearly all world powers, signified the end of a long period devoid of epic and independence in Iranian history, which only became possible because of the blessing of the Islamic Revolution in Iran.

This time Khorramshahr was witness to the birth of a generation of fighters and defenders who had been educated in the lap of the Islamic Revolution and [who] fought not only to defend the nation against the aggressor but [also] to announce and preserve the renewed prestige, power, and life of Islam. Khorramshahr was witness to this birth and was itself also a manifestation, example, and evidence of Islam's rebirth.[55]

That passage demonstrates that protecting the Iranian nation took on even greater significance after the Islamic Revolution, because in the revolution Iran was reborn as an Islamic nation, the Islamic Republic of Iran, the defense of which was a religious duty and imperative, in addition to a nationalist one. Therefore, the concept of a revolution and a religion that transcended national borders, that must not be diminished by nationalism, did not mean that Iranians ceased to be Iranians, or that the Iranian nation ceased to be a nation-state. The Islamic Revolution did not make the Iranian nation or identity obsolete. According to the IRGC, it made Iranian identity true, and the Iranian nation most worthy of defense. And with the Iraqi invasion, this principle became practice, and the imperative of defending the Islamic nation of Iran became real.

Overall, the combination of faith and firepower in both the IRGC sources and in the IRGC itself reflects the amalgamations that define the Islamic Republic – a country that is simultaneously traditional and modern, whose government combines a dictatorial theocracy and a semi-democratic republic, that prosecutes wars with faith and firepower. To attempt to understand Iran by considering only one half without the other is not possible.

---

[55] *Khorramshahr in the Long War*, 2nd ed. (HDRDC, 1998), 14. There is a very similar description in *Guide Atlas 1*, 8.

10 | The Holy Defense Continues
The Iran–Iraq War and Iran's National
Security

"Defying Trump, Iran says will boost missile capabilities," the *Reuters* headline read. The article, posted on September 22, 2017, went on to describe the military parade held in Tehran earlier that day. Among the soldiers and weapons on display at the exhibition was the Khorramshahr ballistic missile developed for the IRGC's Aerospace Force. The missile, *Reuters* noted, had a range of 2,000 kilometers and was "capable of carrying several warheads."[1]

So, there you have it. A defiant Iranian show of force staged to flout the authority of the United States and President Trump. A dangerous new missile with a hard-to-pronounce name. Those ubiquitous Revolutionary Guards taking over and militarizing Iran. What more is there to know?

It turns out that nothing about this story can be understood without accounting for the history and context the *Reuters* report left out.

Iran holds a military parade every year on September 22, the date of the Iraqi invasion of Iran in 1980, to mark the beginning of "Holy Defense Week," the annual commemoration of the Iran–Iraq War. The parade memorializes the country's resistance against a foreign attack and typically features armed forces marching in formation, tributes to those lost and wounded during the conflict, and the unveiling of new weapons. In their speeches, Iranian leaders address not only the legacies of the war but also contemporary security challenges, as the two are closely and explicitly connected.

And that fact was everywhere on display, yet not for the readers of the *Reuters* report. While noting the specifications of the new Khorramshahr missile, and that Iran's development of its missile capabilities represented a "reject[ion]" of US "demands," the story did not mention that the Khorramshahr missile introduced at a parade

---

[1] Bozorgmehr Sharafedin, "Defying Trump, Iran Says Will Boost Missile Capabilities," *Reuters*, September 22, 2017.

commemorating the Iran–Iraq War was named for a city that was captured by Iraqi forces early in that war and that remained under occupation for over a year; or that Iran's retaking of that city marked the culmination of a months-long campaign to expel the Iraqis; or that it represented a turning point not only in the war but in Iran's modern history and a declaration of Iran's determination to defend its independence. As Iranian President Hassan Rouhani said in his speech at the event, "We will increase our military power as a deterrent. We will strengthen our missile capabilities. . . . We will not seek permission from anyone to defend our country."[2] Khorramshahr – the city, the battle, the ballistic missile – therefore signifies how the Iran–Iraq War pervades both the form and content of Iran's security doctrine and how understanding the history of the conflict is essential.

This chapter examines some of the most important ways the Iran–Iraq War and its history impact the IRGC and the Islamic Republic today. These include efforts to derive political and strategic lessons from the conflict and how Iran's experience in the war has given rise to a security doctrine that seeks above all to establish effective deterrence and ensure Iran's independence, in part by integrating Iran into the wider region and utilizing asymmetric and soft power. Running through these and many other aspects of the war's ongoing significance is the conception that the conflict has not ended, and therefore that the Holy Defense continues. An additional aim of this chapter is to put the IRGC's published histories in the broader context of the IRGC, of Iran's ruling establishment, and of how the war's legacies and lessons shape Iranian policy.[3]

Deterrence

The Iran–Iraq War is currently the most important experience influencing Iran's security strategy. According to several of their

---

[2] Ibid.
[3] The discussions in this chapter draw in part on the author's research related to the following: "Perceptions and Narratives of Security," Belfer Center for Science and International Affairs, May 2012; "Beyond Strategic Stability," in *The End of Strategic Stability?*, eds. Lawrence Rubin and Adam N. Stulberg (Georgetown University Press, 2018); Ariane M. Tabatabai and Annie Tracy Samuel, "What the Iran–Iraq War Tells Us About the Future of the Iran Nuclear Deal," *International Security* 42.1 (2017).

publications, one of the reasons the Guards have analyzed and produced studies on the war is to understand the lessons it holds for
national defense. Some of these volumes were designed – often in close
collaboration with IRGC commanders and sometimes by request – to
be used as texts in courses on defense, strategy, and war in IRGC
training centers.[4]

The most fundamental way in which the conflict has shaped Iran's
security outlook is that it generated the determination to prevent a
military attack of the kind Iran experienced in that war and to deter an
armed conflict that could directly threaten its security and territory.
Iranian leaders see the country's lack of deterrent power as one of the
most important factors enabling the outbreak of the Iran–Iraq War.
Iran's blatant susceptibilities, they conclude, provided Iraq with a
powerful impetus to undertake the invasion.

The first volume of the HDRDC's *Analysis* series identifies the
necessity of developing formidable deterrence as the war's foremost
lesson. Studying the conflict is therefore necessary "in order to adopt
appropriate measures ... to prevent or lessen the damages that Iran's
competitors might impose on the country." The fact that during the
war "national security and the preservation of territorial integrity were
in such a difficult position" made the Iranian people and their leaders
"determined to deter neighbors and great powers from invading Iran's
territory" again.[5]

In the years since the war, Iranian officials have developed a strategy
of deterrence that very much reflects this determination and the weaknesses they experienced during the conflict. Iran accordingly views
effective deterrence in very broad terms, as involving efforts to create
not only a formidable military and arsenal but also a strong and unified
society that will be ready and willing to come to the nation's defense. In
other words, the main element running throughout Iran's national
security policy is a doctrine of independent and comprehensive deterrence that accords with the international relations framework of defensive realism.[6]

---

[4] *Battles on the East of the Karun* (HDRDC, 2000), 13; *Analysis of the Iran–Iraq War 1*, 2nd ed. (HDRDC, 2001), 15–16.
[5] *Analysis 1*, 12.
[6] Jack L. Snyder, *The Soviet Strategic Culture* (RAND, 1977); Jeffrey
W. Taliaferro, "Security Seeking Under Anarchy," *International Security* 25.3

Despite their work to develop effective deterrence, Iranian leaders argue that the countries that opposed Iran during the conflict have continued to threaten it after the war's formal end. In 2010, Yahya Rahim Safavi, who served as the head of the IRGC operations unit during the war and as IRGC commander-in-chief from 1997 to 2007, asserted that the countries that "could not realize their hostile plot against Iran during the ... war with Iraq are making efforts to create problems for the Islamic Republic" today.[7] Top IRGC commander Gholam-Ali Rashid similarly contended that those efforts stem from the failure of Iran's enemies to achieve their goals in the course of that conflict. Those foes should know, he avowed in 2011, that just "as they could not isolate or weaken the Iranian nation and could not trample upon [its] rights" through their support for Iraq in the war, "they will not succeed in ignoring [its] inalienable rights" today. That was because, he concluded, Iran "prove[d] its righteousness and managed to promote the level of its internal stability and deterrence against foreign threats through its resistance in the Iraqi imposed war."[8]

As those comments suggest, the Revolutionary Guards support the conviction that Iran will continue to withstand outside opposition by arguing that the country is more powerful now than it was during the war. Even though the Islamic Republic was prevented from winning a decisive victory, they emphasize that the country grew stronger in the war and regard the Holy Defense as a source of Iran's current power. As one IRGC volume states, "what today exists as security, freedom, independence, honor, and pride is indebted to the great epics of the eternal men [who fought in] the Holy Defense."[9]

According to the Guards, the continuation of the enmity that extends from the war is in part the result of Iran's strength, which has led its rivals to adjust, but not to end, their efforts to control and counter it. Mohammad Doroodian, one of the founding IRGC war researchers, characterized the war as a campaign to create "disintegration and instability" and "a tool of regime change." But, he

---

(2000–2001); Kenneth N. Waltz, *Theory of International Politics* (Waveland, 1979).

[7] "Iran Should Be Prepared for Every Imaginable Scenario," *Mehr News*, August 30, 2010.

[8] "Senior Commander Downplays Enemy Plots Against Iran," *Fars News*, April 30, 2011.

[9] *Battles on the East of the Karun*, 21.

affirmed, "none of this happened." He therefore concluded that "those who were behind this war did not achieve any of their demands and as a result Iran became power[ful]. Now the main issue for them became controlling Iran's power."[10]

The convictions that the current policies of Iran's enemies represent the perpetuation of the war and that Iran will resist aggression now as it did then are not held by the Revolutionary Guards alone. That same argument has been employed by Iran's top political leaders, including President Rouhani and Foreign Minister Mohammad Javad Zarif, to portray the country's standoff with world powers over its nuclear program as the continuation of the efforts that began in the war to undermine and weaken Iran. In the words of the former, "the enemy could not achieve its goals in the Imposed War." Therefore, after the war, "under the pretext of the nuclear issue, it imposed an economic war and sanctions against our nation."[11]

In some cases, this view has produced a doctrine of deterrence that can be characterized as aggressively defensive. The wartime precedent for this assertive strategy can be found in the decision to invade Iraq in 1982 and the conviction that Iran must pursue its enemies to ensure their defeat. As described in previous chapters, in their publications the Guards contend that the invasion stemmed from the need to rebuke Iraqi aggression, to compel the international community to do the same, and to ensure that Iran would be safe from future attack. IRGC commander Safavi reiterated that argument in March 2011 when he took part in a pilgrimage to battle sites in Khuzistan Province. "In the period of Holy Defense we taught future aggressors that if they attack Iran we [will] defend our territory," he proclaimed. "We entered Iraqi soil in order to attain a just settlement and to teach the Iraqis and future aggressors that if you attack Iran we will ... defend our territory [and] we will even pursue you ... toward the borders."[12]

---

[10] "Victory in Faw Indicated the Error in Hashemi's Thinking," HDRDC Website, November 30, 2019.

[11] "Confrontation with Iran, Big Mistake of Powers and Reactionaries," President.ir, September 22, 2014 (Persian); Mohammad Javad Zarif, "Iran's Message: Our Counterparts Must Choose Between Agreement and Coercion," YouTube (video), July 3, 2015.

[12] "In the Case of Enemy Attack, We Pursue [the Enemy] to Our Borders, Punish, and Destroy [Him]," *Fars News*, March 11, 2011 (Persian).

Another example of the IRGC's aggressive defensive posture came in its response to the US assassination of IRGC Quds Force commander Qasem Soleimani in January 2020, which IRGC commander-in-chief Hossein Salami described in an address to the Majlis shortly after the fact. He emphasized that the assassination was an aggressive act that inflicted damage on the country and induced a sense of defeat among Iranians. The United States wanted "to say the last word to the Iranian nation" and "to break the Iranian nation forever and to tie our hands," Salami asserted. It "intended to show that the path of our confrontation with it is one-sided and [that] we will not respond." Showing the United States that it did not have such control over the confrontation, that Iran could take action despite US warnings, was therefore necessary. Salami explained that the response to the assassination was designed to demonstrate that Iran would defend itself in an assertive yet proportional manner. He argued that Iran "had to respond quickly" because "powers increase their pressure when they do not face resistance," but that Iran had to respond carefully because "the enemy said it would respond." At the same time, he warned that Iran had "planned for several stages of war, with the possibility of expanding its scope, [as] from our view nothing has ended."[13]

Their embrace of prudence and pragmatism, Iranian leaders affirm, does not mean they will accept compromises that they deem threatening to Iran's security and sovereignty. This, too, can be considered a more aggressive part of their deterrence doctrine, and one that is also guided by their experience in the Iran–Iraq War. For example, during Holy Defense Week in 2019, an IRGC commander in the northern province of Golestan stated that during the war Iran "persisted and did not ... surrender."[14] IRGC researcher Doroodian likewise asserted that Iran's experience in the war made it wary of negotiating and compromising with countries whose opposition to the Islamic Republic was explicit. "Our understanding of the war," he said, "was that [it] was waged to destroy the existence of the system and the revolution; well, will someone who sees the existence of the system in danger be prepared to negotiate? One must establish power and destroy the enemy with power, and the slogan of Saddam's fall

---

[13] "We Have No Desire but to Sacrifice for the Security and Wellbeing of the People," HDRDC Website, January 13, 2020.

[14] "The Way Out of Problems and the Dignity of the Islamic Revolution Is Possible with the Discourse of Resistance," *Fars News*, September 21, 2019 (Persian).

was for that." He noted, however, that "the conditions and assumptions of that time are different from today, and it must be seen whether our understanding of the war will pave the way for [nuclear] negotiations or not."[15]

Independence

One of the primary ways Iran has prepared to deal with possible aggression is by developing a doctrine of deterrence that is based on independence. Iran's commitment to self-sufficiency in protecting its own security stems from its distrust of other countries and the international system and from the isolation it experienced during the Iran–Iraq War. Iranian leaders are quick to recall that the international community failed to condemn both Iraq's aggression in initiating the war and its use of indiscriminate means and methods of warfare in deploying chemical weapons and attacking residential areas, and that Iranian efforts to gain recognition of these injustices were largely unsuccessful. This silence, they argue, encouraged Iraq's continued employment of these practices. At the same time, Iraq effectively utilized international pressure to isolate Iran and to secure military and political advantages. This resulted in the perception that other countries cannot be trusted, and that the international system is unjust.

One of the problems of relying on the protections of international law that was exposed during the war is that they remain meaningless unless countries abide by and enforce them consistently and equitably. Manouchehr Mottaki, then the Iranian foreign minister, articulated this view in an address to the UN Security Council in March 2007, marshaling Iran's experience in the war to object to a resolution calling on Iran to limit its nuclear program by halting its uranium enrichment activities. "This is not the first time the Security Council is asking Iran to abandon its rights," he said. When Saddam invaded Iran in September 1980, the Council "waited seven days so that Iraq could occupy 30,000 square kilometres of Iranian territory." Then it "asked the two sides to stop the hostilities, without asking the aggressor to withdraw. The Council, then too, had effectively asked Iran to suspend ... its right[s]," he continued. "Imagine what would have happened if Iran had complied: We would then be begging the

---

[15] "Victory in Faw."

Council's then sweetheart, President Saddam Hussein, to return our territory."[16] As Mottaki's remarks demonstrate, Iran's leaders view the UNSC's efforts to curb its nuclear program as the continuation of the Council's unfair treatment of Iran that began during the war, and as reaffirming that the world order the Council epitomizes is unjust, biased, and untrustworthy.

These concerns help explain why concluding an agreement to limit its nuclear activities has required Iran to take a leap of faith. So, too, does Iran's distrust of the United States in particular. When the negotiations that produced the Joint Comprehensive Plan of Action (JCPOA) in 2015 were ongoing, IRGC commanders counseled that Iran should be prepared for violations of the agreement by the P5+1 (the five permanent members of the UNSC plus Germany), because the West and especially the United States could not be trusted.[17] According to a report published on the HDRDC website, that was the message former Quds Force commander Soleimani wanted to leave with his compatriots as the Iran–Iraq War was on the brink of its inconclusive end. About a week after his assassination in January 2020, the HDRDC ran a story with the following quote from Soleimani as its headline: "The Superpowers' Friendship with Us Is Like the Friendship of a Wolf and a Sheep." It recounted that this was Soleimani's warning at the final juncture of the war, which he delivered in a speech on August 7, 1988, less than two weeks before the ceasefire terms of Resolution 598 came into effect. The HDRDC included an audio recording and a transcript of a portion of the speech in which Soleimani demonstrated the imprudence of trusting a superpower, saying that befriending such a country is like having "a friend who swallows us whenever he gets hungry."[18]

Although such statements might suggest that the IRGC is categorically opposed to improving relations with the West, and the United States in particular, the Guards do leave room for the possibility of rapprochement, should the United States alter its policy of enmity toward the Islamic Republic. Then Basij Force commander Mohammad Reza Naqdi, for example, declared in 2013 that "the

---

[16] "Security Council Toughens Sanctions Against Iran," UN.org, March 24, 2007.
[17] "Basij Commander: Iran's Problem with US Not Related to Confidence-Building," *Fars News*, December 4, 2013; "We Are Waiting for the West's Real Commitment to Its Promises," *Tasnim News*, November 25, 2013 (Persian).
[18] "The Superpowers' Friendship with Us Is Like the Friendship of a Wolf and a Sheep," HDRDC Website, January 11, 2020.

slogan of death to America continues" because "Iran does not trust America." But, he went on, the slogan "will disappear only with the changing of America's nature."[19] Similarly, then IRGC head Mohammad Ali Jafari stated that the Islamic Revolution cannot accept the "hegemonic system" that the United States leads, "unless the United States' arrogant nature would change, in which case there would remain no cause for enmity."[20]

While their distrust of the international community has made Iranian leaders dubious about pursuing engagement, Iran's isolation has made doing so even less of a possibility, regardless of their level of interest. As discussed in earlier chapters, according to the IRGC and other Iranian sources, during the Iran–Iraq War the Islamic Republic was not just fighting Iraq but also the Western powers. This, they argue, was one of the conflict's defining features. It had a significant impact on the war's course and outcome and continues to affect their views of the West today.

A particularly important aspect of this isolation was how it hindered Iran's ability to defend itself. In 2019, an IRGC commander described how the widespread opposition to the Islamic Republic that was manifest in the war was experienced in Iran. He characterized the period of the conflict as "years of oppression and loneliness [for] a people who were prohibited internationally from acquiring even minimal defensive facilities like barbed wire and bullet[s]."[21] In stark contrast, Iraq had easy access to weapons and a wealth of financial and logistical aid. As Iranian sources often say, this allowed it to be "armed to the teeth."[22]

Together, the distrust of the international community and the experience of isolation gave rise to the conviction that Iran must be able to protect its security and sovereignty independently. Of top priority since the war has been ensuring that Iran possesses a quantity and quality of armaments more equal to those of its adversaries.

[19] "Iran's Distrust of America Persists," *Fars News*, December 12, 2013 (Persian).
[20] "IRGC Commander: Supreme Leader's Words, Nation's Guidelines," *IRNA*, December 12, 2013.
[21] "Resistance to the Islamic Republic Has Led to America's Decline," *Fars News*, September 21, 2019 (Persian).
[22] "Saddam Hussein's Set of Assets Was Destroyed with the Conquest of Khorramshahr," ICANA, May 22, 2011 (Persian); "Which Countries Armed Saddam to the Teeth?," *Parsine*, October 12, 2013 (Persian); "Governor of Eastern Azerbaijan Emphasizes Utilizing the Management Style of the Holy Defense," Ministry of the Interior, September 26, 2015 (Persian).

Maintaining such destructive power would prevent most enemies from attacking in the first place and would make an attack costly for any state that chose to initiate one. Iranian leaders argue that the development of their conventional weapons programs – and their desire to protect themselves from outside domination – developed from the unfavorable position in which they found themselves during the Iran–Iraq War. On the IRGC-affiliated *Fars News*, almost every English-language article about Iran's capabilities notes that Iran launched an indigenous arms development program with the goal of reaching self-sufficiency during the "Iraqi imposed war on Iran to compensate for a US weapons embargo."[23] The announcement and unveiling of new domestically produced missiles and the staging of military exercises often coincide with anniversaries of important events of the war, further indicating the close connections between the war and Iran's current security strategies.[24]

The claim that self-sufficiency is an achievement of the Iran–Iraq War and a rebuke of other countries reflects Iran's long history of exploitation by outside powers, which began well before the 1979 revolution. As one deputy IRGC commander stated in 2011, "the Holy Defense made us Iranians come to ourselves and [made] us realize that others who until yesterday took our oil and in exchange gave us the meagerest aid were only pursuing their own interests."[25] Prior to the war, former IRGC commander Safavi stated, "most of our aircraft and artillery equipment was Western, [but] through the war we achieved independence in the defensive and military industries."[26]

In addition to its determination to establish effective deterrence by independently building up a strong conventional arsenal, the Iran–Iraq War also led Iran to appreciate how indigenous nuclear technology and weapons of mass destruction (WMD) can contribute to a self-sufficient security architecture. Iraq's deployment of chemical weapons

[23] "DM: Iran Plans to Build More Powerful Surface-to-Surface Missile Systems," *Fars News*, April 8, 2014; "Iraqi DM Visits Exhibition on Iran's Military Equipment," *Fars News*, December 30, 2014; "DM: Iran's Defense Capacities Ten Folded," *Fars News*, October 25, 2016.

[24] "Army's Ground Force Kicks Off Massive Military Drills in Central Iran," *Fars News*, May 24, 2017.

[25] "The Value of Holy Defense Must Be Transferred to the Young Generation," *Fars News*, September 24, 2011 (Persian).

[26] "Political Independence and the Training of Managers Were Among the Most Important Achievements of the Holy Defense," *Fars News*, September 24, 2011 (Persian).

during the conflict left Iran with distinct and contradictory conclusions about their utility. On the one hand, Iranians intimately understand the heinousness of WMD and thus maintain a lasting abhorrence of their use. On the other hand, they regard Iraq's employment of chemical weapons as having been very effective because it gave Iraq an important advantage on the battlefield, deterred Iran from launching attacks, and contributed to Tehran's decision to end the war.

Iran's experience with WMD thus helps explain the country's vacillation regarding the possession of both chemical and nuclear weapons.[27] Its long-held stance of refusing to acquiesce to demands for it to halt its nuclear program is also based on the conviction that doing so would erode its independence and security. The way Iranian leaders have framed the nuclear negotiations that produced the JCPOA reflects this amalgamated position – combining independence, non-capitulation, and cooperation. Then defense minister and IRGC commander Hossein Dehqan said that Iran's negotiating team had "followed the path of maintaining dignity and authority" and that the negotiations were a sign of Iran's power.[28] Similarly, in remarks made in August 2015, just after a deal was reached, President Rouhani emphasized the mutual interdependence of these elements. A country must have "power, independence, and stability" in order to "pursue real peace," Rouhani said, adding that these criteria of national strength can be maintained even when negotiating with opposing parties. He also defined deterrence as something that "cannot be obtained with ... military power alone," because it requires "cultural, political, defensive, and economic power."[29]

Regional Integration

As Rouhani's statements indicate, Iranian leaders view security in a comprehensive manner. They maintain that effective deterrence must involve an array of military and nonmilitary elements that are

---

[27] IAEA Board of Governors, "Final Assessment on Past and Present Outstanding Issues Regarding Iran's Nuclear Programme," GOV/2015/68, December 2, 2015; "Iran's Chemical and Biological Programmes," in *Iran's Nuclear, Chemical and Biological Capabilities* (International Institute for Strategic Studies, 2011).

[28] "America Does Not Have the Ability to Confront Our Defensive System," *Fars News*, January 8, 2014 (Persian).

[29] "Text of the President's Speech at the Country's Annual Defensive Industry Day Ceremony," President.ir, August 22, 2015 (Persian).

combined and adjusted in a careful and calculated fashion. As will be discussed below, these elements include regional integration and the conjunction of hard and soft power.

Although the cornerstone of Iran's security strategy is based on maintaining independence, that commitment has been coupled with efforts to promote cooperation with its neighbors and to integrate Iran into the wider region. The experience of isolation in the Iran–Iraq War and the fact that Iran was the object of such widespread enmity constituted an important lesson for its leaders, and they have subsequently adopted strategies for preventing the distension of hostility. While Iranian officials do not usually discuss policies in these terms, in practice these strategies are predicated on the recognition that Iran contributed significantly to its beleaguerment during the war. The result of this recognition, which is an explicit aspect of its policy, has been Iran's effort to portray itself as an important member of the region and the international community, one that can contribute to cooperation and stability.

One part of this policy has involved holding up Iran and the Holy Defense as models that other nations should follow. IRGC leaders argue that Iran's resistance during the war can provide inspiration for those seeking independence, particularly from Western domination.[30] In 2009, for example, IRGC commander Safavi proclaimed that "the strength of Iranian fighters during [the] ... Iran–Iraq [W]ar has turned into an example for all freedom seekers, independence loving people and liberation movements in the world of Islam."[31]

The Guards contend that their efforts have produced some successes. The war between Israel and Hezbollah in 2006, they assert, was an important example of the Holy Defense spreading to other countries. As then Quds Force head Soleimani declared in 2011, "the victory of Lebanese Hezbollah ... was the fruit of the blood spilled in the Holy Defense. Without the Islamic Revolution the victory of Hezbollah is unimaginable. ... Every event of the war ... has been gradually transmitted to other states."[32] Following Soleimani's assassination,

[30] "Basij Makes Iran's Enemies Quake in Their Boots," *Tehran Times*, November 26, 2008.
[31] "Imposed War Brought Sustainable Security to Iran," *Mehr News*, September 26, 2009.
[32] "The Victory of Lebanese Hezbollah in the 33-Day War Was the Fruit of the Blood Spilled in the Eight Years of Holy Defense," *Rasa News*, May 23, 2011 (Persian).

Supreme Leader Khamenei praised the commander for the work he did to implement the model of Holy Defense in the region. Soleimani, he said, "from the Holy Defense to the end of [his] life, bravely went to the heart of danger" in his efforts to support the people of Palestine and Lebanon and to combat US influence. In Iraq, Soleimani's fight against US domination helped thwart efforts to install a regime that would, Khamenei surmised, complacently follow the United States like the one in Saudi Arabia does, whose leaders Khamenei likened to "dairy cattle."[33]

IRGC commanders also view the events of the Arab Spring as a product of the Holy Defense. In February 2011, commander Salami asserted, "the world saw that Islamic Iran could ... emerge victorious and powerful after eight years of war against world dominance. This historical pattern has provided a new path for self-determination."[34] During Holy Defense Week later that year, another commander stated that as a result of the war "Iran became a model in the region," as its experience showed that "the only way to salvation [for] Muslim nations" is by "appealing to self-esteem and self-reliance."[35] Although by 2019 the hope that the Arab Spring had generated was mostly a memory, IRGC leaders continued to claim that the ongoing resistance had "its origin and root in the eight years of the Holy Defense," and that one of the war's achievements "was the export of the thought and culture of resistance, ... the fruits of which we witness today."[36]

This ongoing emphasis on the successful export of the Holy Defense, and of the Islamic Revolution via the Holy Defense, may be compelling because it allows Iran to compensate for the fact that the revolution did not become a pattern on its own and to assuage the failure of the project to make it one. In a sense, the Holy Defense can be more easily accepted as a model for the world than the revolution itself. The latter has not been widely embraced and has not been very successful within

[33] "Supreme Leader in a Visit with the People of Qum," HDRDC Website, January 8, 2020.
[34] "Salami: Egypt Is the Political Life Harbor of the Zionist Regime," *Mashregh News*, February 1, 2011 (Persian).
[35] "Self-Reliance Was the Achievement of the Holy Defense," *Fars News*, September 24, 2011 (Persian).
[36] "The Imposed War Was the Basis of Our Holy Defense," *Fars News*, September 21, 2019 (Persian).

Iran either. The Iran–Iraq War, on the other hand, though costly and inconclusive, did certainly result in the Islamic Republic's survival, and not in a victory for Iraq or for the countries supporting it. The war therefore represents the power of the revolution in action.

Another part of Iran's policy of regional integration has involved reassuring other countries, and particularly its neighbors, that it is not an aggressive or hostile actor. This has been especially important given Iran's efforts to develop its military capabilities, which could easily be seen as menacing to other states. For example, when stating in 2008 that Iranian forces would strike US bases in the Gulf if they were used to attack Iran, then IRGC commander-in-chief Jafari reassured those countries that only the foreign installations would be targeted.[37] The reporting on Iran's military achievements that appears on *Fars News*, mentioned above, stresses that they should not be viewed as a threat to other countries and are intended for deterrence and defense. Thus, in building their deterrent power, the Revolutionary Guards seem to have learned from their experiences in the war, and their statements reflect an awareness that Iran's actions and policies during the conflict were viewed as threatening by other countries.

To further promote its role in the region, Iran has adopted a program of "constructive interaction" to expand effective and meaningful cooperation with other countries.[38] This phraseology serves to affirm Iran's congenial intentions and to emphasize the mutually beneficial nature of its proposed partnerships. It is a message that is directed especially toward countries that have viewed Iran as hostile and have thus seen interaction with it as deleterious rather than constructive.

In some instances, Iranian leaders have attempted to take this message a step further by arguing that cooperation is beneficial not only or primarily for Iran but also for the countries with which it is seeking to engage. Iran's interests align with those of other states, this reasoning

---

[37] "Bush Trying to Foment Discord in Mideast," *Tehran Times*, January 28, 2008.
[38] Mahmoud Vaezi, "Iran in the New Balance of Power in the Middle East," Expediency Council Center for Strategic Research, July 7, 2007 (Persian); Mahmoud Vaezi, "The Strategy of Constructive Interaction and the Requirements of Development-Oriented Foreign Policy," Expediency Council Center for Strategic Research, June 7, 2008 (Persian); Mahmood Ketabi and Ahmad Rastineh, "The Doctrine of Constructive Interaction in Iran's Foreign Policy and the New Geopolitics of Iraq," *Journal of International Political Research* 1.3 (2009) (Persian); "Constructive Interaction Between Iran and Turkey," *IRNA*, August 10, 2015 (Persian).

goes, and in pursuing its aims Iran is also promoting the collective interest. One of the areas in which Iran has fought to take part is the campaign against Sunni extremist groups. During a ceremony marking the beginning of Holy Defense Week in 2015, for example, President Rouhani stated that Iran was "the best defense against terror in the Middle East," pointing to "Iran's role in fighting Da'esh [the Islamic State] in Syria and Iraq."[39]

When its fight to secure a seat at the table does not succeed, Iranian leaders argue that excluding their country ignores the critical role it must play in the region. IRGC commanders made that point after the announcement in 2014 that Iran would not be included in the peace talks convened to try to end the civil war in Syria.[40] Basij Force commander Naqdi "blasted the US attempts to marginalize Tehran in efforts to settle the Syrian crisis." Inviting Iran to the talks "was an opportunity that the Westerners lost," Naqdi said, and he maintained that "[a]ny decision to be taken without the Islamic Republic of Iran's presence will be futile and fruitless."[41] Similarly, IRGC commander Salami declared that the United States could not solve "regional and international problems without Tehran's assistance."[42]

An examination of Iranian sources reveals a notable divergence between the stated goals of Iran's policy and how its relations with other states have developed in practice. The picture of Iran that emerges from the sources alone is of a country earnestly pursuing cooperation, seeking to "avoid tension," and working particularly to improve relations with its neighbors.[43] There is also a recognition, noted above, that the Islamic Republic initially contributed to tensions and its own isolation. In practice, however, Iran has continued to have a very difficult time convincing other countries of its benevolent intentions, and it has not refrained from the sort of rhetoric and action that tend to provoke animosity.

---

[39] "Review of Rouhani's Remarks in World Media," *IRNA*, September 22, 2015 (Persian).

[40] Joe Lauria, "Iran Left Off Invite List for Syria Peace Talks," *The Wall Street Journal*, January 6, 2014.

[41] "Basij Commander: Decisions in Geneva II Fruitless Without Iran's Presence," *Fars News*, January 8, 2014.

[42] "IRGC Commander: US Unable to Resolve Regional Crises Without Iran," *Fars News*, January 11, 2014.

[43] "Iran's National Security in Theory and Practice," Majlis Research Center, 1999 (Persian), 6; "General Policies of the System in the Forthcoming Period," Majlis Research Center, November 3, 2003 (Persian).

Asymmetrical and Soft Power

As was discussed in previous sections, Iranian leaders see the maintenance of a conventional force and arsenal as essential to its comprehensive security strategy. At the same time, they have pursued asymmetrical capabilities to bolster their overall security architecture. That effort derives from the recognition that Iran is a far ways off from establishing conventional parity with its adversaries, and that it is unlikely to be able to match them any time soon. It is also part of a strategy that is based on "multi-lateral defensive deterrence," which combines "symmetric and asymmetric deterrence," and which aims to defend against the breadth and nature of the threats Iran faces.[44]

One aspect of Iran's asymmetric deterrence doctrine is "indirect regional deterrence," which includes alliances with and support for various political and armed groups in the Middle East.[45] These groups play an important role in Iran's deterrence strategy by serving as an extension of Iranian power. The support the IRGC's Quds Force gives to armed groups in Iraq, Lebanon, Syria, and elsewhere can be understood as part of this effort. Hezbollah, for example, gives Iran greater "strategic depth" and increases its deterrence power by standing ready to retaliate for an Israeli attack on Iran.[46] Iran's reliance on such "networked defensive and indirect regional deterrence systems," according to Iranian analysts, is the result of "the lack of strategic symmetry" between Iran and its adversaries, which means that relying on "a system of direct and mutual deterrence could be risky."[47] It also represents a kind of asymmetric security dilemma, as the measures that Iran views as critical to enhancing its deterrent capabilities are regarded by other states as aggressive and as exacerbating instability and insecurity.

---

[44] Rahman Qahremanpour, "Iran's Deterrence Strategy," *Islamic Republic of Iran Diplomacy*, August 25, 2010; Alireza Golshan and Mohsen Baqeri, "The Place of Lebanese Hezbollah in the Islamic Republic of Iran's Deterrence Strategy," *Journal of Political and International Research* 4.11 (2012) (Persian), 135; Ali Baqeri Daulat-Abadi, "The Role of Deterrence in the Military Strategy of Iran," *Journal of Defense Policy* 22.85 (Imam Hossein University, 2013), 41–42; "Eight Deterrence Capabilities of the Islamic Republic of Iran," *Afkar News*, October 11, 2014 (Persian).

[45] Golshan and Baqeri, "The Place of Lebanese Hezbollah," 124.

[46] Ibid., 123–24; "Eight Deterrence Capabilities"; "Victory in Faw."

[47] Golshan and Baqeri, "The Place of Lebanese Hezbollah," 136.

In addition to the military aspects of its comprehensive security strategy, Iran places a high value on nonmilitary factors in promoting effective defense. This, too, is something Iranian leaders came to appreciate firsthand during the Iran–Iraq War when they mobilized a wide variety of military, political, social, economic, and other war-fighting tools. It also reflects the fact that strategies for controlling Iran's power go beyond conventional military means. A serious threat in this regard is the aggressive use of soft power, conceived primarily as the promotion of particular cultural and political values to achieve given ends, or what Iranian leaders term "soft war."[48] Instead of a direct military attack, which would entail greater costs, Iranian leaders assert that Iran's enemies have adopted a strategy of waging a soft war against the regime in order to erode its bases of support, undermine its legitimacy, and bring it down from within.[49] For example, during Holy Defense Week in 2011, an IRGC commander in Gilan Province stated that "our enemies have not been able to achieve their goals with military war or sanctions and therefore they have pursued soft war against the sacred system of the Islamic Republic."[50]

One of the most important nonmilitary factors in promoting security is cultivating unity among the Iranian population and support for the regime. During the Iran–Iraq War, Iranian leaders effectively mobilized the population to fight for the cause by promoting an ideology based on the revolution's founding principles – including independence, opposition to oppression, and sacrifice. The Revolutionary Guards regard their embodiment of this ideology as contributing to Iran's

---

[48] Sayyed Hossein Hejazi, "The Soft Power Capabilities of the Islamic Republic of Iran in Confronting America's Soft Threats," *Report of the Republic* (2008) (Persian), 26–27; Hossein Harsij, Mojtaba Touyserkani, and Leila Jafari, "Iran's Soft Power Geopolitics," *Political Science Research Journal* 4.2 (2009) (Persian); Mahmoud Ketabi, Enayatollah Yazdani, and Masoud Rezaei, "Soft Power and America's Hegemonic Strategy," *Political Knowledge* 8.16 (2012) (Persian); Asghar Eftekhari and Mohammad Janipoor, "The Bases of the Soft Power of Iran's Islamic Revolution," *Islamic Revolution Research Journal* 3.9 (2014) (Persian); "America's Strategic Steps for Influence in Iran," Khamenei.ir, September 19, 2015 (Persian).

[49] Daulat-Abadi, "The Role of Deterrence," 38; "Soft Power, Soft Technology, and Its Effects and Applications in the Defense Sector," Majlis Research Center, 2007 (Persian), 1–3.

[50] "The Will of the Imam Is the Charter of the Revolution," *Fars News*, September 24, 2011 (Persian).

ability to withstand the conflict, and have accordingly sought to champion these principles so they can continue to bolster Iran's security.[51]

Therefore, when it comes to defending the country, the Guards see ideological cohesion as a means to an end. "The thing that gave us an advantage against the enemies and their equipment, and [that] caused us to stand up with courage against them," an IRGC commander asserted during Holy Defense Week in 2019, "was faith in God and the guidance of the Supreme Leader. ... Victory in war is not all about equipment," he affirmed.[52] Soleimani deemed this principle so important that he included it in his will, which was released in early 2020 after his assassination. Among Ayatollah Khomeini's most significant accomplishments, he wrote, "was first that he brought Islam to support Iran and then [that he] put Iran at the service of Islam. If there was no Islam, and if the Islamic spirit did not rule this nation, Saddam would have devoured this country like a predatory wolf, [and] America like a rabid dog would have done the same."[53]

The combination of faith and firepower, the emphasis on unity and loyalty, and the securitization of ideology illustrate the close connection between national and regime security for Iran. In contrast to governments that enjoy a high degree of legitimacy and internal stability, and that are therefore primarily concerned with its external dimension, national security for states like Iran must serve the country and the regime alike.[54] Since its establishment, the Islamic Republic has ruled over a society that is deeply fractured along numerous lines, which have persistently threatened to crack wide open and devour the system. The emergence of a threat from a foreign power, however, provides an embattled regime with precisely the antidote it needs to palliate those internal divisions.

Thus, the idea that the war is still being imposed on Iran reflects the way individuals tend to bind together in the face of a common enemy. For much of the eight years that the war was actually being waged, the

---

[51] "Soft War vs. Holy Defense Values," *IBNA*, March 4, 2011; "Sepah Commander's Tears at the Funeral of Unknown Martyrs," *Fars News*, September 24, 2011 (Persian).

[52] "Faith in God and the Leadership Is the Reason for Our Advantage in the Face of the Enemies' Equipment," *Fars News*, September 21, 2019 (Persian).

[53] "Full Text of Martyr Hajj Qasem Soleimani's Will," HDRDC Website, February 15, 2020.

[54] "Iran's National Security in Theory and Practice," 2–3, 8.

diverse and divided Iranian population came together to confront the external aggressor. The end of the war therefore eliminated one source of insecurity and replaced it with another. Without a clear and common enemy, the unity established during the war was bound to dissolve, and the leaders of the Islamic Republic would be left without an external source to which they could attribute their own shortcomings.

From the perspective of the IRGC, therefore, keeping the war alive comes with political advantages. In a manner not unlike that of other revolutionary states, the Islamic Republic has used the threat of foreign aggression and a focus on past injustice to forge support for the government and unite the people under its mantle. Yet such a strategy would be ineffective if it did not contain some elements of truth, if it did not ring true to a considerable number of Iranians. And the assertions that the Iran–Iraq War ended without resolution and that the conflict was part of a long and ongoing record of foreign countries working to limit Iran's power and independence do indeed reflect the harsh reality of the country's history. Although the past can never be extricated from the present, the tendency of history to linger in the here and now is heightened when it remains unsettled.

11 | Unfinished History

The IRGC and the Holy Defense
Research and Documentation Center
since the War

Why did Iran continue the Iran–Iraq War after the liberation of Khorramshahr? That's the question former IRGC commander-in-chief Mohammad Ali Jafari came to answer. In May 2020, Jafari was over a year into his post-command life, having ended his time as IRGC head in April 2019 after twelve years in that position. His appearance at the Holy Defense Research and Documentation Center conference reflected his new, less-demanding job at one of the organization's cultural institutions. He had traded his dark green military uniform for a blazer and a lightly striped dress shirt. He sat with HDRDC director Dr. Ali-Mohammad Naini and other of the Center's researchers around a glossy table in a well-lit studio auditorium. Behind him were the poster advertising the event and a bookshelf lined with the HDRDC's publications. In front of him sat an audience of a couple dozen, some listening intently, some taking notes, and some checking their phones. The facemasks and empty seats between the attendees indicated that the socially distanced, COVID-19 era had altered but not halted the HDRDC's work.[1]

But back to that question – isn't it one that's already been answered? Wasn't it addressed at length in the HDRDC publications, as discussed in previous chapters? No and yes, respectively. As with so much of this history, it turns out that there remains plenty about the fateful decision to continue the war left to scrutinize, because the history of the IRGC and the history of the Iran–Iraq War both remain unfinished. The penultimate chapter of this book examines those ongoing processes of how the war has continued to shape the IRGC and how the IRGC has continued to shape the history of the war. The former is discussed in the first half of the chapter, which assesses how the war transformed

---

[1] "What Was Iran's Goal in Continuing the War After the Conquest of Khorramshahr?," HDRDC Website, May 19, 2020.

the IRGC into a more complete and professional military and how the organization has used its contributions to the war effort to justify its growing power in the years since; and the latter is discussed in the chapter's second half, which examines how the HDRDC has expanded and promoted its projects, including by reassessing critical questions like why the war continued after Khorramshahr was liberated.

Unfinished History of the IRGC

The Iran–Iraq War fundamentally transformed, and is still transforming, the IRGC. When the conflict began, the Sepah was a disorganized revolutionary armed force. Its roles and identity were in flux. In contrast to the Artesh, the Sepah had no clear-cut precedent or past experience on which to base its methods of organization and operation. The Guards' involvement in the war provided the opportunity and the impetus for them to develop their inchoate existence and to take on new roles without the constraints that institutional norms would have imposed.

One of the most notable features of the Sepah's evolution in the war was its ability to expand while preserving its organizational cohesion. Over the course of the conflict, the Sepah became a full-fledged military with numerous specialized units, but at the same time its branches remained under a central command, which became stronger in the process.[2] It simultaneously continued to operate against anti-revolutionary forces and to maintain its original mission of guarding the Islamic Republic internally.[3] The war thus both transformed and reinforced the Sepah's organizational identity.

Indeed, at the war's end, the Sepah had become a powerful and professional, but still revolutionary, armed force, one that had established a solid basis upon which to further legitimize and expand its authority. While the Guards can and have relied on their ecumenical mandate of "guarding the revolution" to justify their concerted efforts to extend their reach, they have further buttressed their claims to

---

[2] *Chronology of the Iran–Iraq War 33* (HDRDC, 2000), 22; *Chronology of the Iran–Iraq War 37* (HDRDC, 2004), 34; *Chronology of the Iran–Iraq War 43* (HDRDC, 1999), 17–18; *Chronology of the Iran–Iraq War 51* (HDRDC, 2008), 41.

[3] *Survey of the Iran–Iraq War 1*, 4th ed. (HDRDC, 1998), 82–84; *Chronology 51*, 53–55.

power by highlighting their contributions to defending Iran during the war and reconstructing the country after the conflict's end. Without the war, the IRGC would not have been able to assume the power over Iranian society that it has since. The idea that "war made the state and the state made war" therefore applies to both the Islamic Republic and, specifically, to the IRGC: war made the Revolutionary Guards and the Revolutionary Guards made war.[4] Or, in the words of a former Iranian diplomat, the IRGC and the Iran–Iraq War were "born together."[5]

In exploring that process, the IRGC sources portray the Guards' involvement in the conflict as a natural outgrowth of the Sepah's mission of defending the country and the revolution. Yet they also depict its entrance into the war as a very new development for the organization, and one that changed it in fundamental ways. Essentially, prior to the war, the Sepah was not truly or primarily a military organization, but it became one in the war. According to an article in the *Journal of Defense Policy*, published by the IRGC's Imam Hossein University, written by leading IRGC commander Gholam-Ali Rashid, the war was the primary and underlying cause of the Sepah's transformation into a "complete army." This, he affirmed, was something that "was not at all in the mind[s] of the Sepah's first founders." That statement reveals just how fundamental the change was, and how such a metamorphosis required the kind of catalyst that the Iran–Iraq War provided.[6]

The Sepah's evolution into a complete and professional, yet still revolutionary, military was marked by several key developments. First, as discussed in Chapter 5, was the establishment of the Southern Operational Headquarters in 1981. According to Rashid, "the formation of the Southern Operational Headquarters represented

---

[4] Charles Tilly, "Reflections on the History of European State-Making," in *The Formation of National States in Western Europe*, ed. Charles Tilly (Princeton University Press, 1975), 42; Miguel Angel Centeno, "Limited War and Limited States," in *Irregular Armed Forces and Their Role in Politics and State Formation*, eds. Diane E. Davis and Anthony W. Pereira (Cambridge University Press, 2003), 86–87.

[5] In-Person Interview, August 2012.

[6] Gholam-Ali Rashid, "Conditions and Exigencies of the Birth, Development, Consolidation, and Expansion of the Sepah in the War," *Journal of Defense Policy* 7.9 (Imam Hossein University, 1997), 28.

the identification of the Sepah [as a] military organization."[7] That contention and the related discussions in the IRGC sources provide significant insight into how the Revolutionary Guards define a military organization. The argument they put forward reveals that the Guards view cohesion, structure, and command as the defining features of a professional military. As described in earlier chapters, the Guards noticeably lacked those features during their first institutional phase of combatting anti-revolutionary forces. The Sepah's assumption of a military identity in the first year of the war reflects the acute impact the conflict had on the organization.

The second key development marking the Sepah's transformation into a professional military – the establishment of separate ground, naval, and air forces in 1985 – further demonstrates that point, as it also significantly broadened the fields in which the IRGC was involved both during and after the war. According to the volume that focuses on the formation of the Sepah navy, that force's first operations in the Persian Gulf in September 1986 "opened a new chapter in the Imposed War" and invigorated the naval power of the Islamic Republic.[8] At the same time, those missions indicated the Sepah's "operational flexibility" and ability to "adapt to any situation."[9] Thus, the Sepah's initiative and organizational expansion worked together to allow it to have a significant impact on the prosecution of the war. That dynamic reveals the mutually reinforcing process through which the Sepah's involvement in the war promoted its institutional development, which in turn expanded its involvement in the war.

The magnitude of the IRGC's expansion into a complete military remains a key piece of the narrative of the war its commanders present to the public. During Holy Defense Week in 2011, former IRGC commander-in-chief Yahya Rahim Safavi described how the war allowed Iran to achieve "political independence" as well as "independence in the defensive and military industries." What contributed to those outcomes, he continued, was that "a powerful military force was established in Iran," referring not to the formal establishment of the Sepah before the war but to the Sepah's transformation into a military force that occurred in and as a result of the war. "During that period,"

---

[7] Ibid., 3–4.
[8] *The Sepah Pasdaran's First Naval Operations in the Persian Gulf* (HDRDC, 1996), 11, 17.
[9] *Chronology 43*, 19.

he continued, the Sepah, "which had not been a military and [was] considered a security force, [was] transformed into a military power, and now this force plays an effective role as a major weight in the comprehensive defense of Iran."[10]

According to the HDRDC, it was during the war and in the Sepah's transformation into a full military that the IRGC became entrenched and indispensable. In April 2020, the HDRDC published a "half-burned document pertaining to the first Sepah statute that was found after the martyrdom of Shahid Yusuf Kulahduz, the deputy Sepah commander at the time, in his bag." The occasion for the publication of the recovered document, several pictures of which were included in the story, was the anniversary of the Sepah's formation. In its report, the HDRDC related how shortly after the revolution Ayatollah Khomeini issued the command to establish the Sepah "in order to secure and perpetuate the achievement of the Islamic Revolution." Although it "began with a small force and rudimentary facilities to preserve and protect the lasting security and achievements of the revolution," it transformed in and after the "era of Holy Defense" to "become one of the most powerful assemblages of the Islamic system, so much so that today its powerful reputation has shaken the world." Thus, "the position of the Sepah throughout the forty years of its honorable existence is self-explanatory, and the truth of the matter in this regard" can be found in Khomeini's command that "if the Sepah did not exist, the country would also not exist."[11]

While that statement overstates the case, any attempt to equate the existence of the IRGC with the existence of the country would be far less convincing absent the organization's expansion, institutionalization as a military, and role in defending Iran that took place during the Iran–Iraq War. As was the case in the war, the view of the IRGC as indispensable grows when Iran is under threat. Thus, when the United States designated the IRGC as a terrorist organization in April 2019, the slogan championing the IRGC's indispensability was revived on a large scale amidst an unusually popular outpouring of support for the

---

[10] "Political Independence and the Training of Managers Were Among the Most Important Achievements of the Holy Defense,"*Fars News*, September 24, 2011 (Persian).

[11] "Picture of Half-Burned Draft of Sepah Statute," HDRDC Website, April 20, 2020; "If the Sepah Did Not Exist, the Country Would Also Not Exist," Imam-Khomeini.ir, April 10, 2019 (Persian).

Revolutionary Guards. Foreign Minister Zarif showed his backing for the organization following the US designation by visiting with IRGC commanders. He tweeted a picture of the gathering, writing that his defense of the IRGC stemmed in part from the IRGC's defense of the country during the Iran–Iraq War: "Honored to meet top [commanders] of [the] #IRGC. Our armed forces sacrificed to defend our nation, region & the world against Saddam & ISIS. We'll never forget their sacrifice – nor will we allow outlaw bullies to destroy their legacy by fueling insecurity & instability. Nor should the world."[12]

Indeed, in explaining their role in defending Iran today, the Revolutionary Guards point to their experience in the war and argue that they are prepared to protect the nation now as they were then.[13] The combination of faith and firepower that defined its prosecution of the war remains a central tenet of the IRGC's strategy and outlook. As they do in their publications, IRGC commanders emphasize the interconnectedness of the religious and military aspects of Holy Defense when describing both the past and the present. For example, when discussing the liberation of Khorramshahr on the anniversary of that battle in 2011, then defense minister and former head of the Quds Force Ahmad Vahidi characterized the campaign as "one of the greatest prides of the Holy Defense." When "the Basij and the classical military forces entered the battlefields under the command of the late Imam Khomeini," Vahidi said, Iran successfully defended the country.[14]

As it did during the war, the combination of faith and firepower reflects the IRGC's view of the Artesh as a critical and complementary organization within Iran's security establishment. A statement published by the IRGC in the spring of 2011 on the occasion of Army Day, the annual commemoration marking the postrevolutionary transformation of the military, described the factors that allowed the Artesh to become "the impregnable fortress of the revolution and the strong arm of the nation." What accounted for that development, according to the IRGC, were "deep religious spirituality and reliance on God, the

---

[12] Mohammad Javad Zarif (@JZarif), "Honored to meet top cmdrs," Twitter, April 10, 2019.

[13] "IRGC Commander: Basij Forces Boost Iran's Power of Deterrence," *Tasnim News*, November 30, 2015; "Prevailing Global Situation Demands Readiness to Ward Off Threats," *Tehran Times*, September 21, 2003.

[14] "Commander Vahidi: The Liberation of Khorramshahr Was a Great Cultural and Self-Affirming Victory," *IRNA*, May 24, 2011 (Persian).

determination and fortitude of the children of the revolution, the endeavors of the heroic epic of Holy Defense, the achievements in self-sufficiency, ... and the increasing capabilities in military science and defense." As a result, the statement concluded, "all of Iran's forces are ready to respond quickly and decisively to any threat or aggressive plot against the holy land of Iran."[15]

The emphasis on the continuously evolving nature of the IRGC's roles and capabilities is not restricted to the military field. In other areas, too, IRGC commanders contend that their wartime record of adaptation makes the Guards particularly well-suited to addressing the challenges Iran faces today. In 2009, then IRGC commander-in-chief Jafari described how the force had increasingly focused on countering "soft power" threats, noting that the IRGC was building on the "dynamism" that characterized its strategy during the war.[16] In some cases, the Guards look back on their experience in the war to identify areas for improvement. During Holy Defense Week in 2011, former IRGC commander-in-chief Safavi described how rectifying the weaknesses exposed during the conflict helped prepare those who fought to lead Iran through future times of crisis. In the period of the conflict, Safavi conceded, "we were weak in terms of management." The war forced Iranians to remedy that deficiency. "This war trained future managers of the system," Safavi continued, stating that "the war made it possible for these people to manage the country, the war, [and] foreign policy issues together."[17]

The years that have passed since Safavi's statement reveal definitively that managing a proliferating series of crises both familiar and novel has become essential. In the first months of 2020, as Iran and the rest of the world reluctantly realized the serious threat of the new coronavirus pandemic, the Revolutionary Guards stepped up to the challenge and assumed for themselves yet another area of responsibility. On March 1, an IRGC statement published on the HDRDC website attempted to reassure the Iranian people that the Guards would "be on the scene until we completely overcome the coronavirus," and that they had formed a new unit for "preventing and

---

[15] "The Army Is the Impregnable Fortress of the Revolution and the Strong Arm of the Nation," *Fars News*, April 17, 2011 (Persian).

[16] "Commander Stresses Dynamism in IRGC Strategies," *Fars News*, August 15, 2009.

[17] "Political Independence and the Training of Managers."

countering" its spread. For readers who may have thought that epidemiology represented an entirely new field for the IRGC, the statement referred them to the IRGC's record in the Iran–Iraq War. The Guards were prepared to take on the virus, it stated, "thanks to the valuable experiences of the Holy Defense era and the presence on the front of Islamic resistance in confronting threats stemming from microbial wars and chemical bombardments that resulted in serious human injuries."[18]

The HDRDC report on the burned Sepah statute placed the Guards' newest endeavor within the context of their growth over the course of several decades. "From the first days of its formation," the story related, the Sepah "has always performed its service honestly by bearing heavy responsibilities and carrying out serious missions." It went on to describe how those missions have evolved over time. From "the era of the Holy Defense" to "establishing [and] protecting ... the security of the country," in "helping to build and develop Iran," in "the provision of services and relief in the event of natural disasters, and now in the outbreak of the sinister coronavirus," the Guards have stepped up to help and have "continued to shine and grow."[19]

The judiciousness of the IRGC's – or, for that matter, of most governments' – response to the coronavirus has teetered between dubious and disastrous. How this most recent endeavor will affect the IRGC's position and credibility remains to be seen. What is clear now is that the IRGC continues to draw on its role in the Iran–Iraq War to assert its predominance, and that it sees adaptability and expansion as critical to its durability and strength.[20]

The IRGC's response to the nuclear negotiations that produced the Joint Comprehensive Plan of Action in 2015, discussed in Chapter 10, further illustrates that point. While it was assumed that the Guards would oppose engagement and work to undermine the negotiations, they instead remained cautiously open to and conditionally supportive of that process. This stance can be explained in part by their economic interests. The IRGC is sustained not only or primarily by ideology, but by its economic and military endeavors, which have forced the Guards

---

[18] "Sepah Statement: We Will Be on the Scene Until We Completely Overcome the Coronavirus," HDRDC Website, March 1, 2020.

[19] "Picture of Half-Burned Draft of Sepah Statute."

[20] Saeid Golkar, "By Mobilizing to Fight Coronavirus, the IRGC Is Marginalizing the Government," The Washington Institute for Near East Policy, April 8, 2020.

to balance ideology with pragmatism as their interests dictate. Although they are sensitive to aspersions on their military might, the Guards are cognizant of their military weakness relative to the United States. A US attack on Iran, which would have been more likely had the negotiations failed, would have been very costly for Iran and for the IRGC specifically. In contrast, if a deal succeeded and was followed by new economic opportunities, the IRGC might have been able to materially benefit from rapprochement. The IRGC's history shows that the Guards have been able to survive as a powerful institution not by defying all developments that make them uneasy, but by adjusting their organization, strategies, and even their ideology to changing circumstances in order to maintain and expand their authority.[21]

Unfinished History of the War

The Holy Defense Research and Documentation Center has shown a similar ability to adapt and expand. That has especially been the case since Dr. Ali-Mohammad Naini took over as its director in October 2017. The past several years have in fact seen significant growth in both the HDRDC's activities and in the availability of information about those activities online. The HDRDC's own website improved tremendously, although it still has a habit of disappearing in whole or in part for extended periods of time. Its "About Us" pages were updated to include additional information about its history and plans for the future. According to the section that outlines the latter, the HDRDC inaugurated a "new era" in 2008, which was also when it changed its name from the Center for War Studies and Research to its current appellation.[22]

As he looks to the HDRDC's future, Naini also celebrates its past accomplishments as a basis on which it can build. He has called attention to the extensiveness of the HDRDC's archive of primary sources, especially those created by its narrators and in collaboration with IRGC commanders, and to its efforts to digitize and preserve its

---

[21] Annie Tracy Samuel, "Revolutionary Guard Is Cautiously Open to Nuclear Deal," *Iran Matters*, December 20, 2013; Annie Tracy Samuel, "Correcting Misunderstandings of the IRGC's Position on Nuclear Negotiations," *Iran Matters*, February 18, 2014; Hesam Forozan and Afshin Shahi, "The Military and the State in Iran," *The Middle East Journal* 71.1 (2017).
[22] HDRDC "About Us" pages.

collection of documents and to make its work more accessible to researchers.[23] He credited the "favorable position" and repute of the HDRDC to his predecessor, Dr. Hossein Ardestani, and to "the measures, support, and guidance" of former IRGC commander-in-chief Jafari and current commander-in-chief Salami, the latter of whom also serves as the head of the HDRDC's board of directors.[24] Naini expressed confidence in his ability to further build the HDRDC. He noted that in his first two years as president, the number of the HDRDC's research projects has "increased five-fold, ... from 80 to 400 current projects," and that his goal was to increase its output "100-fold" over the course of the next ten years.[25] "I believe that we will certainly witness the further growth and development of the Center's activities," he stated.[26]

Naini has identified several areas on which the HDRDC will focus. First among these is research, the use of "reliable historical documents" and the production of "[well-]documented" histories of the war, which, he noted, is professional work to be carried out by professional historians.[27] He lamented that, although the volume of writings on the war is vast and the general "field of Holy Defense" broad, "the share of research works" in that field "is small." Naini also noted that "the share of student dissertations from research in the field of Holy Defense is small," and that the HDRDC sought to "create a mechanism to support students interested in researching" that subject.[28] One mechanism the HDRDC has adopted to incentivize and promote research works on the war is its creation of the Qasem Soleimani book award shortly after the commander's assassination. Naini emphasized that only research books will be considered for the award, and that "submitted works must meet scholarly criteria."[29]

---

[23] "If the Names and Memories of the Martyrs Are Not Cherished, the Enemy Becomes Dangerous," *Mehr News*, September 25, 2019 (Persian); "Holding of Friendly Meeting with More Than 100 Holy Defense Researchers," *Mehr News*, December 9, 2019 (Persian).

[24] "If the Names and Memories of the Martyrs Are Not Cherished."

[25] Ibid.; "Products of the Documentation Center Increase 100-Fold in the Second Step of the Revolution," *Mehr News*, May 2, 2019 (Persian).

[26] "If the Names and Memories of the Martyrs Are Not Cherished."   [27] Ibid.

[28] "Holding of Friendly Meeting."

[29] "Holding of the 'Commander Martyr Hajj Soleimani Book Award' on the Fortieth Anniversary of the Imposed War," HDRDC Website, February 15, 2020.

The IRGC publications indicate that the aim of increasing research on the war has been long-standing. According to the Guards, the first obstacle to achieving that goal emerged immediately after the conflict's termination, when its study was neglected as a result of "fatigue from the war's prolongation," the death of Khomeini, and the necessity of reconstructing the country.[30] Although the Guards assert that interest grew once the immediate postwar period passed, they maintain that it has not received the attention it requires, and many of their publications are aimed at rectifying that deficiency. One, for example, was published in 2001 in order to "reduce the existing gap in the field of methodical studies and research" about the war, especially because "there are unfortunately very few volunteering to research the eight-year Iran–Iraq War and Holy Defense, and perhaps it could be said that this subject more than any other subject has been neglected, [paid] little attention to, and dealt with unkindly."[31] Considering the enormous amount of activity there has been in Iran to record and commemorate the history of the war, the fact that the Guards maintain nonetheless that it has been neglected further demonstrates the extraordinary significance they attach to analyzing the conflict.

Naini argued that scholarship is particularly important in ensuring that the war remains central in Iran and that its lessons are fully utilized. "For us the Holy Defense is an unmatched national asset," he said, because during the war "the capacities of society were activated and came to the fore." Therefore, "research in the field of Holy Defense can help build the power of the Islamic Republic." Unfortunately, he continued, "despite the importance of research, we have still not been able to have many successes in the field of Holy Defense research." Looking ahead, the HDRDC accordingly "aims to utilize research works in order to exploit the lessons of the Holy Defense, raise the motivation of researchers in this field," and analyze new "angles" of the war.[32] Because "the work of documenting the Holy Defense is not at a desirable point," he said on another occasion, further development will "require jihadist work."[33]

---

[30] *Critique and Review of the Iran–Iraq War 1*, 2nd ed. (HDRDC, 2003), 15; *Chronology of the Iran–Iraq War 4* (HDRDC, 1993), 12.
[31] *Communications and National Security in the Iran–Iraq War* (HDRDC, 2001), 10.
[32] "Holding of Friendly Meeting."
[33] "The Culture of Holy Defense Must Be Extended in the Political and Economic Wars," *Mehr News*, November 3, 2018 (Persian).

Although there is much work to be done to elevate the quality and quantity of research on the war, Naini placed the HDRDC's research publications solidly within the realm of professional history. He has emphasized on several occasions that the HDRDC "endeavors to ... present a true and documented narrative of the history of the war," and that what it has "produced so far are accurate and researched works."[34] He singled out the *Chronology of the Iran–Iraq War* as a particularly noteworthy achievement. The chronologies, he stated, "are the most authoritative historical source of the Islamic Revolution and the Holy Defense and are based on first-hand and unique documents" housed in the HDRDC.[35]

A second and complementary area on which the HDRDC has focused is oral history, and especially the oral histories of the war's commanders. Naini characterized the "oral history of the Holy Defense commanders" as "one of the most important historical research sources" on the war. He emphasized the imperative of recording the commanders' oral histories, as "many of the documents are hidden in the commanders' chests," and noted that "the oral history of the commanders in fact complements the written history of the war." According to Naini, "the Center is the largest organization preparing the oral history of the commanders of the war." It hosts "about 25 commanders almost every week" in order to record their experiences and plans to continue to expand its efforts.[36]

Part of doing so has included work to bring the commanders into conversation with the HDRDC narrators, as combining the oral and documentary records produces a fuller history of the war. This does not mean, however, that the HDRDC is unaware of the ongoing methodological debate about the proper weight historians ought to give to oral accounts of the past. A two-part conference the HDRDC held in early 2020 on the Karbala 4 Operation (a costly and unsuccessful effort on the southern front in December 1986) brought the complementary nature of those sources, as well as debates over their relative veracity and historicity, to the fore. While the first session focused on the views of the commanders, the second featured those of the narrators, a division that indicated the potential for debate and

---

[34] "Operation Karbala 4 Determined the Fate of the War," *Mehr News*, January 7, 2019 (Persian); "Products of the Documentation Center Increase 100-Fold."
[35] "If the Names and Memories of the Martyrs Are Not Cherished."
[36] "The Culture of Holy Defense Must Be Extended."

where the line between the parties was likely to be drawn. And Davud Ranjbar, the narrator embedded with the Sepah during the operation, was ready to make his case. Although he does not appear to have been actively involved in the HDRDC or its publications since the war, he mustered a strong defense of the narrators' work and of the value of documentary evidence.[37]

He described the commanders' views of the operation as "one piece of an extensive puzzle. If we do not put this puzzle [piece] alongside other[s], we will not have a true understanding of the event." Fair enough, but Ranjbar went on to explain that, in his view, one of those pieces is definitely better than the other. The narrators' "narratives are documented. Commanders rely on their memory, but narrators recount [history] by referring to documents they themselves produced." The "narrators' narratives are unimpaired. The commanders' narratives have impairments like forgetting, organizational and professional considerations, etc.; but the narrators' narratives have nothing to do with the events of the day and are free of these impairments."[38] These comments and the HDRDC-sponsored public forum in which they were made demonstrate the IRGC's active engagement in historical scholarship, including but not limited to its own. They make apparent that the Guards are invested in debating even the more enigmatic aspects of the discipline, such as the strengths and weaknesses of its various methodologies.

Working with commanders to record their oral histories is one of several areas in which the HDRDC is seeking to expand its partnerships. In December 2019, the HDRDC announced that it had organized a "friendly meeting with more than 100 Holy Defense researchers." The goal of the gathering, according to Naini, was to "discover priorities, understand problems, and arrive at new ideas ... in an atmosphere of strengthening cooperation and interaction" between the HDRDC and both individuals and other research centers.[39] Regarding the HDRDC's work with individual researchers, Naini noted that at the beginning of his tenure the HDRDC had concluded "only 70 contracts with researchers and experts," as opposed to the "400 contracts" that had then been signed "with more

---

[37] "What Actions Did the Commanders Take After Learning of the Cancellation of the Karbala 4 Operation," HDRDC Website, February 8, 2020.
[38] Ibid.   [39] "Holding of Friendly Meeting."

than 200 researchers and scholars."[40] He emphasized that the HDRDC "is fully ready to support researchers in this field and to support the production of authoritative works with the documents at its disposal."[41] "The doors of this Center," he proclaimed, "are open to all writers and researchers. What is in our possession is a national treasure. All documentarians, researchers, authors, and scholars can use these documents."[42]

As warm and welcoming as Naini's words were, and despite the substantial work the HDRDC has done to elevate its standing and make its publications and documents more widely available, in this case his statements elide the fact that many of the HDRDC's activities remain opaque and exclusive. It is not clear how an interested researcher might go about entering into a "contract" with the HDRDC, what such a contract might entail, or whether the HDRDC's doors are in fact open to everyone or to anyone at all. Although addresses, sometimes phone numbers, and more recently website and e-mail addresses of its "distribution centers" are included in many of its publications, neither they nor the HDRDC's primary location have appeared on the relevant pages of its website. The website for its online bookstore has been distinct from the Center's main website, and neither has consistently provided a link to the other. The "About Us" pages included valuable information on the HDRDC's history, but little on exactly how the HDRDC currently functions, and the "Contact Us" page only had the option to use a form to submit a message.

Despite that discrepancy, on the whole the HDRDC has done much in recent years to publicize and make public its resources and activities. Particularly noteworthy in this regard are the series of meetings and conferences the HDRDC has held and the reports on those activities it published on its website. As in the case of the meeting mentioned in the introduction to this chapter, those events feature not only the HDRDC's director and researchers but also IRGC commanders whose experiences in the war the HDRDC has sought to record. What the proceedings of these conferences reveal so clearly is how the history of the war remains very much unfinished and how the IRGC researchers continue to actively debate what that history is and means.

---

[40] Ibid.   [41] "If the Names and Memories of the Martyrs Are Not Cherished."
[42] "Products of the Documentation Center Increase 100-Fold."

So, going back to the question posed in the beginning of this chapter: What did former commander-in-chief Jafari have to add to the discussion and to the still-open question of why Iran continued the war after the liberation of Khorramshahr? As was discussed in Chapter 6, the question of why Iran invaded Iraq in July 1982 is covered in several of the HDRDC publications. According to the account they contain, Iran was unwilling to end the war at that time because Iraq had not been recognized as the aggressor, because it remained insecure and vulnerable to attack in the absence of such recognition, and because it was seeking not a ceasefire but peace. The invasion was necessary, in other words, to protect and secure the country.[43]

But that's not exactly the story Jafari recounted at the HDRDC conference. On the matter of why Iran decided to continue the war, Jafari echoed the argument found in the IRGC publications that the overarching reason was the nonrecognition of Iran's rights, "which revolved around punishing the aggressor." In the invasion, Iran "sought to have the state of Iraq recognized as an aggressor country, and ... to have Iran's rights, which had been weakened by Iraq's aggression, restored, and if these two things were accomplished, the war would also end." Essentially, he said, "we continued the war after the conquest of Khorramshahr with the aim of ending the war."[44]

But Jafari's explanations for Iran's continuation of the war went further than the IRGC's published accounts and included additional factors that were taken into consideration prior to the invasion of Iraq. First was the complete distrust of Saddam and his intentions on the part of Iranian leaders. "We were confident that Saddam would not withdraw his forces, and it was this distrust that led to the authorization to enter Iraqi territory being given by the Imam," he stated. Second was the need to "maintain the offensive posture of our forces," especially because Saddam was similarly readying "his offensive forces deployed on the border for another attack." Jafari also took on the controversial question of whether the primary goal of the invasion was really to unseat and not merely punish Saddam, and maintained that the fall of the Iraqi regime was not the driving factor. He stated that

---

[43] *Chronology of the Iran–Iraq War 20* (HDRDC, 2002), 18–20.
[44] "What Was Iran's Goal in Continuing the War?"

such an outcome was considered "secondary to the goal" of securing Iran's rights, but also admitted that "our dream was Saddam's fall."[45]

While his answer to the why part of the question added to the IRGC's published accounts, Jafari's comments on the matter of how that decision was made departed from the prevailing explanations provided therein. According to those sources, the IRGC, and particularly wartime commander-in-chief Mohsen Rezaee, played a pivotal role in convincing Khomeini of the necessity and defensive nature of the invasion.[46] That was not the case, according to Jafari. The conference report makes it clear that the debate over who was ultimately responsible for that decision is one of which Jafari and others were very much aware. His comments on that point were introduced as "regarding the decision-making to end the war and whether or not the military commanders were responsible for this decision-making." Not, he said.[47]

As a general matter, Jafari asserted, "beginning war and ending it is not in the hands of the commanders," as a range of "political, cultural, and economic factors" help determine those decisions. Likewise, "when we went into Iraqi territory after the conquest of Khorramshahr, Imam Khomeini's permission was needed for this action, and it was not the case that the fighters did whatever they wanted." He acknowledged that "some proclaimed that Imam Khomeini issued this order because of the insistence of some commanders to continue the war, which is not correct," so "the Imam's decision to continue the war was not [made] because of the insistence of some of the commanders." Yes, "the military commanders informed Imam Khomeini of the possibility of continuing the war on Iraqi soil," but no, "it was not the case that the Imam was pressured."[48]

The decision, he continued, was "difficult" and disputed, but then again why wouldn't it be? "Just as there are differences of opinion in today's conditions and the negotiations with America, in that period there were also differences of opinion about ending or continuing the war." On the whole, however, the order to pursue the aggressor was one the commanders could get behind. They were in consensus that Iran's "military forces had to be strengthened," that "it was necessary to enter Iraqi territory" in order to establish suitable defenses, and that

[45] Ibid.   [46] *Chronology 20*, 18–20.
[47] "What Was Iran's Goal in Continuing the War?"   [48] Ibid.

"Saddam was untrustworthy." Therefore, "since all the commanders believed in victory over the Ba'thist enemy, there was no problem with continuing the war on Iraqi territory."[49]

Although they might not have had a problem with the decision to invade Iraq, Jafari admitted that the commanders did have problems carrying out that invasion in practice. "The conditions of continuing the war on Iraqi soil were difficult" and "complicated," he stated. Did the fact that an IRGC contingent traveled to Lebanon around that time contribute to the difficulty? Quite possibly. When "some of the fighters went to Lebanon," he said, "maybe this issue led some to say that the war with Iraq had to end, because they did not believe that we were capable of fighting on two fronts." Apparently the Supreme Leader had a similar view of the matter. "After being informed" that the Supreme Defense Council had decided to dispatch the forces to Lebanon, Khomeini "commanded that 'the road [to] Quds [Jerusalem] passes through Karbala' and gave the order to return the forces," as their new mission had "overshadowed the war between Iran and Iraq." Jafari's elucidation of Khomeini's oft-quoted statement provides the context essential to interpreting it properly and supports the examination included in the *War Chronology* discussed in Chapter 6. The purpose of the statement, Jafari affirmed, was to emphasize the primacy of ensuring Iran's own security by prioritizing its war with Iraq and limiting its engagement elsewhere if need be.[50]

The discussion of the war's continuation in which Jafari participated illustrates how the HDRDC has contended with the history of the conflict in new and public ways. As this chapter has demonstrated, the HDRDC's development over the past several decades reflects its maturation into a more prominent, professional, and productive research organization. It has proven quite capable of adapting to changing circumstances and of interrogating the war's history in search of lessons that can be applied to emerging realities. As Jafari said in parting, "the experiences of the Holy Defense hold lessons, and we must adapt those to today's conditions."[51]

---

[49] Ibid.   [50] Ibid.   [51] Ibid.

12 | Keeping the War Alive
The IRGC's Commitment to Writing the History of the Iran–Iraq War

This book has examined how the Revolutionary Guards have endeavored to shape the history and memory of the Iran–Iraq War and to ensure that its significance does not wane, particularly by taking on the role of historians of the conflict. The content and vast amount of the material the Guards have published on the war demonstrate clearly the importance they attach to that project. Their commitment to that mission derives from the Guards' extensive involvement in prosecuting the war and the war's formative influence on the IRGC. However, neglect of the IRGC sources and a disinclination for sober analysis have produced controvertible conclusions about the Guards and their roles in the conflict, as well as a failure to comprehend the war's significance in Iran. It is these misinterpretations that this book has sought to correct.

Its analysis has revealed that the IRGC's history of the Iran–Iraq War differs substantially from that found in much of the English-language scholarship, and that the Guards interpret the war very differently than that literature suggests. In the process, it has reaffirmed the imperative of history as a powerful force, not only for recording the past but also for interpreting the present and molding the future. It has likewise shed light on how the war's unfinished history continues to have a significant impact on the IRGC and on Iran's policies and positions today.

Indeed, understanding the Islamic Republic requires not just a basic appreciation of the general significance of the Iran–Iraq War, but a full realization of how pervasive, complex, and persistent the conflict was and is. The historical narrative of the war constructed by the IRGC has great bearing on the views and actions of Iran's leaders. In the lucid words of eminent statesman Ambassador Giandomenico Picco:

The "imposed war" shaped the Iranian narrative in a way many may have underestimated. As always, "narratives" and "national narratives" [must] be understood. They do not have to be right or wrong, but they are the "narratives" which shape the destiny of nations.[1]

The Revolutionary Guards would agree wholeheartedly with that statement. Their conviction that historical narratives shape the destinies of nations further explains the substantial investment they have made in writing the war's history. The concluding chapter of this book will expand on that assessment by arguing that the IRGC has endeavored to write the history of the Iran–Iraq War because of the way the Guards view the importance and meaning of the conflict in Iran today, the way they understand the nature and dynamism of history, and their commitment to what they view as the historical imperative of keeping the war alive.

A Culture of Holy Defense

In addition to constructing the written narrative of the war, the Revolutionary Guards have sought to transmit the lessons of the Holy Defense to the general public in other ways as well. Sometimes the two are one and the same. Each volume of the *Guide Atlas* series, for example, examines the events of the war in one particular Iranian city or province. According to the introduction to the first volume, the series emerged from an earlier project, the *Condensed Atlas of the Land Battles of Iran and Iraq*, as "a simpler edition that could be used by the public, and especially by visitors to the warfronts." The *Guide Atlas* was prepared for that purpose.[2] Organized caravans to the warfronts, known as "passengers of light" (*rahiyan-i nur*), have become an important part of how the war is commemorated in Iran.[3]

The primary forum for connecting the public to the history of the war is Holy Defense Week, which begins annually on September 22, the anniversary of the Iraqi invasion in 1980. Although events and

---

[1] Comments to a private listserv on April 11, 2012, which Amb. Picco gave the author permission to quote. During his twenty years at the UN, Amb. Picco helped negotiate the ceasefire that ended the Iran–Iraq War, the release of Western hostages in Lebanon, and the Soviet withdrawal from Afghanistan, among many other accomplishments.

[2] *Guide Atlas 1*, 5th ed. (HDRDC, 2002), 5.

[3] The IRGC is one of several organizations overseeing these pilgrimages, including as part of the central institution charged with doing so. See www.rahianenoor.com/.

news about the legacies of the war are a daily occurrence throughout the year, they become ubiquitous during Holy Defense Week as Iranians commemorate the war on a national scale. It's a massive undertaking, as the headlines advertising the week's events make clear. On September 21, 2019, for example, *Fars News* carried a panoply of stories announcing the hundreds of Holy Defense Week events sponsored by the IRGC and Basij in cities and counties across Iran. The website covers all of these fully, running several dozen stories on the various aspects of Holy Defense Week each day around that time.[4]

In many of those, the purpose and importance of the commemoration are explicit. When announcing the thirty special programs being put on by the Basij in Damavand, a city about an hour east of Tehran, the force's regional commander emphasized, "our goal during Holy Defense Week is disseminating the culture of sacrifice, endurance, and courage, because everywhere these concepts have taken shape the people of our country have been destined for success and victory, and inversely, everywhere there has been retreat, the enemy has taken a step further."[5] Other stories similarly highlight the now-familiar themes that can be found throughout the IRGC publications.[6]

So, what exactly are these hundreds of events? What can one do during Holy Defense Week? A review of the proceedings attests that the question should really be, what can't one do during Holy Defense Week? The smorgasbord of events is impressive. They are designed for a diverse population and for a wide range of age groups and interests. They're both national and local, with sets of programs held in and for different provinces and cities, often focused on the war's effects and legacies in those particular localities. They're organized by a variety of official and other organizations, including many different branches of the IRGC and the Basij.

---

[4] "Implementation of 300 Programs During Holy Defense Week," *Fars News*, September 21, 2019 (Persian); "More Than 100 Holy Defense Programs Being Held in Baqershahr, Kahrizak, Fashafuyeh," *Fars News*, September 21, 2019 (Persian); "Implementing 50 Distinctive Programs During Holy Defense Week [in] Pardis," *Fars News*, September 21, 2019 (Persian).

[5] "Implementing Thirty Holy Defense Week Special Programs in Damavand," *Fars News*, September 21, 2019 (Persian).

[6] "Commemorating the Holy Defense Adheres to the Values of the Revolution," *Fars News*, September 24, 2011 (Persian); "The Culture of Holy Defense Must Be Put into Action," *Fars News*, September 24, 2011 (Persian).

There are parades, exhibitions of military technologies, dioramas of operations, trips to various Holy Defense museums, and pilgrimages to the fronts.[7] There are motorcycle cavalcades, athletic competitions, hiking trips, prayer stations, Quran competitions, visits with imams, handicraft displays, photo exhibitions, and even a shooting competition (using air guns) especially for young women.[8] There are also events in which giving back to the community rather than commemorating the war is the primary focus, as the week provides opportunities to take part in an addiction prevention conference, to help out a medical team in an underserved area, to visit the elderly, and to rebuild roads and schools.[9]

Even with all this variety, the myriad events are ultimately designed to serve the same goal – ensuring that the Iran–Iraq War is remembered. Many are devoted to preserving and propagating the conflict's history. Exhibitions of Holy Defense books are one of the most common.[10] Some use the week as an opportunity to promote Holy Defense education in schools, with programs including visits and activities with veterans and narrators.[11] There are ceremonies honoring martyrs and veterans and their families, organized visits with those groups, the distribution of martyrs' wills, and trips to the cemeteries where martyrs are buried to pay respects and dust off tombs.[12] To this

---

[7] "Establishment of Exhibition of Holy Defense Achievements in Sanandaj," *Fars News*, September 24, 2011 (Persian); "Sepah's Newest Anti-Ship and Supersonic Missiles on Display," *Fars News*, September 24, 2011 (Persian); "The Unequal War Against Iran Humiliated Arrogance," *Fars News*, September 24, 2011 (Persian); "Holding of Parade of Armed Forces of Markazi Province in 12 Regions," *Fars News*, September 21, 2019 (Persian); "Implementation of 300 Programs During Holy Defense Week"; "More Than 100 Holy Defense Programs Being Held."

[8] "Lurdigan Basiji Women's Shooting Competitions Held," *Fars News*, September 24, 2011 (Persian); "Holding of Parade of Armed Forces of Markazi Province."

[9] "Self-Reliance Was the Achievement of the Holy Defense," *Fars News*, September 24, 2011 (Persian); "Holding of Parade of Armed Forces of Markazi Province"; "More Than 100 Holy Defense Programs Being Held."

[10] "Self-Reliance Was the Achievement of the Holy Defense"; "We Are Still in the Beginning of the Path of Holy Defense," *Fars News*, September 24, 2011 (Persian).

[11] "Holding of Parade of Armed Forces of Markazi Province"; "Implementing 50 Distinctive Programs During Holy Defense Week"; "The Imposed War Was the Basis of Our Holy Defense," *Fars News*, September 21, 2019 (Persian).

[12] "The Imposed War Was the Basis of Our Holy Defense"; "More Than 100 Holy Defense Programs Being Held"; "Self-Reliance Was the Achievement of the Holy Defense."

day, the tally of the war's recognized casualties has not been finalized, as additional victims are still being identified, which reflects yet again the unfinished nature of the conflict. Holy Defense Week provides an opportunity to finally lay the bodies of these victims to rest and to cherish their memories.[13]

Taken together, all these aspects of the IRGC's work to safeguard and sustain the history of the Iran–Iraq War demonstrate the extent of its commitment to that endeavor. They reveal the Guards' recognition that imparting the war's lessons cannot be done successfully in a one-size-fits-all manner, that they must target bibliophobes and bibliophiles alike. And understanding how and how hard the Guards have worked to convey the meaning and significance of the war raises once more the question of why: Why have they spent so much time and effort on this project? The final part of the answer to that question, which this book has sought to address as fully as possible, can be found in the IRGC's philosophy of history.

Theory and War

At the core of the IRGC's philosophy of history is a drive to understand the Iran–Iraq War in all its complexity. The IRGC publications reveal that doing so entails much more than investigating that conflict itself; it requires understanding war and history more fundamentally. It is in their examinations of these subjects that the sophisticated and penetrating nature of their project and the Guards' view of history as an imperative come to the fore most clearly.

Like many historians, the IRGC authors utilize theoretical tools to help them interpret the past. In several of their publications they put the Iran–Iraq War in its broader theoretical context by examining the concept and study of war. *Roots of Invasion*, the first volume of the *Analysis* series that focuses on the outbreak of the conflict, begins its introduction with a theoretical examination. "Why is there war? ... Why do decision-makers go to war?" it asks. To answer those questions, the authors explain that "in the international system, states have conflicting goals and interests and adopt various methods to achieve their goals and resolve disputes," and that war is one of those methods.

---

[13] "Funeral of Two Anonymous Martyrs of the Holy Defense," *Fars News*, September 24, 2011 (Persian).

The question, then, is when do states use "peaceful means to resolve disputes and pursue [their] interests," and when do they "use 'naked force'?"[14] The answer the IRGC authors provide is characteristically multifaceted. "Political and social events," they state, "are not caused by a single factor." In the case of war, causal factors include "geographical boundaries, historical and border disputes, ideological and cultural differences, [and] regional and international links and supporters."[15] In the fifth volume of the series, the Guards invert their approach and attempt to build theory from their case study. Here they set out to examine the lessons of the Iran–Iraq War and to "deduce the general results of the war" in order to bring to light "rules and patterns for studying other wars."[16]

The IRGC authors look to a number of sources when defining what war is and what it means, including social sciences, history, and philosophy. *Roots of Invasion* defines war as "a form of violent and planned action and reaction between two hostile states, which one or both states select to achieve [their] goals and resolve [their] disputes as the dominant pattern of relations between them." In contrast to times of peace, in war "the armed forces are given direct responsibility for implementing the policies adopted" by political leaders. The authors of this volume regard war as the product of "a rational calculation that is governed by rules of human conduct" and as "follow[ing] a relatively fixed and repeated pattern." They accordingly assert that "by accepting this principle, it is possible to examine the emergence of war scientifically, and by gathering the necessary information about the bases, reasons, and factors affecting the outbreak, continuation, and ending of wars, to construct a theoretical model that explains war."[17] This conception of war is firmly grounded in the traditions of military and social science, and echoes particularly Clausewitz's principles of war and the realist school of international relations.[18]

---

[14] *Analysis of the Iran–Iraq War 1*, 2nd ed. (HDRDC, 2001), 18–19.
[15] Ibid., 24, 19. See also *Critique and Review of the Iran–Iraq War 2*, 2nd ed. (HDRDC, 2004), Chapter 1.
[16] Ibid., 17. See also *Critique and Review of the Iran–Iraq War 5* (HDRDC, 2007).
[17] Ibid., 18. Another volume uses a similar definition derived from the Encyclopedia of Social Sciences. *Communications and National Security in the Iran–Iraq War* (HDRDC, 2001), 75.
[18] Carl von Clausewitz, *On War*, trans. Michael Howard and Peter Paret (Oxford University Press, 2007); John J. Mearsheimer, *The Tragedy of Great Power Politics* (W. W. Norton, 2001); Hans J. Morgenthau, *Politics Among Nations*

In other volumes, however, the IRGC authors call into question the contention that a theoretical model can be used to explain war. "War is a complex and multi-dimensional phenomenon," the fiftieth volume of the *War Chronology* states. "Numerous and diverse causes and factors affect its emergence, continuation, developments, and ending." Teasing out these causes and factors presents a formidable challenge. Some "are themselves changed by the effects of the developments that emerge" in the course of the conflict, while "in the various periods of war the extent and manner of their influence and effect are also changed." Very often developments are the product not of "one or several separate causes and factors" but of "causes and factors [that] emerge as an intertwined continuum." Despite the complexity of the causal mechanism, identifying the elements "that affect the emergence of war" and then tracing the course of "their depletion" can help the observer detect when "the signs of the war's end become visible."[19]

The fifth volume of that series similarly challenges the applicability of theory to the reality of war. It notes as "the first point" concerning the analysis of wars that "the particular circumstances and conditions of every war are distinct." As practitioners and historians (rather than social scientists or theoreticians), the IRGC authors appreciate that "what is simple and obvious in theory is equally problematic and complex in practice. No war is apolitical; meaning the outbreak and continuation of war (all wars) ... are not scientific."[20]

The concurrence of divergent takes on the utility of theoretical models of war reveals the internal complexity of the IRGC histories. It also suggests another explanation for the magnitude of studies the Guards have published on the conflict: their engagement with the many different approaches scholars can adopt to examine war. Indeed, the Guards' body of writings encompasses a broad set of methodologies and styles. The IRGC authors often directly address the different approaches they and others use in their analyses and emphasize the

(Alfred A. Knopf, 1948); Stephen M. Walt, *The Origins of Alliances* (Cornell University Press, 1987); Kenneth N. Waltz, *Theory of International Politics* (Waveland Press, 1979).
[19] *Chronology of the Iran–Iraq War 50* (HDRDC, 1999), 1.
[20] *Chronology of the Iran–Iraq War 5* (HDRDC, 1994), 12.

importance of studying war in a way that takes full consideration of how perplexing it is in both theory and practice.[21]

Despite the limitations of theoretical constructions, the IRGC authors nevertheless endeavor to offer more generalized delineations of war that examine its core properties. The fifth volume of the *War Chronology* adopts a much starker definition of war than the rationalist one provided in the other series to underscore war's devastating effects. It states that "war is one kind of connection between humans and human societies in which the will and action of one is utilized against the will and action of the other." War is thus an exceptional state in which people are "allowed to spill blood and take human life and destroy and devastate the human environment."[22]

After stating that definition rather plainly, the volume argues that the manner in which war is studied depends on the particular definition of war in use, and that "the intelligent reader ... wants and has the right to know with whom and with what mental world [the reader] is dealing." While one writer may "believe that 'war is the greatest evil besetting human societies, the source of all evils and moral corruption,'" and may "consider war 'the most horrible thing in life'"; another's "judgment of wars [may] concern truth and falsehood, justice and injustice," and may thus be a writer "who considers war a tool for 'eliminating sedition from the world.'"[23] According to the footnotes included in the text, the first conception of war reflects the views of Immanuel Kant and Leo Tolstoy, and the second reflects those of Ayatollah Khomeini.[24] Although the volume's authors state explicitly that their reader has the right to know how they define war, and that the particular definition of war in use has a determinative impact on their text, they fail to disclose which view they hold. While it might be fair to assume that the Guards espouse Khomeini's position, their initial conception of war as a destructive and violent interaction between competing forces suggests that their definition combines elements of both views, that they conceive of war as something that is

---

[21] *Iran's Economy During the Imposed War* (HDRDC, 2008), 11; *Chronology of the Iran–Iraq War 1* (HDRDC, 1997), 13–14, 18; *Chronology of the Iran–Iraq War 33* (HDRDC, 2000), 13, 39; *Chronology of the Iran–Iraq War 47* (HDRDC, 2002), 17.

[22] *Chronology 5*, 11–12.   [23] Ibid., 13–14.

[24] W. B. Gallie, *Philosophers of Peace and War: Kant, Clausewitz, Marx, Engels and Tolstoy* (Cambridge University Press, 1979).

horrible and devastating but that can also be employed for good if and when it does emerge.

Scholarly Discourse

As their references to Kant and Clausewitz reveal, part of the Guards' effort to understand war as fully as possible involves active engagement with various fields of Western literature. They often cite Western sources to support their own claims, referring, for example, to works from American analyst William F. Hickman and Israeli-British historian Efraim Karsh.[25] In the case of the Iran–Iraq War specifically, the IRGC authors seek to situate their publications within a larger body of scholarship, both domestic and foreign, and to supplement and correct the literature on the war.

In doing so, the Guards examine what distinguishes themselves as historians and emphasize that their roles in the war give their history value and authenticity. They note that, in contrast to their own histories, foreign analyses make limited use of primary sources on the war and present only a basic, often flawed, comprehension of Iranian society.[26] The value they place on primary sources and cultural literacy demonstrates not only that the IRGC authors are well acquainted with the standards of documentation and historical methodology that are accepted in the West, but also that they measure their history against those standards and then use them to give precedence to their own narrative. Their appraisals thus serve both to critique Western understandings of Iran and to highlight what their own publications contribute to the history of the Iran–Iraq War.

A publication produced in 1987 by the IRGC Political Department, for example, takes a jab at ivory tower pedantics. It disparages scholars representing "global arrogance" for being "unable to understand" the Islamic Revolution, "the Imposed War, and the amazing victories of the warriors of Islam, despite holding hundreds of conferences and roundtables [and writing] thousands of analyses and interpretations" on those topics.[27] A volume of the *Survey* cites Western analysts' bewilderment with the faith and commitment displayed by the Iranian forces as another example, asserting that "Westerners . . . have

---

[25] *Survey of the Iran–Iraq War 1*, 4th ed. (HDRDC, 1998), 81.
[26] *Analysis 1*, 15–16.   [27] *Plot Line* (IRGC Political Department, 1987), 7–8.

been unable to understand the presence of popular forces on a broad level and their spirit of martyrdom-seeking." This inability was further exacerbated by Iran's unexpected military successes in the first half of 1982 when it retook most of its occupied territory. It states that in this case foreign analysts were inhibited from understanding the war because of "their intrinsic reluctance to accept the Islamic Republic's political-military advantage ... and the consequences stemming from it in the Persian Gulf and Middle East."[28]

More recent reports indicate that, in the view of the IRGC, the West still struggles to comprehend the Iranian experience in the war. One of the many *Fars News* stories published around the time of Holy Defense Week in 2019 emphasized the ongoing "inability and incapacity" of the West to understand the Iran–Iraq War. It conveyed a statement released by the IRGC provincial guard in Tabriz for that occasion, which connected the bewilderment to misunderstandings of the roles of faith and firepower. The statement attributed Iran's ability to withstand the "cruel and imposed war" not to "facilities, artillery, tanks, [or] military aircraft," but to "the difference of faith," which constituted a "resolute determination" that "astonished the eyes of the world." Even after many years, it laments, "the arrogant politicians and charlatans of the world are unable to analyze those days."[29]

In some cases, the Revolutionary Guards do more than lament; they take on Western mischaracterizations directly. They were compelled to do so at the end of 2013 to correct reporting, originally by *Reuters*, on the IRGC's reaction to the interim nuclear agreement concluded in November of that year.[30] As noted in the previous chapters, the Guards gave their conditional approval to that deal and to the negotiations, although they also warned that Iran's rights had to be respected and that the United States had not proven itself to be trustworthy.[31] *Reuters*, however, construed one set of comments by then IRGC head Jafari as a condemnation of the talks. So the IRGC responded.

---

[28] *Survey 1*, 76.
[29] "Resistance to the Islamic Republic Has Led to America's Decline," *Fars News*, September 21, 2019 (Persian).
[30] Isabel Coles and Marcus George, "Iran Commander Criticizes Government over Influence from West," *Reuters*, December 11, 2013.
[31] "Commander Kazemeini: Geneva Talks Are in the Interest of the Iranian Nation," *ISNA*, November 24, 2013 (Persian); Farhad Rezaei and Somayeh Khodaei Moshirabad, "The Revolutionary Guards: From Spoiler to Accepter of the Nuclear Agreement," *British Journal of Middle Eastern Studies* 45.2 (2018).

A lengthy article on *Fars News*, which had also carried the statement from Jafari that *Reuters* misinterpreted,[32] criticized "Western media outlets" for "misreporting" its story and Jafari's "general comments ... in a bid to portray a confrontation between the IRGC and President Rouhani's government." It argued that *Reuters* had quoted Jafari selectively and employed "a completely out-of-context translation" to "pretend" that the IRGC was in "open confrontation with President Rouhani and his government." *Fars* then invited the reader to "see for yourself" and to review a lengthy series of articles, links to and screenshots of which had been conveniently embedded, to understand the extent of the misreporting that had led "readers to believe that the bone of contention between the IRGC and the government is the recent nuclear deal."[33]

However, and as the engagement with Western scholarship apparent in their publications demonstrates, the Revolutionary Guards are not invariably critical of foreign renderings of Iranian politics and history. In fact, they have worked to promote Western analyses that present a more nuanced picture of the country, that attempt to understand it on its own terms, and that reflect particularly an appreciation of how the Iran–Iraq War impacts Iran today. Those are exactly the qualities that were absent from the myriad articles published in the wake of the assassination of Qasem Soleimani in January 2020, most of which perpetuated hackneyed characterizations of the Islamic Republic, but that were abundantly present in the report the HDRDC translated and featured on its website. That report, written by Bruce Riedel, a senior fellow at Brookings, was published on January 9 with the title "How the Iran–Iraq War shaped the trajectories of figures like Qassem Soleimani."[34] Four days later, the HDRDC website carried a story on the report, introducing it as an analysis that "underscores the vital importance of the Iran–Iraq War in shaping Iran's current and future policy" and in understanding figures like Soleimani.[35]

---

[32] "We Will Not Reduce the Range of Our Missiles," *Fars News*, December 10, 2013 (Persian).

[33] "Western Media Misreport Story to Inspire Public with Widening Rifts in Iran's Political System," *Fars News*, December 24, 2013.

[34] Bruce Riedel, "How the Iran–Iraq War Shaped the Trajectories of Figures Like Qassem Soleimani," Brookings, January 9, 2020.

[35] "Brookings Report on the Effect of the Holy Defense on the Path of Figures Like Martyr Commander Soleimani," HDRDC Website, January 13, 2020.

The Revolutionary Guards, in other words, actively affirm analyses highlighting the war's impact on Iran and themselves. This and other aspects of their engagement with Western scholarship reveal that the Guards see value in comprehending how outside observers assess their own history and policies and in promoting mutual understanding between groups and societies that have often been at odds. At times, however, the reciprocity becomes a bit dizzying: Given that the Guards have translated and publicized my own work on them and their published histories, I now find myself writing about how they have written about how I have written about them writing about themselves.[36]

History and Historians

More broadly, the Guards' scholarly discourse is part of their efforts to critically assess how history is written both in theory and in practice and the many factors that make a work of history more or less sound. Several of those were discussed in Chapter 2, including the availability and accessibility of primary sources, how the research environment affects the historian's work, the benefits of employing a variety of sources and methodologies, the ease with which moments of history can be lost or distorted, and the historical imperative to prevent that from happening by ensuring that history is registered fully and accurately. All of those factors, and history itself, are shaped further by the historian and by the choices historians make about what history is, how it should be written, and what purposes it should serve.

In their publications, the Revolutionary Guards strive to tackle those difficult questions regarding the role of the historian in the writing of history, which constitutes an important part of their philosophy of history. The Guards contend that historians have a number of responsibilities to history and to their readers. Historians must be faithful to the events as they occurred and must serve as trustees or repositories of history.[37] To do so, they must be objective and must work to ensure

---

[36] Annie Tracy Samuel, "The IRGC and the Iran–Iraq War," trans. Abdolmajid Heydari, *Negin Iran* 11.42 (HDRDC, 2012); "Global Post: Sanctions or Military Attack Against Iran Are Useless," *Fars News*, April 3, 2012 (Persian); "Lessons of Iran's Resistance Against Saddam for Today," *Fars News*, August 8, 2012 (Persian).

[37] *Chronology* 5, 11, 13.

that their personal views and values do not interfere in their work. "In controlling the presuppositions and mentalities of the writer," they state, "it is necessary to employ constraint as much as possible."[38] The IRGC authors acknowledge, however, that no history can be free of such inclinations entirely. While there must be a clear and well-protected distinction between "truth and falsehood," the fact that history as we know it is the product of historians means that "the researcher[s'] attitude and insight are imposed on the research" to a certain extent.[39]

The propensity for imposition tends to be exacerbated when those who took part in the events under examination are themselves the examiners. The Revolutionary Guards criticize some studies of the war for falling into that trap. In his forward to the first volume of the *Analysis* series, IRGC commander Rezaee explains that some texts were written to reflect their "authors' political goals or personal motives" or to "showcase their own roles in the war," which had the effect of distorting their analyses.[40] Yet, "the members of the Center for [Holy Defense Documentation] and Research," the *Chronology*'s authors concede, "are no exception to this rule. They have their particular view and attachment to the ideological and defensive eight-year war, but they have tried to help the reader[s] and not to force [them] to either accept the views of the book's preparers or to renounce the utilization of the book" entirely. Therefore, readers of the series need not "agree with the beliefs [and] assumptions ... of its preparers" because "an effort has been made ... to represent the particular attachment and belief but not to impose it on the reader."[41]

In some cases, the IRGC authors push their impartiality too far by leaving the reader with an abundance of information but a dearth of analysis.[42] They do, however, define their approach in a manner that explains this lack of appraisal. According to the thirty-seventh volume of the *War Chronology*, the series addresses "this basic question about the Imposed War: 'Why and how did the war begin, why and how did it continue, and why and how did it end?'" This inquiry, they continue, "can be broken into the two main parts of 'why' and 'how.'" Their

[38] Ibid., 13.   [39] Ibid., 15–16.   [40] *Analysis 1*, 15–16.
[41] *Chronology 5*, 15–16. In this quote the HDRDC's former name was used.
[42] *Analysis 1*, 159–64; *Chronology 1*, 16; *Chronology of the Iran–Iraq War 2* (HDRDC, 1999), 25–27; *Chronology 5*, 13–14; *Chronology of the Iran–Iraq War 37* (HDRDC, 2004), 76.

concern is primarily with the latter rather than the former. The series "was designed firstly to answer questions related to the part of 'how' as comprehensively and precisely as possible; and secondly, in the part of 'why,' to prepare the necessary background for researchers and experts while avoiding presenting answers [that might] limit the field of research."[43]

The Guards further argue that historians have a responsibility to help their readers understand themselves and their methods, and that readers have a right to know what they are reading and who prepared it.[44] The appendix in the *Chronology*'s fourth volume begins with a section on "The Necessity of Introducing the Center [for Holy Defense Documentation] and Research," which explains that "every reader has the right to know what person or persons or what authority has prepared the book" being read and "to what extent" it can be trusted. This, the authors affirm, "is an honorable custom that must be considered," especially in "works that [deal with] sensitive subjects."[45] The fifth volume of that series makes a similar point but argues that the reader also has certain responsibilities in this regard. When assessing "a historical-research book," the "observant researcher" will examine not only "the accuracy of the beliefs and the scientific method" but also "who (or what group) wrote it." Judging the latter requires the reader to "consider that the writer exists within the hierarchy of political power of the day, what position and interests [the writer] might have, and under what exigencies and conditions the book was prepared."[46] These are tenets of historical research that have gained near-universal acceptance among scholars and that are imparted to students throughout their studies. Both the Guards' espousal of those tenets and the fact that in their work the Guards practice what they preach underscore the imperative of taking their work as historians seriously.

The IRGC authors indeed appreciate that presenting history faithfully requires much of the historian. In addition to guarding against the imposition of the subjective, the historian must also prevent the vicissitudes of time from distorting the record. When reconstructing the past, the Guards advise, historians should report events not as they are

---

[43] *Chronology* 37, 17.
[44] *Chronology* 1, 23, 25, 27; *Chronology* 2, 38; *Chronology* 5, 13–14.
[45] *Chronology of the Iran–Iraq War 4* (HDRDC, 1993), 585.
[46] *Chronology* 5, 12–13.

"today" but as they were on "that day," on the day they occurred. As the authors state in the seventh volume of the *War Chronology*:

The recording of events, subjects, and reports must be presented like daily memories [and] in the atmosphere of "that day" and not [of] "today." Presenting the history of the war in this manner is like presenting past days again. Each day of the war is reconstructed as much as possible as it was. The titles, individuals, tone of voice, manner of encounters, and the style of decision-making of each day is particular to that same day. Even the desires and ideals may appear particular to "that day" and will perhaps appear to differ from and contradict the exigencies and conditions of "today."

The authors then explain why preserving the integrity of history requires the adoption of this approach. First, doing so accounts for fluctuations in the power and status of individuals. Second, maintaining a firm distinction between then and now allows historians to extricate themselves more generally from the realities with which they are familiar. "The researcher and writer, disengaged from the exigencies of today and the evolutions of power, works with integrity to reconstruct the facts and events from the most important sources and foundations of scientific and scholarly credibility," they affirm.[47]

They appeal to their readers to do the same – to be aware of their own positions in relation to history and of how the passage of time affects their judgments. In addressing the distinction between "today" and "that day," this volume of the *Chronology* urges the reader to make that distinction as well, to "pass temporarily from the space of today and to settle in the space of that day," and with the appropriate "concerns, pleasures, sorrows, incentives, and disincentives."[48] In a volume of the *Survey* that discusses the liberation of Khorramshahr, the authors describe the position of the reader in a similar manner. Once again readers will travel back to the history and into the battle, and "from an elevated view of the scene will settle in the tempestuous atmosphere resulting from the fluctuations of the various stages of these operations."[49]

Another methodological issue to which the Revolutionary Guards pay close attention is the process through which historians select what to include, and what not to include, in their histories. Part of that

---

[47] *Chronology of the Iran–Iraq War 7-1* (HDRDC, 2006), 17–18. See also *Chronology 4*, 14; *Chronology 5*, 16–17.
[48] Ibid., 18.   [49] *Survey 1*, 15.

challenge is the need to weigh considerations of import against those of interest. The authors acknowledge their concern with holding their readers' attention and state that they "endeavored to establish a balance between presenting the incalculable mass of facts that will cause the reader's mind to recoil, and presenting the reader only with the writer's condensed selection." In the *Chronology* they accordingly tried to combine "reports that will seem important to some but not to others [and] in a way that both prevents the reports from becoming too numerous, scattered, and boring and that avoids eliminating reports that were deemed unimportant."[50] In other volumes the authors provide further information about how the reports were selected, indicating that the main criterion for inclusion was the directness of the report's bearing on the Iran–Iraq War.[51] They recognize that the immense volumes will be too cumbersome for some readers and accordingly included the condensed "Report of the *Chronology*" as well as an index to make the books more accessible.[52]

In some cases, they address the selection of materials in a more philosophical manner. In further discussing the format of the *Chronology*, the authors of the seventh volume pose questions with which all historians grapple. "What must be made of the mass of facts?" There must be some process of selection, as "the reader's patience and tolerance would not permit them all to be presented." In that case, "the facts must be chosen according to their importance. But what is the criterion of importance?" And who selects the criterion? This, too, will be subjective, because "perhaps an issue is not important to the researcher [and] therefore is eliminated or diminished, but the same issue might have particular importance for a diligent and discerning reader." The IRGC authors thus resign themselves to the inevitable, that researchers are left "to select facts with importance" and "to discern the important subjects themselves."[53]

Past and Present

This kind of discerning analysis permeates the IRGC sources. Just as they argue that understanding the Iran–Iraq War requires

---

[50] *Chronology 7-1*, 18.
[51] *Chronology of the Iran–Iraq War 54* (HDRDC, 2013), 50.
[52] *Chronology 1*, 19; *Chronology 5*, 18; *Chronology of the Iran–Iraq War 51* (HDRDC, 2008), 17, 57.
[53] *Chronology 7-1*, 18. See also *Chronology 5*, 17.

understanding war more broadly, the Revolutionary Guards argue
that understanding history is essential to both, because wars, like all
events, can only be understood as part of history. In their publications,
the IRGC authors accordingly spend a substantial amount of time
placing the events of the Iran–Iraq War in historical context, which
they then use as a basis for defining the conflict's meaning and importance. In the *War Chronology*, the first nine books of the fifty-seven-
volume series examine the period before the Iran–Iraq War even
begins. According to the first volume, "the Imposed War can only be
correctly understood if it is studied and comprehended in terms of the
events that preceded Iraq's comprehensive invasion and the planning
of this action."[54]

One reason why historical context is important in understanding
war is because the causes of conflicts originate in the past. According to
the *Analysis*, "the limitations, problems, ideals, goals, conflicts, and
antagonisms of states have roots in the past. It is possible that for a
time they remain hidden from view, sitting around with the dust of
history on them," but in a very short period the dust can be shaken off
and latent goals and disputes can reappear in new and potent forms.[55]
In this context, the force of history is manifest as either the source of
the factors that lead to war or as something that imparts those factors
with greater meaning. Indeed, history was at play in precisely this way
in the Iran–Iraq War, as historical grievances and ambitions did shape
Iraq's behavior and its decision to wage war.[56]

History is similarly indispensable in shaping national identity. In
every country, the IRGC authors write in the very first paragraph of
Battles on the East of the Karun, "history has an important impact on
national identity and strategic orientation. Therefore, recording
historical events" furnishes "a valuable reserve for every nation."
They further specify that "the historical and cultural identity of
nations depends on how they operate" in the course of "difficult events
and crises."[57]

The history of the Iran–Iraq War therefore stands out for its profound and sustained impact on Iran's national life and identity. One of

---

[54] *Chronology 1*, 27.   [55] *Analysis 1*, 19.
[56] Ibid., 32; *Chronology 1*, 16; *Critique and Review 2*, Chapter 3.
[57] *Battles on the East of the Karun* (HDRDC, 2000), 13.

the most important conclusions that must be drawn from the Guards' histories of the conflict is that they view the war's meaning and significance as boundless, as rivaling the repercussions of the Islamic Revolution itself. Because the war and the revolution are bound so closely together, neither one can be understood without the other.[58] As Rezaee wrote in the forward to the first volume of the *Analysis* series,

The Iran–Iraq war is linked closely to the Islamic Revolution, so without a correct understanding of [the war], it is impossible to understand the Islamic Revolution. This [war], because of its vast impact and outcomes, will affect every issue of internal and foreign policy of the Islamic Republic of Iran for at least the next several decades.[59]

Their appreciation of that fact explains why the Guards became and remain committed to writing the history of the conflict and why they assert that it "must be recorded, preserved, collected, and published" and then that it "must be taught and its teachings must be applied."[60] The war, the authors of a volume of the *Critique* series affirm, will remain "part of the reality of Iran's history," the "results and consequences" of which will remain "clear in ... the political, social, cultural, and military life of Iran." The authors of this volume argue that they do not expect that to change. Iran will continue to confront the legacy of the war, and the conflict will continue to "have a fundamental and fateful connection to the political-social life of Iran."[61]

The Holy Defense Research and Documentation Center has likewise continued to stress the seriousness and magnitude of this mission, "because explaining the events of the ... war, with its historical significance and consequences, requires national determination and will."[62] The HDRDC's head, Dr. Naini, noted in September 2019 that over time, and thirty-nine years after the beginning of the conflict, "every day [the war's] importance becomes clearer, and the need to recover that period increases," as "every day" of that era "was a lesson

---

[58] *Analysis 1*, 15; *Chronology 4*, 585; *Chronology 5*, 14. [59] *Analysis 1*, 15.
[60] *Chronology 1*, 15.
[61] *Critique and Review of the Iran–Iraq War 1*, 2nd ed. (HDRDC, 2003), 14–15.
[62] HDRDC "About Us" pages.

learned."[63] Uncovering those lessons would take centuries, Naini asserted.[64]

A Historical Imperative to Keep the War Alive

Indeed, in their publications the Revolutionary Guards argue that the impact of the Iran–Iraq War is so deep and vast that the Islamic Republic of Iran is essentially meaningless unless it is fully, actively, and appropriately recognized. Of particular importance is connecting the generations who did not live through the conflict to its history, and making them understand its meaning and significance. That is often the purpose of the IRGC's efforts to promote the history of the war among the Iranian population, especially during Holy Defense Week, and one that is often stated in its publications as well.[65]

The *Critique* series, for example, was published with the explicit purpose of examining the war's meaning for the Islamic Republic in the period after the conflict ended, of addressing "the difficulty and complexities of dealing with the outcomes of the war and [of how to] connect the generation [born] after the war to the achievements and experiences resulting from [the conflict]."[66] It explains that in the years since the ceasefire, "political, economic, and social changes and the presence of a new generation have changed the space of the country." Accordingly, "the danger of a break between generations and of forgetting or ignoring the legacy and achievements of the decade of revolution and war, and as a result the loss of the new generation's identity, is alarming."[67] This means that "the war and the manner of dealing with it are among the most important and most fundamental issues" that Iranian society has faced.[68]

---

[63] "If the Names and Memories of the Martyrs Are Not Cherished, the Enemy Becomes Dangerous," *Mehr News*, September 25, 2019 (Persian).

[64] "Products of the Documentation Center Increase 100-Fold in the Second Step of the Revolution," *Mehr News*, May 2, 2019 (Persian).

[65] "The Holy Defense Was a Major Test for the System," *Fars News*, September 24, 2011 (Persian); "Sepah Commander's Tears at the Funeral of Unknown Martyrs," *Fars News*, September 24, 2011 (Persian); "The Value of Holy Defense Must Be Transferred to the Young Generation," *Fars News*, September 24, 2011 (Persian); "Faith in God and the Leadership Is the Reason for Our Advantage in the Face of the Enemies' Equipment," *Fars News*, September 21 2019 (Persian); "The Culture of Holy Defense Must Be Put into Action."

[66] *Critique and Review* 1, 11.   [67] Ibid., 10.   [68] Ibid., 14–15.

These concerns reflect the fact that the history of the war will assume ever greater significance as Iranians become increasingly temporally removed from the conflict. The particular manner in which the war is understood is therefore of utmost importance, especially as those with no memory of the war inevitably come to dominate Iranian society. The way the postwar generations conceptualize the conflict will accordingly be "decisive."[69] Indeed, that issue is the decisive factor that will determine the war's impact on the Islamic Republic and the national identity of Iran. The Revolutionary Guards recognize this and have accordingly assumed what they see as the very serious responsibility of ensuring that the war outlives those who experienced it firsthand and is understood by those who will hold the Islamic Republic's future in their hands.

Essentially, then, the Guards are committed to ensuring that the war lives on. As Naini declared, "all of" the IRGC's "efforts are in order to prevent the forgetting of the history of the war."[70] In many instances, the Guards describe the recording of history as "keeping alive" the events of the past.[71] One of the challenges that makes preserving history so difficult is that the truths, realities, or facts of history cannot be obtained easily; the historian must endeavor tirelessly to discover and guard them. According to the IRGC authors, there is something hidden and intangible about history, something that is very difficult for anyone, even the historian, to get at, but that the historian must pursue nonetheless.[72]

This is the mission that lies at the core of the Guards' philosophy of history. As the *Guide Atlas* states, fully "describing these epics and the truths concealed in them is not possible," and even construing those "not remaining concealed required uninterrupted effort and the intertwining of the spirit and soul with the events of that era. But the importance of keeping [it] alive and of preventing its relegation and distortion inspired us to record ... this great epic."[73] The fourth

---

[69] Ibid., 15; *Khorramshahr in the Long War*, 2nd ed. (HDRDC, 1998), 12; *Communications and National Security in the Iran–Iraq War*, 10; *Battles on the East of the Karun*, 18.
[70] "The Culture of Holy Defense Must Be Extended in the Political and Economic Wars," *Mehr News*, November 3, 2018 (Persian).
[71] *Chronology 4*, 15; *Passage of Two Years of War* (IRGC Political Department, 1982), 17.
[72] *Chronology 4*, 11, 15, 590, 592; *Chronology 5*, 22; *Chronology 47*, 17.
[73] *Guide Atlas 1*, 8.

volume of the *War Chronology*, which was the first of the series to be published, echoes this explanation of how and why the IRGC took on the responsibility of recording the conflict. "The primary motivation," the authors explain, was "the fear that the events of the war" would be "erased," and that "the pure blood that had been spilled [would be] wasted."[74]

The Revolutionary Guards therefore regard history as an imperative. They postulate that action is meaningless in the absence of history. If the war was not recorded for history, then it would be worthless; the sacrifices of so many would have been made in vain. Also apparent in these passages is the sense of the fleeting, fragile, and singular nature of history – the idea that history is a collection of moments, any number of which can be lost forever in an instant if they are not kept alive by someone devoted to that mission. The fact that the project of recording the war's history began so early on in the conflict and grew right along with it indicates that the Revolutionary Guards must have immediately understood the transformative impact the war would have on them and on the Islamic Republic as a whole. The combination of that apprehension and the Guards' conviction that history gives meaning and permanence to actions constitutes the imperative that drives their efforts. Taken together, these conclusions reveal both why the Iran–Iraq War continues to pervade all that the Islamic Republic is and does and why the IRGC has devoted itself so earnestly to writing the conflict's unfinished history.

[74] *Chronology 4*, 586. See also *Chronology 1*, 23.

Bibliography

This bibliography includes most of the sources cited in the footnotes, plus additional sources.

Unless otherwise noted, materials were published in Tehran.

URLs for Iranian sources are highly unstable and unreliable. Those cited here reflect the URLs accessed during research and have been included for reference, but may no longer be accurate or active.

Sources Published by the IRGC's Holy Defense Research and Documentation Center (HDRDC) (Persian)

(formerly the Center for War Studies and Research)
(volumes marked * were published under the Center's former name)
Editions cited were those used; contributors, titles, and periodicals may vary by edition.

Chronology of the Iran–Iraq War

1*: *Emergence of the New System, Internal Crises and the Birth of the Armed Forces of the Revolution* (February 10, 1979 – May 6, 1979)
   Contributors: Mehdi Ansari, Alireza Lotfallah-Zadegan, Hadi Nakhai, Mohsen Rashid, Hossein Yekta
   First Edition Published 1997
2*: *Emergence of the New System, Crisis in Khuzistan* (May 7, 1979 – July 15, 1979)
   Contributors: Mehdi Ansari, Alireza Lotfallah-Zadegan, Hadi Nakhai, Mohsen Rashid, Hossein Yekta
   First Edition Published 1999
3: *Chaos in Paveh* (July 16, 1979 – September 6, 1979)
   Not Yet Published
4: *Acceptance of the Shah in America* (September 7, 1979 – November 3, 1979)
   Not Yet Published

5: *The Second Revolution Against America* (November 4, 1979 – January 4, 1980)

Not Yet Published

6: *The Ill-Fated Election of the First President of Iran* (January 5, 1980 – March 19, 1980)

Not Yet Published

7-1*: *America's Rupturing of Relations with Iran* (March 21, 1980 – April 20, 1980)

Contributors: Mehdi Ansari, Hossein Ardestani, Hamidreza Farahani, Mohammad Karami-Rad, Alireza Lotfallah-Zadegan, Sayyed-Mohammad-Baqer Madani, Majid Mokhtari, Hadi Nakhai, Mohsen Rakhsat-Talab

Published 2006–07

7-2: *Tabas to Sanandaj* (April 21, 1980 – May 21, 1980)

Contributors: Mehdi Ansari, Hossein Ardestani, Hamidreza Farahani, Hojjatollah Karimi, Alireza Lotfallah-Zadegan, Hadi Nakhai

Published 2018–19

8: *Economic Siege and the Nojeh Coup* (May 22, 1980 – July 22, 1980)

Not Yet Published

9: *Saddam's Decision for War Against Iran* (July 23, 1980 – September 21, 1980)

Contributors: Mehdi Ansari, Hossein Ardestani, Hamidreza Farahani, Alireza Lotfallah-Zadegan, Hadi Nakhai, Nematollah Soleimani-Khah

Published 2015

4* (now 10): *Full-Scale Invasion, Iraq's Main Offensive and Advances* (September 22, 1980 – October 26, 1980)

Contributors: Mehdi Ansari, Mohammad Doroodian, Martyr Mohammad Garkani, Alireza Lotfallah-Zadegan, Ibrahim Haji Mohammadzadeh, Hadi Nakhai, Davud Ranjbar, Mohsen Rashid, Hossein Yekta, Javad Zamanzadeh, Gholamreza Zarifiyan Shafii

First Edition Published 1993–94

5* (now 11): *Hoveyzeh, The Occupier's Last Steps* (October 27, 1980 – January 17, 1981)

Contributors: Mehdi Ansari, Alireza Lotfallah-Zadegan, Hadi Nakhai, Mohsen Rashid

First Edition Published 1994–95

12: *Establishment of a New Alliance (Cooperation Council) in the Region Against Iran* (January 6, 1981 – March 20, 1981)

Not Yet Published

13-1: *Continuation of the Occupation and Crisis* (March 21, 1981 – April 30, 1981)

Contributors: Mehdi Ansari, Hossein Ardestani, Farhad Darvishi Sehtelani, Hamidreza Farahani, Hojjatollah Karimi, Alireza Lotfallah-Zadegan, Mohammad Mohammadpur, Majid Mokhtari, Hadi Nakhai, Yaqub Nemati

Published 2015

13-2: *Crisis in the Supreme Command of the War* (May 1, 1981 – June 10, 1981)

Not Yet Published

14: *Removal of Bani-Sadr as Commander-in-Chief* (June 11, 1981 – July 22, 1981)

Not Yet Published

15: *Liberation of Iranian Territories, First Step* (July 23, 1981 – October 6, 1981)

Contributors: Mehdi Ansari, Hossein Ardestani, Hamidreza Farahani, Yadollah Izadi, Hojjatollah Karimi, Alireza Lotfallah-Zadegan, Hadi Nakhai

Published 2015–16

16: *Liberation of Iranian Territories, Second Step* (October 7, 1981 – December 21, 1981)

Contributors: Mehdi Ansari, Hossein Ardestani, Hamidreza Farahani, Alireza Lotfallah-Zadegan, Majid Mokhtari, Hadi Nakhai

Published 2015–16

17: *Mohammad Rasullah Operation on the Northern Front* (December 22, 1981 – February 19, 1982)

Not Yet Published

18: *Fath-ul-Mubin Operation* (February 20, 1982 – April 20, 1982)

Not Yet Published

19: *The Liberation of Khorramshahr* (April 21, 1982 – June 21, 1982)

Contributors: Mehdi Ansari, Hossein Ardestani, Hamidreza Farahani, Abolqasem Habibi, Hojjatollah Karimi, Alireza Lotfallah-Zadegan, Leila Saee Manish, Majid Mokhtari, Haniyeh Morshadi, Hadi Nakhai, Baqer Saburi

Published 2018–19

20*: *Crossing the Border; Pursuing the Aggressor in the Ramadan Operations* (June 22, 1982 – August 22, 1982)

Contributors: Mehdi Ansari, Alireza Lotfallah-Zadegan, Hadi Nakhai, Mohsen Rashid

Published 2002–03

21: *Muslim bin Aqil Operation* (August 23, 1982 – October 22, 1982)
    Contributors: Mehdi Ansari, Hossein Ardestani, Hamidreza
    Farahani, Mansur Keshavarz, Alireza Lotfallah-Zadegan,
    Majid Mokhtari, Hadi Nakhai
    Published 2012–13
22: *Muharram Operation* (October 23, 1982 – December 21, 1982)
    Contributors: Mehdi Ansari, Hossein Ardestani, Hamidreza
    Farahani, Mansur Keshavarz, Alireza Lotfallah-Zadegan,
    Majid Mokhtari, Hadi Nakhai
    Published 2014–15
23: *Preliminary Valfajr [Operation]* (December 22, 1982 – February
    19, 1983)
    Contributors: Mehdi Ansari, Hossein Ardestani, Hamidreza
    Farahani, Mansur Keshavarz, Alireza Lotfallah-Zadegan, Hadi
    Nakhai
    Published 2013–14
24: *Valfajr 1 Operation* (February 20, 1983 – April 20, 1983)
    Contributors: Mehdi Ansari, Hossein Ardestani, Hamidreza
    Farahani, Hojjatollah Karimi, Alireza Lotfallah-Zadegan, Hadi
    Nakhai
    Published 2015–16
25: *Dissolution of the Tudeh Party* (April 21, 1983 – June 21, 1983)
    Not Yet Published
26: *Valfajr 2 and 3 Operations* (June 22, 1983 – August 22, 1983)
    Not Yet Published
27: *Preparing Operation Valfajr 4* (August 23, 1983 – October 14, 1983)
    Contributors: Mohammad-Javad Akbarpur-Bazargani, Mehdi
    Ansari, Hossein Ardestani, Hamidreza Farahani, Hojjatollah
    Karimi, Alireza Lotfallah-Zadegan, Hadi Nakhai, Yaqub
    Nemati
    Published 2015–16
28: *First Major Operation in the Northwest* (October 15, 1983 – December
    21, 1983)
    Contributors: Mehdi Ansari, Hossein Ardestani, Hamidreza
    Farahani, Irraj Hemmati, Yadollah Izadi, Hojjatollah Karimi,
    Alireza Lotfallah-Zadegan, Majid Mokhtari
    Published 2015–16
29: *Preparations for War in the Marsh* (December 22, 1983 – February
    19, 1984)
    Not Yet Published

30: *Khaybar Operation* (February 20, 1984 – April 20, 1984)
Not Yet Published

31: *Beginning of the Tanker War* (April 21, 1984 – July 10, 1984)
Contributors: Mehdi Ansari, Hossein Ardestani, Hamidreza Farahani, Hojjatollah Karimi, Alireza Lotfallah-Zadegan, Hadi Nakhai, Mahmud Yazdanfam
Published 2018–19

32: *Stagnation on the Front; Movement in Diplomacy* (July 11, 1984 – September 21, 1984)
Contributors: Mehdi Ansari, Hossein Ardestani, Hamidreza Farahani, Hojjatollah Karimi, Alireza Lotfallah-Zadegan, Hadi Nakhai, Yaqub Nemati
Published 2019–20

33*: *Renewal of Relations of America and Iraq* (September 22, 1984 – November 26, 1984)
Contributors: Mehdi Ansari, Alireza Lotfallah-Zadegan, Hadi Nakhai, Mohsen Rashid
Published 2000

34: *Preparation for the Renewal of War in the Marsh* (November 28, 1984 – February 3, 1985)
Not Yet Published

35: *Badr Operation* (February 4, 1985 – April 7, 1985)
Not Yet Published

36: *Assassination of the Emir of Kuwait* (April 8, 1985 – June 13, 1985)
Not Yet Published

37*: *Expansion of Relations with the Asian Powers* (June 14, 1985 – August 21, 1985)
Contributors: Mehdi Ansari, Hamidreza Farahani, Alireza Lotfallah-Zadegan, Hadi Nakhai, Mohsen Rashid
Published 2004–05

38: *Imam's Command: Establishment of the Three Land, Air, and Naval Forces in the Sepah* (August 22, 1985 – November 6, 1985)
Not Yet Published

39-1: *First Step Toward the Conquest of Faw* (November 7, 1985 – December 14, 1985)
Contributors: Mehdi Ansari, Hossein Ardestani, Hamidreza Farahani, Alireza Lotfallah-Zadegan, Hadi Nakhai
Published 2015

39-2: *Intensification of Efforts for the Conquest of Faw* (December 15, 1985
– January 20, 1986)
Contributors: Mehdi Ansari, Hossein Ardestani, Hamidreza
Farahani, Hojjatollah Karimi, Alireza Lotfallah-Zadegan, Hadi
Nakhai
Published 2016–17
40: *Conquest of Faw and Iran's Readiness to End the War Justly and the
Negative Reaction of the International System* (January 21, 1986 –
February 25, 1986)
Not Yet Published
41: *Valfajr 9 Operation* (February 26, 1986 – April 29, 1986)
Not Yet Published
42-1: *Continuation of Iraq's Mobile Defense Strategy* (April 30, 1986 – June
4, 1986)
Contributors: Mehdi Ansari, Hossein Ardestani, Hamidreza
Farahani, Hojjatollah Karimi, Mehdi Haji Khodavardi-Khan,
Alireza Lotfallah-Zadegan, Hadi Nakhai
Published 2019–20
42-2: *Liberation of Mehran* (June 5, 1986 – July 8, 1986)
Contributors: Mehdi Ansari, Hossein Ardestani, Hamidreza
Farahani, Hojjatollah Karimi, Mehdi Haji Khodavardi-Khan,
Alireza Lotfallah-Zadegan, Hadi Nakhai
Published 2019–20
43*: *In Preparation for the Decisive Operations* (July 9, 1986 – September
11, 1986)
Contributors: Mehdi Ansari, Yahya Fauzi, Alireza Lotfallah-
Zadegan, Hadi Nakhai, Mohsen Rashid
Published 1999–2000
44*: *McFarlane's Adventure* (September 12, 1986 – November 13, 1986)
Contributors: Mehdi Ansari, Hossein Ardestani, Yahya Fauzi,
Alireza Lotfallah-Zadegan, Hadi Nakhai
First Edition Published 2001–02
45: *Consequences of the Disclosure of McFarlane's Adventure* (November
14, 1986 – December 25, 1986)
Not Yet Published
46: *Karbala 5 Operation* (December 26, 1986 – February 19, 1987)
Not Yet Published
47*: *Last Struggles in the South* (February 20, 1987 – April 11, 1987)
Contributors: Mehdi Ansari, Mohammad-Hossein Jamshidi,
Alireza Lotfallah-Zadegan, Hadi Nakhai, Mohsen Rashid,
Mahmud Yazdanfam
First Edition Published 2002–03

48: *Karbala 10 Operation* (April 12, 1987 – June 1, 1987)
Not Yet Published

49: *Approval of Resolution 598* (June 2, 1987 – July 20, 1987)
Contributors: Mehdi Ansari, Hossein Ardestani, Hamidreza Farahani, Alireza Lotfallah-Zadegan, Hadi Nakhai, Ahmad Nasrati, Mohsen Rakhsat-Talab
Published 2008–09

50*: *Escort of Tankers* (July 21, 1987 – September 22, 1987)
Contributors: Alireza Lotfallah-Zadegan, Mahmud Yazdanfam
First Edition Published 1999–2000

51*: *Limited War of Iran and America in the Persian Gulf* (September 23, 1987 – November 18, 1987)
Contributors: Mehdi Ansari, Hossein Ardestani, Hamidreza Farahani, Alireza Lotfallah-Zadegan, Hadi Nakhai, Mohsen Rakhsat-Talab, Mahmud Yazdanfam
First Edition Published 2008–09

52*: *Worldwide Search to End the War* (November 19, 1987 – January 14, 1988)
Contributors: Mehdi Ansari, Hossein Ardestani, Alireza Lotfallah-Zadegan, Hadi Nakhai, Mohsen Rashid, Khosru Shah-Mohammadi
First Edition Published 2003–04

53-1: *Major Winter Battle on the Northern Front* (January 15, 1988 – February 12, 1988)
Contributors: Mehdi Ansari, Hossein Ardestani, Hamidreza Farahani, Yadollah Izadi, Hojjatollah Karimi, Alireza Lotfallah-Zadegan, Hadi Nakhai, Ahmad Nasrati
Published 2019–20

53-2: *Preparation of the Valfajr 10 Operation* (February 13, 1988 – March 12, 1988)
Not Yet Published

54: *Valfajr 10 Operation, Chemical Bombardment of Halabja, International Pressure on Iran to Accept Resolution 598* (March 13, 1988 – April 16, 1988)
Contributors: Mehdi Ansari, Hossein Ardestani, Hamidreza Farahani, Yadollah Izadi, Mansur Keshavarz, Alireza Lotfallah-Zadegan, Hadi Nakhai
Published 2013–14

55: *Iraq's Single Success in Faw with the Use of Chemical Materials* (April 17, 1988 – May 26, 1988)
Not Yet Published

56: *Acceptance of Resolution 598* (May 27, 1988 – July 18, 1988)
Not Yet Published
57: *Defeat of Iraq in Its Renewed Occupation of Khuzistan, Ceasefire* (July 19, 1988 – August 20, 1988)
Not Yet Published

Analysis of the Iran–Iraq War

1*: *Roots of Invasion*
Contributors: Farhad Darvishi, Khosru Shah-Mohammadinezhad, Beha-Aldin Sheikh-Alislami
Second Edition Published 2001–02
2*: *War, Regaining Stability*
Contributors: Mohammad Doroodian, Khosru Shah-Mohammadi, Beha-Aldin Sheikh-Alislami
Published 1999–2000
3*: *Punishing the Aggressor*
Contributors: Hossein Ardestani, Majid Mokhtari, Mohsen Rashid, Khosru Shah-Mohammadinezhad
Second Edition Published 2005–06

Survey of the Iran–Iraq War

1*: *Khuninshahr to Khorramshahr*
Contributors: Mehdi Ansari, Mohammad Doroodian, Beha-Aldin Sheikh-Alislami
Fourth Edition Published 1998–99
2*: *Khorramshahr to Faw*
Contributors: Mohammad Doroodian, Beha-Aldin Sheikh-Alislami
Fifth Edition Published 1999–2000
3*: *From Faw to Shalamcheh*
Contributors: Mohammad Doroodian, Gholam-Ali Rashid, Beha-Aldin Sheikh-Alislami
First Edition Published 1994–95
4*: *Shalamcheh to Halabjah*
Contributors: Mehdi Ansari, Mohammad Doroodian, Beha-Aldin Sheikh-Alislami
Third Edition Published 2002–03
5*: *End of the War*
Contributors: Mohammad Doroodian, Beha-Aldin Sheikh-Alislami
Published 1999–2000

6*: *Beginning to End*
    Contributors: Mehdi Ansari, Mohammad Doroodian, Beha-Aldin
      Sheikh-Alislami
    First Edition Published 1997–98

Critique and Review of the Iran–Iraq War

1*: *Basic Questions of the War*
    Contributors: Mohammad Doroodian, Beha-Aldin Sheikh-Alislami
    Second Edition Published 2003–04
2*: *The Inevitability of the War*
    Contributors: Mehdi Ansari, Mohammad Doroodian, Beha-Aldin
      Sheikh-Alislami
    Second Edition Published 2004–05
3*: *Reasons for the War's Continuation*
    Contributors: Mehdi Ansari, Mohammad Doroodian, Beha-Aldin
      Sheikh-Alislami
    Published 2003–04
4: *The Process of Ending the War*
    Contributors: Mohammad Doroodian, Gholam-Ali Rashid, Beha-
      Aldin Sheikh-Alislami
    Fourth Edition Published 2015–16
5*: *Strategic Choices of the War*
    Contributors: Mohammad Doroodian, Gholam-Ali Rashid
    Published 2007–08

Guide Atlas

1*: *Khuzistan in the War*
    Contributors: Mehdi Ansari, Abolqasem Habibi, Mohsen Rashid
    Fifth Edition Published 2002–03
2*: *Khorramshahr in the War*
    Contributors: Abolqasem Habibi, Mohsen Rashid
    First Edition Published 2001–02
3*: *Ilam in the War*
    Contributors: Mehdi Ansari, Mohsen Rashid, Amir Razzaqzadeh
    Published 2001–02
4: *Dasht-e Azadegan in the War*
    Contributors: Mehdi Ansari, Abolqasem Habibi, Mohsen Rashid
    Third Edition Published 2011–12

5*: *Record of Land Battles*
    Contributors: Mehdi Ansari, Hassan Dorri, Mohsen Rashid
    Published 2002–03
6*: *Abadan in the War*
    Contributors: Mehdi Ansari, Abolqasem Habibi, Mohsen
        Rakhsat-Talab
    Published 2003–04
7*: *Kermanshah in the War*
    Contributors: Mehdi Ansari, Hassan Dorri, Mohsen Rashid
    Published 2004–05
8*: *Dezful, Shush, Andimeshk in the War*
    Contributors: Mehdi Ansari, Abolqasem Habibi, Mohsen
        Rakhsat-Talab
    Published 2006–07
9: *Kurdistan in the Counterinsurgency War and the Holy Defense*
    Published 2011–12
10: *Mehran in the War*
    Published 2011–12
11: *Paveh in the Counterinsurgency War and the Holy Defense*
    Published 2012–13
12: *Western Azerbaijan in the War with the Counter-Revolution and the
        Holy Defense*
    Published 2012–13

Unit Atlases

Atlas of the 7th Vali-Asr Division in the Period of Holy Defense
    Contributors: Abdolmohammad Kuchak, Akbar Rostami
    Published 2019–20
Atlas of the 31st Ashura Division in the Period of Holy Defense
    Contributors: Jalal Mabudi, Mohsen Rashid
    Published 2019–20
Atlas of the 41st Sarollah Division in the Eight Years of Holy Defense
    Contributors: Hossein Ardestani, Abbas Mirzaei, Mohsen Rashid
    Published 2016–17

Other Atlases

Atlas of the Epic of Khorramshahr
    Contributors: Mohsen Rakhsat-Talab, Mohsen Rashid
    Published 2019–20

Atlas of the Iran–Iraq War: Concise Summary of Land Battles
   Third Edition Published 2013–14
Atlas of Khuzistan in the Iran–Iraq War
   Contributors: Majid Mokhtari, Ali Shamkhani
   Published 2013–14
Statistical Atlas of the War of the Cities
   Contributors: Mehdi Ansari, Maryam Haqani Montazeri, Musa
      Kazemi, Sayyed-Naser Keshavarz, Mohsen Rashid, Ali Sadeqi
   Published 2018–19

Monographs about Specific Battles

*Battles on the East of the Karun According to the Commanders'
   Narrative**
   Contributors: Mehdi Ansari, Sayyed-Ali Bani-Luhi, Mohsen
      Mohammadi, Hadi Moradpiri, Gudarz Nowruzi, Yahya Safavi
   First Edition Published 2000
*Khorramshahr in the Long War**
   Contributors: Mehdi Ansari, Mohammad Doroodian, Hadi Nakhai
   Second Edition Published 1998–99
*The Sepah Pasdaran's First Naval Operations in the Persian Gulf, Battle of
   al-Omayyeh**
   Contributors: Mehdi Ansari, Martyr Sayyed-Mohammad Ishaqi, Mehdi
      Khodavardikhan, Hadi Nakhai, Beha-Aldin Sheikh-Alislami
   Published 1996–97

Other Books and Periodicals

*Communications and National Security in the Iran–Iraq War**
   Contributors: Hossein Ardestani, Mohammad-Baqer Heshmatzadeh,
      Majid Mokhtari
   Published 2001
*Introduction to the War 1: Short Report**
   Contributors: Mehdi Ansari, Mohsen Rashid
   Published 1999–2000
The Iran–Iraq War: Roots and Reasons of Occurrence (Collection of Articles)
   Published 2009–10
Iran's Economy During the Imposed War
   Contributors: Mehdi Ansari, Farhad Dezhpasand, Hamid-Reza Raufi
   Published 2008–09
Negin Iran
   www.defamoghaddas.ir/portal/journal/type/92

Current Editors: Mohammad-Javad Akbarpour Bazargani, Hamid
    Aslani,Ali Fadavi, Mostafa Izadi, Ali-Mohammad Naini, Yahya
    Niazi, Hossein Salami
Yahyavi, Sayyed-Hossein, "War of the Cities," 10.36 (2011).

Articles from the Center's Website

www.defamoghaddas.ir
http://shop.hdrdc.ir/

"About Us" Pages – www.defamoghaddas.ir/portal/page/48, www
    .defamoghaddas.ir/portal/page/47
"Brookings Report on the Effect of the Holy Defense on the Path of Figures
    Like Martyr Commander Soleimani," January 13, 2020, www
    .defamoghaddas.ir/portal/news/print/93.
"Full Text of Martyr Hajj Qasem Soleimani's Will," February 15, 2020,
    www.defamoghaddas.ir/portal/news/print/128.
"Holding of the 'Commander Martyr Hajj Soleimani Book Award' on the
    Fortieth Anniversary of the Imposed War," February 15, 2020, www
    .defamoghaddas.ir/portal/news/print/129.
"Picture of Half-Burned Draft of Sepah Statute," April 20, 2020,
    www.defamoghaddas.ir/portal/news/print/315.
"Sepah Statement: We Will Be on the Scene Until We Completely Overcome
    the Coronavirus," March 1, 2020, www.defamoghaddas.ir/portal/
    news/print/143.
"The Superpowers' Friendship with Us Is Like the Friendship of a Wolf
    and a Sheep," January 11, 2020, www.defamoghaddas.ir/portal/
    news/print/88.
"Supreme Leader in a Visit with the People of Qum," January 8, 2020,
    www.defamoghaddas.ir/portal/news/print/86.
"Victory in Faw Indicated the Error in Hashemi's Thinking," November 30,
    2019, www.defamoghaddas.ir/portal/news/print/24.
"We Have No Desire but to Sacrifice for the Security and Wellbeing of the
    People," January 13, 2020, http://www.defamoghaddas.ir/portal/news/
    print/92.
"What Actions Did the Commanders Take After Learning of the
    Cancellation of the Karbala 4 Operation," February 8, 2020, www
    .defamoghaddas.ir/portal/news/print/117.
"What Was Iran's Goal in Continuing the War After the Conquest of
    Khorramshahr?," May 19, 2020, www.defamoghaddas.ir/portal/news/
    print/353.

Other IRGC Branches (Persian)

Journal of Defense Policy
(Imam Hossein University, Periodical), https://dpj.ihu.ac.ir/.

Daulat-Abadi, Ali Baqeri, "The Role of Deterrence in the Military Strategy of Iran," 22.85 (2013).
Mohammad-Pur, Said, "The Impact of the Ramazan Garrison's Irregular Operations in the Imposed War," 12.47 (2004).
Rashid, Gholam-Ali, "Conditions and Exigencies of the Birth, Development, Consolidation, and Expansion of the Sepah in the War," 7.19 (1997).

Others

Message of Revolution (IRGC, Periodical).
Passage of Two Years of War (IRGC Political Department, 1982–83).
Plot Line (IRGC Political Department, 1987).
Toward Karbala (IRGC, 1981).

Materials Published by the Iranian Government and Leaders (Persian)

Majlis (Islamic Consultative Assembly, Parliament)

Constitution, http://rc.majlis.ir/fa/law/show/132239.
"General Policies of the System in the Forthcoming Period," Majlis Research Center, November 3, 2003, https://rc.majlis.ir/fa/law/show/132299.
"Iran's National Security in Theory and Practice," Majlis Research Center, 1999, https://rc.majlis.ir/fa/report/show/732615.
"Saddam Hussein's Set of Assets Was Destroyed with the Conquest of Khorramshahr," ICANA, May 22, 2011, www.icana.ir/Fa/News/165109.
"Soft Power, Soft Technology, and Its Effects and Applications in the Defense Sector," Majlis Research Center, 2007, https://rc.majlis.ir/fa/report/show/732797.

Others

Jafari, Mohammad Ali, *Dusty Overlays* (Soore Mehr, 2016).
Khamenei, Ali, "America's Strategic Steps for Influence in Iran," September 19, 2015, https://farsi.khamenei.ir/others-note?id=30796.

"The Leader of the Revolution's Answers to Ten Questions About the Historical Struggle of the Iranian Nation with America," December 6, 2012, http://farsi.khamenei.ir/print-content?id=21721.

Khomeini, Ruhollah, "If the Sepah Did Not Exist, the Country Would Also Not Exist," April 10, 2019, www.imam-khomeini.ir/fa/NewsPrint .aspx?ID=2240.

Ministry of the Interior, "Governor of Eastern Azerbaijan Emphasizes Utilizing the Management Style of the Holy Defense," September 26, 2015, www.moi.ir/fa/%D8%A7%D8%AE%D8%A8%D8%A7% D8%B1/35829.

Rezaee, Mohsen, Online Archive, http://rezaee.ir/fa/archive.

Rafsanjani, Akbar Hashemi, Online Memoirs, https://rafsanjani.ir/diaries.

Rouhani, Hassan, "Confrontation with Iran, Big Mistake of Powers and Reactionaries," September 22, 2014, http://president.ir/fa/81065.

"Text of the President's Speech at the Country's Annual Defensive Industry Day Ceremony," August 22, 2015, www.president.ir/fa/ 88805/printable.

Safavi, Yahya, Website, www.yahyasafavi.com/index.php/fa/.

War Information Headquarters, Supreme Defense Council, *The Imposed War: Defense vs. Aggression*, 5 Volumes (1983–87) (English).

Zarif, Mohammad Javad (@JZarif), "Honored to meet top cmdrs," Twitter, April 10, 2019 (English), https://twitter.com/JZarif/status/ 1115962335313657856?s=20.

"Iran's Message: Our Counterparts Must Choose Between Agreement and Coercion," YouTube (video), July 3, 2015 (English), www.youtube.com/watch?v=cw71HMKDpco.

US Government Materials

CIA World Factbook: Iran, www.cia.gov/library/publications/the-world-fact book/geos/ir.html.

CIA World Factbook: Iraq, www.cia.gov/library/publications/the-world-fact book/geos/iz.html.

CIA, "Khuzestan: Iran's Achilles Tendon" (Undated), www.cia.gov/library/ readingroom/docs/CIA-RDP09-00438R000100380001-7.pdf.

McLaurin, R. D., "Technical Memorandum 13-82, Military Operations in the Gulf War: The Battle of Khorramshahr (Aberdeen Proving Ground, MD: US Army Human Engineering Laboratory, July 1982).

Metz, Helen Chapin, ed., *Iran: A Country Study* (Washington: GPO for the Library of Congress, 1987).

Iraq: A Country Study (Washington: GPO for the Library of Congress, 1988).
"Report of the President's Special Review Board (Tower Commission)," February 26, 1987, https://archive.org/details/TowerCommission/mode/2up.
US Navy, "Formal Investigation into the Circumstances Surrounding the Attack on the *USS Stark* (FFG 31) on May 17, 1987," June 12, 1987, www.jag.navy.mil/library/investigations/USS%20STARK%20BASIC.pdf.

United Nations Materials

IAEA Board of Governors, "Final Assessment on Past and Present Outstanding Issues Regarding Iran's Nuclear Programme," GOV/2015/68, December 2, 2015, www.iaea.org/sites/default/files/gov-2015-68.pdf.
"No. 14903 Iran and Iraq," *Treaty Series: Treaties and International Agreements Registered or Filed and Recorded with the Secretariat of the United Nations, Volume 1017* (New York: United Nations, 1986), https://treaties.un.org/doc/Publication/UNTS/Volume%201017/v1017.pdf.
"Security Council Toughens Sanctions Against Iran, Adds Arms Embargo, with Unanimous Adoption of Resolution 1747 (2007)," March 24, 2007, www.un.org/press/en/2007/sc8980.doc.htm.
"Secretary-General Dismayed at Iraq's Intention to Resume Attacks on Iran's Civilian Areas," *UN Chronicle* 22.7 (July 1985).
UN Security Council, "Resolution 479 (1980) of 28 September 1980," https://digitallibrary.un.org/record/16029?ln=en.
"Resolution 514 (1982) of 12 July 1982," https://digitallibrary.un.org/record/31564?ln=en.
"Resolution 598 (1987) of 20 July 1987," https://peacemaker.un.org/iraqiran-resolution598.

Iranian News Sources and Websites

Defa Press (Persian)

"Note from Mohammad Doroodian: Recalling the Founders of the Sepah Political Bureau," May 31, 2014, www.defapress.ir/fa/print/20511.
"Visit of the Head of the Holy Defense Research and Documentation Center [with] the Holy Defense News Agency," September 15, 2019, https://defapress.ir/fa/print/361789.

Fars News (Persian)

"America Does Not Have the Ability to Confront Our Defensive System," January 8, 2014, www.farsnews.ir/printnews/13921018000867.

"The Army Is the Impregnable Fortress of the Revolution and the Strong Arm of the Nation," April 17, 2011, www.farsnews.ir/printnews/9001280173.

"Commander Jazayeri: Those Who Put Confidence in America Are Not Familiar with America or [Its] Policy," September 24, 2013, www.farsnews.ir/printnews/13920702000676.

"Commemorating the Holy Defense Adheres to the Values of the Revolution," September 24, 2011, www.farsnews.ir/printnews/13900702000440.

"The Culture of Holy Defense Must Be Put into Action," September 24, 2011, www.farsnews.ir/printnews/13900702000117.

"Establishment of Exhibition of Holy Defense Achievements in Sanandaj," September 24, 2011, www.farsnews.ir/printnews/13900702000373.

"Faith in God and the Leadership Is the Reason for Our Advantage in the Face of the Enemies' Equipment," September 21, 2019, www.farsnews.ir/printnews/13980630001213.

"Full Text of the Imam's Letter on the Acceptance of Resolution 598," July 20, 2007, www.farsnews.com/printable.php?nn=8604170080.

"Funeral of Two Anonymous Martyrs of the Holy Defense," September 24, 2011, www.farsnews.ir/printnews/13900702000137.

"Global Post: Sanctions or Military Attack Against Iran Are Useless," April 3, 2012, www.farsnews.ir/printnews/13910115000949.

"Holding of Parade of Armed Forces of Markazi Province in 12 Regions," September 21, 2019, www.farsnews.ir/printnews/13980630000697.

"The Holy Defense Was a Major Test for the System," September 24, 2011, www.farsnews.ir/printnews/13900702000370.

"How the Operation of Martyr Ghayur Asli Was Carried Out," October 2, 2008, www.farsnews.ir/printnews/8706311053.

"Implementation of 300 Programs During Holy Defense Week," September 21, 2019, www.farsnews.ir/printnews/13980630000656.

"Implementing 30 Holy Defense Week Special Programs in Damavand," September 21, 2019, www.farsnews.ir/printnews/13980630001174.

"Implementing 50 Distinctive Programs During Holy Defense Week [in] Pardis," September 21, 2019, www.farsnews.ir/printnews/13980630000986.

"The Imposed War Was the Basis of Our Holy Defense," September 21, 2019, www.farsnews.ir/printnews/13980630001049.

"In the Case of Enemy Attack, We Pursue [the Enemy] to Our Borders, Punish, and Destroy [Him]," March 11, 2011, www.farsnews.ir/print news/8912200233.

"Iran's Distrust of America Persists," December 12, 2013, www.farsnews.ir/printnews/13920921000867.

"Lessons of Iran's Resistance Against Saddam for Today," August 8, 2012, www.farsnews.ir/printnews/13910517000675.

"Lurdigan Basiji Women's Shooting Competitions Held," September 24, 2011, www.farsnews.ir/printnews/13900701000516.

"More Than 100 Holy Defense Programs Being Held in Baqershahr, Kahrizak, Fashafuyeh," September 21, 2019, www.farsnews.ir/print news/13980630000971.

"Political Independence and the Training of Managers Were Among the Most Important Achievements of the Holy Defense," September 24, 2011, www.farsnews.ir/printnews/13900702000045.

"Resistance to the Islamic Republic Has Led to America's Decline," September 21, 2019, www.farsnews.ir/printnews/13980630000519.

"Self-Reliance Was the Achievement of the Holy Defense," September 24, 2011, www.farsnews.ir/printnews/13900702000472.

"Sepah Commander's Tears at the Funeral of Unknown Martyrs," September 24, 2011, www.farsnews.ir/printnews/13900702000344.

"Sepah's Newest Anti-Ship and Supersonic Missiles on Display," September 24, 2011, www.farsnews.ir/printnews/13900702000043.

"The Unequal War Against Iran Humiliated Arrogance," September 24, 2011, www.farsnews.ir/printnews/13900702000461.

"The Value of Holy Defense Must Be Transferred to the Young Generation," September 24, 2011, www.farsnews.ir/printnews/13900702000310.

"The Way Out of Problems and the Dignity of the Islamic Revolution Is Possible with the Discourse of Resistance," September 21, 2019, www .farsnews.ir/printnews/13980630001019.

"We Are Still in the Beginning of the Path of Holy Defense," September 24, 2011, www.farsnews.ir/printnews/13900702000476.

"We Will Not Reduce the Range of Our Missiles," December 10, 2013, https://web.archive.org/web/20150424025615/http://www.farsnews .com/newstext.php?nn=13920919001701.

"The Will of the Imam Is the Charter of the Revolution," September 24, 2011, www.farsnews.ir/printnews/13900701000552.

Fars News (English)

"Army's Ground Force Kicks Off Massive Military Drills in Central Iran," May 24, 2017, https://en.farsnews.ir/newstext.aspx?nn=13960303000974.

"Basij Commander: Decisions in Geneva II Fruitless Without Iran's Presence," January 8, 2014, https://en.farsnews.ir/newstext.aspx?nn= 13921018001136.

"Basij Commander: Iran's Problem with US Not Related to Confidence-Building," December 4, 2013, https://en.farsnews.ir/newstext.aspx? nn=13920913000880.

"Commander Stresses Dynamism in IRGC Strategies," August 15, 2009, http:// english.farsnews.com/newstext.php?nn=8805241281.

"DM: Iran Plans to Build More Powerful Surface-to-Surface Missile Systems," April 8, 2014, https://en.farsnews.ir/newstext.aspx?nn= 13930119001275.

"DM: Iran's Defense Capacities Ten Folded," October 25, 2016, https://en .farsnews.ir/newstext.aspx?nn=13950804000962.

"Iraqi DM Visits Exhibition on Iran's Military Equipment, Missile Capabilities," December 30, 2014, https://en.farsnews.ir/newstext .aspx?nn=13931009001466.

"IRGC Commander: US Unable to Resolve Regional Crises Without Iran," January 11, 2014, https://en.farsnews.ir/newstext.aspx?nn=13921021001163.

"Senior Commander Downplays Enemy Plots Against Iran," April 30, 2011, http://english.farsnews.com/newstext.php?nn=9002101259.

"Western Media Misreport Story to Inspire Public with Widening Rifts in Iran's Political System," December 24, 2013, https://en.farsnews.ir/ newstext.aspx?nn=13921003001600.

Iran Book News Agency (IBNA) (Persian)

"IBNA Interview with Mohsen Rashid About the First War Writers," April 20, 2009, www.ibna.ir/fa/doc/tolidi/37946/.

"Journey to the Depths of War," January 31, 2006, www.ibna.ir/vdcaiwn6 .49nmo15kk4.html.

Islamic Republic News Agency (IRNA) (Persian)

"Commander Vahidi: The Liberation of Khorramshahr Was a Great Cultural and Self-Affirming Victory," May 24, 2011, http://irna.ir/ NewsShow.aspx?NID=30399686.

"Constructive Interaction Between Iran and Turkey," August 10, 2015, www.irna.ir/news/81714363/.

"Review of Rouhani's Remarks in World Media: Iran Is the Best Defense Against Terror in the Middle East," September 22, 2015, www.irna.ir/ fa/News/81769710/.

Iranian Students' News Agency (ISNA) (Persian)

"Commander Kazemeini: Geneva Talks Are in the Interest of the Iranian Nation," November 24, 2013, www.isna.ir/news/92090302177/.

"A Memoir for Hadi Nakhai, Imposed War Narrator," December 13, 2018, www.isna.ir/news/97092211104/.

Mehr News (Persian)

"Commander Naini Becomes Head of the Sepah Holy Defense Research and Documentation Center," October 3, 2018, mehrnews.com/xJSY.

"The Culture of Holy Defense Must Be Extended in the Political and Economic Wars," November 3, 2018, mehrnews.com/xMPGM.

"Holding of Friendly Meeting with More Than 100 Holy Defense Researchers During Research Week," December 9, 2019, mehrnews.com/xQLhS.

"If the Names and Memories of the Martyrs Are Not Cherished, the Enemy Becomes Dangerous," September 25, 2019, mehrnews.com/xQcfT.

"Operation Karbala 4 Determined the Fate of the War," January 7, 2019, mehrnews.com/xNjYc.

"Products of the Documentation Center Increase 100-Fold in the Second Step of the Revolution," May 2, 2019, mehrnews.com/xP9tm.

Mehr News (English)

"Imposed War Brought Sustainable Security to Iran: Ex-IRGC Chief," September 26, 2009, en.mehrnews.com/news/36073/.

"Iran Should Be Prepared for Every Imaginable Scenario: General," August 30, 2010, en.mehrnews.com/news/41629/.

Tasnim News (Persian)

"Commander Naini Becomes Head of the Sepah Holy Defense Research and Documentation Center," October 3, 2017, https://tn.ai/1535450.

"The Issue-Oriented and Documented Approach to the Holy Defense," May 13, 2013, https://tn.ai/55298.

"A Look at Naini's Records," August 2, 2014, https://tn.ai/448127.

"We Are Waiting for the West's Real Commitment to Its Promises," November 25, 2013, https://tn.ai/201725.

Other (Persian)

"Eight Deterrence Capabilities of the Islamic Republic of Iran," *Afkar News*, October 11, 2014, www.afkarnews.com/fa/tiny/news-368327.

"The Commander Who Drove Saddam Back Behind Bostan with 40 People," *Tabnak*, October 12, 2011, www.tabnak.ir/fa/print/196577.

Doroodian, Mohammad, Website, www.m-doroodian.ir/.

　"Interview with Book News Agency," May 14, 2014, www.m-doroodian .ir/post/133, www.m-doroodian.ir/post/135.

"Hadi Nakhai Passed Away," *Feydus*, December 10, 2016, http://feydus.ir/ fa/print/32782.

"Overview of the Research Activities of the Center for War Studies and Research," Resource Center for Holy Defense Sciences and Education, May 26, 2010, http://dsrc.ir/view/articleFrame.aspx?ID=1001&PF=true.

Rashid, Mohsen, Website, http://mohsenrashid.persianblog.ir/.

"Salami: Egypt Is the Political Life Harbor of the Zionist Regime," *Mashregh News*, February 1, 2011, mshrgh.ir/27572.

"The Victory of Lebanese Hezbollah in the 33-Day War Was the Fruit of the Blood Spilled in the Eight Years of Holy Defense, " *Rasa News*, May 23, 2011, https://rasanews.ir/fa/print/105241.

"Which Countries Armed Saddam to the Teeth?," *Parsine*, October 12, 2013, www.parsine.com/000e6J.

Other (English)

"Basij Makes Iran's Enemies Quake in Their Boots," *Tehran Times*, November 26, 2008, www.tehrantimes.com/news/183368/Basij-makes-Iran-s-enemies-quake-in-their-boots.

"Bush Trying to Foment Discord in Mideast: IRGC Commander," *Tehran Times*, January 28, 2008, www.tehrantimes.com/news/162107/Bush-trying-to-foment-discord-in-Mideast-IRGC-commander.

"Historical Photos: 23 May 1981, Khorramshahr Liberation Day," Photos by *IRNA*, *Payvand*, May 23, 2009, www.payvand.com/news/09/may/ 1248.html.

"IRGC Commander: Basij Forces Boost Iran's Power of Deterrence," *Tasnim News*, November 30, 2015, https://tn.ai/207033.

"IRGC Commander: Supreme Leader's Words, Nation's Guidelines," *IRNA*, December 12, 2013, https://en.irna.ir/news/80947665/IRGC-C ommander-Supreme-Leader-s-Words-Nation-s-Guidelines.

"Prevailing Global Situation Demands Readiness to Ward Off Threats: Substitute Commander," *Tehran Times*, September 21, 2003, www

.tehrantimes.com/news/104622/Prevailing-Global-Situation-Demands-R-eadiness-to-Ward-off-Threats.

Qahremanpour, Rahman, "Iran's Deterrence Strategy," *Islamic Republic of Iran Diplomacy*, August 25, 2010, www.irdiplomacy.ir/en/news/8481/iran-s-deterrence-strategy.

"Soft War vs. Holy Defense Values," *IBNA*, March 4, 2011, www.ibna.ir/vdcgnw9y.ak97z4j5ra.html.

Other Persian Sources

Eftekhari, Asghar and Mohammad Janipoor, "The Bases of the Soft Power of Iran's Islamic Revolution," *Islamic Revolution Research Journal* 3.9 (2014), https://rjir.basu.ac.ir/article_674.html.

Golshan, Alireza and Mohsen Baqeri, "The Place of Lebanese Hezbollah in the Islamic Republic of Iran's Deterrence Strategy," *Journal of Political and International Research* 4.11 (2012), www.sid.ir/Fa/Journal/ViewPaper.aspx?id=193884.

Harsij, Hossein, Mojtaba Touyserkani, and Leila Jafari, "Iran's Soft Power Geopolitics," *Political Science Research Journal* 4.2 (2009), www.ipsajournal.ir/article_91_353b96bfff668efd00dd68fd25cd2663.pdf.

Hejazi, Sayyid Hossein, "The Soft Power Capabilities of the Islamic Republic of Iran in Confronting America's Soft Threats," *Report of the Republic*, 2008.

Ketabi, Mahmood and Ahmad Rastineh, "The Doctrine of Constructive Interaction in Iran's Foreign Policy and the New Geopolitics of Iraq," *Journal of International Political Research* 1.3 (2009), www.magiran.com/volume/57422.

Ketabi, Mahmoud, Enayatollah Yazdani, and Masoud Rezaei, "Soft Power and America's Hegemonic Strategy,"*Political Knowledge* 8.16 (2012), http://pkn.journals.isu.ac.ir/article_1332.html.

Vaezi, Mahmoud, "Iran in the New Balance of Power in the Middle East," Expediency Council Center for Strategic Research, July 7, 2007, www.isrjournals.com/en/experts/660-archive-special-articles-farsi-79.html.

"The Strategy of Constructive Interaction and the Requirements of Development-Oriented Foreign Policy," Expediency Council Center for Strategic Research, June 7, 2008, www.isrjournals.com/fa/special-articles/636-archive-special-articles-farsi-56.html.

English-Language Books and Articles

Abdulghani, Jasim M., *Iraq and Iran: The Years of Crisis* (Baltimore: Johns Hopkins University Press, 1984).

Abedin, Mahan, "Iran's Revolutionary Guards: Ideological but Not Praetorian," *Strategic Analysis* 35.3 (2011).

Abrahamian, Ervand, *Iran Between Two Revolutions* (Princeton: Princeton University Press, 1982).

Adelman, Jonathan, *Revolution, Armies, and War: A Political History* (Boulder: Lynne Rienner, 1985).

Adib-Moghaddam, Arshin, "Inventions of the Iran–Iraq War," *Critique: Critical Middle Eastern Studies* 16.1 (2007).

Ahmadi, Kourosh, *Islands and International Politics in the Persian Gulf: Abu Musa and the Tunbs in Strategic Perspective* (Milton Park: Routledge, 2008).

Al-i Ahmad, Jalal, *Occidentosis: A Plague from the West*, trans. R. Campbell (Berkeley: Mizan Press, 1984).

Alemzadeh, Maryam, "The Islamic Revolutionary Guards Corps in the Iran–Iraq War: An Unconventional Military's Survival," *British Journal of Middle Eastern Studies* 46.4 (2019).

Alfoneh, Ali, "All the Guard's Men," *World Affairs* 173.3 (2010).

   Iran Unveiled: How the Revolutionary Guards Is Turning Theocracy into Military Dictatorship (Washington: American Enterprise Institute Press, 2013).

   "Review of *The Twilight War: The Secret History of America's Thirty-Years Conflict with Iran* by David Crist," *Middle East Quarterly* 20.3 (2013).

   "The Revolutionary Guards' Role in Iranian Politics," *Middle East Quarterly* 15.4 (Fall 2008).

Ali, Javed, "Chemical Weapons and the Iran–Iraq War: A Case Study in Noncompliance," *The Nonproliferation Review* 8.1 (Spring 2001).

Amirahmadi, Hooshang and Manoucher Parvin, eds., *Post-Revolutionary Iran* (Boulder: Westview Press, 1988).

Arjomand, Said Amir, *The Turban for the Crown: The Islamic Revolution in Iran* (New York: Oxford University Press, 1988).

Asgharzadeh, Alireza, *Iran and the Challenge of Diversity* (New York: Palgrave Macmillan, 2007).

Ashton, Nigel and Bryan Gibson, eds., *The Iran–Iraq War: New International Perspectives* (London: Routledge, 2013).

Bajoghli, Narges, *Iran Reframed: Anxieties of Power in the Islamic Republic* (Stanford: Stanford University Press, 2019).

Bakhash, Shaul, "Center–Periphery Relations in Nineteenth-Century Iran," *Iranian Studies* 14.1–2 (1981).

   The Reign of the Ayatollahs: Iran and the Islamic Revolution (New York: Basic Books, 1990).

Banuazizi, Ali and Myron Weiner, eds., *The State, Religion, and Ethnic Politics: Afghanistan, Iran, and Pakistan* (Syracuse: Syracuse University Press, 1986).

Batatu, Hanna, *The Old Social Classes and the Revolutionary Movements of Iraq* (Princeton: Princeton University Press, 1978).

Beck, Lois, "Tribes and the State in Nineteenth- and Twentieth-Century Iran," in *Tribes and State Formation in the Middle East*, eds. Philip S. Khoury and Joseph Kostiner (Berkeley: University of California Press, 1990).

Blight, James G., et al., *Becoming Enemies: U.S.–Iran Relations and the Iran–Iraq War, 1979–1988* (Lanham: Rowman & Littlefield, 2012).

Bolourchi, Neda, "The Sacred Defense: Sacrifice and Nationalism Across Minority Communities in Post-Revolutionary Iran," *Journal of the American Academy of Religion* 86.3 (2018).

Boroujerdi, Mehrzad, "Contesting Nationalist Constructions of Iranian Identity," *Critique: Critical Middle Eastern Studies* 7.12 (1998).

Boroujerdi, Mehrzad and Kourosh Rahimkhani, *Postrevolutionary Iran: A Political Handbook* (Syracuse: Syracuse University Press, 2018).

Brands, Hal and David Palkki, "'Conspiring Bastards': Saddam Hussein's Strategic View of the United States," *Diplomatic History* 36.3 (2012).

Brown, Ian, *Khomeini's Forgotten Sons: The Story of Iran's Boy Soldiers* (London: Grey Seal, 1990).

Bulloch, John and Harvey Morris, *The Gulf War: Its Origins, History and Consequences* (London: Methuen, 1989).

Centeno, Miguel Angel, "Limited War and Limited States," in *Irregular Armed Forces and Their Role in Politics and State Formation*, eds. Diane E. Davis and Anthony W. Pereira (Cambridge: Cambridge University Press, 2003).

"Chapter Seven: Middle East and North Africa," in *The Military Balance* (London: International Institute for Strategic Studies, 2017).

Chorley, Katharine, *Armies and the Art of Revolution* (Boston: Beacon Press, 1973).

Chubin, Shahram, "Iran and the War: From Stalemate to Ceasefire," in *The Iran–Iraq War: Impact and Implications*, ed. Efraim Karsh (Houndmills: Macmillan, 1989).

  Iran's National Security Policy: Intentions, Capabilities & Impact (Washington: The Carnegie Endowment for International Peace, 1994).

  "The Last Phase of the Iran–Iraq War: From Stalemate to Ceasefire," *Third World Quarterly* 11.2 (1989).

Chubin, Shahram and Charles Tripp, *Iran and Iraq at War* (London: I.B. Tauris, 1988).

Chubin, Shahram and Sepehr Zabih, *The Foreign Relations of Iran: A Developing State in a Zone of Great-Power Conflict* (Berkeley: University of California Press, 1974).

Von Clausewitz, Carl, *On War*, trans. Michael Howard and Peter Paret (Oxford: Oxford University Press, 2007).

Cole, Juan R. and Nikki R. Keddie, eds., *Shi'ism and Social Protest* (New Haven: Yale University Press, 1986).

Coles, Isabel and Marcus George, "Iran Commander Criticizes Government over Influence from West," *Reuters*, December 11, 2013, www.reuters .com/article/us-iran-military/iran-commander-criticizes-government-over-influence-from-west-idUSBRE9BA0CI20131211.

Confino, Alon, "Collective Memory and Cultural History: Problems of Method," *The American Historical Review* 102.5 (1997).

Cordesman, Anthony, *The Lessons of Modern War, Vol. II: The Iran–Iraq War* (Boulder: Westview Press, 1991).

The Correlates of War, "Inter-State War Data," www.correlatesofwar.org/ data-sets/COW-war.

Crist, David, *The Twilight War: The Secret History of America's Thirty-Year Conflict with Iran* (New York: Penguin, 2012).

Cronin, Stephanie, "Riza Shah and the Disintegration of Bakhtiyari Power in Iran, 1921–1934," *Iranian Studies* 33.3–4 (2000).

Dabashi, Hamid, *Theology of Discontent: The Ideological Foundation of the Islamic Revolution in Iran* (New York: New York University Press, 1993).

Davis, Diane E., "Contemporary Challenges and Historical Reflections on the Study of Militaries, States, and Politics," in *Irregular Armed Forces and Their Role in Politics and State Formation*, eds. Diane E. Davis and Anthony W. Pereira (Cambridge: Cambridge University Press, 2003).

Davis, Eric, "The Uses of Historical Memory," *Journal of Democracy* 16.3 (2005).

Deeb, Marius, "Shi'a Movements in Lebanon: Their Formation, Ideology, Social Basis, and Links with Iran and Syria," *Third World Quarterly* 10.2 (1988).

Dekker, Ige F. and Harry H. G. Post, eds., *The Gulf War of 1980–1988: The Iran–Iraq War in International Legal Perspective* (Dordrecht: Martinus Nijhoff, 1992).

Donovan, Jerome, *The Iran–Iraq War: Antecedents and Conflict Escalation* (London: Routledge, 2011).

Donovan, Jerome, et al., "Strategic Interaction and the Iran–Iraq War: Lessons to Learn for Future Engagement?," *Digest of Middle East Studies* 24.2 (2015).

Ehsani, Kaveh, "War and Resentment: Critical Reflections on the Legacies of the Iran–Iraq War," *Middle East Critique* 26.1 (2017).

Ellis, John, *Armies in Revolution* (London: Croom Helm, 1973).

Entessar, Nader, *Kurdish Ethnonationalism* (Boulder: Lynn Rienner, 1992).
    "The Kurdish Mosaic of Discord," *Third World Quarterly* 11.4 (1989).

"The Kurds in Post-Revolutionary Iran and Iraq," *Third World Quarterly* 6.4 (1984).

"The Military and Politics in the Islamic Republic of Iran," in *Post-Revolutionary Iran,* eds. Hooshang Amirahmadi and Manoucher Parvin (Boulder: Westview Press, 1988).

Farhi, Farideh, "The Antinomies of Iran's War Generation," in *Iran, Iraq, and the Legacies of War,* eds. Lawrence Potter and Gary Sick (New York: Palgrave Macmillan, 2004).

"Crafting a National Identity Amidst Contentious Politics in Contemporary Iran," *Iranian Studies* 38.1 (2005).

Farrokh, Kaveh, *Iran at War: 1500-1988* (London: Bloomsbury, 2011).

Farzaneh, Mateo Mohammad, "Shi'i Ideology, Iranian Secular Nationalism and the Iran–Iraq War (1980–1988)," *Studies in Ethnicity and Nationalism* 7.1 (2007).

Ferretti, Matthew J., "The Iran–Iraq War: United Nations Resolution of Armed Conflict," *Villanova Law Review* 35.1 (1990).

Forozan, Hesam, *The Military in Post-Revolutionary Iran: The Evolution and Roles of the Revolutionary Guards* (London: Routledge, 2016).

Forozan, Hesam and Afshin Shahi, "The Military and the State in Iran: The Economic Rise of the Revolutionary Guards," *The Middle East Journal* 71.1 (2017).

Frick, Matthew M., "Iran's Islamic Revolutionary Guard Corps: An Open Source Analysis," *Joint Force Quarterly* 49 (2008).

Gallie, W. B., *Philosophers of Peace and War: Kant, Clausewitz, Marx, Engels and Tolstoy* (Cambridge: Cambridge University Press, 1979).

Gause, F. Gregory III, "Iraq's Decisions to Go to War, 1980 and 1990," *The Middle East Journal* 56.1 (2002).

Genocide in Iraq: The Anfal Campaign Against the Kurds (New York: Human Rights Watch, 1993).

Ghamari-Tabrizi, Behrooz, "Memory, Mourning, Memorializing: On the Victims of the Iran–Iraq War, 1980–Present," *Radical History Review* 105 (2009).

Gibson, Bryan R., *Covert Relationship: American Foreign Policy, Intelligence, and the Iran–Iraq War, 1980–1988* (New York: Praeger, 2010).

Gieling, Saskia, *Religion and War in Revolutionary Iran* (London: I.B. Tauris, 1999).

Golkar, Saeid, "By Mobilizing to Fight Coronavirus, the IRGC Is Marginalizing the Government," The Washington Institute for Near East Policy, April 8, 2020, www.washingtoninstitute.org/policy-analy sis/view/by-mobilizing-to-fight-coronavirus-the-irgc-is-marginalizing-the-government.

Captive Society: The Basij Militia and Social Control in Iran (New York: Columbia University Press, 2015).

Hamzeh, A. Nizar, "Lebanon's Hizbullah: From Islamic Revolution to Parliamentary Accommodation," *Third World Quarterly* 14.2 (1993).

Harris, Kevan, "All the Sepah's Men: Iran's Revolutionary Guards in Theory and Practice," in *Businessmen in Arms: How the Military and Other Armed Groups Profit in the MENA Region*, eds. Elke Grawert and Zeinab Abul-Magd (Lanham: Rowman & Littlefield, 2016).

A Social Revolution: Politics and the Welfare State in Iran (Berkeley: University of California Press, 2017).

Helfgott, Leonard M., "The Structural Foundations of the National Minority Problem in Revolutionary Iran," *Iranian Studies* 13.1–4 (1980).

Hen-Tov, Elliot and Nathan Gonzalez, "The Militarization of Post-Khomeini Iran: Praetorianism 2.0," *Washington Quarterly* 34.1 (2010–11).

Hickman, William F., "How the Iranian Military Expelled the Iraqis," *Brookings Review* 1.3 (1983).

Hiltermann, Joost R., *A Poisonous Affair: America, Iraq, and the Gassing of Halabja* (Cambridge: Cambridge University Press, 2007).

Hiro, Dilip, *The Longest War: The Iran–Iraq Military Conflict* (London: Grafton, 1989).

Hunter, Shireen T., "Iran and the Spread of Revolutionary Islam," *Third World Quarterly* 10.2 (1988).

Huntington, Samuel, *Political Order in Changing Societies* (New Haven: Yale University Press, 1968).

Soldier and the State: The Theory and Politics of Civil-Military Relations (Cambridge: Harvard University Press, 1957).

"Iran's Chemical and Biological Programmes," in *Iran's Nuclear, Chemical and Biological Capabilities* (London: International Institute for Strategic Studies, 2011).

Jaber, Hala, *Hezbollah: Born with a Vengeance* (New York: Columbia University Press, 1997).

Janowitz, Morris, *The Military in the Political Development of New Nations* (Chicago: University of Chicago Press, 1964).

Johnson, Robert, *The Iran–Iraq War* (London: Palgrave Macmillan, 2011).

Kansteiner, Wulf, "Finding Meaning in Memory: A Methodological Critique of Collective Memory Studies," *History and Theory* 41.2 (2002).

Karsh, Efraim, "Geopolitical Determinism: The Origins of the Iran–Iraq War," *Middle Journal* 44.2 (1980).

"Introduction," in *The Iran–Iraq War: Impact and Implications*, ed. Efraim Karsh (Houndmills: Macmillan, 1989).

The Iran–Iraq War (Oxford: Osprey, 2002).

"Military Power and Foreign Policy Goals: The Iran–Iraq War Revisited," *International Affairs* 64.1 (1987–88).

Katzman, Kenneth, *The Warriors of Islam: Iran's Revolutionary Guard* (Boulder: Westview Press, 1993).

Keddie, Nikki R., *Modern Iran: Roots and Results of Revolution* (New Haven: Yale University Press, 2003).

Khakpour, Arta, Mohammad Mehdi Khorrami, and Shouleh Vatanabadi, eds., *Moments of Silence: Authenticity in the Cultural Expressions of the Iran–Iraq War, 1980–1988* (New York: New York University Press, 2016).

Khosronejad, Pedram, ed., *Unburied Memories: The Politics of Bodies of Sacred Defense Martyrs in Iran* (New York: Routledge, 2013).

Khosronejad, Pedram, *War in Iranian Cinema: Religion, Martyrdom and National Identity* (London: I.B. Tauris, 2012).

Kornbluh, Peter and Malcolm Byrne, eds., *The Iran–Contra Scandal: The Declassified History* (New York: The New Press, 1993).

Lauria, Joe, "Iran Left Off Invite List for Syria Peace Talks," *The Wall Street Journal*, January 6, 2014, www.wsj.com/articles/no-headline-available-1389041917?tesla=y#printMode.

Lob, Eric, *Iran's Reconstruction Jihad: Rural Development and Regime Consolidation After 1979* (Cambridge: Cambridge University Press, 2020).

Marinova, Nadejda K., *Ask What You Can Do for Your (New) Country: How Host States Use Diasporas* (Oxford: Oxford University Press, 2017).

Martin, Vanessa, *Creating an Islamic State: Khomeini and the Making of a New Iran* (London: I.B. Tauris, 2003).

McNaugher, Thomas L., "Ballistic Missiles and Chemical Weapons: The Legacy of the Iran–Iraq War," *International Security* 15.2 (1990).

Mearsheimer, John J., *The Tragedy of Great Power Politics* (New York: W. W. Norton, 2001).

Mehr, Farhang, *A Colonial Legacy: The Dispute Over the Islands of Abu Musa, and the Greater and Lesser Tumbs* (Lanham: University Press of America, 1997).

Menashri, David, "Iran's Revolutionary Politics: Nationalism and Islamic Identity," in *Ethnic Conflict and International Politics in the Middle East*, ed. Leonard Binder (Gainesville: University of Florida Press, 1999).

Milani, Mohsen, *The Making of Iran's Islamic Revolution: From Monarchy to Islamic Republic*, 2nd ed. (Boulder: Westview Press, 1994).

Mohamedi, Fareed, "The Oil and Gas Industry," The Iran Primer (United States Institute of Peace, 2010), https://iranprimer.usip.org/resource/oil-and-gas-industry.

Morgenthau, Hans J., *Politics Among Nations: The Struggle for Power and Peace* (New York: Alfred A. Knopf, 1948).

Moslem, Mehdi, *Factional Politics in Post-Khomeini Iran* (Syracuse: Syracuse University Press, 2002).

Murray, Williamson and Kevin M. Woods, *The Iran–Iraq War: A Military and Strategic History* (New York: Cambridge University Press, 2014).

Nader, Alireza, "The Revolutionary Guards," The Iran Primer (United States Institute of Peace, 2010), https://iranprimer.usip.org/resource/revolution ary-guards.

Nakash, Yitzhak, *The Shi'is of Iraq* (Princeton: Princeton University Press, 1994).

Natali, Denise, *The Kurds and the State: Evolving National Identity in Iraq, Turkey, and Iran* (Syracuse: Syracuse University Press, 2005).

Noori, Neema, "Rethinking the Legacies of the Iran–Iraq War: Veterans, the Basij, and Social Resistance in Iran," in *Political and Military Sociology*, Annual Review 40, eds. Neovi M. Karakatsanis and Jonathan Swarts (New York: Routledge, 2013).

O'Ballance, Edgar, *The Gulf War* (London: Brassey's Defence, 1988).

O'Hern, Steven, *Iran's Revolutionary Guard: The Threat That Grows While America Sleeps* (Dulles: Potomac Books, 2012).

Ostovar, Afshon, *Vanguard of the Imam: Religion, Politics, and Iran's Revolutionary Guards* (Oxford: Oxford University Press, 2016).

Ottolenghi, Emanuele, *The Pasdaran: Inside Iran's Islamic Revolutionary Guard Corps* (Washington: Foundation for the Defense of Democracies, 2011).

The Peace Research Institute Oslo, "Battle Deaths Dataset," www.prio.no/ Data/Armed-Conflict/Battle-Deaths/.

Pelletiere, Stephen C., *The Iran–Iraq War: Chaos in a Vacuum* (New York: Praeger, 1992).

Pelletiere, Stephen C. and Douglas V. Johnson II, *Lessons Learned: The Iran–Iraq War* (Carlisle Barracks: Strategic Studies Institute, US Army War College, 1991).

Pereira, Anthony W., "Conclusion: Armed Forces, Coercive Monopolies, and Changing Patterns of State Formation and Violence," in *Irregular Armed Forces and Their Role in Politics and State Formation*, eds. Diane E. Davis and Anthony W. Pereira (Cambridge: Cambridge University Press, 2003).

Potter, Lawrence and Gary Sick, eds., *Iran, Iraq, and the Legacies of War* (New York: Palgrave Macmillan, 2004).

Rajaee, Farhang, ed., *Iranian Perspectives on the Iran–Iraq War* (Gainesville: University of Florida Press, 1997).

Ramazani, Rouhollah K., *Iran's Foreign Policy, 1941–1973: A Study of Foreign Policy in Modernizing Nations* (Charlottesville: University of Virginia Press, 1975).

Revolutionary Iran: Challenge and Response in the Middle East (Baltimore: Johns Hopkins University Press, 1986).

Razi, G. Hossein, "An Alternative Paradigm to State Rationality in Foreign Policy: The Iran–Iraq War," *The Western Political Quarterly* 41.4 (1988).

Razoux, Peirre, *The Iran–Iraq War*, trans. Nicholas Elliott (Cambridge: Belknap Press/Harvard University Press, 2015).

Rezaei, Farhad and Somayeh Khodaei Moshirabad, "The Revolutionary Guards: From Spoiler to Accepter of the Nuclear Agreement," *British Journal of Middle Eastern Studies* 45.2 (2018).

Riedel, Bruce, "How the Iran–Iraq War Shaped the Trajectories of Figures Like Qassem Soleimani," Brookings, January 9, 2020, www.brookings .edu/blog/order-from-chaos/2020/01/09/how-the-iran-iraq-war-shaped-the-trajectories-of-figures-like-qassem-soleimani/.

Rizvi, M. Mahtab Alam, "Evaluating the Political and Economic Role of the IRGC," *Strategic Analysis* 36.4 (2012).

Roberts, Mark J., *Khomeini's Incorporation of the Iranian Military*, McNair Paper 48 (Washington: Institute for National Strategic Studies, National Defense University, 1996).

Rolston, Bill, "When Everywhere Is Karbala: Murals, Martyrdom and Propaganda in Iran," *Memory Studies* 13.1 (2020).

Safshekan, Roozbeh and Farzan Sabet, "The Ayatollah's Praetorians: The Islamic Revolutionary Guard Corps and the 2009 Election Crisis," *Middle East Journal* 64.4 (2010).

Saleh, Alam, *Ethnic Identity and the State in Iran* (New York: Palgrave Macmillan, 2013).

Salzman, Philip C., "National Integration of the Tribes in Modern Iran," *Middle East Journal* 25.3 (1971).

Schahgaldian, Nikola, *The Iranian Military Under the Islamic Republic* (Santa Monica: RAND, 1987).

Schofield, Richard N., "Evolution of the Shatt al-'Arab Boundary Dispute," Menas Studies in Continuity & Change in the Middle East and North Africa (Cambridgeshire: Middle East & North African Studies, 1986).

Shanahan, Rodger, "Shi'a Political Development in Iraq: The Case of the Islamic Da'wa Party," *Third World Quarterly* 25.5 (2004).

Sharafedin, Bozorgmehr, "Defying Trump, Iran Says Will Boost Missile Capabilities," *Reuters*, September 22, 2017, www.reuters.com/article/ us-iran-military-usa/defying-trump-iran-says-will-boost-missile-capabil ities-idUSKCN1BX0J7.

Sinkaya, Bayram, *Revolutionary Guards in Iranian Politics: Elites and Shifting Relations* (London: Routledge, 2016).

Skocpol, Theda, "Social Revolutions and Mass Military Mobilization," *World Politics* 40.2 (1988).

States and Social Revolutions (Cambridge: Cambridge University Press, 1979).

Snyder, Jack L., *The Soviet Strategic Culture: Implications for Limited Nuclear Operations* (Santa Monica: RAND, 1977).

"Supreme Council for Islamic Revolution in Iraq (SCIRI)," National Consortium for the Study of Terrorism and Responses to Terrorism, University of Maryland (June 2015), www.start.umd.edu/baad/narra tives/supreme-council-islamic-revolution-iraq-sciri.

Tabaar, Mohammad Ayatollahi, "Factional Politics in the Iran–Iraq War," *Journal of Strategic Studies* 42.3–4 (2019).

Tabatabai, Ariane M. and Annie Tracy Samuel, "What the Iran–Iraq War Tells Us About the Future of the Iran Nuclear Deal," *International Security* 42.1 (2017).

Tahir-Kheli, Shirin and Shaheen Ayubi, eds., *The Iran–Iraq War: New Weapons, Old Conflicts* (New York: Praeger, 1983).

Takeyh, Ray, *Guardians of the Revolution: Iran and the World in the Age of the Ayatollahs* (Oxford: Oxford University Press, 2009).

"The Iran–Iraq War: A Reassessment," *The Middle East Journal* 64.3 (2010).

Taliaferro, Jeffrey W., "Security Seeking Under Anarchy: Defensive Realism Revisited," *International Security* 25.3 (2000–01).

This Week, ABC, September 29, 2013, http://abcnews.go.com/ThisWeek/ week-transcript-president-bill-clinton-iranian-foreign-minister/story? id=20407450.

Tilly, Charles, "Reflections on the History of European State-Making," in *The Formation of National States in Western Europe*, ed. Charles Tilly (Princeton: Princeton University Press, 1975).

Tracy Samuel, Annie, "Beyond Strategic Stability: Deterrence, Regional Balance, and Iranian National Security," in *The End of Strategic Stability?: Nuclear Weapons and the Challenge of Regional Rivalries*, eds. Lawrence Rubin and Adam N. Stulberg (Washington: Georgetown University Press, 2018).

"Correcting Misunderstandings of the IRGC's Position on Nuclear Negotiations," *Iran Matters*, February 18, 2014, www.belfercenter .org/publication/correcting-misunderstandings-irgcs-position-nuclear- negotiations.

"Guarding the Nation: The Iranian Revolutionary Guards, Nationalism and the Iran–Iraq War," in *Constructing Nationalism in Iran: From the Qajars to the Islamic Republic*, ed. Meir Litvak (London: Routledge, 2017).

"Perceptions and Narratives of Security: The Iranian Revolutionary Guards Corps and the Iran–Iraq War," Belfer Center for Science and International Affairs, Harvard Kennedy School, May 2012, www.belfercenter.org/sites/ default/files/files/publication/samuel_perceptions.pdf.

"Revolutionary Guard Is Cautiously Open to Nuclear Deal," *Iran Matters*, December 20, 2013, www.belfercenter.org/publication/revolu tionary-guard-cautiously-open-nuclear-deal-1.

"Viewpoint Iran: The Past and Present of the U.S.–Iran Standoff," *Origins: Current Events in Historical Perspective* 7.1 (2013).

Uskowi, Nader, *Temperature Rising: Iran's Revolutionary Guards and Wars in the Middle East* (Lanham: Rowman & Littlefield, 2019).

Vahabzadeh, Peyman, "Secularism and the Iranian Militant Left: Political Misconception or Cultural Issues?," *Comparative Studies of South Asia, Africa and the Middle East* 31.1 (2011).

Vali, Abbas, *Kurds and the State in Iran: The Making of Kurdish Identity* (London: I.B. Tauris, 2011).

Varzi, Roxanne, *Warring Souls: Youth, Media, and Martyrdom in Post-Revolution Iran* (Durham: Duke University Press, 2006).

Vazeri, Haleh, "Iran's Involvement in Lebanon: Polarization and Radicalization of Militant Islamic Movements," *Journal of South Asian and Middle Eastern Studies* 16.2 (1992).

Walt, Stephen M., *The Origins of Alliances* (Ithaca: Cornell University Press, 1987).

Waltz, Kenneth N., *Theory of International Politics* (Long Grove: Waveland Press, 1979).

Ward, Steven R., *Immortal: A Military History of Iran and Its Armed Forces* (Washington: Georgetown University Press, 2009).

Weber, Max, "Politics as a Vocation" (1918), in *From Max Weber: Essays in Sociology*, trans. and eds. H. H. Gerth and C. Wright Mills (New York: Oxford University Press, 1946).

Wehrey, Frederic, et al., *The Rise of the Pasdaran: Assessing the Domestic Roles of Iran's Islamic Revolutionary Guards Corps* (Santa Monica: RAND, 2009).

Winter, Jay and Emmanuel Sivan, eds., *War and Remembrance in the Twentieth Century* (Cambridge: Cambridge University Press, 1999).

Woods, Kevin M., et al., *Saddam's War: An Iraqi Military Perspective on the Iran–Iraq War* (Washington: Institute for National Strategic Studies, National Defense University, 2009).

Woods, Kevin M., David D. Palkki, and Mark E. Stout, *The Saddam Tapes: The Inner Workings of a Tyrant's Regime, 1978–2001* (Cambridge: Cambridge University Press, 2011).

Zabih, Sepehr, *The Iranian Military in Revolution and War* (London: Routledge, 1988).

Index

Lightning Source UK Ltd.
Milton Keynes UK
UKHW020800180222
398873UK00004B/176